THE LOEB CLASSICAL LIBRARY

FOUNDED BY JAMES LOEB

EDITED BY

G. P. GOOLD

PREVIOUS EDITORS

T. E. PAGE   E. CAPPS

W. H. D. ROUSE   L. A. POST

E. H. WARMINGTON

JEROME

SELECT LETTERS

LCL 262

JEROME

SELECT LETTERS

WITH AN ENGLISH TRANSLATION BY

F. A. WRIGHT

DISCARD

L.C.C. LIBRARY

HARVARD UNIVERSITY PRESS
CAMBRIDGE, MASSACHUSETTS
LONDON, ENGLAND

First published 1933
Reprinted 1954, 1963, 1975, 1980, 1991, 1999

LOEB CLASSICAL LIBRARY® is a registered trademark
of the President and Fellows of Harvard College

ISBN 0-674-99288-1

Printed in Great Britain by St Edmundsbury Press Ltd,
Bury St Edmunds, Suffolk, on acid-free paper.
Bound by Hunter & Foulis Ltd, Edinburgh, Scotland.

CONTENTS

INTRODUCTION   vii

I. The Woman Struck by Seven Swords   2

VII. Family Affairs   18

XIV. The Ascetic Life   28

XXII. The Virgin's Profession   52

XXXVIII. A Good Woman   158

XL. Onasus the Windbag   166

XLIII. The Country Life   170

XLIV. A Letter of Thanks   176

XLV. Innocent Friendships   178

LII. A Clergyman's Duties   188

LIV. Widows   228

LX. A Letter of Consolation   264

LXXVII. The Eulogy of Fabiola   308

CVII. A Girl's Education   338

CXVII. Dangerous Friendships   370

CXXV. Good and Bad Monks   396

CXXVII. Marcella and the Sack of Rome   438

CXXVIII. Feminine Training   466

APPENDICES   483

INDEX OF PROPER NAMES   503

INTRODUCTION

(a) LIFE OF JEROME

JEROME—or, to give him his significant Greek name, Eusebius Hieronymus—was born about 345 A.D. at Stridon in Dalmatia, a small town near Aquileia, which was partly destroyed by the Goths during their invasion of 377. His father, Eusebius, and his mother were Christians of moderate wealth and were alive in 373 when Jerome first went to the East, but probably died when Stridon was taken by the barbarians. Jerome himself received a good education at his local school, and then, like most young provincials of talent, he was attracted to Rome, where he studied rhetoric under the great grammarian Aelius Donatus, returning with his friend Bonosus to Aquileia in 370. In that town he established his first society of ascetics, which lasted for three years until some event—referred to by him variously as ‘ a sudden storm ’ and ‘ a monstrous rending asunder ’—broke up the fellowship, and Jerome with a few of his closer associates went eastwards to Antioch. But even this small company did not remain long together, and a meeting with the old hermit Malchus made Jerome resolve to seek complete solitude. The adjacent desert of Chalcis was already full of hermits living under the rule of Theodosius, and Jerome soon became one of their number, sleeping in a bare cell,

clothed in sackcloth, submitting himself to rigorous
penances, and for five years giving all his days to
devotional exercise and to the study of the Scriptures.

This first period of Jerome's life ended in 379 when
he returned to Antioch and was ordained presbyter
by Bishop Paulinus. With Paulinus he attended
the Second General Council at Constantinople,
where he met Gregory Nazianzen and Gregory of
Nyssa, and in his bishop's company he came to Rome
for the Church Council held there in 382, and for the
next three years lived in the great city. The Pope
at that time was Damasus, the clerical dilettante
who made the catacombs a show place for the world,
and Jerome soon became his intimate friend and
trusted adviser, constantly consulted on all points
of biblical knowledge and finally commissioned to
write a revised Latin version of the Psalms and the
New Testament. This was a task of pure scholar-
ship, but Jerome also found amid the luxury and
splendour of Rome a few ardent souls, most of them
women, who were ready to embrace and follow his
ascetic rule. One of his disciples was Paula, the
heiress of the great Aemilian family, who brought
over her two daughters Blesilla and Eustochium.
Another was the wealthy Marcella, at whose palace
on the Aventine master and pupils used to come
together for the study of Hebrew, to join in earnest
prayer, and to sing psalms. During these months
Jerome was perhaps as happy as he ever thought it
right to be, but the death of his protector Damasus
unchained against him all the enmities that his
rigorous virtues had challenged and his bitter
sarcasms provoked. The new Pope Siricius regarded
him as a dangerous rival; the mob were enraged by

the sudden death of Blesilla, which was believed to have been caused by her prolonged fastings and penances; the cry was raised ' The monks to the Tiber ': and Jerome left Rome and Europe for ever.

Then began the third period in Jerome's life. He resolved that he would no longer sing the Lord's song in a strange land, and taking Paula and Eustochium with him he went once more to the East, the true home of ascetic belief, and after some little delay settled down in Judaea at Bethlehem, where he remained for the last thirty-four years of his existence. At Bethlehem he built a monastery of which he was head, a convent over which first Paula and then Eustochium presided, a church where both communities assembled for worship, and a hospice to lodge the pilgrims who came from all parts of the world to that holy ground. The expenses of these various institutions were borne by Paula until even her great wealth was exhausted, and then by Jerome himself, who sold the remains of his family property for their support. Their administration must have occupied a portion of his time, but the greater part of his energy was given at Bethlehem, as everywhere, to writing and study. Not that his life was peaceful, or that he passed his days in quietude. His own character always ensured a certain amount of friction; he quarrelled bitterly with the Bishop of Jerusalem; his health was never of the best; and the calm of his monastery was continually being broken by rumours of wars and by the actual shock of invasion.

The sack of Rome in 410, for example, spread terror even in Palestine, and it is from Jerome perhaps that we get the clearest idea of the con-

sternation caused throughout the world by the
fall of the imperial city. In the preface to his
Ezekiel he writes: ' I was so stupefied and dismayed
that day and night I could think of nothing but the
welfare of the Roman community. It seemed to me
that I was sharing the captivity of the saints and I
could not open my lips until I received some more
definite news. All the while, full of anxiety, I
wavered between hope and despair, torturing myself
with the misfortunes of others. But when I heard
that the bright light of all the world was quenched,
or rather that the Roman Empire had lost its head
and that the whole universe had perished in one city:
then indeed, " I became dumb and humbled myself
and kept silence from good words." ' But however
troubled at heart Jerome might be, neither public
calamity nor private sorrow could stop his labours.
Paula passed away from him in Palestine; Marcella
only survived the barbarities of the sack of Rome for
a short period; even Eustochium, although she was
of a younger generation, succumbed to the rigours
of the ascetic life. But the old man, nearly blind
and over seventy, was still working at his commentary on Jeremiah when his last illness came. He
died September 20th, 420, and his body was buried
beside Paula near the grotto of the Nativity at
Bethlehem, in later days to be transferred and to be
the cause of many a miracle at the Church of Santa
Maria Maggiore in Rome.

(b) Jerome's Works

The literary works of Jerome, apart from the
Letters, are very voluminous, for he lived a long life,

INTRODUCTION

was a quick writer, and possessed enormous powers of industry. The following list is given by Canon Fremantle.

I. Bible Translations.

(*a*) From the Hebrew.—The Vulgate of the Old Testament, written at Bethlehem, begun 391 and finished 404.

(*b*) From the Septuagint.—The Psalms as used at Rome, written in Rome 383, and the Psalms as used in Gaul, written at Bethlehem 388, this Gallican Psalter being collated with the Hebrew. The Book of Job, written at Bethlehem 386–392.

(*c*) From the Chaldee.—The Books of Tobit and Judith. Bethlehem, 398.

(*d*) From the Greek.—The Vulgate version of the New Testament, made at Rome, 382–385.

II. Commentaries.

(*a*) Original.—Ecclesiastes, 385. Isaiah, 410. Jeremiah i–xxxii, 419. Ezekiel, 410–414. Daniel, 407. Minor Prophets, 391–406. St. Matthew, 398. Galatians, Ephesians, Titus, Philemon, 388. All these written at Bethlehem.

(*b*) Translated from the Greek of Origen.—Jeremiah and Ezekiel, Bethlehem, 381. St. Luke, Bethlehem, 389. Canticles, Rome and Bethlehem, 385–387.

A commentary on Job and a translation of Origen's Isaiah are also often attributed to Jerome.

III. Books on Scriptural Subjects.

(*a*) A glossary of proper names in the Old Testament, 388.

(*b*) Questions on Genesis, 388.

(*c*) A translation of Eusebius ' On the sites and names of Hebrew places,' 388.

(*d*) A translation of Didymus ' On the Holy Spirit,' 385–387.

All these written at Bethlehem.

IV. Books on Church History and Controversy.

(*a*) Book of Illustrious Men, Bethlehem, 392.

(*b*) Dialogue with a Luciferian, Antioch, 379.

(*c*) Lives of the Hermits: Paulus. Desert of Chalcis, 374. Hilarion and Malchus, Bethlehem, 390.

(*d*) Translation of the Rule of Pachomius, Bethlehem, 404.

(*e*) Against Helvidius, Rome, 384. Against Jovinian, Bethlehem, 393. Against Vigilantius, Bethlehem, 406. Against John of Jerusalem, Bethlehem, 398. Against Rufinus, Bethlehem, 402–404.

V. General History.

Translation, with additions, of the Chronicle of Eusebius, Constantinople, 382.

Few writers in any age or in any country can surpass this catalogue. Among Latin authors Cicero, Livy, and Augustine come nearest to Jerome, but even they fall short of his immense productiveness. The Vulgate alone would be a full life's work, and yet it forms only a small part of Jerome's labours. History, biography, theological controversy, scriptural exegesis, all flowed with equal readiness from his pen, and like Cicero, who is his closest exemplar in Latin literature, he writes on all subjects with equal skill. The two men in character are altogether

different: Cicero wished to please everybody, Jerome wished to please no one; Cicero was wrapped up in the things of this world, Jerome fixed his gaze steadfastly on the world to come; Cicero reserved his deepest feelings of unselfishness for his son and daughter, Jerome would seem to discourage all procreation and child-bearing. But they are alike in one respect: they are both, first and foremost, men of letters, and when Jerome has a subject that gives scope for skill, subjects such as he finds in his controversy with Jovinian, in the lives of the three hermits Paul, Hilarion and Malchus, and in many of his Letters, he shows himself a wonderful master of words.

(c) The Letters

The four most famous collections of letters in Latin literature are those of Cicero, Seneca, Pliny and Jerome. Of these the letters of Cicero and of Jerome are the largest in bulk and the most important in substance, and even if Cicero has some advantage in wit and grace of style, there can be no doubt that for a Christian reader the subjects with which Jerome deals make him infinitely the more valuable. We have now extant one hundred and twenty-six epistles from his pen, written between the years 370 and 419, and varying in length from a few lines to several thousand words, which in Hilberg's edition fill nearly sixteen hundred pages. The difficulty of selection has been mainly a difficulty of what letters to omit, and a few words may be said here of those that appear in this volume. Letter I is probably the earliest of Jerome's compositions and is interesting by reason both of its style and its

subject, which shows that Jerome, like Augustine, was a sturdy believer in miracles. Letter VII is one of the very few in which Jerome mentions his own family: it is short and pithy, and may be compared with XL, XLIII, XLIV, XLV, which exhibit the various sides of his personal character. The first of these four shows him as a violent satirist, the second as a lover of nature, the third is a graceful letter of thanks, and the fourth a vigorous defence of his friendships with women, this last being in a way a pendant to Letter CXVII. Another group of three letters, XIV, LII, LX, is concerned with Heliodorus, Bishop of Altinum, the first reproaching him for his abandonment of the ascetic life, the second laying down for his nephew Nepotian the duties of a clergyman, the third, one of the finest letters, consoling him for Nepotian's death. Letter CXXV, treating of monasticism, draws a vivid picture of the good and bad monk, and the remaining seven letters deal with the other of Jerome's two main interests, the position of woman in the Christian Church as virgin, wife and widow. Three of them, XXXVIII, LXXVII, CXXVII, are elaborate portraits of married women, two others, CVII, CXXVIII, are concerned with the education of girls. Letter LIV instructs a widow in the best means of maintaining her widowhood, which Jerome holds to be the second of the three degrees of chastity; and Letter XXII, the most famous in the collection, is a fervent panegyric of the life of virginity.

(d) Text and Bibliography

The text used for this translation is that of the masterly edition of Isidor Hilberg (Vienna, 3 vols.,

1910–1918). The few divergencies from his text
are noted where they occur, and for the many
variant readings of the MSS. the reader is referred to
his very copious *apparatus criticus*.

The chief manuscripts are given by Hilberg thus:

Γ	Lugdunensis	6th century
ε	Parisinus	6th „
G	Neapolitanus	6th–7th century
K	Spinaliensis	8th „
H	Monacensis	8th–9th „
Σ	Turicensis Augiensis	9th century
W	Parisinus	9th „
L	Coloniensis	9th „
A	Berolinensis	9th „
D	Vaticanus	9th–10th century
C	Vaticanus	10th „
B	Berolinensis	12th „

The Editio Princeps of the Letters appeared in
Rome, 1470. The next edition of independent value
is that of Erasmus (Basle, 1516–1520), followed by
that of Marianus Victorius (Rome, 1560). Then
comes the Benedictine edition of Martianay and
Pouget (Paris, 1693), which like all its predecessors
was superseded by that of Dominic Vallarsi (Verona,
1734–1742). This last was reprinted by Migne and
held the field until in its turn it was superseded by
the edition of Isidor Hilberg mentioned above.

Of modern works on Jerome it will be sufficient to
mention three: ' Hieronymus, Sein Leben und
Wirken ' (O. Zöckler, Gotha, 1865), ' Saint Jérôme '
(A. Thierry, Paris, 1867), and ' The Principal Works
of St. Jerome ' (Fremantle, Oxford, 1893), this last

a book to which the present translation is under especial obligations. For a general account of the early Latin Fathers, including Jerome, two recent books may be consulted: ' Latin Christianity ' (P. de Labriolle, London, 1925), and ' Fathers of the Church ' (F. A. Wright, London, 1928).

We now have the text and translation by J. Labourt, 2 vols., Budé, Paris, 1949–1951; edition by I. Hilberg, 3 vols., Vienna: New York, 1910, reprints 1961 (1912–1918) and selections ed. by C. Favez, Brussels, 1950. Also, C. C. Mierow, *Letters of Jerome* in *Ancient Christian Writers*, vols. 31–32, 1960.

The Editors wish to thank the Rev. Father Sharpe, of More Hall, Stroud, for help in finding some abstruse references.

SELECT LETTERS OF
ST. JEROME

SANCTI EUSEBII HIERONYMI EPISTULAE

I

AD INNOCENTIUM PRESBYTERUM DE SEPTIES PERCUSSA

1. SAEPE a me, Innocenti carissime, postulasti, ut de eius miraculo rei, quae in nostram aetatem inciderat, non tacerem. Cumque ego id verecunde et vere, ut nunc experior, negarem meque adsequi posse diffiderem, sive quia omnis humanus sermo inferior esset laude caelesti, sive quia otium quasi quaedam ingenii robigo parvulam licet facultatem pristini siccasset eloquii, tu e contrario adserebas in Dei rebus non possibilitatem inspici debere, sed animum, neque eum posse verba deficere, qui credidisset in verbo.

2. Quid igitur faciam ? Quod inplere non possum, negare non audeo. Super onerariam navem rudis vector inponor, et homo, qui necdum scalmum in lacu rexi, Euxini Maris credor fragori. Nunc mihi evanescentibus terris ' caelum undique et undique

---

[1] A member of Jerome's first band of ascetics in Aquileia; he accompanied Jerome to Antioch where he died in 374.

2

SELECT LETTERS OF
ST. JEROME

LETTER I

To Innocentius

The woman struck by seven swords

Written A.D. 370

You have often in the past asked me, my dearest Innocent,[1] to relate that miraculous happening which occurred in my lifetime. To that request I gave a modest, and as I now find by trial, a justified refusal. I distrusted my power of achievement, both because all the language of man is inadequate to the praise of heaven, and also because lack of exercise, like rust upon the mind, has dried up any slight power of eloquence that in the past I might have possessed. You on the other hand declared that in the things of God one ought to consider not the possibility, but the will, and that he who believed in the Word could not find words fail him.

What then shall I do? I cannot fulfil this task, but I do not dare to refuse it. A novice in ship-craft, I am put on board a vessel heavily laden; a poor fellow who has never steered a skiff upon a lake, I am entrusted to the roar of the Euxine Sea. The land fades from sight, around me now ' on every side is

3

pontus,' nunc unda tenebris horrescens et caeca
nocte nimborum spumei fluctus canescunt. Hortaris,
ut tumida malo vela suspendam, rudentes explicem,
clavum regam. Pareo iam iubenti et, quia caritas
omnia potest, spiritu sancto cursum prosequente
confidam habiturus in utraque parte solacium: si me
ad optatos portus aestus adpulerit, gubernator puta-
bor; si inter asperos orationis anfractus inpolitus
sermo substiterit, facultatem forsitan quaeras, voluntatem certe flagitare non poteris.

3. Igitur Vercellae Ligurum civitas haud procul
a radicibus Alpium sita, olim potens, nunc raro habi-
tatore semiruta. Hanc cum ex more consularis
inviseret, oblatam sibi quandam mulierculam una
cum adultero—nam id crimen maritus inpegerat—
poenali carceris horrore circumdedit. Neque multo
post, cum lividas carnes ungula cruenta pulsaret et
sulcatis lateribus dolor quaereret veritatem, infeli-
cissimus iuvenis volens conpendio mortis longos vitare
cruciatus, dum in suum mentitur sanguinem, accusa-
vit alienum solusque omnium miser meritus visus est
percuti, quia non reliquit innoxiae, unde posset
negare. At vero mulier sexo fortior suo, cum eculeus
corpus extenderet et sordidas paedore carceris manus

4

sky, on every side the sea ';[1] darkness roughens
the waves and in the black night of the storm-clouds
the billows show white with foam. You bid me
hoist the swelling sails to the mast top, to let the
sheets run loose and take the tiller in my hand. To-
day I obey your command: love is all-powerful, and
with the Holy Spirit guiding my course, I may feel
confident that in either case I shall find comfort. If
the surging waves drive me to the desired haven, I
shall be considered a skilful steersman: if my
unvarnished tale strikes the rocks among the rough
windings of my story, you may perhaps find me
lacking in ability but you certainly will not be able to
challenge my good-will.

Vercellae then is a Ligurian city near the foothills
of the Alps, once a place of importance, but now
lying half in ruins with only a few inhabitants.
When the governor paid it his usual visit, a woman
and her lover were brought before him accused by
the husband of adultery, and were by him consigned
to the dread torture chamber of the public prison.
There by agony the truth was sought; and the
unhappy youth soon gave way. As the blood-
stained hook furrowed his sides and tore his blackened
flesh, he determined to escape from his long-drawn
torments by the short road of death, and lying against
his own body accused another's as well. So for once
a miserable wretch seemed to deserve his fate, for
he left an innocent person no chance of denying the
charge brought against her. But the woman for her
part showed a courage superior to her sex. Her
body was stretched upon the rack, and her hands
black with the prison filth were bound with cords

[1] Virgil, *Aeneid*, III. 193.

post tergum vincula cohiberent, oculis, quos tantum tortor alligare non poterat, suspexit ad caelum et volutis per ora lacrimis: 'Tu,' inquit, 'testis, domine Iesu, cui occultum nihil est, qui es scrutator renis et cordis, non ideo me negare velle, ne peream. At tu, miserrime homo, si interire festinas, cur duos interimis innocentes? Equidem et ipsa cupio mori, cupio invisum hoc corpus exuere, sed non quasi adultera. Praesto iugulum, micantem intrepida excipio mucronem, innocentiam tantum mecum feram. Non moritur, quisquis victurus occiditur.'

4. Igitur consularis pastis cruore luminibus, ut fera, quae gustatum semel sanguinem semper sitit, duplicare tormenta iubet et saevum dentibus frendens similem carnifici minitatus est poenam, nisi confiteretur sexus infirmior, quod non potuerat robur virile reticere.

5. 'Succurre, domine Iesu : ad unum hominem tuum quam plura sunt inventa supplicia!' Crines ligantur ad stipitem et toto corpore ad eculeum fortius alligato vicinus pedibus ignis adponitur, utrumque latus carnifex fodit nec papillis dantur indutiae: inmota mulier manet et a dolore corporis spiritu separato, dum conscientiae bono fruitur, vetuit circa se saevire tormenta. Iudex crudelis quasi superatus adtollitur, illa dominum deprecatur;

6

behind her; but the torturer could not chain her
eyes, and with them she looked up to heaven, and
cried as the tears rolled down her cheeks: ' Thou,
Lord Jesus, from whom nothing is hidden, who dost
search out the reins and the heart, Thou art my witness
that it is not to save myself from death that I wish to
deny this, but that it is to save myself from sin that I
refuse to tell a lie. As for you, unhappy man, if
you are in haste to perish, why take two innocent
lives? I for my part long to strip off this hateful
body, I long to meet death, but not as a woman
convicted of adultery. I offer my throat to the
gleaming sword, I welcome it without a shudder;
only I must take my innocence with me. He does
not perish, who dies to live again.'

The governor had been feasting his eyes on the
gory spectacle, like some wild animal that has once
tasted blood and is for evermore athirst. At this
he ordered her tortures to be redoubled, and gnashing
his teeth in fury, threatened the executioner with a
like fate, unless he made the weaker sex confess a
crime which manly strength had not been able to
conceal.

' O Lord Jesus, bring help: how many punishments
have been discovered for this one creature of thine!'
Her hair is fastened to the stake, her whole body
bound more tightly to the rack, and fire is put to her
feet. The executioner stabs her on both sides, and
even her breasts are not spared. Still the woman remains firm: her spirit feels not bodily pain, and enjoy-
ing still a good conscience she forbids the torture to
vent its rage upon her. The cruel judge starts from
his seat as though he were defeated; she still prays
to the Lord. Her limbs are torn from their joints;

7

solvuntur membra conpagibus, illa oculos ad caelum tendit; de communi scelere alius confitetur, illa pro confitente negat et periclitans ipsa alium vindicat periclitantem.

6. Una interim vox: ' Caede, ure, lacera; non feci. Si dictis tollitur fides, veniet dies, quae hoc crimen diligenter excutiat; habebo iudicem meum.' Iam lassus tortor suspirabat in gemitum nec erat novo vulneri locus, iam victa saevitia corpus, quod laniarat, horrebat: extemplo ira excitus consularis: ' Quid miramini,' inquit, ' circumstantes, si torqueri mavult mulier, quam perire ? Adulterium certe sine duobus committi non potest et esse credibilius reor noxiam ream negare de scelere, quam innocentem iuvenem confiteri.'

7. Pari igitur prolata in utrumque sententia damnatos carnifex trahit. Totus ad spectaculum populus effunditur, et prorsus quasi migrare civitas putaretur, stipatis proruens portis turba densatur. Et quidem miserrimi iuvenis ad primum statim ictum amputatur gladio caput truncumque in suo sanguine volutatur cadaver. Postquam vero ad feminam ventum est et flexis in terram poplitibus super trementem cervicem micans elevatus est gladius et exercitatam carnifex dexteram totis viribus concitavit, ad primum corporis tactum stetit mucro letalis et leviter perstringens cutem rasurae modicae sanguinem aspersit. Inbellem manum percussor

she only lifts her eyes to heaven. Another confesses their common guilt; she on his behalf denies what he confessed, and in danger herself tries to save another from danger.

Her cry was still the same : 'Beat me, burn me, tear me in pieces. I did not do it. If you do not believe my words, the day will soon come that will sift this charge aright. I have One who will judge me.' By this time the torturer was sighing and groaning. There was no room for fresh wounds. The man himself shuddered to see the body he had so mangled, and even his ferocity gave way. But the governor was only roused to fresh rage, and cried out forthwith: 'Why does it surprise you, bystanders, that a woman prefers torture to death? Obviously it takes two persons to commit adultery, and I consider that it is far more likely that a guilty woman should deny a crime than that an innocent youth should confess one.'

The same sentence, therefore, was passed upon both, and the executioner dragged away his victims. The whole populace rushed out to see the sight, pouring in dense masses from the crowded gates, so that you might have thought the entire city was migrating. At the very first stroke of the sword the miserable youth's head was cut off, and his headless corpse rolled over in its own blood. Then came the woman's turn. With bent knees she sank to the ground, and over her quivering neck the gleaming sword was raised. The executioner brought down his well-trained arm with all his might, but directly it touched her body the deadly sword was stayed, and lightly grazing the skin made a scratch just sufficient to draw blood. At his hand's defeat the striker

expavit, et victam dexteram gladio marcescente miratus in secundos impetus torquet. Languidus rursum in feminam mucro delabitur et, quasi ferrum ream timeret adtingere, circa cervicem torpet innoxium. Itaque furens et anhelus lictor paludamento in cervicem retorto, dum totas expedit vires, fibulam, quae chlamydis mordebat oras, in humum excussit ignarusque rei ensem librat in vulnus et : ' En tibi,' ait mulier, ' ex umero aurum ruit. Collige multo quaesitum labore, ne pereat.'

8. Rogo, quae est ista securitas? Impendentem non timet mortem, laetatur percussa, carnifex pallet; oculi gladium non videntes tantum fibulam vident et, ne parum esset, quod non formidabat interitum, praestabat beneficium saevienti. Iam igitur et tertius ictus : sacramentum frustraverat trinitatis. Iam speculator exterritus et non credens ferro mucronem aptabat in iugulum, ut, qui secare non poterat, saltim premente manu corpori conderetur : O omnibus inaudita res saeculis !—ad capulum gladius reflectitur, et velut dominum suum victus aspiciens confessus est se ferire non posse.

9. Huc, huc mihi trium exempla puerorum, qui inter frigidos flammarum globos hymnos edidere pro fletibus, circa quorum sarabara sanctamque caesariem

trembled and looked in amazement at his conquered arm: then swinging high the craven blade he prepared to give a second stroke. Again the sword fell feebly on the woman and lay still and harmless on her neck, as though the steel feared to touch the accused. Thereupon the headsman, panting now with rage, flung his cloak back over his shoulders, so that he might exert all his strength without hindrance. The action loosened the brooch that fastened his garment, and it fell to the ground, unnoticed by the man, who was poising his sword for another blow. ' Look,' cried the woman, ' your gold brooch has fallen from your shoulder. Pick it up, or you will lose something for which you have worked hard.'

What, I ask, is the secret of such confidence? She has no fear of the death that threatens her, she rejoices in her wounds, it is the executioner who turns pale. Her eyes do not see the sword, they only see the brooch. It is not enough for her to feel no dread of death, she does an act of kindness to her savage tormentor. And now the third blow fell, only to be rendered vain by the sacred power of the Trinity. By this time the soldier was completely frightened, and no longer trusting the blade put the sword point to her throat, with the idea that though it could not cut, the pressure of his hand might force it into her body. But the sword—O marvel unheard of through all the ages!—bent back to the hilt, and in its defeat seemed to look at its master, as if confessing that it could not strike.

Now, now let me recall the example of the three children, who amid the cool circles of the fire sang hymns instead of shedding tears, while the flames played harmlessly about their turbans and their holy

innoxium lusit incendium. Huc beati Danihelis revocetur historia, iuxta quem adulantibus caudis praedam suam leonum ora timuerunt. Nunc Susanna nobilis fide mentes omnium subeat, quae iniquo damnata iudicio sancto spiritu puerum replente servata est. Ecce non dispar in utraque misericordia domini : illa liberata per iudicem, ne iret ad gladium, haec a iudice damnata absoluta per gladium est.

10. Tandem ergo ad feminam vindicandam populus armatur. Omnis aetas, omnis sexus carnificem fugat et coetu in circulum coeunte non credit paene unusquisque, quod vidit. Turbatur tali nuntio urbs propinqua et tota lictorum caterva glomeratur. E quibus medius, ad quem damnatorum cura pertinebat, erumpens et ' canitiem immundam perfuso pulvere turpans ': ' Meum,' inquit, ' O cives, petitis caput, me illi vicarium datis! Si misericordes, si clementes estis, si vultis servare damnatam, innocens certe perire non debeo.' Quo fletu vulgi concussus est animus maestusque se per omnes torpor insinuat et mirum in modum voluntate mutata, cum pietatis fuisset, quod ante defenderant, pietatis visum est genus, ut paterentur occidi.

11. Novus igitur ensis, novus percussor adponitur.

locks. Let me repeat again the story of the blessed
Daniel, before whom the lions crouched with fawning
tails, and trembled at the man who was to be their
prey. Let all men remember once more the grandeur
of Susanna's faith, who, condemned by an unjust
judgment, was saved by a lad inspired by the Holy
Spirit. Not unlike was the mercy of the Lord in both
cases: Susanna was set free by the judge and saved
from the sword: this woman was condemned by the
judge but by the sword acquitted.

So at length the populace took up arms to defend
the woman. People of every age and every sex join
in driving off the headsman. The whole crowd form
into a ring about her and hardly one among them can
believe his own eyes. The news of their action throws
the neighbouring city into confusion, and the governor's attendants muster in force. From their midst
the officer charged with the care of condemned
criminals dashed forth, and as he

' Poured defiling dust upon grey hair befouled '[1]

cried: 'It is my life that you are taking, fellow-
countrymen. You are making me her substitute.
Even if you do feel mercy and compassion, even
if you are set on rescuing a woman condemned
to death, surely it is not right for an innocent man
like myself to die.' This lamentable appeal shook
the people's resolution, and a spirit of gloomy
torpor soon became universal. Men's feelings were
strangely changed. It had seemed their duty to
defend the woman, it now seemed their duty in a
way to allow her to be executed.

Accordingly a new sword and a new executioner

[1] Virgil, *Aeneid*, XII. 611.

Stat victima Christo tantum favente munita. Semel percussa concutitur, iterum repetita quassatur, tertio vulnerata prosternitur et—O divinae potentiae sublimanda maiestas!—quae prius fuerat quarto percussa nec laesa, ideo paululum visa est mori, ne pro ea periret innoxius.

12. Clerici, quibus id officii erat, cruentum linteo cadaver obvolvunt et fossam humum lapidibus construentes ex more tumulum parant. Festinato sol cursu occasum petit, et misericordiam domini celatura nox advenit. Subito feminae palpitat pectus et oculis quaerentibus lucem corpus animatur ad vitam: iam spirat, iam videt, iam sublevatur et loquitur, iam in illam potest vocem erumpere: ' Dominus, auxiliator meus, non timebo, quid faciat mihi homo.'

13. Anus interim quaedam, quae ecclesiae sustentabatur opibus, debitum caelo spiritum reddidit, et quasi de industria ordine currente rerum vicarium tumulo corpus operitur. Dubia adhuc luce in lictore zabulus occurrit, quaerit cadaver occisae, sepulchrum sibi monstrari petit; vivere putat, quam mori potuisse miratur. Recens a clericis caespes ostenditur et dudum superiecta humus cum his vocibus ingeritur flagitanti: ' Erue scilicet ossa iam condita, infer novum sepulchro bellum, et si hoc parum est,

appeared. The victim takes her place, protected only by the favour of Christ. The first blow makes her shake, at the second she totters, the third brings her wounded to the ground. O majesty of God's power, how wondrous, how sublime! Previously she had received four strokes without injury: now for a little while she seemed to die, merely that an innocent man might not suffer in her stead.

Those of the clergy, whose duty it was to perform this office, wrapped the blood-stained corpse in a sheet, and then prepared to dig a grave and duly cover it over with stones. The sun sets in haste, and night comes on to conceal God's mercy in its darkness. Suddenly the woman's breast heaves, her eyes seek the light, her body is quickened to life again. She sighs, she looks round, she rises, she speaks. At last she is able to cry aloud: ' The Lord is on my side. I will not fear. What can man do unto me? '[1]

In the meantime an aged female, who had been maintained at the expense of the Church, rendered back her soul to heaven. So opportunely her corpse took the woman's place, and was buried in the tomb. Before dawn the devil came on the scene in the person of the headsman, who began to look about for the body of the woman he had slain, and asked to be shown the place where she was buried. He thought that she was still alive, for he wondered that she was able to die. At his demand the clergy showed him the fresh turf and the ground which now for some time had been heaped up, crying out: ' Dig up the bones forsooth which now have been laid to rest, make new war upon her tomb, and if that does not satisfy you, scatter her limbs for vultures and wild

[1] Psalm cxviii. 6.

avibus ferisque lanianda membra discerpe; septies percussa debet aliquid morte plus perpeti.'

14. Tali invidia carnifice confuso clam domi mulier focilatur et, ne forte creber ad ecclesiam medici commeatus suspicionis panderet viam, cum quibusdam virginibus ad secretiorem villulam secto crine transmittitur. Ibi paulatim virili habitu veste mutata in cicatricem vulnus obducitur. Et—' O vere ius summum summa malitia!'—post tanta miracula adhuc saeviunt leges.

15. En quo me gestorum ordo protraxit! Iam enim ad Evagrii nostri nomen advenimus. Cuius ego pro Christo laborem si arbitrer a me dici posse, non sapiam, si penitus tacere velim, voce in gaudium erumpente non possim. Quis enim valeat digno canere praeconio Auxentium Mediolanii incubantem huius excubiis sepultum paene ante quam mortuum, Romanum episcopum iam paene factionis laqueis inretitum et vicisse adversarios et non nocuisse superatis?

' Verum haec ipse equidem spatiis exclusus iniquis
Praetereo atque aliis post me memoranda relinquo.'

---

[1] Terence, *Heaut. Tim.* 796.
[2] Evagrius, a presbyter of Antioch, later (c. 388) consecrated bishop of that see; often referred to by Jerome (Letters III, IV, V, and XV); also by Basil, Letter CXXXVIII.

beasts to mangle; a woman who has received seven
strokes of the sword ought to suffer something more
than death.'

The odium of such an action sent the executioner
away in confusion, and the woman was secretly cared
for indoors. Finally, lest the doctor's frequent visits
to the church should give rise to suspicion, she had
her hair cut short, and in company with some
virgins was sent to a lonely house in the country.
There for a little time she put on men's clothes until
the scars formed over her wound. And yet to-day—
' How true it is that complete legality is complete
injustice ! ' [1]—after all these wondrous happenings
the laws are still raging against her.

See now to what point the order of events has
brought me. At last we have reached the name of
our friend Evagrius.[2] If I were to think that I could
describe all his labours on Christ's behalf, I should
indeed be foolish. Were I minded to pass them over
completely, I could not do so, for my voice of itself
would burst into cries of joy. Who could write a
fitting panegyric of the man whose vigilance put
Auxentius,[3] that pest of Milan, into the grave before
the time of his death, and enabled the bishop of
Rome to escape from the entangling snares of
faction, to overcome his enemies and to show them
mercy in defeat? But

> ' This I must leave for others to relate,
> Shut out myself by time and unkind fate.' [4]

---

[3] Auxentius, the Arian bishop of Milan, Ambrose's predecessor, died 374.
[4] Virgil, *Georgics*, IV. 147.

Praesentis tantum rei fine contentus sum : imperatorem industria adit, precibus fatigat, merito lenit, sollicitudine promeretur, ut redditam vitae redderet libertati.

VII

AD CHROMATIUM, IOVINUM, EUSEBIUM

1. Non debet charta dividere, quos amor mutuus copulavit, nec per singulos officia mei sunt partienda sermonis, cum sic invicem nos ametis, ut non minus tres caritas iungat, quam duos natura sociavit. Quin potius, si rei condicio pateretur, sub uno litterulae apice nomine indiviso concluderem vestris quoque ita me litteris provocantibus, ut et in uno tres et in tribus unum putarem. Nam postquam sancto Evagrio transmittente in ea ad me heremi parte delatae sunt, quae inter Syros et Sarracenos vastum limitem ducit, sic gavisus sum, ut illum diem Romanae felicitatis, quo primum Marcelli apud Nolam proelio post Cannensem pugnam superba Hannibalis agmina conciderunt, ego vicerim. Et licet supra dictus frater saepe me visitet atque ita ut sua in Christo viscera foveat, tamen longo a me spatio seiunctus

---

[1] This letter written in A.D. 374 to three young friends (who all later became bishops) from the desert of Chalcis, where Jerome then was living, gives some details of the

I am satisfied to record the end of my present story.
Evagrius seeks a special interview with the Emperor:
wearies him with his prayers, secures his sympathy
by the merits of his case, and finally by anxious care
wins the day. The Emperor restored to freedom the
woman who had been thus restored to life.

LETTER VII

To Chromatius, Jovinus and Eusebius [1]

Family affairs

THOSE whom mutual love has joined together
ought not to be separated on a written page. Therefore I must not divide between you individually the
words that I owe to you all. Two of you, as brothers,
are already natural partners, but so strong is the love
which you feel for one another that affection unites
the three in a bond that is equally close. Indeed,
if actual conditions allowed, I would make one
abbreviation include all your names without division;
for your letter challenged me to regard you as
three in one and one in three. That letter was
handed to me by the saintly Evagrius in that part of
the desert which forms a broad boundary line
between the Syrians and the Saracens, and it filled
me with joy, a joy surpassing even the exultation
felt at Rome over the victory of Marcellus at Nola,
when for the first time after Cannae Hannibal's
proud hosts were defeated. The above-named
brother often pays me a visit, and cherishes me in
Christ like his own flesh; but he is separated from me

writer's sister, whose name is unknown, and of the condition
of the church in Dalmatia. Cf. p. 308, note 2.

non minus mihi dereliquit abeundo desiderium,
quam adtulerat veniendo laetitiam.

2. Nunc cum vestris litteris fabulor, illas amplexor,
illae mecum loquuntur, illae hic tantum Latine
sciunt. Hic enim aut barbarus seni sermo discendus
est aut tacendum est. Quotiensque carissimos
mihi vultus notae manus referunt inpressa vestigia,
totiens aut ego hic non sum aut vos hic estis. Credite
amori vera dicenti : et cum has scriberem, vos
videbam. Quibus hoc primum queror, cur tot
interiacentibus spatiis maris et terrarum tam parvam
epistulam miseritis, nisi quod ita merui, qui vobis, ut
scribitis, ante non scripsi. Chartam defuisse non
puto Aegypto ministrante commercia. Et si aliqui
Ptolomaeus maria clausisset, tamen rex Attalus
membranas e Pergamo miserat, ut penuria chartae
pellibus pensaretur ; unde pergamenarum nomen
ad hanc usque diem tradente sibi invicem posteritate
servatum est. Quid igitur? Arbitrer baiulum
festinasse? Quamvis longae epistulae una nox
sufficit. An vos aliqua occupatione detentos? Nulla
necessitas maior est caritate. Restant duo, ut aut
vos piguerit aut ego non meruerim. E quibus malo
vos incessere tarditatis, quam me condemnare non
meriti. Facilius enim negligentia emendari potest,
quam amor nasci.

3. Bonosus, ut scribitis, quasi filius ἰχθύος aquosa
petit, nos pristina contagione sordentes quasi reguli

---

[1] *I.e.* has been baptized. ἰχθύς = Ἰησοῦς Χριστὸς Θεοῦ Υἱὸς
Σωτήρ. Bonosus, Jerome's foster-brother, studied with him
at Rome, joined his band of ascetics at Aquileia, and when
this broke up retired to live as a hermit on a small island
near Aquileia.

by a great distance, and his departure always causes me as much regret as his coming has brought delight.

Now I talk to your letter, I embrace it, it carries on a conversation with me, it is the only thing here that knows Latin. In this place an old man has either to learn a barbarous jargon, or else to hold his tongue. The handwriting I know so well brings your dear faces before my eyes; and then either I am no longer here or else you are here with me. Believe love when it tells you the truth: as I write this letter I see you before me. However, I have one complaint to make first. Why is it that with such stretches of sea and land between us you sent me so short a letter? Perhaps I deserved it; for as you say, I did not write first. Paper, I imagine, cannot have failed you now that Egypt supplies the market. Even if some Ptolemy had closed the seas, King Attalus was there to send you skins from Pergamum, and by parchment you could have made up for lack of paper. The very word parchment as it exists to-day, handed down from generation to generation, reveals its origin. Well, am I to suppose that your messenger was pressed for time? One night is sufficient to write a letter in, however long the letter be. Were you prevented by some urgent business? Nothing has a greater claim on you than affection. Two reasons are left; either you felt disinclined, or else I was not deserving. I prefer to accuse you of sloth rather than condemn myself as unworthy. The correction of carelessness is an easier matter than the birth of love.

You tell me that Bonosus, like a true son of the Fish, makes for watery places.[1] For myself, I am

21

et scorpiones arentia quaeque sectamur. Ille iam
calcat super colubri caput, nos serpenti terram ex
divina sententia comedenti adhuc cibo sumus. Ille
potest summum graduum psalmum scandere, nobis
adhuc in primo ascensu flentibus nescio an dicere
aliquando contingat : ' Levavi oculos meos in montes,
unde veniat auxilium mihi.' Ille inter minaces
saeculi fluctus in tuto insulae, hoc est ecclesiae
gremio, sedens ad exemplum Iohannis librum forte
iam devorat, ego in scelerum meorum sepulchro
iacens et peccatorum vinculis conligatus dominicum
de evangelio expecto clamorem : ' Hieronyme, veni
foras.' Bonosus, inquam,—quia secundum prophetam
omnis diaboli virtus in lumbo est—trans Euphraten
tulit lumbare suum ibi illud in foramine petrae
abscondens et postea scissum repperiens cecinit :
' Domine, tu possedisti renes meos; disrupisti
vincula mea; tibi sacrificabo hostiam laudis,'
me verus Nabuchodonosor ad Babylonem, id est
confusionem mentis meae, catenatum duxit; ibi
mihi captivitatis iugum inposuit, ibi ferri circulum
innectens de canticis Sion cantare praecepit. Cui
ego dixi : ' Dominus solvit conpeditos, dominus
inluminat caecos '; et, ut breviter coeptam dis-
similitudinem finiam, ego veniam deprecor, ille
expectat coronam.

4. Soror mea sancti Iuliani in Christo fructus est :

---

[1] Psalm cxxi. 1. The so-called "Psalms of degrees," cxx-
cxxxiv, chanted on the steps of the Temple, are taken as a
type of the Christian's progress.

[2] Revelation, x. 9, 10.

[3] Jeremiah, xiii. 4-5.

[4] Psalm cxxxix. 13.

[5] Psalm cxxxvii. 3. [6] Psalm cxlvi. 7, 8.

[7] P. 18. n. 1: her conversion is again referred to in

still foul with my ancient stains, and like the
basilisk and scorpion I seek out any place that is dry.
Bonosus to-day treads the serpent's head beneath his
heel; I am still food for the creeping monster who
by God's decree devours the earth. Bonosus can
climb to the highest step in the psalms of degrees;
I am still weeping at the beginning of the ascent, and
scarcely know whether it will ever be my lot to say[1]:
'I lifted up mine eyes unto the hills, from whence
cometh my help.' Bonosus amid the threatening
billows of the world sits in the safe retreat of his
island, the bosom of the Church, and perhaps, like
John, he is even now eating God's book;[2] I lie
in the tomb of my sins, bound in the chains of iniquity, and wait for the Lord's gospel cry: 'Jerome,
come forth.' Bonosus, I say—for according to the
prophet all the devil's strength is in the loins—has
carried his loin-cloth across the Euphrates[3] to hide it
in a hole of the rock, and after he found it torn he
has sung: 'O Lord, thou hast possessed my reins.
Thou hast broken my bonds in sunder. I will offer
to thee the sacrifice of thanksgiving.'[4] As for me, a
real Nebuchadnezzar has led me in chains to Babylon,
that is, to the babel of a distracted mind. There he
has laid upon me the yoke of captivity, there he has
fastened an iron ring upon me and bidden me sing
one of the songs of Sion.[5] To him I have made
reply: 'The Lord looseth the prisoners; the Lord
openeth the eyes of the blind.'[6] In fact, to complete
this comparison of differences in a simple sentence,
I pray for mercy, Bonosus awaits a crown.

My sister[7] is the fruit in Christ of the saintly

Letter VI, addressed to this same Julian, a deacon of the
Church at Aquileia.

ille plantavit, vos rigate, dominus incrementum dabit. Hanc mihi Iesus pro eo vulnere, quod diabolus inflixerat, praestitit vivam reddendo pro mortua. Huic ego, ut ait gentilis poeta, omnia etiam tuta timeo.[1] Scitis ipsi lubricum adolescentiae iter, in quo et ego lapsus sum et vos non sine timoris transitis. Hoc illa cum maxime ingrediens omnium fulcienda praeceptis, omnium est sustentanda solaciis, id est crebris vestrae sanctitudinis epistulis roboranda, et quia caritas omnia sustinet, obsecro ut etiam a papa[2] Valeriano[3] ad eam confortandam litteras exigatis. Nostis puellares animos his rebus plerumque solidari, si se intellegant curae esse maioribus.

5. In mea enim patria rusticitatis vernacula deus venter est et de die vivitur: sanctior est ille, qui ditior est. Accessit huic patellae iuxta tritum populi proverbium dignum operculum, Lupicinus sacerdos—secundum illud quoque, de quo semel in vita Crassum ait risisse Lucilius: ' Similem habent labra lactucam asino cardus comedente '—videlicet[4] ut perforatam navem debilis gubernator regat et caecus caecos ducat in foveam talisque sit rector, quales illi qui reguntur.[5]

6. Matrem communem, quae, cum vobis sanctitate

---

[1] Virgil, *Aeneid*, IV. 298.

[2] For the term " Pope " cf. p. 308, note 2.

[3] A priest or bishop of Stridon, a Spaniard by birth, who was at variance with Jerome probably because he opposed monasticism.

[4] Cicero, *De Fin.* v. 30.

[5] For this proverb (the precise point of which is not clear) cf. also Eugenius, *Carm.* 89 (Migne, *Patrolog. Lat.*, LXXXVII, II. Carm. 50, p. 393): *Carduus et spina, cum pastum praebet asello, lactuca labris compar est.*

Julian. He planted, you must water, the Lord will give the increase. Jesus has given her to me as compensation for the wound which the devil inflicted. He has brought her back from death to life. But, as the heathen poet says, for her

' All things, though safe in semblance, I do fear.' [1]

You know yourselves how treacherous is the path of youth, a path where I fell and which you are now traversing not without fear. At this moment, when she is entering upon it, she needs to be supported by all men's encouragement, confirmed by all men's advice; in other words, strengthened by such frequent letters as your saintliness will suggest. Love endureth all things; and I therefore beg you to get a letter from Pope Valerian [2] also, so that her courage may be increased. You know that a girl's spirit is often fortified by the thought that her elders are interested in her.

As for my own country, it is enslaved to barbarism, and men's family God is their belly. People live only for the day, and the richer you are the more saintly you are held to be. Furthermore, to use a well-worn popular saying, the cover there is worthy of the dish; for Lupicinus [3] is their priest. It bears out the proverb which, as Lucilius tells us, made Crassus laugh for the only time in his life [4]: ' When an ass eats thistles up, his lips have lettuce like themselves.' [5] I mean that in my country a crippled helmsman steers a leaking ship, a blind man leads the blind into a pit; as the ruler is, so are the ruled.

I send my greetings to your mother, who is a

25

societur, in eo vos praevenit, quia tales genuit, cuius vere venter aureus potest dici, eo salutamus honore, quo nostis; una quoque suspiciendas cunctis sorores, quae sexum vicere cum saeculo, quae oleo ad lampadas largiter preparato sponsi opperiuntur adventum. O beata domus, in qua morantur Anna vidua, virgines prophetissae, geminus Samuhel nutritus in templo! O tecta felicia, in quibus cernimus Macchabaeorum martyrum coronis cinctam martyrem matrem! Nam licet cotidie Christum confiteamini, dum eius praecepta servatis, tamen ad privatam gloriam publica haec accessit vobis et aperta confessio, quod per vos ab urbe vestra Arriani quondam dogmatis virus exclusum est. Et miremini forsitan, quod in fine iam epistulae rursus exorsus sim. Quid faciam? Vocem pectori negare non valeo. Epistulae brevitas conpellit tacere, desiderium vestri cogit loqui. Praeproperus sermo; confusa turbatur oratio; amor ordinem nescit.

mother to us all, with the deep respect which you know I feel. She is your close associate in holy life; but she has one advantage over you in that she is the mother of such sons as yourselves. Truly her womb may be called golden. I salute your sisters also, for they are worthy of universal respect. They have triumphed over sex and the world, and now await the Bridegroom's coming, their lamps well filled with oil. How happy is the house, where dwells a widowed Anna, virgins that are prophetesses, and twin Samuels[1] reared in the temple precincts. How fortunate the roof that shelters for us the martyr mother of the martyr Maccabees all girt with crowns.[2] Though every day you confess Christ by keeping his commandments, you have added to this private glory the public fame of an open confession, and it was by your efforts in the past that the poison of the Arian heresy was expelled from your city.[3] Perhaps you may wonder at my beginning thus afresh at the end of a letter. What am I to do? I cannot preclude my heart from utterance. The brief limits of a letter force me to be silent, but my longing for your company compels me to speak. My words pour out in eager haste; my language is confused and disjointed; but love knows nothing of order.

[1] *I.e.* Chromatius and Eusebius, cf. sect. v.
[2] Cf. 2 Maccabees, vii.   [3] Aquileia.

XIV

AD HELIODORUM MONACHUM

1. QUANTO studio et amore contenderim, ut pariter in heremo moraremur, conscium mutuae caritatis pectus agnoscit. Quibus lamentis, quo dolore, quo gemitu te absentem persecutus sim, istae quoque litterae testes sunt, quas lacrimis cernis interlitas. Verum tu quasi parvulus delicatus contemptum rogantis per blandimenta fovisti et ego incautus, quid tunc agerem, nesciebam. Tacerem? Sed quod ardenter volebam, moderate dissimulare non poteram. Impensius obsecrarem? Sed audire nolebas, quia similiter non amabas. Quod unum potuit, spreta caritas fecit. Quem praesentem retinere non valuit, quaerit absentem. Quoniam igitur et tu ipse abiens postularas, ut tibi, postquam ad deserta migrassem, invitatoriam a me scriptam transmitterem, et ego facturum receperam, invito, iam propera. Nolo pristinarum necessitatum recorderis—nudos amat heremus—nolo te antiquae peregrinationis terreat difficultas. Qui in Christo credis, et eius crede sermonibus: ' Quaerite primum regnum Dei, et haec omnia adponentur nobis.' Non pera tibi sumenda, non virga est; adfatim dives est, qui cum Christo pauper est.

LETTER XIV

To Heliodorus

The ascetic life

Written A.D. 374

Your own heart conscious of our mutual affection knows with what loving zeal I urged you to let us stay together in the desert. This letter even, blotted, as you see, with tears, bears witness to the grief, the sobs, and the lamentations wherewith I accompanied your departure. You, like some spoilt child, smoothed over your contemptuous refusal then with soft words and I in my folly did not know what to do. Ought I to have held my tongue? I could not conceal my ardent desires under a cloak of indifference. Ought I to have pleaded with more urgency? You would not have listened, for you did not love me as I loved you. The affection you scorned has done the one thing it could. It was not able to keep you when present, but it now comes to seek you when you are far away. At your departure you asked me to send you a letter of invitation when I took up my home in the desert, and I promised that I would do so. That letter of invitation I now send: come, and come quickly. Do not think of old ties— the desert loves the naked—do not be deterred by the hardships of our former travels. As you believe in Christ, believe also in his words: ' Seek ye first the kingdom of God, and all these things shall be added unto you '![1] You need not take scrip nor staff; he is abundantly rich who is poor with Christ.

[1] St. Matthew, vi. 33.

2. Sed quid ago? Rursus inprovidus obsecro? Abeant preces, blandimenta discedant; debet amor irasci. Qui rogantem contempseras, forsitan audies obiurgantem. Quid facis in paterna domo, delicate miles? Ubi vallum, ubi fossa, ubi hiemps acta sub pellibus? Ecce de caelo tuba canit, cum nubibus debellaturus orbem imperator armatus egreditur, eoce bis acutus gladius ex regis ore procedens obvia quaeque metit: et tu mihi de cubiculo ad aciem, de umbra egrederis ad solem? Corpus adsuetum tunica loricae onus non suffert, caput opertum linteo galeam recusat, mollem otio manum durus exasperat capulus. Audi edictum regis tui: ' Qui mecum non est, contra me est; et qui mecum non colligit, spargit.' Recordare tirocinii tui diem, quo Christo in baptismate consepultus sacramenti verba iurasti: pro nomine eius non te matri parciturum esse, non patri. Ecce adversarius in pectore tuo Christum conatur occidere; ecce donativum, quod militaturus acceperas, hostilia castra suspirant. Licet parvulus ex collo pendeat nepos, licet sparso crine et scissis vestibus ubera, quibus nutrierat, mater ostendat, licet in limine pater iaceat, per calcatum

LETTER XIV

But what am I doing? Why these imprudent
entreaties for the second time? A truce to prayers,
enough of soft words. It is the duty of offended love
to show resentment. You despised my request;
perhaps you will listen to my reproof. What
business have you, pampered soldier, in your father's
house? Where now are the rampart, the trench,
and the winter under canvas? Lo, the trumpet
sounds from heaven! Lo, our general fully armed
comes forth amid the clouds to subdue the world!
Lo, from our king's mouth proceeds a sword twice
sharpened, which cuts down all that is in its path!
Are you coming out, pray, from your chamber to the
battle-field, from the shade to the sun? A body
that is used to a tunic cannot support a cuirass, a
head that has worn a linen hood shrinks from a
helmet, a hand that idleness has softened is galled by
a hard sword-hilt. Hear your king's proclamation:
' He that is not with me is against me, and he that
gathereth not with me scattereth.'[1] Remember
the day when you enlisted as a recruit, when, buried
with Christ in baptism, you took the oath of allegiance
to Him, declaring that in His name you would spare
neither father nor mother. Lo, the adversary
within your own heart is trying now to slay Christ!
Lo, the enemy's camp is sighing now for the bounty
which you received before your service began.
Though your little nephew[2] hang on your neck,
though your mother with dishevelled hair and torn
raiment show you the breasts that gave you suck,
though your father fling himself upon the threshold,
trample your father underfoot and go your way, fly

[1] St. Matthew, xii. 30.
[2] Nepotian. Cf. Letters LII and LX.

perge patrem, siccis oculis ad vexillum crucis vola!
Pietatis genus est in hac re esse crudelem.

3. Veniet postea dies, quo victor revertaris in
patriam, quo Hierosolymam caelestem vir fortis
coronatus incedas. Tunc municipatum cum Paulo
capies, tunc et parentibus tuis eiusdem civitatis ius
petes, tunc et pro me rogabis, qui, ut vinceres,
incitavi. Neque vero nescio, qua te nunc dicas
conpede praepediri. Non est nobis ferreum pectus
nec dura praecordia, non ex silice natos Hyrcanae
nutriere tigrides. Et nos per ista transivimus.
Nunc tibi blandis vidua soror haeret lacertis, nunc
illi, cum quibus adolevisti, vernulae aiunt: ' Cui nos
servituros relinquis?' Nunc et gerula quondam,
iam anus, et nutricius, secundus post naturalem
pietatis pater, clamitat: ' Morituros expecta paulisper et sepeli.' Forsitan et laxis uberum pellibus,
arata rugis fronte antiquum referens mamma lallare
congeminet. Dicant, si volunt, et grammatici:
' In te omnis domus inclinata recumbit.' Facile
rumpit haec vincula amor Christi et timor gehennae.
' At scriptura praecipit parentibus obsequendum ':
sed quicumque eos supra Christum amat, perdit
animam suam. Gladium tenet hostis, ut me peri-
mat, et ego de matris lacrimis cogitabo? Propter

with tearless eyes to the standard of the Cross. In these matters to be cruel is a son's duty.

The day will come later when you shall return in triumph to your true country, when, crowned as a man of might, you shall walk the streets of the heavenly Jerusalem. Then you shall share with Paul the franchise of that city, and ask the same privilege for your parents. Yes, and for me also you shall intercede, who urged you on to victory. I know full well the fetters which you will say impede you. My breast is not of iron nor my heart of stone. I was not born from a rock or suckled by Hyrcanian tigers.[1] I too have passed through all this. Your widowed sister clings to you to-day with loving arms; the house-slaves, in whose company you grew to manhood, cry ' To what master are you leaving us? ' Your old nurse and her husband, who have the next claim to your affection after your own father, exclaim, ' Wait for a few months till we die and then give us burial.' Perhaps your foster mother with sagging breasts and wrinkled face may remind you of your old lullaby and sing it once again. Your tutors even, if they wish, may say with Virgil : [2]

' On you the whole house resting leans.'

The love of Christ and the fear of hell easily break such bonds as these.

But, you will say, the Scripture bids us to obey our parents. Nay, whosoever loves his parents more than Christ loses his own soul. The enemy takes up his sword to slay me: shall I think of my mother's tears? Shall I desert from my army because of my

---

[1] Cf. *Aeneid*, IV. 366.   [2] *Aeneid*, XII. 59.

patrem militiam deseram, cui sepulturam Christi causa non debeo, quam etiam omnibus eius causa debeo? Domino passuro timide consulens Petrus scandalum fuit. Paulus retinentibus fratribus, ne Hierosolymam pergeret, respondit: ' Quid facitis plorantes et conturbantes cor meum? Ego non solum ligari, sed mori in Hierusalem paratus sum pro nomine domini nostri Iesu Christi.' Aries iste pietatis, quo fides quatitur, evangelii retundendus est muro: ' Mater mea et fratres mei hi sunt, quicumque faciunt voluntatem patris mei, qui in caelis est.' Si credunt in Christo, faveant mihi pro eius nomine pugnaturo; si non credunt, ' mortui sepeliant mortuos suos.'

4. ' Sed hoc,' ais, ' in martyrio.' Erras, frater, erras, si putas umquam Christianum persecutionem non pati; et nunc cum maxime oppugnaris, si te oppugnari nescis. Adversarius noster tamquam leo rugiens aliquem devorare quaerens circuit, et tu pacem putas? ' Sedet in insidiis cum divitibus in occultis, ut interficiat innocentem; oculi eius in pauperem respiciunt; insidiatur in occulto sicut leo in spelunca sua; insidiatur ut rapiat pauperem ': et tu frondosae arboris tectus umbraculo molles somnos, futura praeda, carpis? Inde me persequitur luxuria, inde avaritia conatur inrumpere,

father, to whom in Christ's cause I owe no rites of burial, although in Christ's cause I owe them to all men? Peter with his craven counsel was an offence to Our Lord before His passion. Paul's answer to his brothers, who would have stayed his journey to Jerusalem, was this: ' What mean ye, to weep and to break my heart? For I am ready not to be bound only, but also to die at Jerusalem for the name of the Lord Jesus.' [1] The battering-ram of affection which shakes faith must be beaten back by the wall of the Gospel: ' My mother and my brethren are these, whosoever do the will of my father which is in heaven.' [2] If men believe in Christ, they should cheer me on as I go to fight in His name. If they do not believe, ' let the dead bury their dead.' [3]

All this is well enough, you reply, if one is a martyr. Ah, you are mistaken, grievously mistaken, my brother, if you think that there is ever a time when the Christian is not suffering persecution. At this very moment you are being furiously attacked when you do not know that any attack is being made. ' Our adversary as a roaring lion walketh about seeking whom he may devour,' [4] and do you think you are at peace? ' He sitteth in ambush with the rich in secret to murder the innocent, his eyes are privily set against the poor. He lieth in wait secretly as a lion in his den; he lieth in wait to catch the poor,' [5] and do you, his destined prey, enjoy your soft slumbers under the shady covering of a leafy tree? On one side self-indulgence pursues me, on another avarice tries to break in, on another my belly

[1] Acts, xxi. 13.　　　　　　[2] St. Matthew, xii. 50.
[3] St. Matthew, viii. 22.　　[4] 1 St. Peter, v. 8.
[5] Psalm x. 8.

inde venter meus vult mihi deus esse pro Christo,
conpellit libido, ut habitantem in me spiritum
sanctum fugem, ut templum eius violem, persequitur me, inquam, hostis, ' cui nomina mille, mille
nocendi artes ': et ego infelix victorem me putabo,
dum capior ?

5. Nolo, frater carissime, examinato pondere delic-
torum minora arbitreris idolatriae crimina esse,
quae diximus ; immo apostoli disce sententiam, qui
ait : ' Hoc enim scitote intellegentes, quia omnis
fornicator aut immundus, aut fraudator, quod est
idolatria, non habet hereditatem in regno Dei et
Christi.'   Et quamquam generaliter adversum Deum
sapiat, quidquid diaboli est, et quod diaboli est,
idolatria sit, cui omnia idola mancipantur, tamen et
in alio loco speciatim nominatimque determinat
dicens : ' Mortificate membra vestra, quae in terra
sunt, exponentes fornicationem, immunditiam et
concupiscentiam malam et cupiditatem, quae sunt
idolorum servitus, propter quae venit ira Dei.'   Non
est tantum in eo servitus idoli, si quis duobus digitulis tura comprehensa in bustum arae iaciat aut
haustum patera fundat merum.   Neget avaritiam
idolatriam, qui potest triginta argenteis dominum
venditum appellare iustitiam ; neget sacrilegium in
libidine, sed is qui membra Christi et hostiam vivam
placentem Deo cum publicarum libidinum victimis

wishes to be my god in Christ's place: lust urges me to drive away the Holy Spirit that dwells within me and to violate His temple; I am pursued, I repeat. by an enemy who has

' A thousand names, a thousand arts for ill '; [1]

and shall I, poor wretch, deem myself a conqueror when I am being led into captivity?

Do not weigh one transgression too closely against another, dearest brother, nor think that the sins I have mentioned are less heinous than idolatry. Nay, listen to the apostle's verdict: ' For this we know, that no whoremonger or unclean person, nor covetous man, who is an idolater, hath any inheritance in the kingdom of Christ and of God.' [2] Speaking generally all that is of the devil savours of enmity to God, and what is of the devil is idolatry, since all idols are in his service. But in another place the apostle lays down a special law, saying expressly: ' Mortify your members which are upon the earth, laying aside fornication, uncleanness, evil concupiscence and covetousness, which are idolatry, for which things' sake the wrath of God cometh.' [3] Idolatry is not confined to taking some grains of incense in two fingers and throwing them upon an altar fire, nor to pouring a libation of wine from a bowl. Let him deny that avarice is idolatry, who can assert that the selling of the Lord for thirty pieces of silver was a righteous act. Let him, but only him, deny that there is sacrilege in carnal lust, who has polluted the living offering of his body pleasing to God by shameful intercourse with the victims of public

---

[1] Virgil, *Aeneid*, VII. 337.   [2] Ephesians, v. 5.
[3] Colossians, iii. 5.

nefaria conluvione violavit; non fateatur idolatras eos, sed similis eorum, qui in Actibus Apostolorum ex patrimonio suo partem pretii reservantes praesenti periere vindicta. Animadverte, frater: non tibi licet de tuis quicquam habere rebus. ' Omnis,' inquit dominus, ' qui non renuntiaverit cunctis quae possidet, non potest meus esse discipulus.'

6. Cur timido animo Christianus es? Respice cum patre relictum rete, respice surgentem de teloneo publicanum, statim apostolum. ' Filius hominis non habet, ubi caput reclinet ': et tu amplas porticus et ingentia tectorum spatia metaris? Hereditatem expectas saeculi, coheres Christi? Interpretare vocabulum monachi, hoc est nomen tuum: quid facis in turba, qui solus es? Et haec ego non integris rate vel mercibus quasi ignaros fluctuum doctus nauta praemoneo, sed quasi nuper naufragio eiectus in litus timida navigaturis voce denuntio. In illo aestu Charybdis luxuriae salutem vorat, ibi ore virgineo ad pudicitiae perpetranda naufragia Scyllaceum renidens libido blanditur; hic barbarum litus, hic diabolus pirata cum sociis portat vincla capiendis. Nolite credere, nolite esse securi. Licet in morem stagni fusum aequor adrideat, licet vix summa iacentis elementi spiritu terga crispentur, magnus hic campus montes habet,

---

[1] Acts, v. 1.   [2] St. Luke, xiv. 33.

vice. Let him not confess that those men were idolaters, who in the Acts of the Apostles [1] kept back part of the price of their inheritance, and perished by an instant penalty, but only if he is himself like them. Take heed, brother : it is not lawful for you to keep anything that you possess. ' Whosoever he be of you,' says the Lord, ' that forsaketh not all that he hath, he cannot be my disciple '! [2]

Why are you such a timid Christian? Consider him who left his father and his nets, and how the publican rising from the receipt of custom became at once an apostle. ' The Son of man hath not where to lay his head,' [3] and are you planning wide colonnades and spacious halls? Are you looking for an inheritance in this world, you who are joint-heir with Christ? Consider the meaning of the word monk, your proper designation. [4] What are you, a solitary, doing in a crowd? These warnings of mine are not those of a skilled sailor, with ship and cargo intact, addressed to people ignorant of the sea; nay, rather, like some shipwrecked mariner just cast ashore, I address my faltering words to others who are about to set sail. On one side of the strait the Charybdis of self-indulgence engulfs our salvation; on the other the Scylla of lust, with a smile upon her girlish cheek, lures us on to make shipwreck of our chastity. To the right is a savage coast, to the left the devil with his pirate crew carrying chains for his future captives. Be not credulous, be not over-confident. Though the sea be now as smooth and smiling as a pond, though the mighty monster's back be scarcely ruffled by a breath of air, yet that huge plain contains mountains within

---

[3] St. Matthew, viii. 20.   [4] Μόναχος, solitary.

intus inclusum est periculum, intus est hostis. Expedite rudentes, vela suspendite. Crux antemnae figatur in frontibus: tranquillitas ista tempestas est.

'Quid ergo? quicumque in civitate sunt, Christiani non sunt?' Non est tibi eadem causa, quae ceteris. Dominum ausculta dicentem: 'Si vis perfectus esse, vade, vende omnia tua et da pauperibus et veni, sequere me.' Tu autem perfectum te esse pollicitus es. Nam cum derelicta militia castrasti te propter regnum caelorum, quid aliud quam perfectam sectatus es vitam? Perfectus autem servus Christi nihil praeter Christum habet; si praeter Christum habet, perfectus non est. Et si perfectus non est, cum se perfectum Deo fore pollicitus sit, ante mentitus est. 'Os,' autem, 'quod mentitur, occidit animam.'[2] Igitur, ut concludam, si perfectus es, cur bona paterna desideras? Si perfectus non es, dominum fefellisti. Divinis evangelium vocibus tonat: 'Non potestis duobus dominis servire,' et audet quisquam mendacem Christum facere mamonae et domino serviendo? Vociferatur ille saepe: 'Si quis vult post me venire, abneget se ipsum et tollat crucem suam et sequatur me.' Et ego onustus auro arbitror me Christum sequi? 'Qui dicit se in Christo manere, debet, quomodo ille ambulavit, et ipse ambulare.'

7. Quodsi nihil habes, ut responsurum te scio, cur

---

[1] St. Matthew, xix. 21.   [2] Wisdom, i. 11.

it. There is danger in its depths, the foe is lurking there. Stow your tackle, reef your sails, and let the cross which the yard-arm makes be fastened on your front. That stillness means a tempest.

Well, you may say, are not all my fellow-townsmen Christians? Your case is not the same as that of other men. Listen to the Lord speaking: ' If thou wilt be perfect go and sell that thou hast, and give to the poor, and come and follow me.'[1] You promised to be perfect. When you gave up the army and made yourself an eunuch for the kingdom of heaven's sake, what other purpose had you in view save the perfect life? A perfect servant of Christ has nothing beside Christ: if he has anything beside Christ he is not perfect. And if he is not perfect, when he promised God that he would be perfect, his first promise was a lie. Now ' the mouth that lieth slayeth the soul.'[2] To conclude, then, if you are perfect why do you hanker after your father's property? If you are not perfect, you have played the Lord false. The Gospel thunders with God's own voice: ' Ye cannot serve two masters ';[3] and does any man dare to make Christ a liar by serving Mammon and the Lord together? Often does He cry: ' If any one will come after me let him deny himself and take up his cross and follow me.'[4] Do I think that I am following Christ when I load myself with gold? ' He that saith he abideth in Him ought himself also to walk even as He walked.'[5]

I know what your reply will be—' I possess nothing.' When you are so well equipped for war, why do you

---

[3] St. Matthew, vi. 24.   [4] St. Matthew, xvi. 24.
[5] 1 John, ii. 6.

tam bene paratus ad bella non militas? Nisi forte
in patria tua te arbitraris hoc facere, cum in sua
dominus signa non fecerit. Et cur id? Cum auctoritate sume rationem: ' Nemo propheta in sua patria
honorem habet.' ' Non quaero,' inquies, ' honorem;
sufficit mihi conscientia mea.' Neque dominus
quaerebat, quippe qui, ne a turbis rex constitueretur,
aufugit. Sed ubi honor non est, ibi contemptus est;
ubi contemptus, ibi frequens iniuria; ubi autem
iniuria, ibi et indignatio; ubi indignatio, ibi quies
nulla; ubi quies non est, ibi mens a proposito saepe
deducitur; ubi autem per inquietudinem aliquid
aufertur ex studio, minus fit ab eo, quod tollitur, et
ubi minus est, perfectum non potest dici. Ex hac
supputatione illa summa nascitur, monachum perfectum in patria sua esse non posse. Perfectum
autem esse nolle delinquere est.

8. Sed de hoc gradu pulsus provocabis ad clericos:
' An de his aliquid audeam dicere, qui certe in suis
urbibus commorantur?' Absit ut quicquam de his
sinistrum loquar, qui apostolico gradui succedentes
Christi corpus sacro ore conficiunt, per quos nos
etiam Christiani sumus, qui claves regni caelorum
habentes quodammodo ante iudicii diem iudicant,
qui sponsam domini sobria castitate conservant.
Sed alia, ut ante praestruxi, monachi causa est, alia
clericorum. Clerici oves pascunt, ego pascor; illi
de altario vivunt, mihi quasi infructuosae arbori
securis ponitur ad radices, si munus ad altare non

---

[1] Cf. p. 412, note 1.

not take the field? Perhaps you think you can do
so in your own country, although the Lord could
do no signs in His. Why could He not? Hear the
reason that has His authority: 'No prophet has
honour in his own country.' 'I do not seek honour,'
you will say; 'my own conscience is enough for me.'
Neither did the Lord seek it; for when the crowds
would have made Him king He fled away. But
where there is no honour, there is contempt; where
there is contempt, insult is frequent; where there is
insult, there is indignation; where there is indignation, there is no rest; where there is no rest, the
mind is often diverted from its purpose. Moreover,
where through restlessness something of zeal is lost,
zeal is lessened by what it loses, and when a thing is
lessened it cannot be called perfect. We may sum
up our account by saying that a monk cannot be
perfect in his own country; and not to wish to be
perfect is a sin.

Shifted from this position you will appeal to the
clergy. 'Do you dare to criticize them,' you will
say, 'who yet assuredly remain in their own cities?'
Heaven forbid that I should say anything unfavourable about the men who, as successors to the
apostles, make the body of Christ for us with holy
words; who baptize us as Christians; who hold
the keys of the kingdom of heaven, and in a way
judge us before the Judgment Day; who in
sober chastity guard the bride of Christ. But, as
I have laid down already, the case of a monk is
different from that of the clergy.[1] The clergy feed
Christ's sheep; I, a monk, am of their flock. The
clergy live of the altar; if I bring no gift to the altar
steps, I am a barren tree and the axe is laid to my

defero. Nec possum obtendere paupertatem, cum in evangelio anum videam duo, quae sola sibi supererant, aera mittentem. Mihi ante presbyterum sedere non licet; illi, si peccavero, licet tradere me Satanae in interitum carnis, ut spiritus salvus fiat.

Et in veteri quidem lege, quicumque sacerdotibus non obtemperasset, aut extra castra positus lapidabatur a populo aut gladio cervice subiecta contemptum expiabat cruore. Nunc vero inoboediens spiritali mucrone truncatur aut eiectus de ecclesia rabido daemonum ore discerpitur. Quod si te quoque ad eundem ordinem pia fratrum blandimenta sollicitant, gaudebo de ascensu, timebo de lapsu. 'Qui episcopatum desiderat, bonum opus desiderat.' Scimus ista, sed iunge, quod sequitur: 'Oportet autem huiusmodi inreprehensibilem esse, unius uxoris virum, sobrium, pudicum, prudentem, ornatum, hospitalem, docibilem, non vinolentum, non percussorem, sed modestum.' Et ceteris de eo, quae sequuntur, explicitis non minore in tertio gradu adhibuit diligentiam dicens: 'Diaconos similiter pudicos, non bilingues, non multo vino deditos, non turpilucros, habentes mysterium fidei in conscientia pura. Et hi autem probentur primum et sic ministrent nullum crimen habentes.' Vae illi homini, qui vestem non habens nuptialem ingreditur ad cenam! Nihil superest, nisi ut statim audiat: 'Amice, quomodo

---

[1] 1 Corinthians, v. 5.   [2] Deut., xvii. 12.

roots. I cannot plead poverty, for in the Gospel I
see the aged woman offering the last two pennies
she had left. It is not permitted me to sit in the
presence of a presbyter: it is permitted him, if I
sin, to deliver me to Satan, for the destruction of the
flesh that the spirit may be saved.[1]

Under the old law anyone who refused obedience
to the priests was put outside the camp and stoned
by the people, or else he was beheaded and expiated
his contempt with his blood.[2] To-day the dis-
obedient are smitten with the spiritual sword, or
they are expelled from the Church and torn in
pieces by the ravening jaws of demons. If the
pious persuasion of your brethren invites you to take
clerical orders, I shall rejoice at your present rise
and fear a future fall. 'If a man desire the office
of a bishop, he desireth a good work.'[3] We know
the passage: you must continue the quotation:
'Such an one must be blameless, the husband of
one wife, sober, chaste, of good behaviour, given to
hospitality, apt to teach, not given to wine, no
striker but patient.'[4] After setting out some
further details the apostle shows no less care in
dealing with clergy of the third degree. 'Likewise
must the deacons be grave,' he says, 'not double-
tongued, not given to much wine, not greedy of
filthy lucre, holding the mystery of the faith in a
pure conscience. And let these also first be proved;
then let them minister, being found blameless.'[5]
Woe to the man who enters the feast without a
wedding garment! Nothing remains for him but
the quick challenge, 'Friend, how camest thou in

[3] 1 Timothy, iii. 1.   [4] 1 Timothy, iii. 2.
[5] 1 Timothy, iii. 8.

huc venisti?' et illo obmutescente dicatur ministris:
'Tollite illum pedibus et manibus et mittite eum in
tenebras exteriores; ibi erit fletus et stridor dentium.'
Vae illi, qui acceptum talentum in sudario ligans
ceteris lucra facientibus id tantum, quod acceperat,
reservarit! Ilico indignantis domini clamore ferie-
tur: 'Serve nequam, quare non dedisti pecuniam
meam ad mensam, et ego veniens cum usuris exegis-
sem?' id est: 'deposuisses ad altare, quod ferre
non poteras. Dum enim tu, ignavus negotiator,
denarium tenes, alterius locum, qui pecuniam duplicare poterat, occupasti.' Quam ob rem sicut is, qui
bene ministrat, bonum gradum sibi adquirit, ita,
qui indigne ad calicem domini accedit, reus erit
dominici corporis et sanguinis.

9. Non omnes episcopi episcopi. Adtendis
Petrum, sed et Iudam considera. Stephanum sus-
picis, sed et Nicolaum respice, quem dominus in
Apocalypsi sua odit; qui tam turpia et nefanda
commentus est, ut Ophitarum heresis ex illa radice
nascatur. Probet se unusquisque et sic accedat.
Non facit ecclesiastica dignitas Christianum. Cornelius centurio adhuc ethnicus dono spiritus sancti
inundatur; presbyteros Danihel puer iudicat; Amos
ruborum mora destringens repente propheta est;
David pastor adlegitur in regem; minimum dis-
cipulum Iesus amat plurimum. Inferius, frater,

---

[1] St. Matthew, xxii. 11.   [2] St. Luke, xix. 23.
[3] The assumed founder of the sect of the Nicolaitanes,
Rev., ii. 6.

hither?' And as he stands speechless, the servants will be bidden: 'Bind him hand and foot, and take him away, and cast him into outer darkness; there shall be weeping and gnashing of teeth.'[1] Woe to the man who receives a talent and ties it in a napkin, merely keeping what he has received while others make a profit! At once his angry lord's rebuke shall strike him: 'Thou wicked servant, wherefore gavest thou not my money into the bank, that at my coming I might have required mine own with usury?'[2] That is, 'You should have laid down at the altar what you yourself were not able to carry. For while you, a slothful trader, keep a penny back, you occupy the place of another who could have doubled the money.' Wherefore, as he who ministers well wins for himself an honourable place, so he who comes to the Lord's cup unworthily shall be guilty of the body and blood of the Lord.

Not all bishops are true bishops. You notice Peter; but mark Judas as well. You look up to Stephen; but consider also Nicolas[3] whom the Lord in His Apocalypse abominates, the man whose foul and shameful teachings gave rise to the Ophite[4] heresy. Let a man examine himself and so let him come. Ecclesiastical rank does not make a man a Christian. The centurion Cornelius was still a heathen when he was cleansed by the gift of the Holy Spirit. Daniel was but a child when he judged the elders. Amos was plucking blackberries when in a moment he was made a prophet. David was only a shepherd when he was chosen to be king. The least of his disciples was the one whom Jesus loved most. My brother, sit down in the lower place,

---

[4] The Ophites were an obscure Gnostic sect.

accumbe, ut minore veniente sursum iubearis
accedere. Super quem dominus requiescit, nisi
super humilem et quietum et trementem verba sua?
Cui plus creditur, plus ab eo exigitur. ' Potentes
potenter tormenta patientur.' Nec sibi quisquam
de corporis tantum mundi castitate supplaudat, cum
omne verbum otiosum, quodcumque locuti fuerint
homines, reddituri sint pro eo rationem in die iudicii,
cum etiam convicium in fratrem homicidii sit reatus.
Non est facile stare loco Pauli, tenere gradum iam
cum Christo regnantium, ne forte veniat angelus,
qui scindat velum templi tui, qui candelabrum tuum
loco moveat. Aedificaturus turrem futuri operis
sumptus supputa. Infatuatum sal ad nihilum est
utile, nisi ut proiciatur foras et a porcis conculcetur.
Monachus si ceciderit, rogabit pro eo sacerdos; pro
sacerdotis lapsu quis rogaturus est?

10. Sed quia e scopulosis locis enavigavit oratio
et inter cavas spumeis fluctibus cautes fragilis in
altum cumba processit, expandenda vela sunt ventis
et quaestionum scopulis transvadatis laetantium more
nautarum epilogi celeuma cantandum est. O desertum Christi floribus vernans! O solitudo, in qua
illi nascuntur lapides, de quibus in Apocalypsi
civitas magni regis extruitur! O heremus familiari
Deo gaudens! Quid agis, frater, in saeculo, qui
maior es mundo? Quam diu te tectorum umbrae

that when one less honourable comes you may be bidden to go up higher. Upon whom does the Lord rest save upon him that is lowly and of a contrite spirit and that trembleth at his words? The more that is entrusted to a man, the more is demanded from him: ' The mighty will suffer torments mightily.'[1] Let no man applaud himself because of his bodily chastity alone on the day of judgment, for men shall render account for every idle word they have spoken, and abuse of a brother shall be counted as the sin of murder. It is no easy thing to stand in Paul's place and to hold the rank of those who now reign with Christ. Perchance an angel may come to rend the veil of your temple and to remove your candlestick from its place. If you are thinking of building a tower, reckon up the cost of the structure first. Salt that has lost its savour is worthless: it can only be cast out and trodden underfoot by swine. If a monk falls, a priest will intercede for him; but who shall intercede for a fallen priest?

My discourse has now sailed clear of the reefs, and from the midst of hollow crags with foaming waves my frail bark has won her way into deep water. Now I may spread my canvas to the wind, and leaving the rocks of controversy astern, like some merry sailor sing a cheerful epilogue. O wilderness, bright with Christ's spring flowers! O solitude, whence come those stones wherewith in the Apocalypse the city of the mighty king is built! O desert, rejoicing in God's familiar presence! What are you doing in the world, brother, you who are more than the universe? How long is the shade of a roof going

[1] Wisdom, vi. 6.

premunt? Quam diu fumeus harum urbium carcer includit? Crede mihi, nescio quid plus lucis aspicio. Libet sarcina carnis abiecta ad purum aetheris volare fulgorem. Paupertatem times? sed beatos pauperes Christus appellat. Labore terreris? sed nemo athleta sine sudoribus coronatur. De cibo cogitas? sed fides famem non sentit. Super nudam metuis humum exesa ieiuniis membra conlidere? sed dominus tecum iacet. Squalidi capitis horret inculta caesaries? sed caput tuum Christus est. Infinita heremi vastitas terret? sed tu paradisum mente deambula. Quotienscumque illuc cogitatione conscenderis, totiens in heremo non eris. Scabra sine balneis adtrahitur cutis? sed qui in Christo semel lotus est, non illi necesse est iterum lavare. Et, ut breviter, ad cuncta apostolum audias respondentem: ' Non sunt condignae passiones huius saeculi ad superventuram gloriam, quae revelabitur in nobis.' Delicatus es, carissime, si et hic vis gaudere cum saeculo et postea regnare cum Christo.

11. Veniet, veniet illa dies, qua corruptivum hoc et mortale incorruptionem induat et immortalitatem. Beatus servus, quem dominus invenerit vigilantem. Tunc ad vocem tubae pavebit terra cum populis, tu gaudebis. Iudicaturo domino lugubre mundus immugiet; tribus ad tribum ferient pectora; potentissimi quondam reges nudo latere

to confine you? How long shall the smoky prison of these cities shut you in? Believe me, I see something more of light than you behold. How sweet it is to fling off the burden of the flesh, and to fly aloft to the clear radiance of the sky! Are you afraid of poverty? Christ calls the poor blessed. Are you frightened by the thought of toil? No athlete gains his crown without sweat. Are you thinking about food? Faith feels not hunger. Do you dread bruising your limbs worn away with fasting on the bare ground? The Lord lies by your side. Is your rough head bristling with uncombed hair? Your head is Christ. Does the infinite vastness of the desert seem terrible? In spirit you may always stroll in paradise, and when in thought you have ascended there you will no longer be in the desert. Is your skin rough and scurfy without baths? He who has once washed in Christ needs not to wash again. Listen to the apostle's brief reply to all complaints: ' The sufferings of this present time are not worthy to be compared with the glory which shall come after them, which shall be revealed in us.' [1] You are a pampered darling indeed, dearest brother, if you wish to rejoice here with this world and afterwards to reign with Christ.

The day, the day will come when this corrupt and mortal body shall put on incorruptibility and become immortal. Happy the servant whom the Lord then shall find on the watch. Then at the voice of the trumpet the earth with its peoples shall quake, and you will rejoice. When the Lord comes to give judgment the universe will utter a mournful groan; the tribes of men will beat their breasts; kings once

[1] Romans, viii. 18.

palpitabunt; exhibebitur cum prole sua vere tunc ignitus Iuppiter; adducetur et cum suis stultus Plato discipulis; Aristoteli argumenta non proderunt. Tunc tu rusticanus et pauper exultabis, ridebis et dices: ' Ecce crucifixus Deus meus, ecce iudex, qui obvolutus pannis in praesepio vagiit. Hic est ille operarii et quaestuariae filius, hic, qui matris gestatus sinu hominem Deus fugit in Aegyptum, hic vestitus coccino, hic sentibus coronatus, hic magus daemonium habens et Samarites. Cerne manus, Iudaee, quas fixeras; cerne latus, Romane, quod foderas. Videte corpus, an idem sit, quod dicebatis clam nocte tulisse discipulos.' Ut haec tibi, frater, dicere, ut his interesse contingat, qui nunc labor durus est?

XXII

Ad Eustochium

1. 'Audi, filia, et vide et inclina aurem tuam et obliviscere populum tuum et domum patris tui; et concupiscet rex decorem tuum.' In quadragesimo quarto psalmo Deus ad animam loquitur humanam,

most mighty will shiver with naked flanks; Jupiter
with all his offspring will then be shown amid real
fires; Plato with his disciples will be revealed as but
a fool; Aristotle's arguments will not help him.
Then you the poor rustic will exult, and say with a
smile: ' Behold my crucified God, behold the judge.
This is he who once was wrapped in swaddling clothes
and uttered baby cries in a manger. This is the
son of a working man and a woman who served for
wages. This is he who, carried in his mother's
arms, fled into Egypt, a God from a man. This
is he who was clad in a scarlet robe and crowned
with thorns. This is he who was called a magician,
a man with a devil, a Samaritan. Behold the
hands, ye Jews, that you nailed to the cross.
Behold the side, ye Romans, that you pierced. See
whether this is the same body that you said the
disciples carried off secretly in the night.'

O my brother, that it may be yours to say these
words and to be present on that day, what labour
now can seem hard?

LETTER XXII

To Eustochium

The virgin's profession

Written A.D. 384

' HEAR, O daughter, and consider, and incline
thine ear; forget also thine own people and thy
father's house, and the king shall desire thy beauty.' [1]
So in the forty-fourth Psalm God speaks to the

[1] Psalm xlv. 11. (Vulg. Psalm xliv.)

ut secundum exemplum Abrahae exiens de terra sua
et de cognatione sua relinquat Chaldaeos, qui ' quasi
daemonia' interpretantur, et habitet in regione
viventium, quam alibi propheta suspirat, dicens:
' Credo videre bona domini in terra viventium.'
Verum non sufficit tibi exire de patria, nisi obliviscaris populi et domum patris tui et carne contempta
sponsi iungaris amplexibus. ' Ne respexeris,' inquit,
' retro nec steteris in tota circa regione; in montem
salvum te fac, ne forte comprehendaris.' Non
expedit adprehenso aratro respicere post tergum
nec de agro reverti domum nec post Christi tunicam
ad tollendum aliud vestimentum tecta descendere.
Grande miraculum: pater filiam cohortatur: ' Ne
memineris patris.' ' Vos de patre diabolo estis et
desideria patris vestri vultis facere' dicitur ad
Iudaeos et alibi: ' Qui facit peccatum, de diabolo
est.' Tali primum parente generati nigri sumus et
post paenitentiam necdum culmine virtutis ascenso
dicimus: ' Nigra sum et speciosa filia Hierusalem.'

Exivi de domo infantiae meae, oblita sum patris,
renascor in Christo. Quid pro hoc mercedis accipio?
Sequitur: ' Et concupiscet rex decorem tuum.' Hoc
ergo illud magnum est sacramentum: ' Propter hoc
relinquet homo patrem et matrem et adhaerebit
uxori suae et erunt ambo—in carne una?' Iam

---

[1] Psalm xxvii. 13. [2] Genesis, xix. 17.
[3] St. John, viii. 44. [4] 1 John, iii. 8.
[5] Song of Solomon, i. 5. Jerome's text here differs from
the Vulgate: *Nigra sum sed formosa, filiae Jerusalem*. Vulg.
Cant., i. 4. [6] Ephesians, v. 31.

human soul, that, following Abraham's example, it should go out from its own land and from its kinsmen, and leave the Chaldaeans, that is the demons, and dwell in the country of the living, for which elsewhere the prophet sighs, saying: ' I trust to see the good things of the Lord in the land of the living.' [1] But for you it is not enough to go out from your own land, unless you forget your people and your father's house, so that despising the flesh you may be joined to your bridegroom's embrace. ' Look not behind thee,' the Scripture says, ' neither stay in all the part around; escape to the mountain; lest thou be caught.' [2] It is not right for one who has grasped the plough to look behind him or to return home from the field, or after putting on Christ's tunic to descend from the roof for other raiment. A wonder: a father charges his daughter: ' Do not remember your father.' ' Ye are of your father the devil, and the lusts of your father it is your will to do.' [3] So it was said to the Jews. And in another place. ' He that committeth sin is of the devil.' [4] Born of such a parent first we are black by nature, and even after repentance, until we have climbed to virtue's height, we may say, ' I am black and comely, a daughter of Jerusalem.' [5]

You may say—I have gone out from my childhood's home, I have forgotten my father, I am born again in Christ. What reward do I receive for this? The context tells you—' And the king shall desire thy beauty.' This then is the great sacrament. ' For this cause shall a man leave his father and his mother and shall be joined unto his wife, and they two shall be,' [6] no longer, as there, ' of one flesh,'

non, ut ibi, in una carne, sed spiritu. Non est sponsus tuus adrogans, non superbus: Aethiopissam duxit uxorem. Statim ut volueris sapientiam veri audire Salomonis et ad eum veneris, confitebitur tibi cuncta, quae novit, et inducet te rex in cubiculum suum et mirum in modum colore mutato sermo tibi ille conveniet: 'Quae est ista, quae ascendit dealbata?'

2. Haec idcirco, mi domina Eustochium—dominam quippe debeo vocare sponsam domini mei—ut ex ipso principio lectionis agnosceres non me nunc laudes virginitatis esse dicturum, quam probasti optime, eam cum secuta es, nec enumeraturum molestias nuptiarum, quomodo uterus intumescat, infans vagiat, cruciet paelex, domus cura sollicitet, et omnia, quae putantur bona, mors extrema praecidat— habent enim et maritatae ordinem suum, honorabiles nuptias et cubile immaculatum—sed ut intellegeres tibi exeunti de Sodoma timendum esse Loth uxoris exemplum. Nulla in hoc libello adulatio—adulator quippe blandus inimicus est—nulla erit rhetorici pompa sermonis, quae te iam inter angelos statuat et beatudine virginitatis exposita mundum subiciat pedibus tuis.

3. Nolo tibi venire superbiam de proposito, sed timorem. Onusta incedis auro, latro vitandus est. Stadium est haec vita mortalibus: hic contendimus, ut alibi coronemur. Nemo inter serpentes et scorpiones securus ingreditur. 'Inebriatus est,'

but of one spirit. Your bridegroom is not arrogant,
not haughty; He has married a woman of Ethiopia.
As soon as you resolve to hear the wisdom of the
true Solomon, and come to Him, He will avow to
you all His knowledge; He will lead you as a king
to His chamber; your colour will be miraculously
changed, and to you the words will be fitting: ' Who
is this that goeth up and hath been made white? ' [1]

I am writing this to you, Lady Eustochium (I am
bound to call my Lord's bride ' Lady '), that from the
very beginning of my discourse you may learn that
I do not to-day intend to sing the praises of the
virginity which you have adopted and proved to be
so good. Nor shall I now reckon up the disadvantages of marriage, such as pregnancy, a
crying baby, the tortures of jealousy, the cares of
household management, and the cutting short by
death of all its fancied blessings. Married women
have their due allotted place, if they live in honourable marriage and keep their bed undefiled. My
purpose in this letter is to show you that you are
fleeing from Sodom and that you should take warning
by Lot's wife. There is no flattery in these pages.
A flatterer is a smooth-spoken enemy. Nor will
there be any pomp of rhetoric in expounding the
beatitude of virginity, setting you among the angels
and putting the world beneath your feet.

I would have you draw from your vows not pride
but fear. When you walk laden with gold you must
beware of robbers. For mortals this life is a race:
we run it on earth that we may receive our crown
elsewhere. No man can walk secure amid serpents
and scorpions. The Lord says: ' My sword hath

[1] Song of Solomon, viii. 5. (Septuagint.)

inquit dominus, ' gladius meus in caelo,' et tu pacem arbitraris in terra, quae tribulos generat et spinas, quam serpens comedit? ' Non est nobis conluctatio adversus carnem et sanguinem, sed adversus principatus et potestates huius mundi et harum tenebrarum, adversus spiritalia nequitiae in caelestibus.' Magnis inimicorum circumdamur agminibus, hostium plena sunt omnia. Caro fragilis et cinis futura post modicum pugnat sola cum pluribus.

Cum autem fuerit dissoluta et venerit princeps mundi istius et invenerit in ea nihil, tunc secura audies per prophetam : ' Non timebis a timore nocturno, a sagitta volante per diem, a negotio perambulante in tenebris, ab incursu et daemonio meridiano. Cadent a latere tuo mille et decem milia a dextris tuis, ad te autem non adpropinquabit.' Quodsi eorum te multitudo turbaverit et ad singula incitamenta vitiorum coeperis aestuare et dixerit tibi cogitatio tua : ' Quid faciemus ? ' respondit Heliseus : ' Noli timere, quoniam plures nobiscum sunt, quam cum illis,' et orabit et dicet : ' Domine, adaperi oculos puellae tuae et videat.' Et apertis oculis videbis igneum currum, qui te ad exemplum Heliae in astra sustollat, et tunc laeta cantabis : ' Anima nostra quasi passer erepta est de laqueo venantium : laqueus contritus est et nos liberati sumus.'

4. Quamdiu hoc fragili corpusculo continemur, quamdiu ' habemus thesaurum istum in vasis ficti-

---

[1] Isaiah, xxxiv. 5.   [2] Ephesians, vi. 12.
[3] Psalm xci. 5.   [4] 2 Kings, vi. 16.
[5] Psalm cxxiv. 7.   [6] 2 Corinthians, iv. 7.

drunk its fill in heaven ';[1] and do you expect peace
on the earth, which yields only thorns and thistles
and is itself the serpent's food? 'Our wrestling is
not against flesh and blood, but against the principalities, against the powers, against the world rulers
of this darkness, against the spiritual hosts of wickedness in the heavenly places.'[2] We are surrounded
by the thronging hosts of our foes, our enemies are
on every side. The flesh is weak and soon it will be
ashes, but to-day it fights alone against a multitude.

But when the flesh has been melted away and the
Prince of yonder world has come and found in it no
sin, then in safety you shall listen to the prophet's
words: 'Thou shall not be afraid for the terror by
night nor for the arrow that flieth by day; nor for
the trouble which haunteth thee in the darkness;
nor for the demon and his attacks at noonday. A
thousand shall fall at thy side and ten thousand at
thy right hand; but it shall not come nigh thee.'[3]
If the hosts of the enemy beset you, if the allurements of sin begin to burn within your breast, if in
your troubled thoughts you ask—'What shall I do?'
Elisha's words will give you an answer: 'Fear not,
for they that be with us are more than they that be
with them.'[4] He will pray for you and will say:
'Lord, open the eyes of thy handmaid that she may
see.' And when your eyes have been opened you
will see a chariot of fire which will carry you, as it
carried Elijah, up to the stars; and then you will
joyfully sing: 'Our soul is escaped as a sparrow out
of the snare of the fowlers: the snare is broken and
we are escaped.'[5]

As long as we are held down by this frail body;
as long as we keep our treasure in earthen vessels,[6]

59

libus' et concupiscit spiritus adversus carnem et
caro adversus spiritum, nulla est certa victoria.
Adversarius noster diabolus tamquam leo rugiens
aliquid devorare quaerens circuit. ' Posuisti,' ait
David, ' tenebras et facta est nox. In ipsa pertran-
sibunt omnes bestiae silvae, catuli leonum rugientes,
ut rapiant et quaerant a Deo escam sibi.' Non
quaerit diabolus homines infideles, non eos, qui
foris sunt et quorum carnes rex in olla succendit
Assyrius : de ecclesia Christi rapere festinat. Escae
eius secundum Ambacum electae sunt : Iob subver-
tere cupit et devorato Iuda ad cribrandos apostolos
expetit potestatem. Non venit salvator pacem
mittere super terram, sed gladium. Cecidit Lucifer,
qui mane oriebatur, et ille, qui in paradiso deliciarum
nutritus est, meruit audire : ' Si alte feraris ut aquila,
inde te detraham, dicit dominus.' Dixerat enim
in corde suo : ' Super sidera caeli ponam sedem
meam et ero similis altissimo.' Unde cotidie ad eos,
qui per scalam Iacob somniante descendunt, loquitur
Deus : ' Ego dixi : dii estis et filii altissimi omnes.
Vos autem sicut homines moriemini et tamquam unus
de principibus cadetis.' Cecidit enim primus diabolus, et cum stet Deus in synagoga deorum, in medio
autem deos discernat, apostolus eis, qui dii esse
desinunt, scribit : ' Ubi enim in vobis dissensiones et
aemulationes, nonne homines estis et secundum
hominem ambulatis ? '

5. Si Paulus apostolus, vas electionis et preparatus
in evangelium Christi, ob carnis aculeos et incentiva

[1] Psalm civ. 20.
[2] Reference doubtful, but perhaps cf. Jeremiah xxix. 22.
[3] Habakkuk, i. 16.   [4] Isaiah, xiv. 13.
[5] Psalm lxxxii. 6.   [6] 1 Corinthians, iii. 3.

and the flesh lusteth against the spirit, the spirit
against the flesh: so long can there be no sure
victory. Our adversary the devil goeth about as a
roaring lion seeking whom he may devour. David
says: 'Thou makest darkness and it is night;
wherein all the beasts of the forest do creep forth.
The young lions roar after their prey and seek their
meat from God.'[1] The devil does not look for unbelievers or for those who are without, whose flesh
the Assyrian king roasted in a pot:[2] it is the Church
of Christ that he hastens to ravish. According to
Habakkuk: 'His dainty morsels are of the choicest.'[3]
He desires Job's ruin, and after devouring Judas he
seeks power to put all the apostles through his
sieve. The Saviour came not to send peace upon the
earth but a sword. Lucifer fell, Lucifer who used
to rise with the dawn; and he who was nurtured in a
paradise of delight heard the well-earned sentence:
'Though thou exalt thyself as the eagle, thence will
I bring thee down, saith the Lord.'[4] For he had said
in his heart: 'I will exalt my throne above the stars
of God and I will be like the Most High.' Wherefore God every day says to the angels as they go
down the stairway which Jacob saw in his dream:
'I have said ye are Gods and all of you are children
of the Most High. But ye shall die like men and fall
like one of the princes.'[5] The devil fell first, and
since God stands in the congregation of the Gods
and judges them in the midst, the apostle writes to
those who are ceasing to be Gods: 'Whereas there is
among you envying and strife, are ye not carnal and
walk as men?'[6]

The apostle Paul, who was a chosen vessel set
apart for the gospel of Christ, because of the spur of

61

vitiorum reprimit corpus suum et servituti subicit,
ne aliis praedicans ipse reprobus inveniatur, et
tamen videt aliam legem in membris suis repugnantem legi mentis suae et captivantem se in lege
peccati, si post nuditatem, ieiunia, famem, carcerem,
flagella, supplicia in semet versus exclamat: ' Infelix
ego homo, quis me liberabit de corpore mortis huius? '[1]
tu te putas securam esse debere? Cave, quaeso, ne
quando de te dicat Deus: ' Virgo Israhel cecidit:
non est, qui suscitet eam.'[2] Audenter loquor: cum
omnia Deus possit, suscitare virginem non potest
post ruinam. Valet quidem liberare de poena, sed
non valet coronare corruptam. Timeamus illam
prophetiam, ne in nobis etiam conpleatur: ' et
virgines bonae deficient.'[3] Observa, quid dicat: ' et
virgines bonae deficient ': quia sunt et virgines
malae. ' Qui viderit,' inquit, ' mulierem ad concupiscendum iam moechatus est eam in corde suo.'[4]
Perit ergo et mente virginitas. Istae sunt virgines
malae, virgines carne, non spiritu, virgines stultae,
quae oleum non habentes excluduntur ab sponso.

6. Si autem et illae virgines virgines sunt, ob alias
tamen culpas virginitate corporum non salvantur,
quid fiet illis, quae prostituerunt membra Christi et
mutaverunt templa Sancti Spiritus in lupanar? Ilico
audient: ' Descende, sede in terra, virgo filia
Babylonis, sede in terra: non est thronus filiae

---

[1] Romans, vii. 24.   [2] Amos, v. 2.
[3] Amos, viii. 13.   [4] St. Matthew, v. 28.

the flesh and the allurements of sin, keeps his body down and subjects it to slavery, lest in preaching to others he himself be found a reprobate. But still he sees that there is another law in his members fighting against the law of his will, and that he is still led captive to the law of sin. After nakedness, fasting, hunger, prison, scourging and torture, he turns back upon himself and cries: ' Oh, wretched man that I am, who shall deliver me from the body of this death ? ' [1] If that is so with him, do you think that you ought to lay aside all fear ? Beware, pray, lest God some day should say of you: ' The virgin of Israel is fallen and there is none to raise her up.' [2] I will say it boldly; though God can do all things, he cannot raise a virgin up after she has fallen. He is able to free one who has been corrupted from the penalty of her sin, but he refuses her the crown. Let us be fearful lest in our case also the prophecy be fulfilled: ' Good virgins shall faint.' [3] Note that it is of good virgins he speaks, for there are bad ones as well. The Scripture says: ' Whosoever looketh on a woman to lust after her hath committed adultery with her already in his heart.' [4] Virginity therefore can be lost even by a thought. Those are the evil virgins, virgins in the flesh, but not in the spirit: foolish virgins, who, having no oil in their lamps, are shut out by the Bridegroom.

But if even those virgins are virgins, and yet are not saved by their bodily virginity when they have other faults, what shall be done to those who have prostituted the members of Christ and changed the temple of the Holy Spirit into a brothel ? Straightway they shall hear the words : ' Come down and sit in the dust, O virgin daughter of Babylon; sit in the dust, for there

Chaldaeorum; non vocaberis ultra mollis et delicata. Accipe molam, mole farinam, discoperi velamentum, denuda crura tua, transi flumina et revelabitur ignominia tua et apparebunt opprobria tua,' et hoc post Dei Filii thalamos, post oscula fratruelis et sponsi illa, de qua quondam sermo propheticus concinebat: ' Adstitit regina a dextris tuis in vestitu deaurato, circumdata varietate.' Nudabitur et posteriora eius ponentur in facie ipsius; sedebit ad aquas solitudinis et posito vase divaricabit pedes suos omni transeunti et usque ad verticem polluetur. Rectius fuerat homini subisse coniugium, ambulasse per plana, quam ad altiora tendentem in profundum inferi cadere.

Non fiat, obsecro, civitas meretrix fidelis Sion, ne post trinitatis hospitium ibi daemones saltent et sirenae nidificent et hiricii. Non solvatur fascia pectoralis, sed statim ut libido titillaverit sensum, ut blandum voluptatis incendium dulci nos calore perfuderit, erumpamus in vocem: ' Dominus auxiliator meus, non timebo, quid faciat mihi caro.' Cum paululum interior homo inter vitia et virtutes coeperit fluctuare, dicito: ' Quare tristis es, anima mea, et quare conturbas me? Spera in domino, quoniam confitebor illi, salutare vultus mei et Deus meus.' Nolo sinas cogitationem crescere; nihil in

---

[1] Isaiah, xlvii. 1.　　　[2] Psalm xliv. 10.　Vulgate.
[3] Ezekiel, xvi. 25. cf. Jeremiah, xiii. 26.　[4] Psalm cxviii. 6.
[5] Psalm xlii. 11.

64

is no throne for the daughter of the Chaldaeans; no more shalt thou be called tender and delicate. Take the millstone and grind meal; uncover thy locks, make bare thy legs, pass over the rivers; thy nakedness shall be uncovered, yea, thy shame shall be seen.'[1] And this, after the bride-chamber of God the Son, after the kisses of her kinsman and her bridegroom, she of whom once the word of the prophet sang: 'Upon thy right hand stood the queen in a vestment of gold wrought about with divers colours.'[2] But now she shall be made naked and her skirts shall be placed upon her face: she shall sit by the waters of loneliness and lay down her pitcher; and shall open her feet to every one that passeth by and shall be polluted to the crown of her head.[3] Better had it been for her to have submitted to marriage with a man and to have walked on the plain, rather than to strain for the heights and fall into the depths of hell.

Let not the faithful city of Sion become a harlot, I pray you; let not demons dance and sirens and satyrs nest in the place that once sheltered the Trinity. Loose not the belt that confines the bosom. As soon as lust begins to tickle the senses and the soft fires of pleasure envelop us with their delightful warmth, let us break forth and cry: 'The Lord is on my side: I will not fear what the flesh can do unto me.'[4] When for a moment the inner man shows signs of wavering between vice and virtue, say: 'Why art thou cast down, O my soul, and why art thou disquieted within me? Hope thou in God, for I shall yet praise Him who is the health of my countenance and my God.'[5] I would not have you allow any such thoughts to rise. Let nothing disorderly,

te Babylonium, nihil confusionis adolescat. Dum parvus est hostis, interfice; nequitia elidatur in semine. Audi psalmistam loquentem: ' Filia Babylonis misera, beatus, qui retribuet tibi retributionem tuam; beatus qui tenebit et adlidet parvulos tuos ad petram.' Quia ergo inpossibile est in sensum hominis non inruere notum medullarum calorem, ille laudatur, ille praedicatur beatus, qui, statim ut coeperit cogitare, interfecit cogitatus et elidit eos ad petram: petra autem est Christus.

7. O quotiens in heremo constitutus et in illa vasta solitudine, quae exusta solis ardoribus horridum monachis praestat habitaculum, putavi me Romanis interesse deliciis! Sedebam solus, quia amaritudine repletus eram. Horrebam sacco membra deformis, squalida cutis situm Aethiopicae carnis adduxerat. Cotidie lacrimae, cotidie gemitus et, si quando repugnantem somnus imminens oppressisset, nuda humo vix ossa haerentia conlidebam. De cibis vero et potu taceo, cum etiam languentes aqua frigida utantur et coctum aliquid accepisse luxuriae sit. Ille igitur ego, qui ob gehennae metum tali me carcere ipse damnaveram, scorpionum tantum socius et ferarum, saepe choris intereram puellarum. Pallebant ora ieiuniis et mens desideriis aestuabat

---

[1] Psalm cxxxvii. 9.

nothing that is of Babylon find shelter in your breast. Slay the enemy while he is small: nip evil in the bud. Hearken to the words of the Psalmist: ' Hapless daughter of Babylon, happy shall he be that rewardeth thee as thou hast served us. Happy shall he be that taketh and dasheth thy little ones against the stones.'[1] It is impossible that the body's natural heat should not sometimes assail a man and kindle sensual desire; but he is praised and accounted blessed, who, when thoughts begin to rise, gives them no quarter, but dashes them straightway against the rock: ' And the Rock is Christ.'[2]

Oh, how often, when I was living in the desert, in that lonely waste, scorched by the burning sun, which affords to hermits a savage dwelling-place, how often did I fancy myself surrounded by the pleasures of Rome! I used to sit alone; for I was filled with bitterness. My unkempt limbs were covered in shapeless sackcloth; my skin through long neglect had become as rough and black as an Ethiopian's. Tears and groans were every day my portion; and if sleep ever overcame my resistance and fell upon my eyes, I bruised my restless bones against the naked earth. Of food and drink I will not speak. Hermits have nothing but cold water even when they are sick, and for them it is sinful luxury to partake of cooked dishes. But though in my fear of hell I had condemned myself to this prison-house, where my only companions were scorpions and wild beasts, I often found myself surrounded by bands of dancing girls. My face was pale with fasting; but though my limbs were cold

[2] 1 Corinthians, x. 4.

in frigido corpore et ante hominem suum iam carne praemortua sola libidinum incendia bulliebant.

Ita omni auxilio destitutus ad Iesu iacebam pedes, rigabam lacrimis, crine tergebam et repugnantem carnem ebdomadarum inedia subiugabam. Non erubesco infelicitatis meae, quin potius plango non esse, quod fuerim. Memini me clamantem diem crebro iunxisse cum nocte nec prius a pectoris cessasse verberibus, quam domino rediret increpante tranquillitas. Ipsam quoque cellulam meam quasi cogitationum consciam pertimescebam et mihimet iratus et rigidus solus deserta penetrabam. Sicubi concava vallium, aspera montium, rupium praerupta cernebam, ibi meae orationi locus, illud miserrimae carnis ergastulum ; et, ut mihi ipse testis est dominus, post multas lacrimas, post caelo oculos inhaerentes nonnunquam videbar mihi interesse agminibus angelorum et laetus gaudensque cantabam: ' Post te in odorem unguentorum tuorum currimus.'

8. Si autem haec sustinent illi, qui exeso corpore solis cogitationibus oppugnantur, quid patitur puella, quae deliciis fruitur ? Nempe illud apostoli : ' Vivens mortua est.' Si quid itaque in me potest esse consilii, si experto creditur, hoc primum moneo, hoc obtestor, ut sponsa Christi vinum fugiat pro veneno. Haec adversus adulescentiam prima arma sunt daemonum. Non sic avaritia quatit, inflat superbia,

---

[1] Song of Solomon, i. 3.   [2] 1 Timothy, v. 6.

as ice my mind was burning with desire, and the fires of lust kept bubbling up before me when my flesh was as good as dead.

And so, when all other help failed me, I used to fling myself at Jesus' feet; I watered them with my tears, I wiped them with my hair; and if my flesh still rebelled I subdued it by weeks of fasting. I do not blush to confess my misery; nay, rather, I lament that I am not now what once I was. I remember that often I joined night to day with my wailings and ceased not from beating my breast till tranquillity returned to me at the Lord's behest. I used to dread my poor cell as though it knew my secret thoughts. Filled with stiff anger against myself, I would make my way alone into the desert; and when I came upon some hollow valley or rough mountain or precipitous cliff, there I would set up my oratory, and make that spot a place of torture for my unhappy flesh. There sometimes also—the Lord Himself is my witness—after many a tear and straining of my eyes to heaven, I felt myself in the presence of the angelic hosts and in joy and gladness would sing: 'Because of the savour of thy good ointments we will run after thee.' [1]

If such are the temptations of men whose bodies are emaciated with fasting so that they have only evil thoughts to withstand, how must it fare with a girl who clings to the enjoyment of luxuries? Surely, as the apostle says: 'She is dead while yet she liveth.' [2] Therefore, if I may advise you and if experience gives my advice weight, I would begin with an urgent exhortation. As Christ's spouse avoid wine as you would avoid poison. Wine is the first weapon that devils use in attacking the young. The restlessness of greed, the windiness of pride, the

delectat ambitio. Facile aliis caremus vitiis: hic hostis intus inclusus est. Quocumque pergimus, nobiscum portamus inimicum. Vinum et adulescentia duplex incendium voluptatis. Quid oleum flammae adicimus? Quid ardenti corpusculo fomenta ignium ministramus?

Paulus ad Timotheum: ' Iam noli,' inquit, ' aquam bibere, sed vinum modicum utere propter stomachum et frequentes tuas infirmitates.' Vide, quibus causis vini potio concedatur: vix hoc stomachi dolor et frequens meretur infirmitas. Et ne nobis forsitan de aegrotationibus blandiremur, modicum praecepit esse sumendum, medici potius consilio quam apostoli —licet et apostolus sit medicus spiritalis—et, ne Timotheus inbecillitate superatus evangelii praedicandi non posset habere discursus. Alioquin se dixisse meminerat et: ' vinum, in quo est luxuria,' et: ' bonum est homini vinum non bibere et carnem non manducare.' Noe vinum bibit et inebriatus est rudi adhuc saeculo; et tunc primum plantavit vineam: inebriare vinum forsitan nesciebat. Et ut intellegas scripturae in omnibus sacramentum— margarita quippe est sermo Dei et ex omni parte forari potest—post ebrietatem nudatio femorum subsecuta est, libido iuncta luxuriae. Prius venter et statim cetera; manducavit enim populus et bibit, ' et surrexerunt ludere.' Loth, amicus Dei, in monte

---

1 1 Timothy, v. 23.   2 Ephesians, v. 18.
3 Romans, xiv. 21.   4 Exodus, xxxii. 6.

delights of ostentation are nothing to this. Other vices we easily forgo: this is an enemy within our walls and wherever we go we carry our foe with us. Wine and Youth—behold a double source for pleasure's fire. Why throw oil on the flame; why give fresh fuel to a wretched body that is already ablaze?

Paul says to Timothy: 'Drink no longer water, but use a little wine for thy stomach's sake, and for thine often infirmities.'[1] Notice the reasons why wine is allowed: it is to cure pain in the stomach and to relieve a frequent infirmity and hardly then. And lest perchance we should indulge ourselves on the ground of illness, Paul recommends that but a little wine should be taken, advising rather as a physician than as an apostle—although indeed an apostle is a spiritual physician. He was afraid that Timothy might be overcome by weakness and might not be able to complete the many journeys that the preaching of the Gospel rendered necessary. In any case, he remembered that he had said elsewhere: 'Wine, wherein is wantonness'[2] and 'It is good for a man neither to drink wine nor to eat flesh.'[3] Noah took wine and became drunken. But living in the rude age after the Flood, when the vine first was planted, he was unaware perhaps of its inebriating qualities. And that you may see the mystery of the Scripture in all its fullness—for the word of God is a pearl and may be pierced right through—note that after his drunkenness there followed the uncovering of his thighs: lust was near neighbour to wantonness. First the belly is swollen, then the other members are roused. 'The people sat down to eat and drink and rose up to play.'[4] Lot, the friend of God, after

salvatus et de tot millibus populis solus iustus inventus inebriatur a filiabus suis; et licet putarent genus hominum defecisse et hoc facerent liberorum magis desiderio quam libidinis, tamen virum iustum sciebant hoc nisi ebrium non esse facturum; denique, quid fecerit ignoravit; et—quamquam voluntas non sit in crimine, error in culpa est—inde nascuntur Moabitae et Ammanitae, inimici Israhel qui usque ad quartam et decimam progeniem et usque in aeternum non ingrediuntur ecclesiam Dei.

9. Helias, cum Iezabel fugeret et sub quercu fessus iaceret, veniente ad se angelo suscitatur et dicitur ei: ' " Surge et manduca." Et respexit, et ecce ad caput eius panis olyrae et vas aquae.' Revera non poterat Deus conditum ei merum mittere et ex oleo cibos et carnes contusione mutatas? Heliseus filios prophetarum invitat ad prandium et herbis agrestibus eos alens consonum prandentium audit clamorem: ' Mors in olla, homo Dei.' Non iratus est cocis—lautioris enim mensae consuetudinem non habebat—sed farina desuper iacta amaritudinem dulcoravit eadem spiritus virtute, qua Moyses mutaverat Merra. Necnon et illos, qui ad se con-prehendendum venerant, oculis pariter ac mente caecatos, cum Samariam nescios induxisset, qualibus epulis refici imperarit, ausculta: ' Pone eis panem et

---

[1] Genesis, xix. 16, 35. [2] Deuteronomy, xxiii. 3.
[3] 1 Kings, xix. 4–7. [4] 2 Kings, iv. 40.

he had been saved upon the mountain as the one man found righteous among all those thousands, was intoxicated by his daughters.[1] They may have thought that the human race had ended and have acted rather from a desire for offspring than from love of sinful pleasure; but they knew full well that the righteous man would not abet them unless he were drunken. In fact he did not know what he was doing: but although there be no wilfulness in his sin the error of his fault remains. As the result he became the father of Moab and Ammon, Israel's enemies, who ' even to the fourteenth generation shall not enter into the congregation of the Lord for ever.'[2]

When Elijah in his flight from Jezebel was lying weary and alone beneath the oak tree, an angel came and raised him up and said, ' " Arise and eat." And he looked, and behold there was a cake and a cruse of water at his head.'[3] Could not God have sent him spiced wine and foods cooked in oil and tenderly basted meats, if He had willed? Elisha invited the sons of the prophets to dinner, and when he gave them field herbs to eat he heard his guests cry out with one accord, 'There is death in the pot, O man of God.'[4] He, however, was not angry with the cooks—for he was not used to very sumptuous fare— but threw some meal upon the herbs and thus sweetened their bitterness by the same spiritual virtue wherewith Moses once sweetened the waters of Marah. Again, when the men sent to seize the prophet had been blinded alike in eyes and understanding, that he might bring them unawares to Samaria, notice the food with which Elisha ordered them to be refreshed. ' Set bread and water before

aquam; et manducent et bibant et remittantur ad
dominum suum.' Potuit et Danihelo de regis
ferculis opulentior mensa transferri, sed Ambacum
messorum prandium portat, arbitror, rusticanum.
Ideoque et ' desideriorum vir ' appellatus est, quia
panem desiderii non manducavit et vinum con-
cupiscentiae non bibit.

10. Innumerabilia sunt scripturis respersa divinis,
quae gulam damnent et simplices cibos praebeant;
verum quia nunc non est praepositum de ieiuniis
disputare et universa exsequi sui est tituli et voluminis, haec sufficiant pauca de plurimis. Alioquin
ad exemplum horum potes tibi ipsa colligere,
quomodo et primus de paradiso homo ventri magis
oboediens quam Deo in hanc lacrimarum deictus est
vallem et ipsum dominum fame Satanas temptaverit
in deserto et apostolus clamitet: ' Esca ventri et
venter escae, Deus autem et hunc et illa destruet,'
et de luxuriosis: ' Quorum deus venter est.' Id
enim colit unusquisque, quod diligit. Ex quo
sollicite providendum est, ut, quos saturitas de
paradiso expulit, reducat esuries.

11. Quodsi volueris respondere te nobili stirpe
generatam, semper in deliciis, semper in plumis, non
posse a vino et esculentioribus cibis abstinere nec
his legibus vivere districtius, respondebo: ' Vive
ergo lege tua, quae Dei non potes.' Non quo Deus,
universitatis creator et dominus, intestinorum

---

[1] 2 Kings, vi. 18 ff.   [2] Daniel, i. 8.

[3] Apoc. Bel and the Dragon, 33.

[4] Cf. Dan. x. 11, ' a man greatly beloved ' (A. and R. V.);
the Septuagint has ἀνὴρ ἐπιθυμιῶν; the Vulgate *desideriorum
vir.*

[5] 1 Corinthians, vi. 13.   [6] Philippians, iii. 19.

them,' he said; 'let them eat and drink and go
back to their master.'[1]   Daniel too might have had
rich dishes served him from the king's table,[2] but
it was a mower's breakfast that Habakkuk brought,[3]
which must, methinks, have been but country fare.
Therefore he was called 'the man of desires,'[4] because he refused to eat the bread of desire or drink
the wine of lustfulness.

From the Scriptures we may collect countless divine
answers condemning gluttony and approving simple
food.   But as it is not my present purpose to discuss
the question of fasting, and an exhaustive inquiry
would need a volume to itself, these few remarks
from the many I could make must suffice.   In
any case the examples I have given will enable you
to understand why the first man, obeying his belly
rather than God, was cast down from Paradise into
this vale of tears.   You will see also why Satan
tempted Our Lord Himself with hunger in the
wilderness, and why the apostle cries: ' Meats for
the belly and the belly for meats, but God shall
destroy both it and them,'[5] and why he says of the
wanton: ' Whose God is their belly.'[6]   Every
man worships what he loves.   Wherefore we must
take all care that abstinence may bring back to
Paradise those whom repletion once drove out.

You may choose perhaps to answer that a girl of
good family like yourself, accustomed to luxury and
down pillows, cannot do without wine and tasty food
and would find a stricter rule of life impossible.   To
that I can only say: ' Live then by your own rule,
since you cannot live by God's.'   Not that God, the
Lord and Creator of the universe, takes any delight
in the rumbling of our intestines or the emptiness of

nostrorum rugitu et inanitate ventris pulmonumque
delectetur ardore, sed quo aliter pudicitia tuta esse
non possit. Iob Deo carus et testimonio ipsius
inmaculatus et simplex, audi, quid de diabolo
suspicetur: ' Virtus eius in lumbis et potestas eius
in umbilico.' Honeste viri mulierisque genitalia
inmutatis sunt appellata nominibus. Unde et de
lumbis David super sedem eius promittitur esse
sessurus; et septuaginta et quinque animae introi-
erunt Aegyptum, quae exierunt de femore Iacob, et
postquam conluctante Deo latitudo femoris eius
emarcuit, a liberorum opere cessavit; et qui pascha
facturus est, accinctis mortificatisque lumbis facere
praecipitur; et ad Iob dicit Deus: ' Accingere sicut
vir lumbos tuos '; et Iohannes zona pellicia cingitur
et apostoli iubentur accinctis lumbis habere in
manibus evangelii lucernas. Ad Hierusalem vero,
quae respersa sanguine in campo invenitur erroris, in
Ezechiel dicitur: ' Non est praecisus umbilicus tuus.'
Omnis igitur adversus viros diaboli virtus in lumbis
est, omnis in umbilico contra feminas fortitudo.

12. Vis scire ita esse, ut dicimus? Accipe exempla.
Sampson leone fortior, saxo durior et qui unus et
nudus mille est persecutus armatos, in Dalilae
mollescit amplexibus; David secundum cor domini
electus et qui venturum Christum sancto saepe ore
cantaverat, postquam deambulans super tectum
domus suae Betsabee captus est nuditate, adulterio
iunxit homicidium. Ubi et illud breviter adtende,

---

our stomach or the inflammation of our lungs; but because this is the only way of preserving chastity. Job was dear to God, his purity and frankness witnessed by God's own testimony; yet hear what he thinks of the devil: ' His strength is in the loins and his force is in the navel.'[1] The words are used for decency's sake, but the male and female generative organs are meant. So the descendant of David, destined according to the promise to sit upon his throne, is said to come from his loins. The seventy-five souls who entered into Egypt are said in the same way to have come from Jacob's thigh. And when after wrestling with the Lord the stoutness of his thigh shrank away Jacob begat no more children. Those who celebrate the Passover also are bidden to do so with their loins girded and mortified. God says to Job: ' Gird up thy loins like a man.'[2] John wears a leather girdle; and the apostles are bidden to gird their loins before they take the lamps of the Gospel. Ezekiel tells us how Jerusalem is found in the plain of wandering, all bespattered with blood, and he says: ' Thy navel has not been cut.'[3] In his assaults on men therefore all the devil's strength is in the loins: against women his force is in the navel.

Would you like to be sure that it is as I say? Here are some examples. Samson was stronger than a lion and harder than rock; alone and unprotected he chased a thousand armed men; but in Dalilah's soft arms his vigour melted away. David was chosen as a man after God's heart, and his lips had often sung of the future coming of Christ with holy voice: but as he walked upon his housetop he was fascinated by Bathsheba's nakedness and added murder to adultery. Notice for a moment that even in one's own house the

quod nullus sit, etiam in domo, tutus aspectus.
Quapropter ad Deum paenitens loquitur: ' Tibi soli
peccavi et malum coram te feci.' Rex enim alium
non timebat. Salomon, per quem se cecinit ipsa
sapientia, qui disputavit ' a cedro Libani usque ad
hysopum, quae exit per parietem,' recessit a domino,
quia amator mulierum fuit. Et ne aliquis etiam de
sanguinis sibi propinquitate confideret, in inlicitum
Thamar sororis Amnon frater exarsit incendium.

13. Piget dicere, quot cotidie virgines ruant,
quantas de suo gremio mater perdat ecclesia, supra
quot sidera superbus inimicus ponat thronum suum,
quot petras excavet et habitet coluber in foraminibus
earum. Videas plerasque viduas ante quam nuptas
infelicem conscientiam mentita tantum veste pro-
tegere, quas nisi tumor uteri et infantum prodiderit
vagitus, erecta cervice et ludentibus pedibus incedunt.
Aliae vero sterilitatem praebebunt et necdum sati
hominis homicidium faciunt. Nonnullae, cum se
senserint concepisse de scelere, aborti venena
meditantur et frequenter etiam ipsae commortuae
trium criminum reae ad inferos perducuntur, homi-
cidae sui, Christi adulterae, necdum nati filii parri-
cidae. Istae sunt, quae solent dicere: ' Omnia
munda mundis. Sufficit mihi conscientia mea. Cor
mundum desiderat Deus. Cur me abstineam a
cibis, quos Deus creavit ad utendum ? ' Et si quando

---

[1] Psalm li. 4.   [2] 1 Kings, iv. 33.
[3] *I.e.* unmarried women who pretend to be widows.

eyes are never safe from danger. Therefore in
repentance he says to the Lord: 'Against Thee,
Thee only, have I sinned and done this evil in thy
sight.'[1] He was a king and feared no one else but
God. Solomon too, by whose lips Wisdom herself
used to speak, who knew of all plants 'from the cedar
of Lebanon to the hyssop that grows out of the wall,'[2]
went back from God because he became a lover of
women. And that no one may trust in kinship by
blood, remember that Amnon was fired by an illicit
passion for his sister Thamar.

It wearies me to tell how many virgins fall daily,
what notable women Mother Church loses from her
bosom: over how many stars the proud enemy sets
his throne, how many hollow rocks the serpent
pierces and makes his habitation. You may see
many women who have been left widows before
they were ever wed,[3] trying to conceal their
consciousness of guilt by means of a lying garb.
Unless they are betrayed by a swelling womb or by
the crying of their little ones they walk abroad with
tripping feet and lifted head. Some even ensure
barrenness by the help of potions, murdering human
beings before they are fully conceived. Others,
when they find that they are with child as the result
of their sin, practise abortion with drugs, and so
frequently bring about their own death, taking with
them to the lower world the guilt of three crimes:
suicide, adultery against Christ, and child murder.
Yet these are the women who will say: 'To the
pure all things are pure. My conscience is enough
for me. A pure heart is what God craves. Why
should I refrain from the food which God made for
enjoyment?' When they wish to appear bright and

lepidae et festivae volunt videri et se mero ingur-
gitaverint, ebrietati sacrilegium copulantes aiunt:
'Absit, ut ego me a Christi sanguine abstineam.'
Et quam viderint tristem atque pallentem, miseram
et monacham et Manicheam vocant, et consequenter;
tali enim proposito ieiunium heresis est. Hae sunt,
quae per publicum notabiliter incedunt et furtivis
oculorum nutibus adulescentium gregem post se
trahunt, quae semper audiunt per prophetam:
'Facies meretricis facta est tibi, impudorata es tu.'
Purpura tantum in veste sit tenuis, et laxius, ut
crines decidant, ligatum caput, soccus vilior et per
humeros maforte volitans, strictae manicae bracchiis
adhaerentes et solutis genibus fractus incessus:
haec est apud illas tota virginitas. Habeant istiusmodi laudatores suos et sub virginali nomine lucros-
ius pereant: libenter talibus non placemus.

14. Pudet dicere, pro nefas! Triste, sed verum
est: unde in ecclesias agapetarum pestis introiit?
Unde sine nuptiis aliud nomen uxorum? Immo unde
novum concubinarum genus? Plus inferam: unde
meretrices univirae? Eadem domo, uno cubiculo,
saepe uno tenentur et lectulo, et suspiciosos nos
vocant, si aliquid aestimemus. Frater sororem
virginem deserit, caelibem spernit virgo germanum,
et, cum in eodem proposito esse se simulent, quaerunt alienorum spiritale solacium, ut domi habeant

---

[1] Jeremiah, iii. 3.

merry, they drench themselves with wine, and then joining profanity to drunkenness they cry : ' Heaven forbid that I should abstain from the blood of Christ.' When they see a woman with a pale sad face, they call her ' a miserable Manichaean nun ': and quite logically too, for on their principles fasting is heresy. As they walk the streets they try to attract attention and with stealthy nods and winks draw after them troops of young men. Of them the prophet's words are true: ' Thou hast a whore's forehead: thou refusest to be ashamed.' [1] Let them have only a little purple in their dress, and loose bandeau on their head to leave the hair free ; cheap slippers, and a Maforte [2] fluttering from their shoulders; sleeves fitting close to their arms, and a loose-kneed walk: there you have all their marks of virginity. Such women may have their admirers, and it may cost more to ruin them because they are called virgins. But to such virgins as these I prefer to be displeasing.

There is another scandal of which I blush to speak ; yet, though sad, it is true. From what source has this plague of ' dearly beloved sisters ' found its way into the Church? Whence come these unwedded wives, these new types of concubines, nay, I will go further, these one-man harlots? They live in the same house with their male-friend; they occupy the same room and often even the same bed; and yet they call us suspicious if we think that anything is wrong. A brother leaves his virgin sister; a virgin, scorning her unmarried brother, seeks a stranger to take his place. Both alike pretend to have but one object: they are seeking spiritual consolation among

[2] The ' Maforte ' was a sort of cape, usually of a lilac colour.

carnale commercium. Istiusmodi homines in Proverbiis Salomonis arguit Deus dicens: ' Alligabit quis
ignem in sinu et vestimenta eius non conburentur?
aut ambulabit supra carbonis ignis et pedes illius non
ardebunt? '

15. Explosis igitur et exterminatis his, quae
nolunt esse virgines, sed videri, nunc ad te mihi
omnis dirigitur oratio, quae quanto prima Romanae
urbis virgo nobilis esse coepisti, tanto tibi amplius
laborandum est, ne et praesentibus bonis careas et
futuris. Et quidem molestias nuptiarum et incerta
coniugii de domestico exemplo didicisti, cum soror
tua Blesilla aetate maior, sed proposito minor, post
acceptum maritum septimo mense viduata est. O
infelix humana condicio et futuri nescia! Et
virginitatis coronam et nuptiarum perdidit voluptatem. Et quamquam secundum pudicitiae gradum
teneat, tamen quas illam per momenta sustinere
aestimas cruces spectantem cotidie in sorore, quod
ipsa perdiderit, et, cum difficilius experta careat
voluptate, minorem continentiae habere mercedem?
Sit tamen et illa secura, sit gaudens: centesimus et
sexagesimus fructus de uno sunt semine castitatis.

16. Nolo habeas consortia matronarum, nolo ad
nobilium accedas domos, nolo te frequenter videre,
quod contemnens virgo esse voluisti. Si sibi solent

---

[1] Proverbs, vi. 27.

strangers: but their real aim is to indulge at home in carnal intercourse. About such folk as these Solomon in Proverbs speaks the scornful words: ' Can a man take fire in his bosom and his clothes not be burned? Can one go upon hot coals and not burn his feet? ' [1]

Let us therefore drive off and expel from our company such women as only wish to seem and not to be virgins. Now I would direct all my words to you who, inasmuch as you have been at the beginning the first virgin of high rank at Rome, will now have to labour the more diligently so as not to lose your present and your future happiness. As for the troubles of wedded life and the uncertainties of marriage, you know of them by an example in your own family. Your sister Blesilla, superior to you in age but inferior in firmness of will, has become a widow seven months after taking a husband. How luckless is our mortal state, how ignorant of the future! She has lost both the crown of virginity and the pleasures of wedlock. Although the widowed state ranks as the second degree of chastity, can you not imagine the crosses which every moment she must bear, seeing in her sister daily that which she herself has lost? It is harder for her than for you to forgo the delights that she once knew, and yet she receives a less reward for her present continence. Still, she too may rejoice and be not afraid. The fruit that is an hundredfold and that which is sixtyfold both spring from one seed, the seed of chastity.

I would not have you consort overmuch with married women or frequent the houses of the great. I would not have you look too often on what you spurned when you desired to be a virgin. Women

adplaudere mulierculae de iudicibus viris et in aliqua positis dignitate, si ad imperatoris uxorem concurrit ambitio salutantium, cur tu facias iniuriam viro tuo? Ad hominis coniugem Dei sponsa quid properas? Disce in hac parte superbiam sanctam, scito te illis esse meliorem. Neque vero earum te tantum cupio declinare congressus, quae maritorum inflantur honoribus, quas eunuchorum greges saepiunt et in quarum vestibus adtenuata in filum metalla texuntur, sed etiam eas fuge, quas viduas necessitas fecit, non quo mortem optare debuerint maritorum, sed quo datam occasionem pudicitiae libenter arripere. Nunc vero tantum veste mutata pristina non mutatur ambitio. Praecedit caveas basternarum ordo semivir et rubentibus buccis cutis farsa distenditur, ut eas putes maritos non amisisse, sed quaerere. Plena adulatoribus domus, plena convivis. Clerici ipsi, quos et magisterio esse oportuerat et timori, osculantur capita patronarum et extenta manu, ut benedicere eos putes velle, si nescias, pretium accipiunt salutandi. Illae interim, quae sacerdotes suo vident indigere praesidio, eriguntur in superbiam et, quia maritorum expertae dominatum viduitatis praeferunt libertatem, castae vocantur et nonnae et post cenam dubiam apostolos somniant.

17. Sint tibi sociae, quas videris quod ieiunia

of the world, you know, plume themselves if their husband is a judge or holds some high position. Even if an eager crowd of visitors flocks to greet the Emperor's wife, why should you insult your Husband? Why should you, who are God's bride, hasten to visit the wife of a mortal man? In this regard you must learn a holy pride; know that you are better than they. And not only do I desire you to avoid the company of those who are puffed up by their husbands' honours, who surround themselves with troops of eunuchs, and wear robes inwrought with fine threads of gold: you must also shun such women as are widows from compulsion, not choice. Not that they ought to have desired their husbands' death; but they have been unwilling to accept their opportunity for chastity. As it is, they only change their dress: their old love of show remains unchanged.

Look at them as they ride in their roomy litters with a row of eunuchs walking in front: see their red lips and their plump sleek skins: you would not think they had lost a husband, you would fancy they were looking for one. Their houses are full of flatterers, full of guests. The very clergy, whose teaching and authority ought to inspire respect, kiss these ladies on the forehead, and then stretch out their hand—you would think, if you did not know, that they were giving a benediction—to receive the fee for their visit. The women meanwhile, seeing that priests need their help, are lifted up with pride. They know by experience what a husband's rule is like, and they prefer their liberty as widows. They call themselves chaste nuns, and after a diversified dinner they dream apostles.

Let your companions be those who are pale of face

tenuant, quibus pallor in facie est, quas et aetas
probavit et vita, quae cotidie in cordibus canunt:
' Ubi pascis? ubi cubas in meridie?' Quae ex
affectu dicunt: ' Cupio dissolui et esse cum Christo.'
Esto subiecta parentibus, imitare sponsum tuum.
Rarus sit egressus in publicum: martyres tibi quaer-
antur in cubiculo tuo. Nunquam causa deerit
procedendi, si semper, quando necesse est, pro-
cessura sis. Moderatus cibus et nunquam venter
repletus. Plurimae quippe sunt, quae, cum vino
sunt sobriae, ciborum largitate sunt ebriae. Ad
orationem tibi nocte surgenti non indigestio ructum
faciat, sed inanitas. Crebrius lege et disce quam
plurima. Tenenti codicem somnus obrepat et
cadentem faciem pagina sancta suscipiat. Sint tibi
cotidiana ieiunia et refectio satietatem fugiens.
Nihil prodest biduo triduoque transmisso vacuum
portare ventrem, si pariter obruitur, si compensatur
saturitate ieiunium. Ilico mens repleta torpes-
cit et inrigata humus spinas libidinum germinat. Si
quando senseris exteriorem hominem florem adulescentiae suspirare et accepto cibo cum te in lectulo
conpositam dulcis libidinum pompa concusserit,
arripe scutum fidei, in quo ignitae diaboli extin-
guuntur sagittae. ' Omnes adulterantes, quasi
clibanus ' corda eorum.

At tu Christi comitata vestigiis et sermonibus eius
intenta dic: ' Nonne cor nostrum erat ardens in via,

---

[1] Song of Solomon, i. 7.
[2] Philippians, i. 23.
[3] A visit to a martyr's shrine was often made an excuse
for going abroad.
[4] Hosea, vii. 4.

and thin with fasting, approved by their years and their conduct, who daily within their hearts sing the words: 'Tell me where thou feedest thy flock, where thou makest it to rest at noon,'[1] and lovingly say: 'I have a desire to depart and to be with Christ.'[2] Follow your Husband's example, and like Him be subject to your parents. Walk not often abroad, and if you wish the help of the martyrs seek it in your own chamber.[3] You will never lack a reason for going out if you always go out when there is need. Take food in moderation and never overload your stomach. Many women are temperate over wine, but intemperate as to the amount of food they take. When you rise at night to pray, let any uneasiness of breath be caused not by indigestion but by an empty stomach. Read often and learn all you can. Let sleep steal upon you with a book in your hand, and let the sacred page catch your drooping head. Let your fasts be of daily occurrence, and let refreshment ever avoid satiety. It is of no avail to carry an empty stomach for two or three days if that fast is to be made up for by a clogging repletion. The mind when cloyed straightway grows sluggish and the watered ground puts forth the thorns of lust. If ever you feel that your outward being is sighing for the bloom of youth, and if, as you lie on your couch after a meal, you are shaken by the vision of lust's alluring train, then catch up the shield of faith, and it will quench the devil's fiery darts. 'They are all adulterers,' says the prophet, 'they have made their hearts like an oven.'[4]

But do you keep close to Christ's footsteps and be ever intent upon his words. Say to yourself: 'Did not our heart burn within us by the way, while

cum aperiret nobis Iesus scripturas?' et illud:
'Ignitum eloquium tuum, et servus tuus dilexit illud.'
Difficile est humanam animam non amare et necesse
est, ut in quoscumque mens nostra trahatur affectus.
Carnis amor spiritus amore superatur; desiderium
desiderio restinguitur. Quidquid inde minuitur, hinc
crescit. Quin potius semper ingemina: 'Super lectum meum in noctibus quaesivi, quem dilexit anima
mea.' 'Mortificate,' ait apostolus, 'membra vestra
super terram.' Unde et ipse confidenter aiebat:
'Vivo autem iam non ego, vivit autem in me Christus.'
Qui mortificavit membra sua et in imagine peram-
bulabat, non timet dicere: '" Factus sum tanquam
uter in pruina"; quidquid enim in me fuit umoris,
excoctum est,' et: 'Infirmata sunt in ieiunio genua
mea,' et: 'Oblitus sum manducare panem meum;
a voce gemitus mei adhaesit os meum carni meae.'

18. Esto cicada noctium. Lava per singulas noctes
lectum tuum, in lacrimis stratum tuum riga. Vigila
et fiere sicut passer in solitudine. Psalle spiritu,
psalle et mente: 'Benedic, anima mea, dominum
et ne obliviscaris omnes retributiones eius, qui pro-
pitiatur cunctis iniquitatibus tuis, qui sanat omnes
infirmitates tuas et redimit ex corruptione vitam
tuam.' Quis nostrum ex corde dicere potest:
'Quia cinerem quasi panem manducavi et potionem
meam cum fletu miscebam'? An non flendum est,

---

¹ St. Luke, xxiv. 32.   ² Psalm cxix. 140 (cviii. Vulg.).
³ Song of Solomon, iii. 1.   ⁴ Colossians, iii. 5.
⁵ Galatians, ii. 20.
⁶ Psalm cxix. 83. A. V. has *smoke* for *frost*. Jerome quotes
the Vulgate (cxviii.).   ⁷ Psalm cix. 24.   ⁸ Psalm cii. 5.
⁹ *I.e.* Be as active at night as the grasshopper is in the day-

Jesus opened to us the Scriptures?'[1] and again:
'Thy word is tried to the uttermost, and thy servant
loveth it.'[2] It is hard for the human soul not to love
something, and our mind of necessity must be drawn
to some sort of affection. Carnal love is overcome
by spiritual love: desire is quenched by desire:
what is taken from the one is added to the other.
Nay rather, as you lie upon your couch, say these
words and repeat them continually: 'By night
have I sought Him whom my soul loveth.'[3]
'Mortify your members on earth,'[4] says the
apostle; and because he did so himself, he could
afterwards boldly say: 'I live, yet not I but Christ
liveth in me.'[5] He who mortifies his members, and
as he walks through this world knows it to be vanity,
is not afraid to say: '"I am become like a leather
bottle in the frost."'[6] For whatever there was in me of
the moisture of lust has dried away.' And again:
'My knees are weak with fasting.'[7] 'I forget to eat
my bread. By reason of the voice of my groaning
my bones cleave to my skin.'[8]

Be thou the grasshopper of the night.[9] Wash
your bed and water your couch nightly with
tears. Keep vigil and be like the sparrow alone
upon the housetop. Let your spirit be your harp,
and let your mind join in the psalm: 'Bless the
Lord, O my soul, and forget not all his benefits;
who forgiveth all thine iniquities; who healeth all
thy diseases; who redeemeth thy life from destruction.'[10] Who of us can say from our heart:
'I have eaten ashes like bread and mingled my
drink with weeping'?[11] And yet ought I not to

time when he is always heard. Cf. Virg. *Ec.* II. 13, *sole sub
ardenti resonant arbusta cicadis.*
[10] Psalm ciii. 2.   [11] Psalm cii. 9.

89

non gemendum, cum me rursus serpens invitat ad inlicitos cibos? cum de paradiso virginitatis eiectum tunicis vult vestire pelliciis, quas Helias ad paradisum rediens proiecit in terram? Quid mihi et voluptati, quae in brevi perit? Quid cum hoc dulci et mortifero carmine sirenarum? Nolo illi subiacere sententiae, quae in hominem est lata damnatum: in doloribus et anxietatibus paries, mulier—lex ista non mea est—'Et ad virum conversio tua.' Sit conversio illius ad maritum, quae virum non habet Christum, et ad extremum 'morte morieris' finis iste coniugii. Meum propositum sine sexu est. Habeant nuptiae suum tempus et titulum: mihi virginitas in Maria dedicatur et Christo.

19. Dicat aliquis: 'Et audes nuptiis detrahere, quae a domino benedictae sunt?' Non est detrahere nuptiis, cum illis virginitas antefertur. Nemo malum bono conparat. Glorientur et nuptae, cum a virginibus sunt secundae. 'Crescite,' ait, 'et multiplicamini et replete terram.' Crescat et multiplicetur ille, qui inpleturus est terram: tuum agmen in caelis est. 'Crescite et multiplicamini.' Hoc expletur edictum post paradisum et nuditatem et ficus folia auspicantia pruriginem nuptiarum. Nubat et nubatur ille, qui in sudore faciei comedit panem suum, cui terra tribulos generat et spinas, cuius herba sentibus

---

[1] Genesis, iii. 16.   [2] Genesis, ii. 17.
[3] Genesis, i. 28.

weep and groan when the serpent again invites me
to take forbidden fruit, and when, after driving us
from the Paradise of virginity, he tries to clothe us
in tunics of skin, such as Elijah on his return to
Paradise threw upon the ground? What have I to
do with the short-lived pleasures of sense? What
have I to do with the sirens' sweet and deadly songs?
You must not be subject to the sentence whereby
condemnation was passed upon mankind: ' In pain
and in sorrow shalt thou bring forth children.' [1]
Say to yourself: ' That is a Law for a married woman,
but not for me.' ' And thy desire shall be to thy
husband.' Say to yourself: ' Let her desire be to
her husband who has not a Husband in Christ;' and
at the last ' Thou shalt surely die.' [2] Say once more:
' Death is the end of marriage. But my vows are
independent of sex. Let married women keep to
their own place and title: for me virginity is consecrated in the persons of Mary and of Christ.'

Some one may say: ' Do you dare to disparage wedlock, a state which God has blessed?'
It is not disparaging wedlock to prefer virginity.
No one can make a comparison between two
things, if one is good and the other evil. Let
married women take their pride in coming next after
virgins. ' Be fruitful,' God said, ' and multiply
and replenish the earth.' [3] Let him then be fruitful
and multiply who intends to replenish the earth:
but your company is in heaven. The command to
increase and multiply is fulfilled after the expulsion
from Paradise, after the recognition of nakedness,
after the putting on of the fig leaves which augured
the approach of marital desire. Let them marry
and be given in marriage who eat their bread in the
sweat of their brow, whose land brings forth thorns

suffocatur: meum semen centena fruge fecundum est.

'Non omnes capiunt verbum Dei, sed hi quibus datum est.' Alium eunuchum necessitas faciat, me voluntas. 'Tempus et amplexandi et tempus abstinendi manus a conplexu; tempus mittendi lapides et tempus colligendi.' Postquam de duritia nationum generati sunt filii Abraham, coeperunt sancti lapides volvi super terram. Pertranseunt quippe mundi istius turbines et in curru Dei rotarum celeritate volvuntur. Consuant tunicas, qui inconsutam desursum tunicam perdiderunt, quos vagitus delectat infantum in ipso lucis exordio fletu lugente, quod nati sunt. Eva in paradiso virgo fuit: post pellicias tunicas initium nuptiarum. Tua regio paradisus. Serva quod nata es, et dic: 'Revertere, anima mea, in requiem tuam.'

Et ut scias virginitatem esse naturae, nuptias post delictum: virgo nascitur caro de nuptiis in fructu reddens, quod in radice perdiderat. 'Exiet virga de radice Iesse et flos de radice ascendet.' Virga mater est domini, simplex, pura, sinceris nullo extrinsecus germine cohaerente et ad similitudinem Dei unione fecunda. Virgae flos Christus est dicens: 'Ego flos campi et lilium convallium.' Qui et in alio loco lapis praedicatur de monte sine manibus significante propheta virginem nasciturum de virgine. Manus

---

[1] St. Matthew, xix. 11. [2] Ecclesiastes, iii. 5.
[3] Psalm cxvi. 7. [4] Isaiah, xi. 1. (Vulgate.)
[5] A pun on *virga, virgo*. [6] Song of Solomon, ii. 1.
[7] Daniel, ii. 45.

and thistles, and whose crops are choked with brambles. My seed produces fruit a hundredfold.

' Not all men can receive God's saying, but only those to whom it is given.'[1] Some men may be eunuchs of necessity : I am one by choice. ' There is a time to embrace, and a time to refrain from embracing. There is a time to cast away stones, and a time to gather stones together.'[2] Now that out of the hardness of the Gentiles sons have been born to Abraham, they begin to be holy stones rolling upon the earth. So they pass through the storms of this world and roll on with rapid wheels in God's chariot. Let those stitch themselves coats who have lost that raiment which was woven from the top in one piece, and delight in the cries of infants lamenting that they are born as soon as they see the light of day. Eve in Paradise was a virgin : it was only after she put on a garment of skins that her married life began. Paradise is your home. Keep therefore as you were born, and say : ' Return unto thy rest, O my soul.'[3]

That you may understand that virginity is natural and that marriage came after the Fall, remember that what is born of wedlock is virgin flesh and that by its fruit it renders what in its parent root it had lost. ' There shall come forth a rod out of the stem of Jesse, and a flower shall grow out of his roots.'[4] That virgin[5] rod is the mother of Our Lord, simple, pure, unsullied ; drawing no germ of life from without, but like God Himself fruitful in singleness. The flower of the rod is Christ, who says : ' I am the rose of Sharon and the lily of the valleys.'[6] In another passage He is foretold to be ' a stone cut out of the mountain without hands,'[7] the prophet signifying thereby that He will be born a virgin of a

quippe accipiuntur pro opere nuptiarum, ut ibi:
' Sinistra eius sub capite meo et dextera eius amplexabitur me.' In huius sensus congruit voluntatem
etiam illud, quod animalia, quae a Noe bina in arcam
inducuntur, immunda sunt—inpar numerus est
mundus—quod Moyses et Iesus Nave nudis in
sanctam terram pedibus iubentur incedere, et
discipuli sine calciamentorum onere et vinculis
pellium ad praedicationem evangelii destinantur;
quod milites vestimentis Iesu sorte divisis caligas non
habuere, quas tollerent. Nec enim potuerat habere
dominus, quod prohibuerat in servis.

20. Laudo nuptias, laudo coniugium, sed quia mihi
virgines generant: lego de spinis rosas, de terra
aurum, de concha margaritum. Numquid, qui
arat, tota die arabit? Nonne et laboris sui fruge
laetabitur? Plus honorantur nuptiae, quando, quod
de illis nascitur, plus amatur. Quid invides, mater,
filiae? Tuo lacte nutrita est, tuis educata visceribus
in tuo adolevit sinu, tu illam sedula pietate servasti:
indignaris, quod noluit militis uxor esse, sed regis?
Grande tibi beneficium praestitit: socrus Dei esse
coepisti.

' De virginibus,' inquit apostolus, ' praeceptum
domini non habeo ': cur? Quia, et ipse ut esset
virgo, non fuit imperii, sed propriae voluntatis.
Neque enim audiendi sunt, qui eum uxorem habuisse

---

[1] Song of Solomon, ii. 6.   [2] 1 Corinthians, vii. 25.

virgin. The word ' hands ' is to be taken as meaning the marital act, as in the passage : ' His left hand is under my head and his right hand doth embrace me.' [1] It agrees also with this interpretation, that the unclean animals are led into Noah's ark in pairs, while of the clean an uneven number is taken. In the same way Moses and Joshua were bidden to take off their shoes before they walked on holy ground. When the disciples were appointed to preach the new Gospel they were told not to burden themselves with shoes or shoe-latchets. And when the soldiers cast losts for Jesus' garments they found no shoes that they could take away. For the Lord could not Himself possess what He had forbidden to His servants.

I praise wedlock, I praise marriage ; but it is because they produce me virgins. I gather the rose from the thorn, the gold from the earth, the pearl from the oyster. Shall the ploughman plough all day ? Shall he not also enjoy the fruit of his labour ? Wedlock is the more honoured when the fruit of wedlock is the more loved. Why, mother, grudge your daughter her virginity ? She has been reared on your milk, she has come from your body, she has grown strong in your arms. Your watchful love has kept her safe. Are you vexed with her because she chooses to wed not a soldier but a King ? She has rendered you a high service : from to-day you are the mother by marriage of God.

The apostle says : ' Concerning virgins I have no commandment of the Lord.' [2] Why so ? Because he himself was a virgin, not by order but of his own free will. Those people must not be listened to who pretend that he had a wife. When he is discussing

confingunt, cum de continentia disserens et suadens perpetuam castitatem intulerit : ' Volo autem omnes esse sicut me ipsum,' et infra : ' Dico autem innuptis et viduis : bonum est illis, si sic permaneant, sicut et ego,' et in alio loco : ' Numquid non habemus potestatem uxores circumducendi sicut et ceteri apostoli ? ' Quare non habet domini de virginitate praeceptum ? Quia maioris est mercis, quod non cogitur et offertur, quia, si fuisset virginitas imperata, nuptiae videbantur ablatae et durissimum erat contra naturam cogere angelorumque vitam hominibus extorquere et id quodam more damnare, quod conditum est.

21. Alia fuit in veteri lege felicitas. ' Beatus, qui habet semen in Sion et domesticos in Hierusalem,' et maledicta sterilis, quae non pariebat, et : ' Filii tui sicut novella olivarum in circuitu mensae tuae,' et repromissio divitiarum, et : ' Non erit infirmus in tribubus tuis.' Nunc dicitur : ' Ne te lignum arbitreris aridum ; habes locum pro filiis et filiabus in caelestibus sempiternum ' ;[6] nunc benedicuntur pauperes et Lazarus diviti praefertur in purpura ; nunc, qui infirmus est, fortior est. Vacuus erat orbis, et ut de typis taceam, sola erat benedictio liberorum. Propterea et Abraham iam senex Cetturae copulatur et Iacob mandragoris redimitur

---

[1] 1 Corinthians, vii. 7, 8.   [2] 1 Corinthians, ix. 5.
[3] Isaiah, xxxi. 9. LXX. version.   [4] Psalm cxxviii. 3.

continence and recommending perpetual chastity, he says: 'I wish that all men were even as I myself.'[1] And later: 'I say therefore to the unmarried and widows, it is good for them if they abide even as I.' And in another place: 'Have we not power to lead about wives even as the other apostles?'[2] Why then has he no commandment from the Lord concerning virginity? Because that which is freely offered is worth more than what is extorted by force, and to command virginity would have been to abrogate wedlock. It would have been a stern task to force men against their nature and to extort from them the life that angels enjoy: moreover it would have meant condemning in a way what has been ordained.

The old law had a different ideal of felicity. There it is said: 'Blessed is he who hath seed in Zion and a family in Jerusalem':[3] and cursed is the barren woman who beareth not children. And again: 'Thy children shall be as olive plants around thy table.'[4] To such men riches are promised, and we are told that 'there was not one feeble man among the tribes.'[5] But to-day the word is: 'Think not that you are a dry tree; for instead of sons and daughters you have a place for ever in heaven.'[6] Now the poor are blessed, and Lazarus is set before Dives in his purple. Now he who is weak has thereby the greater strength. But in the old days the world was empty of people, and, omitting those whose childlessness was but a type for the future, the only benediction possible was the gift of children. It was for this reason that Abraham in his old age married Keturah; that Jacob was hired with mandrakes; and that

[5] Psalm cv. 37.   [6] Cf. Isaiah, lvi. 3.

et conclusam vulvam in ecclesiae figuram Rachel pulchra conqueritur.

Paulatim vero increscente segete messor inmissus est. Virgo Helias, Helisaeus virgo, virgines multi filii prophetarum. Hieremiae dicitur: ' Et tu ne accipias uxorem.' Sanctificatus in utero captivitate propinquante uxorem prohibetur accipere. Aliis verbis id ipsud apostolus loquitur: ' Existimo ergo hoc bonum esse propter instantem necessitatem, quoniam bonum est homini sic esse.' Quae est ista necessitas, quae aufert gaudia nuptiarum? ' Tempus breviatum est; reliquum est, ut et qui habent uxores sic sint, quasi non habentes.' In proximo est Nabuchodonosor. Promovit se leo de cubili suo. Quo mihi superbissimo regi servitura coniugia? Quo parvulos, quos propheta conploret dicens: ' Adhaesit lingua lactantis ad faucem ipsius in siti. Parvuli postulaverunt panem, et, qui frangeret eis, non erat'? Inveniebatur ergo, ut diximus, in viris tantum hoc continentiae bonum et in doloribus iugiter Eva pariebat. Postquam vero virgo concepit in utero et peperit nobis puerum, ' cuius principatus in umero eius,' Deum fortem, patrem futuri saeculi, soluta maledictio est. Mors per Evam, vita per Mariam. Ideoque et ditius virginitatis donum fluxit in feminas, quia coepit a femina. Statim ut Filius Dei ingressus

---

[1] 1 Corinthians, vii. 26.   [2] 1 Corinthians, vii. 29.
[3] Lamentations, iv. 4.

fair Rachel—a type of the Church—complained of the closing of her womb.

But gradually the crop grew high and the reaper was sent in. Elijah was a virgin, and so was Elisha, and so were many of the sons of the prophets. Jeremiah was told that he must not take a wife. He had been sanctified in his mother's womb, and now that the captivity was drawing near he was forbidden to marry. The apostle gives the same injunction in different words: 'I think therefore that this is good by reason of the present distress, namely that it is good for a man to be as he is.'[1] What is this distress which abrogates the joys of wedlock? The apostle tells us: 'The time is short: it remaineth that those who have wives be as though they had none.'[2] Now is Nebuchadnezzar again drawing nigh. Now has the lion come out from his den. What to me is a wife, if she shall fall as a slave to some proud king? What good will little ones do, if their lot must be that which the prophet deplores: 'The tongue of the sucking child cleaveth to the roof of his mouth for thirst; the young children ask for bread and there was none to break it'?[3] In the old days, as I have said, the virtue of continence was confined to men, and Eve continually bore children in travail. But now that a virgin has conceived in the womb a child, upon whose shoulders is government, a mighty God, Father of the age to come, the fetters of the old curse are broken. Death came through Eve: life has come through Mary. For this reason the gift of virginity has been poured most abundantly upon women, seeing that it was from a woman it began. As soon as the

est super terram, novam sibi familiam instituit, ut,
qui ab angelis adorabatur in caelo, haberet angelos in
terris. Tunc Olofernae caput Iudith continens
amputavit; tunc Aman, quod interpretatur 'ini-
quitas,' suo igne conbustus est; tunc Iacobus et
Iohannes relicto patre, rete, navicula, secuti sunt
salvatorem affectum sanguinis et vincula saeculi et
curam domus pariter relinquentes; tunc primum
auditum est: 'Qui vult venire post me, neget se
ipsum sibi et tollat crucem suam et sequatur me.'[1]

Nemo enim miles cum uxore pergit ad proelium.
Discipulo ad sepulturam patris ire cupienti non
permittitur. 'Vulpes foveas habent et volucres
caeli nidos; filius autem hominum non habet, ubi
caput reclinet'[2]; ne forsitan contristeris, si anguste
manseris. 'Qui sine uxore est, sollicitus est ea, quae
domini sunt, quomodo placeat Deo, qui autem cum
uxore est, sollicitus est, quae sunt huius mundi,
quomodo placeat uxori. Divisa est mulier et virgo:
quae non est nupta, cogitat, quae sunt domini, ut
sit sancta corpore et spiritu; nam quae nupta est,
cogitat, quae sunt mundi, quomodo placeat viro.'[3]

22. Quantas molestias habeant nuptiae et quot
sollicitudinibus vinciantur, in eo libro, quem adversus
Helvidium de beatae Mariae perpetua virginitate
edidimus, puto breviter expressum. Nunc eadem
replicare perlongum est et, si cui placet, de illo
potest haurire fonticulo.[4] Verum, ne penitus videar

---

[1] St. Mark, viii. 34.   [2] St. Matthew, viii. 20.
[3] 1 Corinthians, vii. 32–34.   [4] Cf. App., p. 489.

Son of God set foot on earth, He formed for Himself a new household, that as He was adored by angels in heaven He might have angels also on earth. Then chaste Judith once more cut off the head of Holofernes. Then Haman—whose name means ' iniquity '—was once more burned in his own fire. Then James and John forsook father and net and ship, and followed the Saviour: they put behind them the love of their kin, the ties of this world, and the care of their home. Then first the words were heard: ' Whosoever will come after me, let him deny himself and take up his cross and follow me.' [1]

For no soldier takes a wife with him when he is marching into battle. Even when a disciple was fain to go and bury his father, the Lord forbade him and said: ' Foxes have holes and the birds of the air have nests: but the Son of Man hath not where to lay his head.' [2] So you must not complain if you are scantily lodged. ' He that is unmarried careth for the things that belong to the Lord, how he may please the Lord: but he that is married careth for the things of the world, how he may please his wife. There is a difference also between a wife and a virgin. The unmarried woman cares for the things of the Lord, that she may be holy both in body and spirit; but she that is married cares for the things of the world, how she may please her husband.' [3]

How great are the inconveniences involved in wedlock, and how many anxieties encompass it, I think I have briefly described in my treatise against Helvidius [4] on the perpetual virginity of the blessed Mary. It would be tedious to go over the same ground again, and anyone who wishes to can draw from my little spring. But lest I should be thought

omisisse, nunc dicam, quod cum apostolus sine intermissione orare nos iubeat et, qui in coniugio debitum solvit, orare non possit, aut oramus semper et virgines sumus, aut orare desinimus, ut coniugio serviamus. ' Et si nupserit,' inquit, ' virgo, non peccat; tribulationem tamen carnis habebunt huiusmodi.' Et in principio libelli praefatus sum me de angustiis nuptiarum aut nihil omnino aut pauca dicturum et nunc eadem admoneo. At, si tibi placet scire, quot molestiis virgo libera, quot uxor adstricta sit, lege Tertulliani ad amicum philosophum et de virginitate alios libellos et beati Cypriani volumen egregium et papae Damasi super hac re versu prosaque conposita et Ambrosii nostri quae nuper ad sororem scripsit opuscula. In quibus tanto se fudit eloquio, ut, quidquid ad laudem virginum pertinet, exquisierit, ordinarit, expresserit.

23. Nobis diverso tramite inceditur: virginitatem non efferimus, sed servamus. Nec sufficit scire, quod bonum est, nisi custodiatur adtentius, quod electum est, quia illud iudicii est, hoc laboris, et illud commune cum pluribus, hoc cum paucis. ' Qui perseveraverit,' inquit, ' usque ad finem, hic salvus erit,' et : ' Multi vocati, pauci autem electi.' Itaque obtestor te coram Deo et Christo Iesu et electis angelis eius, ne vasa templi, quae solis sacerdotibus videre concessum est, facile in publicum proferas, ne sacrarium

---

[1] 1 Corinthians, vii. 28. [2] Not extant.

[3] The *De habitu virginum* of Cyprian, Bishop of Carthage (fl. 258), is still extant, as are the three books *De Virginibus* of Ambrose, Bishop of Milan, which were written for Marcellina (pp. 187 and 485); the treatise of Damasus is now lost.

[4] St. Matthew, xxiv. 13. [5] St. Matthew, xx. 16.

to have passed over this subject completely, I will say now that the apostle bids us pray without ceasing, and that the man who in the married state renders his wife her due cannot so pray. Either we pray always and are virgins; or we cease to pray that we may perform our marital service. The apostle says also: ' If a virgin marry she hath not sinned. Nevertheless such shall have trouble in the flesh.' [1] At the outset of my book I promised that I should say little or nothing of the troubles of wedlock, and now I give you the same warning again. But if you wish to know from how many vexations a virgin is free and by how many a wife is fettered, you should read Tertullian's ' To a philosophic friend,' [2] and his other treatises on virginity; the blessed Cyprian's notable book; the writings of Pope Damasus in prose and verse; and the essays recently written by our own Ambrose for his sister. [3] In these he has poured forth his soul with such eloquence that he has sought out, set forth, and arranged all that bears on the praise of virgins.

I must proceed by a different path. Far from trumpeting the praises of virginity, I only wish to keep it safe. To know what is good is not enough; when you have chosen it you must guard it with jealous care. The first is a matter of judgment and we share it with many: the second calls for labour and for that few care. The Lord says: ' He that shall endure unto the end, the same shall be saved,' [4] and ' Many are called but few are chosen.' [5] Therefore before God and Jesus Christ and His chosen angels I adjure you to guard what you have, and not lightly to expose to the public gaze the vessels of the Lord's temple which priests alone are allowed to see. No man that is profane may look upon God's

Dei quisquam profanus inspiciat. Ozias arcam, quam non licebat, adtingens subita morte prostratus est. Neque enim aureum vas et argenteum tam carum Deo fuit, quam templum corporis virginalis. Praecessit umbra, nunc veritas est. Tu quidem simpliciter loqueris et ignotos quoque blanda non despicis, sed aliter inpudici vident oculi. Non norunt animae pulchritudinem considerare, sed corporum. Ezechias thesaurum Dei monstrat Assyriis, sed Assyrii videre, quod cuperent. Denique frequentibus bellis Iudaea convulsa vasa primum domini capta atque translata sunt et inter epulas et concubinarum greges, quia palma vitiorum est honesta polluere, Baltasar potat in fialis.

24. Ne declines aurem tuam in verba mala. Saepe indecens aliquid loquentes temptant mentis arbitrium. Si libenter audias, virgo, quod dicitur, si ad ridicula quaeque solvaris, quidquid dixeris, laudant; quidquid negaveris, negant. Facetam vocant et sanctam et in qua nullus sit dolus, ' Ecce vera Christi ancilla,' dicentes, ' ecce tota simplicitas, non ut illa horrida, turpis, rusticana, terribilis et quae ideo forsitan maritum invenire non potuit.' Naturali ducimur malo: adulatoribus nostris libenter favemus et, quamquam nos respondeamus indignos et calidus rubor ora perfundat, tamen ad laudem suam intrinsecus anima laetatur.

Sponsa Christi arca est testamenti extrinsecus et

---

[1] 2 Samuel, vi. 6, 7.   [2] 2 Kings, xx. 15.   [3] Daniel, v. 2.

sanctuary. When Uzziah laid hands upon the ark,[1] which it was not lawful to touch, he was struck down by sudden death. And no vessel of gold or silver was ever so dear to God as the temple of a virgin's body. What was shadowed in the past presaged the reality of to-day. You indeed may speak frankly to strangers and look at them with kindly eyes: but the unchaste see differently. They cannot appreciate the beauty of the soul, they only regard the beauty of the body. Hezekiah showed God's treasure to the Assyrians, but the Assyrians only saw in it something to covet.[2] And so it was that Judaea was rent asunder by continual wars, and that the first things taken and carried away were the Lord's vessels. From them as drinking cups Belshazzar quaffed his wine—for the crown of vice is to pollute what is noble—surrounded by his concubines at the feast.[3]

Never incline your ear to words of mischief. Men often make an improper remark, that they may test a virgin's real purpose. If you hear it with pleasure and are ready to unbend at a joke, they approve of all you say, and anything you deny they deny also. They call you both merry and good, one in whom there is no guile. ' Behold,' they cry, ' a true handmaid of Christ: behold complete frankness. She is not like that rough, ugly country fright who probably could not find a husband just for that reason.' A natural weakness easily beguiles us. We willingly smile on such flatterers, and although we may blush and say we are unworthy of their praise, the soul within us rejoices to hear their words.

Like the ark of the covenant Christ's bride should be overlaid with gold within and without; she should

intrinsecus deaurata, custos legis domini. Sicut in illa nihil aliud fuit nisi tabulae testamenti, ita et in te nullus sit extrinsecus cogitatus. Super hoc propitiatorio quasi super cherubim sedere vult dominus. Mittit discipulos suos, ut in pullo asinae curis te saecularibus solvant, ut paleas et lateres Aegypti derelinquens Moysen sequaris in heremo et terram repromissionis introeas. Nemo sit, qui prohibeat, non mater, non soror, cognata, germanus; dominus te necessariam habet. Quod si voluerint inpedire, timeant flagella Pharaonis, qui populum Dei ad colendum eum nolens dimittere passus est illa, quae scripta sunt. Iesus ingressus templum omnia, quae templi non erant, proiecit. Deus enim zelotes est et non vult domum patris fieri speluncam latronum. Alioquin, ubi aera numerantur, ubi sunt caveae columbarum et simplicitas enecatur, ubi in pectore virginali saecularium negotiorum cura aestuat, statim velum templi scinditur; sponsus consurgit iratus et dicit: ' Relinquetur vobis domus vestra deserta.'

Lege evangelium et vide, quomodo Maria ad pedes domini sedens Marthae studio praeferatur—et certe Martha sedulo hospitalitatis officio domino atque discipulis convivium praeparabat: ' Martha,' inquit, ' Martha, sollicita es et turbaris circa plurima; pauca autem necessaria sunt aut unum. Maria bonam partem elegit, quae non auferetur ab ea.' Esto et tu Maria, cibis praeferto doctrinam. Sorores tuae

---

[1] St. Matthew, xxiii. 38.   [2] St. Luke, x. 41.

guard the law of the Lord. As in the ark there was nothing but the tablets of the covenant, so in you let there be no thought of anything outside. On that mercy seat it is God's pleasure to sit as once He sat upon the cherubim. He sends His disciples, that as He rode upon the foal of an ass, so He may ride upon you, setting you free from the cares of this world so that you may leave the bricks and straw of Egypt and follow Him, the true Moses, through the wilderness and enter the land of promise. Let no one prevent you, neither mother nor sister nor kinswoman nor brother: the Lord hath need of you. If they seek to hinder, let them fear the scourges that fell on Pharaoh, who, because he would not let God's people go to worship Him, suffered what is written in the Scriptures. Jesus entered into the temple and cast out those things which were not of the temple. For God is jealous and He does not allow His Father's house to be made a den of robbers. In any case, where money is counted, where there are pens of doves for sale, where simplicity is slain, where a virgin's breast is disturbed by thoughts of worldly business, there at once the veil of the temple is rent and the Bridegroom rising in anger says: 'Your house is left unto you desolate.'[1]

Read the Gospel, and see how Mary sitting at the feet of the Lord is preferred to the busy Martha. Martha, in her anxious and hospitable zeal, was preparing a meal for the Lord and His disciples: but Jesus said to her: 'Martha, Martha, thou art careful and troubled about many things. But few things are needful or one. And Mary hath chosen that good part which shall not be taken away from her.'[2] Be thou too Mary, and prefer the Lord's

cursitent et quaerant, quomodo Christum hospitem
habeant; tu insemel saeculi onere proiecto sede ad
pedes domini et dic: ' Inveni eum, quem quaerebat
anima mea; tenebo eum et non dimittam eum,' et
ille respondeat: ' Una est columba mea, perfecta
mea; una est matri suae, electa genetrici suae,'
caelesti videlicet Hierusalem.

25. Semper te cubiculi tui secreta custodiant,
semper tecum sponsus ludat intrinsecus. Oras:
loqueris ad sponsum; legis: ille tibi loquitur, et,
cum te somnus oppresserit, veniet post parietem et
mittet manum suam per foramen et tanget ventrem
tuum, et tremefacta consurges et dices: ' Vulnerata
caritatis ego sum,' et rursus ab eo audies: ' Hortus
conclusus soror mea sponsa; hortus conclusus, fons
signatus.' Cave ne domum exeas, ne velis videre
filias regionis alienae, quamvis fratres habeas patri-
archas et Israhel parente laeteris: Dina egressa
corrumpitur. Nolo te sponsum quaerere per plateas,
nolo circumire angulos civitatis. Dicas licet: ' Sur-
gam et circumibo in civitate, in foro et in plateis et
quaeram quem dilexit anima mea,' et interroges:
' Nunquid, quem dilexit anima mea, vidistis?' nemo
tibi respondere dignabitur. Sponsus in plateis non
potest inveniri—' Arta et angusta via est, quae ducit
ad vitam '—denique sequitur: ' Quaesivi eum et non
inveni eum, vocavi eum et non respondit mihi.'

---

¹ Song of Solomon, iii. 4.   ² Song of Solomon, vi. 9.
³ *I.e.* to pull the latch open.   ⁴ Song of Solomon, v. 8.
⁵ Song of Solomon, iv. 12.   ⁶ Genesis, xxxiv. 1.
⁷ Song of Solomon, iii. 2.   ⁸ St. Matthew, vii. 14.

teaching to food. Let your sisters run to and fro, and seek how they may entertain Christ as a guest. Do you once for all cast away the burden of this world and sit at the Lord's feet, and say : ' I have found him whom my soul sought; I will hold him, I will not let him go.'[1] And He will answer : ' My dove, my undefiled is but one; she is the only one of her mother, she is the choice one of her that bare her.'[2] And that mother is the Jerusalem that is in heaven.

Let the seclusion of your own chamber ever guard you; ever let the Bridegroom sport with you within. If you pray, you are speaking to your Spouse : if you read, He is speaking to you. When sleep falls on you, He will come behind the wall and will put His hand through the hole in the door[3] and will touch your flesh. And you will awake and rise up and cry : ' I am sick with love.'[4] And you will hear Him answer : ' A garden inclosed is my sister, my spouse; a garden shut up, a fountain sealed.'[5] Go not from home nor visit the daughters of a strange land, though you have patriarchs for brothers and rejoice in Israel as your father. Dinah went out and was seduced.[6] I would not have you seek the Bridegroom in the public squares; I would not have you go about the corners of the city. You may say : ' I will rise now and go about the city : in the streets and in the broad ways I will seek Him whom my soul loveth.'[7] But though you ask the watchmen : ' Saw ye Him whom my soul loveth ? ' no one will deign to answer you. The Bridegroom cannot be found in the city squares. ' Strait and narrow is the way that leadeth unto life.'[8] And the Song goes on : ' I sought him but I could not find him : I called him but he gave me no answer.'

Atque utinam non invenisse sufficiat. Vulnera-
beris, nudaberis et gemebunda narrabis: ' Invene-
runt me custodes, qui circumeunt civitatem;
percusserunt me, vulneraverunt me, tulerunt
theristrum meum a me.' Si autem hoc exiens
patitur illa, quae dixerat: ' Ego dormio et cor meum
vigilat,' et: 'Fasciculus stactae fratruelis meus
mihi, in medio uberum meorum commorabitur,' quid
de nobis fiet, quae adhuc adulescentulae sumus,
quae sponsa intrante cum sponso remanemus extrinsecus? Zelotypus est Iesus, non vult ab aliis
videri faciem tuam. Excuses licet atque causeris:
' Adducto velamine ora contexi, te quaesivi, tibi dixi:
" Adnuntia mihi, quem dilexit anima mea, ubi pascis,
ubi cubas in meridie, nequando fiam sicut cooperta
super greges sodalium tuorum," ' indignabitur, tu-
mebit, et dicet: ' Si non cognoveris temet ipsam, o
pulchra in mulieribus, egredere tu in vestigiis gre-
gum et pasce haedos tuos in tabernaculis pastorum.'
' Sis,' inquit, ' pulchra et inter omnes mulieres species
tua diligatur ab sponso, nisi te cognoveris et omni
custodia servaveris cor tuum, nisi oculos iuvenum
fugeris, egredieris de thalamo meo et pasces haedos,
qui staturi sunt a sinistris.'

26. Itaque, mi Eustochia, filia, domina, conserva,
germana—aliud enim aetatis, aliud meriti, illud
religionis, hoc caritatis est nomen—audi Esaiam

---

[1] Song of Solomon, v. 7.   [2] Song of Solomon, i. 13.
[3] Song of Solomon, i. 7.   [4] Song of Solomon, i. 8.

Would that failure to find Him were all. You will be wounded and stripped, you will lament and say: 'The watchmen who go about the city found me: they smote me, they wounded me, they took away my veil from me.' [1] If this was the punishment that going forth brought to her who said: 'I sleep but my heart waketh,' and 'A bundle of myrrh is my cousin unto me; he shall lie all night between my breasts'; [2] if she, I say, suffered so much because she went abroad, what shall be done to us who are but young girls, to us who, when the bride goes in with the Bridegroom, still remain without? Jesus is jealous: He does not wish others to see your face. You may excuse yourself and say: 'I have drawn my veil, I have covered my face, I have sought Thee there, and I have said: "Tell me, O Thou whom my soul loveth, where Thou feedest Thy flock, where Thou makest it to rest at noon. For why should I be as one that is veiled beside the flocks of Thy companions?"' [3] But He will be wroth and angry, and He will say: 'If thou know not thyself, O thou fairest among women, go thy way forth by the footsteps of the flock and feed thy goats beside the shepherd's tents.' [4] 'Though you be fair,' says He, 'and though of all faces yours be dearest to the Bridegroom, yet unless you know yourself and keep your heart with all diligence and avoid the eyes of lovers, you will be turned from My bridal-chamber to feed the goats which shall be set on the left hand.'

Therefore, my Eustochium, daughter, lady, fellow-servant, sister—for the first name suits your age, the second your rank, the third our religion, and the last our affection—hear the words of Isaiah: 'Come,

loquentem: ' Populus meus, intra in cubicula tûa, claude ostium tuum, abscondere pusillum quantulum, donec pertranseat ira domini.' Foris vagentur virgines stultae, tu intrinsecus esto cum sponso, quia, si ostium cluseris et secundum evangelii praeceptum in occulto oraveris patrem tuum, veniet et pulsabit et dicet: ' Ecce ego sto ante ianuam et pulso. Si quis mihi aperuerit, intrabo et cenabo cum eo et ipse mecum,' et tu statim sollicita respondebis: ' Vox fratruelis mei pulsantis: aperi mihi, soror mea, proxima mea, columba mea, perfecta mea.' Nec est, quod dicas: ' Dispoliavi me tunicam meam, quomodo induar eam? Lavi pedes meos, quomodo inquinabo eos?' Ilico surge et aperi, ne te remorante pertranseat et postea conqueraris dicens: ' Aperui fratruelis meo, fratruelis meus pertransiit.' Quid enim necesse est, ut cordis tui ostia clausa sint sponso? Aperiantur Christo, claudantur diabolo secundum illud: ' Si spiritus potestatem habentis ascenderit super te, locum ne dederis ei.' Danihel in cenaculo suo—neque enim manere poterat in humili—fenestras ad Hierusalem apertas habuit: te tu habeto fenestras apertas, sed unde lumen intro-eat, unde videas civitatem Dei. Ne aperias illas fenestras, de quibus dicitur: ' Mors intravit per fenestras vestras.'

27. Illud quoque tibi vitandum est cautius, ne vanae gloriae ardore capiaris. ' Quomodo,' inquit Iesus, ' potestis credere gloriam ab hominibus accipientes?' Vide, quale malum sit, quod qui

---

[1] Isaiah, xxvi. 20.   [2] Revelation, iii. 20.
[3] Song of Solomon, v. 2, 3.   [4] Song of Solomon, v. 6.
[5] Ecclesiastes, x. 4.   [6] Jeremiah, ix. 21.

my people, enter thou into thy chambers, and shut thy doors about thee: hide thyself as it were for a little moment, until the indignation of the Lord be over-past.' [1] Let foolish virgins roam abroad; do you for your part stay within with the Bridegroom. If you shut your door, and according to the Gospel precept pray to your Father in secret, He will come and knock, and He will say: ' Behold I stand at the door and knock: if any man open, I will come in to him and will sup with him, and he with me.' [2] And you forthwith will eagerly make reply: ' It is the voice of my beloved that knocketh, saying " Open to me, my sister, my nearest, my dove, my undefiled."' You must not say: ' I have put off my coat; how shall I put it on? I have washed my feet; how shall I defile them?' [3] Arise straightway and open: lest, if you linger, He pass on and leave you mournfully to cry: ' I opened to my cousin, but my cousin was gone.' [4] Why need the door of your heart be closed to the Bridegroom? Let it be open to Christ but closed to the devil, according to the saying: ' If the spirit of him who hath power rise up against thee, leave not thy place.' [5] Daniel when he could no longer remain below withdrew to an upper room, but he kept its windows open towards Jerusalem. Do you too keep your windows open on the side where light may enter and you may see the City of God. Open not those other windows of which it is said: ' By our windows death came in.' [6]

You must also avoid with especial care the traps that are set for you by a desire for vainglory. Jesus says: ' How can ye believe, which receive glory one from another?' [7] Consider then how evil that thing

[7] St. John, v. 44.

habuerit, non potest credere. Nos vero dicamus:
' Quoniam gloriatio mea es tu,' et: ' Qui gloriatur,
in domino glorietur,' et: ' Si adhuc hominibus
placerem, Christi servus non essem,' et: ' Mihi
absit gloriari, nisi in cruce domini mei Iesu Christi,
per quem mihi mundus crucifixus est et ego mundo,'
et illud: ' In te laudabimur tota die,' et: ' In
domino laudabitur anima mea.'

Cum facis elemosynam, Deus solus videat. Cum
ieiunas, laeta sit facies tua. Vestis nec satis munda
nec sordida et nulla diversitate notabilis, ne ad te
obvia praetereuntium turba consistat et digito
demonstreris. Frater est mortuus, sororis est
corpusculum deducendum: cave ne, dum hoc
saepius facis, ipsa moriaris. Ne satis religiosa velis
videri nec plus humilis, quam necesse est, ne gloriam
fugiendo quaeras. Plures enim paupertatis, misericordiae atque ieiunii arbitros declinantes in hoc ipso
placere cupiunt, quod placere contemnunt; et
mirum in modum laus, dum vitatur, adpetitur.
Ceteris perturbationibus, quibus mens hominis
gaudet, aegrescit, sperat et metuit, plures invenio
extraneos; hoc vitio pauci admodum sunt qui
caruerint, et ille est optimus, qui quasi in pulchro
corpore rara naevorum sorde respergitur.

Neque vero moneo, ne de divitiis glorieris, ne de
generis nobilitate te iactes, ne te ceteris praeferas:
scio humilitatem tuam; scio te ex affectu dicere:
' Domine, non est exaltatum cor meum neque elati

---

[1] 1 Corinthians, i. 31.   [2] Galatians, i. 10.
[3] Galatians, vi. 14.   [4] Psalm xliv. 8.

must be whose presence forbids belief. Let us rather say: ' Thou art my glorying,' and, ' He that glorieth, let him glory in the Lord,' [1] and, ' If I yet pleased men I should not be the servant of Christ,' [2] and, ' Far be it from me to glory save in the cross of our Lord Jesus Christ, through whom the world hath been crucified unto me and I unto the world,' [3] and again, ' In God we boast all the day long; my soul shall make her boast in the Lord.' [4]

When you are giving alms, let God alone see you. When you are fasting, keep a cheerful face. Let your dress be neither elegant nor slovenly, and let it not be noticeable by any strangeness that might attract the notice of passers-by and make people point their fingers at you. If a brother dies or the body of a beloved sister has to be carried to burial, take care that you do not attend such funerals too often, or you may die yourself. Do not try to seem very devout nor more humble than is necessary. It is possible to seek glory by avoiding it. Many men who screen from view their poverty, charity, and fasting, reveal their desire for admiration by the very fact that they spurn it, and, strangely enough, seek praise while avoiding it. From the other perturbations of the mind, from exultation, despondency, hope and fear I find many free; but desire for praise is a fault which few escape, and that man is best whose character, like a fair skin, is disfigured by the fewest blemishes.

I am not going to warn you against boasting of your wealth, or priding yourself on your birth, or setting yourself up as superior to others. I know your humility. I know that you can say from your heart: ' Lord, my heart is not haughty nor my eyes

sunt oculi mei.' Novi et apud te et apud matrem tuam superbiam, per quam diabolus cecidit, locum penitus non habere. Unde et super ea scribere supersedi. Stultissimum quippe est docere, quod noverit ille, quem doceas. Sed ne hoc ipsud tibi iactantiam generet, quod saeculi iactantiam contempsisti, ne cogitatio tacita subrepat, ut quia in auratis vestibus placere desisti, placere coneris in sordibus et, quando in conventu fratrum veneris vel sororum, humili sedeas scabello, te causeris indignam, vocem ex industria quasi confecta ieiuniis tenues et deficientis imitata gressum umeris innitaris alterius. Sunt quippe nonnullae exterminantes facies suas, ut pareant hominibus ieiunare; quae, statim ut aliquem viderint, ingemescunt, demittunt supercilium et operta facie vix unum oculum liberant ad videndum; vestis pulla, cingulum sacceum et sordidis manibus pedibusque; venter solus, quia videri non potest, aestuat cibo; his cotidie psalmus ille cantatur: 'Deus dissipavit ossa hominum sibi placentium.' Aliae virili habitu, veste mutata, erubescunt feminae esse, quod natae sunt, crinem amputant et inpudenter erigunt facies eunuchinas. Sunt, quae ciliciis vestiuntur et cucullis fabrefactis, ut ad infantiam redeant, imitantur noctuas et bubones.

28. Sed ne tantum videar disputare de feminis,

---

[1] Psalm cxxxi. 1.   [2] Psalm liii. 5. (Roman Psalter.)

lofty.'[1] I know that with you, as with your mother, the pride through which the devil fell finds no lodging. Therefore it would be superfluous to write to you on this subject: for indeed it is the height of folly to teach a pupil what he already knows. But beware lest your contempt for the world's boastfulness breed in you a boastfulness of another kind. Harbour not the secret thought that as you have ceased to please in cloth of gold you may now try to please in home-spun. When you come into a gathering of brethren and sisters, do not sit in too lowly a place or pretend that you are unworthy of a footstool. Do not lower your voice on purpose, as though you were worn out by fasting; nor yet lean upon a friend's shoulder imitating the gait of one who is completely exhausted. Some women indeed actually disfigure themselves, so as to make it obvious that they have been fasting. As soon as they catch sight of anyone they drop their eyes and begin sobbing, covering up the face, all but a glimpse of one eye, which they just keep free to watch the effect they make. They wear a black dress and a girdle of sackcloth; their feet and hands are unwashed: their stomach alone—because it cannot be seen—is busy churning food. Of these the psalm is sung every day: ' The Lord will scatter the bones of them that please themselves.'[2] Other women change their garb and put on men's dress; they cut their hair short and lift up their chins in shameless fashion; they blush to be what they were born to be—women, and prefer to look like eunuchs. Others again dress themselves in goat's hair, and returning to their childhood's fashions put on a baby's hood and make themselves look like so many owls.

Women are not the only persons of whom I must

viros quoque fuge, quos videris catenatos, quibus feminei contra apostolum crines, hircorum barba, nigrum pallium et nudi in patientiam frigoris pedes. Haec omnia argumenta sunt diaboli. Talem olim Antimum, talem nuper Sofronium Roma congemuit. Qui postquam nobilium introierint domos et deceperint mulierculas ' oneratas peccatis, semper discentes et numquam ad scientiam veritatis pervenientes,' tristitiam simulant et quasi longa ieiunia furtivis noctium cibis protrahunt; pudet reliqua dicere, ne videar invehi potius quam monere.

Sunt alii—de mei ordinis hominibus loquor—qui ideo ad presbyterium et diaconatum ambiunt, ut mulieres licentius videant. Omnis his cura de vestibus, si bene oleant, si pes laxa pelle non folleat. Crines calamistri vestigio rotantur, digiti de anulis radiant et, ne plantas umidior via spargat, vix imprimunt summa vestigia. Tales cum videris, sponsos magis aestimato quam clericos. Quidam in hoc omne studium vitamque posuerunt, ut matronarum nomina, domos moresque cognoscant.

E quibus unum, qui huius artis est princeps, breviter strictimque describam, quo facilius magistro cognito discipulos recognoscas. Cum sole festinus exsurgit; salutandi ei ordo disponitur; viarum

---

[1] 2 Corinthians, xi. 14.   [2] Unknown.
[3] 2 Timothy, iii. 6.

warn you. Avoid those men also whom you see
loaded with chains and wearing their hair long like a
woman's, in contravention of the apostle's precept;[1]
and with all this a shaggy goat's beard, a black cloak,
and bare feet braving the cold. All these things
are plain signs of the devil. Antimus[2] some time
ago was the sort of man I mean, and just lately Sophronius[2] has been another for Rome to groan over.
Such men as these make their way into noble houses,
and deceive ' silly women laden with sins, ever
learning and never able to come to the knowledge of
the truth.'[3] They put on a mournful face and
pretend to make long fasts, which for them are
rendered easy by secret nocturnal banquets. I am
ashamed to say more, lest I should seem to be using
the language of invective rather than of admonition.

There are other men—I speak of those of my own
order—who only seek the office of presbyter and
deacon that they may be able to visit women freely.
These fellows think of nothing but dress; they must
be nicely scented, and their shoes must fit without
a crease. Their hair is curled and still shows traces
of the tongs; their fingers glisten with rings; and if
there is wet on the road they walk across on tiptoe
so as not to splash their feet. When you see these
gentry, think of them rather as potential bridegrooms
than as clergymen. Indeed some of them devote
their whole life and all their energies to finding out
about the names, the households, and the characters
of married ladies.

I will give you a brief and summary portrait of the
chief practitioner in this line, that from the master's
likeness you may recognize his disciples. He rises
with the sun in haste; the order of his morning calls

conpendia requiruntur, et paene usque ad cubilia
dormientium senex inportunus ingreditur. Si pul-
villum viderit, si mantele elegans, si aliquid domes-
ticae supellectilis, laudat, miratur, adtrectat, et se
his indigere conquerens non tam inpetrat quam
extorquet, quia singulae metuunt veredarium urbis
offendere. Huic inimica castitas, inimica ieiunia;
prandium nidoribus probat et altilem quae vulgo
' ποππύζων ' nominatur. Os barbarum et procax
et in convicia semper armatum. Quocumque
te verteris, primus in facie est. Quidquid novum
insonuerit, aut auctor aut exaggerator est famae.[1]
Equi per horarum momenta mutantur tam nitidi,
tam feroces, ut illum Thracii regis putes esse germanum.

29. Variis callidus hostis pugnat insidiis. Sapientior erat coluber omnibus bestiis, quas fecerat dominus
Deus super terram.[2] Unde et apostolus: ' Non,'
inquit, ' ignoramus eius astutias.'[3] Nec affectatae
sordes nec exquisitae munditiae conveniunt Christianis. Si quid ignoras, si quid de scripturis dubitas,
interroga eum, quem vita commendat, excusat
aetas, fama non reprobat, qui possit dicere: ' De-
sponsavi enim vos uni viro, virginem castam exhibere
Christo.'[4] Aut si non est, qui possit exponere,
melius est aliquid nescire securam, quam cum
periculo discere. Memento, quoniam in medio

---

[1] Cf. Virgil, *Aeneid*, I. 752. Diomede was a great horseman.
[2] Genesis, iii. 1.
[3] 2 Corinthians, ii. 11.
[4] 2 Corinthians, xi. 2.

LETTER XXII

is duly arranged; he takes short cuts, and importunately thrusts his old head almost into the bedchambers of ladies still asleep. If he sees a cushion, or an elegant table cover, or indeed any article of furniture that he fancies, he begins praising and admiring it and takes it in his hand, and so, lamenting that he has nothing like this, he begs or rather extorts it from the owner, as all the women are afraid to offend the town gossip. He hates chastity and he hates fasting: what he likes is a savoury lunch—say a plump young bird such as is commonly called a cheeper. He has a rough and saucy tongue always well equipped with abusive words. Wherever you betake yourself, he is the first man you see. Whatever news is noised abroad, he either originates the story or else exaggerates it. He changes horses every hour; and his nags are so sleek and spirited that you might take him to be own brother to Diomede of Thrace.[1]

Our cunning enemy fights against us with many varied stratagems. 'The serpent was more subtile than any beast of the field which the Lord God had made.'[2] So the apostle says: 'We are not ignorant of his devices.'[3] Neither an affected shabbiness nor an elaborate elegance of attire becomes a Christian. If you feel ignorant or have any doubt about some passage in Scripture, ask advice from some man whose life commends him, whose age puts him above suspicion, and whose reputation stands high with all; one who can say: 'I have espoused you to one husband, a chaste virgin to present to Christ.'[4] If there is no one at hand able to resolve your difficulty, remember that peaceful ignorance is better than dangerous instruc-

laqueorum ambulas et multae veteranae virgines castitatis indubitatam in ipso mortis limine coronam perdidere de manibus.

Si quae ancillae sunt comites propositi tui, ne erigaris adversus eas, ne infleris ut domina. Unum sponsum habere coepistis, simul psallitis Christo, simul corpus accipitis, cur mensa diversa sit? Provocentur et aliae. Honor virginum sit invitatio ceterarum. Quodsi aliquam senseris infirmiorem in fide, suscipe, consolare, blandire et pudicitiam illius fac lucrum tuum. Si qua simulat fugiens servitutem, huic aperte apostolum lege: ' Melius est nubere quam uri.'

Eas autem virgines viduasque, quae otiosae et curiosae domus circumeunt matronarum, quae rubore frontis adtrito parasitos vicere mimorum. quasi quasdam pestes abice. ' Corrumpunt mores bonos confabulationes pessimae.' Nulla illis nisi ventris cura est et quae ventri proxima. Istiusmodi hortari solent et dicere: ' Mi catella, rebus tuis utere et vive, dum vivis,' et: ' Numquid filiis tuis servas?' Vinosae atque lascivae quidvis mali insinuant, ac ferreas quoque mentes ad delicias molliunt, et ' cum luxuriatae fuerint in Christo, nubere volunt habentes damnationem, quia primam fidem inritam fecerunt.'

---

[1] 1 Corinthians, vii. 9.   [2] 1 Corinthians, xv. 33.
[3] 1 Timothy, v. 11.

tion. You walk in the midst of snares, and many
veteran virgins, whose chastity never was doubted,
on the very threshold of death have let the crown slip
from their hands.

If any of your handmaids have taken the vow with
you, do not lift yourself up against them or pride
yourself as being the mistress. From now you all
have one Bridegroom; you sing psalms together;
together you receive the Body of Christ. Why then
should you separate at meals? You must challenge
other mistresses: let the respect paid to your virgins
be an invitation for the rest to do the same. If you
find one of your girls weak in faith, take her aside,
comfort and caress her, make her chastity your
treasure. But if one merely pretends to have a
vocation in order to escape from service, read aloud
to her the apostle's words: 'It is better to marry
than to burn.' [1]

Cast from you like the plague those idle and
inquisitive virgins and widows who go about to
married women's houses and surpass the very para-
sites in a play by their unblushing effrontery. 'Evil
communications corrupt good manners,' [2] and these
women care for nothing but their belly and its
adjacent members. Creatures of this sort will give
you wheedling advice: 'My pretty pet, make the
best of what you have and live your own life. What
is the use of saving for your children?' Flown with
wine and wantonness, they instil all sorts of mischief
into a girl's mind, and tempt even the firmest soul
with the soft delights of pleasure. 'And when they
have begun to wax wanton against Christ they will
marry, having condemnation because they have
rejected their first faith.' [3]

Nec tibi diserta multum velis videri aut lyricis festiva carminibus metro ludere. Non delumbem matronarum salivam delicata secteris, quae nunc strictis dentibus, nunc labiis dissolutis, balbutientem linguam in dimidiata verba moderantur, rusticum putantes omne, quod nascitur. Adeo illis adulterium etiam linguae placet. ' Quae enim communicatio luci ad tenebras, qui consensus Christo et Belial?' Quid facit cum psalterio Horatius? cum evangeliis Maro? cum apostolo Cicero? Nonne scandalizatur frater, si te viderit in idolio recumbentem? Et licet ' omnia munda mundis et nihil reiciendum sit, quod cum gratiarum actione percipitur,' tamen simul bibere non debemus calicem Christi et calicem daemoniorum. Referam tibi meae infelicitatis historiam.

30. Cum ante annos plurimos domo, parentibus, sorore, cognatis et, quod his difficilius est, consuetudine lautioris cibi propter caelorum me regna castrassem et Hierosolymam militaturus pergerem, bybliotheca, quam mihi Romae summo studio ac labore confeceram, carere non poteram. Itaque miser ego lecturus Tullium ieiunabam; post noctium crebras vigilias, post lacrimas, quas mihi praeteritorum recordatio peccatorum ex imis visceribus eruebat, Plautus sumebatur in manibus. Si quando in memet reversus prophetam legere coepissem, sermo horrebat incultus, et quia lumen caecis oculis non videbam, non oculorum putabam culpam esse, sed solis. Dum

---

[1] 2 Corinthians, vi. 14.

Do not seek to appear over-eloquent or compose trifling songs in verse. Do not in false refinement follow the sickly taste of those married ladies who habitually speak with a lisp and clip all their words, now pressing their teeth together, and now opening their lips wide, fancying that anything produced naturally is countrified. So much do they like adultery even of the tongue. 'What communion hath light with darkness? What concord hath Christ with Belial?'[1] What has Horace to do with the Psalter, Virgil with the Gospels and Cicero with Paul? Is not a brother made to stumble if he sees you sitting at table in an idol's temple? Although unto the pure all things are pure and nothing is to be refused if it be received with thanksgiving, still we ought not to drink the cup of Christ and the cup of devils at the same time. I will tell you the story of my own unhappy experience.

Many years ago for the sake of the kingdom of heaven I cut myself off from home, parents, sister, relations, and, what was harder, from the dainty food to which I had been used. But even when I was on my way to Jerusalem to fight the good fight there, I could not bring myself to forgo the library which with great care and labour I had got together at Rome. And so, miserable man that I was, I would fast, only to read Cicero afterwards. I would spend many nights in vigil, I would shed bitter tears called from my inmost heart by the remembrance of my past sins; and then I would take up Plautus again. Whenever I returned to my right senses and began to read the prophets, their language seemed harsh and barbarous. With my blind eyes I could not see the light: but I attributed the fault not to my eyes

ita me antiquus serpens inluderet, in media ferme
quadragesima medullis infusa febris corpus invasit
exhaustum et sine ulla requie—quod dictu quoque
incredibile sit—sic infelicia membra depasta est, ut
ossibus vix haererem.

Interim parabantur exsequiae et vitalis animae
calor toto frigente iam corpore in solo tam tepente
pectusculo palpitabat, cum subito raptus in spiritu
ad tribunal iudicis pertrahor, ubi tantum luminis et
tantum erat ex circumstantium claritate fulgoris,
ut proiectus in terram sursum aspicere non auderem.
Interrogatus condicionem Christianum me esse
respondi: et ille, qui residebat, 'Mentiris,' ait,
'Ciceronianus es, non Christianus; "ubi thesaurus
tuus, ibi et cor tuum."' Ilico obmutui et inter
verbera—nam caedi me iusserat—conscientiae magis
igne torquebar illum mecum versiculum reputans:
'In inferno autem quis confitebitur tibi?' Clamare
tamen coepi et heiulans dicere: 'Miserere mei,
domine, miserere mei.' Haec vox inter flagella
resonabat. Tandem ad praesidentis genua pro-
voluti, qui adstiterant, precabantur, ut veniam
tribueret adulescentiae, ut errori locum paenitentiae
commodaret exacturus deinde cruciatum, si gentilium

---

[1] St. Matthew, vi. 21.

but to the sun. While the old serpent was thus mocking me, about the middle of Lent a fever attacked my weakened body and spread through my inmost veins. It may sound incredible, but the ravages it wrought on my unhappy frame were so persistent that at last my bones scarcely held together.

Meantime preparations were made for my funeral: my whole body grew gradually cold, and life's vital warmth only lingered faintly in my poor throbbing breast. Suddenly I was caught up in the spirit and dragged before the Judge's judgment seat: and here the light was so dazzling, and the brightness shining from those who stood around so radiant, that I flung myself upon the ground and did not dare to look up. I was asked to state my condition and replied that I was a Christian. But He who presided said: ' Thou liest; thou art a Ciceronian, not a Christian. " For where thy treasure is there will thy heart be also." ' [1] Straightway I became dumb, and amid the strokes of the whip—for He had ordered me to be scourged—I was even more bitterly tortured by the fire of conscience, considering with myself the verse: ' In the grave who shall give thee thanks? ' [2] Yet for all that I began to cry out and to bewail myself, saying: ' Have mercy upon me, O Lord, have mercy upon me ': and even amid the noise of the lash my voice made itself heard. At last the bystanders fell at the knees of Him who presided, and prayed Him to pardon my youth and give me opportunity to repent of my error, on the understanding that the extreme of torture should be inflicted on me if ever I read again the works of

[2] Psalm vi. 5.

litterarum libros aliquando legissem. Ego, qui tanto constrictus articulo vellem etiam maiora promittere, deiurare coepi et nomen eius obtestans dicere: 'Domine, si umquam habuero codices saeculares, si legero, te negavi.'

In haec sacramenti verba dimissus revertor ad superos et mirantibus omnibus oculos aperio tanto lacrimarum imbre perfusos, ut etiam incredulis fidem facerent ex dolore. Nec vero sopor ille fuerat aut vana somnia, quibus saepe deludimur. Teste est tribunal, ante quod iacui, iudicium teste est, quod timui—ita mihi numquam contingat talem incidere quaestionem!—liventes habuisse me scapulas, plagas sensisse post somnum et tanto dehinc studio divina legisse, quanto mortalia ante non legeram.

31. Avaritiae quoque tibi vitandum est malum, non quo aliena non adpetas—hoc enim et leges publicae puniunt,—sed quo tua, quae sunt aliena, non serves. 'Si in alieno,' inquit, 'fideles non fuistis, quod vestrum est, quis dabit vobis?' Aliena nobis auri argentique sunt pondera, nostra possessio spiritalis est, de qua alibi dicitur: 'Redemptio viri propriae divitiae.' 'Nemo potest duobus dominis servire; aut enim unum odiet et alterum amabit, aut unum patietur et alterum contemnet. Non potestis

---

[1] St. Luke, xvi. 12.   [2] Proverbs, xiii. 8.

Gentile authors. In the stress of that dread hour
I should have been willing to make even larger
promises, and taking oath I called upon His name:
' O Lord, if ever again I possess worldly books or
read them, I have denied thee.'

After swearing this oath I was dismissed, and
returned to the upper world. There to the surprise
of all I opened my eyes again, and they were so
drenched with tears, that my distress convinced even
the incredulous. That this experience was no sleep
nor idle dream, such as often mocks us, I call to witness the judgment seat before which I fell and the
terrible verdict which I feared. May it never be my
lot again to come before such a court as that! I
profess that my shoulders were black and blue, and
that I felt the bruises long after I awoke from my
sleep. And I acknowledge that henceforth I read
the books of God with a greater zeal than I had ever
given before to the books of men.

You must also avoid the sin of love of money.
Not merely must you refuse to claim what belongs
to another, for that is an offence punished by the
laws of the State; you must also give up clinging
to your own property, which has now become no
longer yours. The Lord says: ' If ye have not
been faithful in that which is another man's,
who shall give you that which is your own?' [1]
' That which is another man's ' is a mass of gold
and silver; ' that which is your own ' is the
spiritual heritage of which it is said elsewhere:
' The ransom of a man's life is his riches.' [2] ' No
man can serve two masters, for either he will hate
the one and love the other; or else he will hold to
the one and despise the other. Ye cannot serve

Deo servire et mammonae,' id est divitiis. Nam gentili Syrorum lingua ' mammona ' divitiae nuncupantur Cogitatio victus spinae sunt fidei, radix avaritiae, cura gentilium.

At dices: ' Puella sum delicata et quae meis manibus laborare non possum. Si ad senectam venero, si aegrotare coepio, quis mei miserebitur?' Audi ad apostolos loquentem Iesum: ' Ne cogitetis in corde vestro, quid manducetis, neque corpori vestro, quid induamini. Nonne anima plus est quam esca et corpus plus est quam vestimentum? Respicite volatilia caeli, quoniam non serunt neque metunt neque congregant in horrea et pater vester caelestis pascit illa.' Si vestis defuerit, lilia proponentur; si esurieris, beatos audies pauperes et esurientes; si aliquis adflixerit dolor, legito: ' Propter hoc conplaceo mihi in infirmitatibus meis,' et: ' Datus est mihi stimulus carnis meae, angelus Satanae, qui me colafizet,' ne extollar. Laetare in omnibus iudiciis Dei; ' Exultaverunt,' enim, ' filiae Iudae in omnibus iudiciis tuis, domine.' Illa tibi semper in ore vox resonet: ' Nudus exivi de utero matris meae, nudus et redeam,' et: ' Nihil intulimus in hunc mundum nec auferre quid possumus.'

32. At nunc plerasque videas armaria stipare vestibus, tunicas mutare cotidie et tamen tineas non posse superare. Quae religiosior fuerit, unum exterit vestimentum et plenis arcis pannos trahit. Inficitur

---

[1] St. Matthew, vi. 24.   [2] St. Matthew, vi. 25.
[3] St. Matthew, vi. 28.   [4] 2 Corinthians, xii. 7, 10.
[5] Psalm xcvii. 8.   [6] Job, i. 21.   [7] 1 Timothy, vi. 7.

God and Mammon.'[1] By Mammon understand
riches: for in the heathen tongue of the Syrians
riches are so called. The thorns that choke our faith
are the taking thought for our subsistence. Care for
the things of the Gentiles is the root of love of money.

But you say: 'I am a delicate girl and I cannot
work with my hands. If I reach old age and fall
sick who will take pity on me?' Hear Jesus speaking to the apostles: 'Take no thought what ye shall
eat; nor yet for your body what ye shall put on.
Is not the life more than meat and the body more
than raiment? Behold the fowls of the air; for they
sow not, nor reap nor gather into barns: yet your
heavenly Father feedeth them.'[2] If clothing fail
you, the lilies shall be put before you.[3] If you are
hungry, you shall hear how blessed are the poor
and hungry among men. If any pain afflict you,
read the words: 'Therefore I take pleasure in my
infirmities,' and, 'There was given to me a thorn
in the flesh, the messenger of Satan to buffet me,
lest I should be exalted above measure.'[4] Rejoice
in all God's judgments; for does not the psalmist
say: 'The daughters of Judah rejoiced because
of thy judgments, O Lord'?[5] Let the words be
ever on your lips: 'Naked came I out of my
mother's womb and naked shall I return thither,'[6]
and, 'We brought nothing into this world, and it is
certain we can carry nothing out.'[7]

But to-day you see many women packing their
wardrobes with dresses, putting on a fresh frock every
day, and even so unable to get the better of the moth.
The more scrupulous sort wear one dress till it is
threadbare, but though they go about in rags their
boxes are full of clothes. Parchments are dyed

membrana colore purpureo, aurum liquescit in litteras, gemmis codices vestiuntur et nudus ante fores aerum Christus emoritur. Cum manum porrexerint, bucinant; cum ad agapen vocaverint, praeco conducitur. Vidi nuper—nomina taceo, ne saturam putes—nobilissimam mulierum Romanarum in basilica beati Petri semiviris antecedentibus propria manu, quo religiosior putaretur, singulos nummos dispertire pauperibus. Interea—ut usu nosse perfacile est—anus quaedam annis pannisque obsita praecurrit, ut alterum nummum acciperet; ad quam cum ordine pervenisset, pugnus porrigitur pro denario et tanti criminis reus sanguis effunditur.

' Radix malorum omnium est avaritia,' ideoque et ab apostolo idolorum servitus appellatur. ' Quaere primum regnum Dei et haec omnia adponentur tibi.' Non occidet dominus fame animam iusti: ' Iuvenior fui et senui et non vidi iustum derelictum nec semen eius quaerens panem.' Helias corvis ministrantibus pascitur; vidua Sareptena ipsa cum filiis nocte moritura prophetam pascit esuriens et mirum in modum capsace conpleto, qui alendus venerat, alit. Petrus apostolus: ' Argentum,' inquit, ' et aurum non habeo; quod autem habeo, hoc tibi do. In nomini domini Iesu Christi surge et ambula.' At nunc multi, licet sermone taceant, re loquuntur: ' Fidem et misericordiam non habeo; quod autem

---

[1] In the early Church the Eucharist was preceded by an ' agape,' or love-feast. All contributed, all sat down together, and the meal ended with a psalm.

[2] 1 Timothy, vi. 10.

[3] St. Matthew, vi. 33.

[4] Psalm xxxvii. 25.

[5] Acts, iii. 6.

purple, gold is melted for lettering, manuscripts are decked with jewels: and Christ lies at their door naked and dying. When they hold a hand out to the needy, they sound the trumpet. When they invite to a love-feast,[1] they hire a crier. Just lately I saw the greatest lady in Rome—I will not give her name, for this is not a satire—standing in the church of the blessed Peter with her band of eunuchs in front. She was giving money to the poor with her own hand to increase her reputation for sanctity; and she gave them each a penny! At that moment —as you might easily know by experience—an old woman, full of years and rags, ran in front of the line to get a second coin; but when her turn came she got, not a penny, but the lady's fist in her face, and for her dreadful offence she had to pay with her blood.

'The love of money is the root of all evil,'[2] and therefore the apostle calls it slavery to idols. 'Seek ye first the kingdom of God and all these things shall be added unto you.'[3] The Lord will never let a righteous soul die of hunger. The psalmist says: 'I have been young and now am old, yet have I not seen the righteous forsaken nor his seed begging bread.'[4] Elijah was fed by ministering ravens. The widow of Zarephath, herself and her sons within an ace of death that night, went hungry that she might feed the prophet: by a miracle the flour barrel was filled and he who had come to be fed supplied food. The apostle Peter says: 'Silver and gold have I none, but such as I have give I thee. In the name of Jesus Christ, rise up and walk.'[5] To-day many people, though they do not say it in words, by their deeds declare: 'Faith and pity have I

133

habeo, aurum et argentum non do tibi.'[1] Habentes
igitur victum et vestimentum his contenti sumus.
Audi, Iacob in sua oratione quid postulet: ' Si fuerit
dominus Deus mecum et servaverit me in via hac,
per quam ego iter facio, et dederit mihi panem ad
manducandum et vestem ad induendum.' Tantum
necessaria deprecatus est et post annos viginti dives
dominus et ditior pater ad terram revertitur Chanaan.
Infinita de scripturis exempla subpeditant, quae et
avaritiam doceant esse fugiendam.

33. Verum quia nunc ex latere de ea dicitur et
suo, si Christus adnuerit, volumini reservatur, quid
ante non plures annos Nitriae gestum sit, referam.
Quidam e fratribus parcior magis quam avarior et
nesciens triginta argenteis dominum venditum
centum solidos, quos lina texendo quaesierat, moriens
dereliquit. Initum inter monachos consilium—nam
in eodem loco circiter quinque milia divisis cellulis
habitant[2]—quid facto opus est. Alii pauperibus
distribuendos esse dicebant, alii dandos ecclesiae,
nonnulli parentibus remittendos. Macarius vero et
Pambos et Isidorus et ceteri, quos patres vocant,
sancto in eis loquente spiritu decreverunt infodiendos
esse cum domino suo dicentes: ' Pecunia tua tecum
in perditionem.'[3] Nec hoc crudeliter quisquam
factum putet: tantus per totam Aegyptum cunctos
terror invasit, ut unum solidum dimisisse sit
criminis.

34. Et quoniam monachorum fecimus mentionem
et te scio libenter audire, quae sancta sunt, aurem
paulisper adcommoda. Tria sunt in Aegypto genera

---

[1] Genesis, xxviii. 20.
[2] Cf. Index and Appendix, p. 484.   [3] Acts, viii. 20.

none; but such as I have, gold and silver, these give I thee not.' Having food and raiment let us be content. Hear the words of Jacob in his prayer: ' If God will be with me and will keep me in this way that I go, and will give me bread to eat and raiment to put on, [then shall the Lord be my God.'][1] He prayed only for necessities; yet twenty years afterwards he returned to the land of Canaan, rich in goods and richer still in children. Endless are the examples that Scripture supplies teaching us to beware of love of money.

As I have touched on this subject—if Christ allows I keep it for a special book—I will relate an incident that occurred not many years ago at Nitria. A brother, rather thrifty than avaricious, forgetting that the Lord was sold for thirty pieces of silver, left behind him at his death a hundred gold coins which he had earned by weaving linen. The monks held a council as to what was to be done with it, for there were about five thousand of them in the neighbourhood living in separate cells; some said that the money should be distributed among the poor; others that it should be given to the Church; others that it should be sent back to the dead man's parents. But Macarius, Pambos, Isidore,[2] and the other Fathers, the Holy Spirit speaking by them, decreed that the coins should be buried with their owner, saying: ' Thy money perish with thee.' [3] Let no one think their decision too harsh; for so great a fear has fallen upon all in Egypt that it is now a crime to leave a single gold piece.

Since I have mentioned the monks, and know that you like to hear about holy things, lend me your ear awhile. There are in Egypt three classes of

monachorum : coenobium, quod illi ' sauhes ' gentili
lingua vocant, nos ' in commune viventes ' possumus
appellare ; anchoretae, qui soli habitant per deserta
et ab eo, quod procul ab hominibus recesserint,
nuncupantur ; tertium genus est, quod dicunt
' remnuoth,' deterrimum atque neglectum et quod
in nostra provincia aut solum aut primum est. Hi
bini vel terni nec multo plures simul habitant suo
arbitratu ac dicione viventes, et de eo, quod labora-
verint, in medium partes conferunt, ut habeant ali-
menta communia. Habitant autem quam plurimum
in urbis et castellis, et, quasi ars sit sancta, non vita,
quidquid vendiderint, maioris est pretii. Inter hos
saepe sunt iurgia, quia suo viventes cibo non patiuntur
se alicui esse subiectos. Re vera solent certare
ieiuniis et rem secreti victoriae faciunt. Apud hos
affectata sunt omnia : laxae manicae, caligae folli-
cantes, vestis grossior, crebra suspiria, visitatio
virginum, detractatio clericorum, et si quando festior
dies venerit, saturantur ad vomitum.

35. His igitur quasi quibusdam pestibus exterminatis veniamus ad eos, qui plures in commune
habitant, id est, quos vocari coenobium diximus.
Prima apud eos confoederatio est oboedire maioribus
et, quidquid iusserint, facere. Divisi sunt per
decurias atque centurias, ita ut novem hominibus
decimus praesit et rursus decem praepositos sub se
centesimus habeat. Manent separati, sed iunctis

---

[1] From κοινὸς βίος, living a life in common.
[2] An Egyptian word not elsewhere found.
[3] From ἀναχωρεῖν, to withdraw.
[4] Monks who lived in groups under no fixed rule. Cf.
Cassian. *Collat.* xviii. 7.
[5] *I.e.* Pannonia.

monks. First, there are the cenobites,[1] called in their Gentile tongue Sauhes,[2] or, as we should say, men living in a community. Secondly, there are the anchorites,[3] who live in the desert as solitaries, so called because they have withdrawn from the society of men. Thirdly, there is the class called Remnuoth,[4] a very inferior and despised kind, though in my own province[5] they are the chief if not the only sort of monks. These men live together in twos and threes, seldom in larger numbers, and live according to their own will and ruling. A portion of what they make they contribute to a common fund which provides food for all. In most cases they live in cities or in villages, and anything they sell is very dear, the idea being that their workmanship, not their life, is sanctified. Quarrels are frequent among them; for while they supply their own food, they will not brook subordination. It is true that they compete with one another in fasting, making what should be a private matter an occasion for a triumph. Everything with them is done for effect: loose sleeves, big boots, clumsy dress, constant sighing, visiting virgins, disparaging the clergy, and when a feast day comes, they eat so much that they make themselves ill.

Avoiding these then as though they were the plague, let us come to the more numerous class who live together and are called, as we have said, cenobites. Among them the first principle of their association is to obey superiors and do whatever they command. They are divided into sections of ten and a hundred; each tenth man is over nine others, while the hundredth has ten such officers under him. They live apart from each other, but

cellulis. Usque ad horam nonam quasi iustitium est: nemo pergit ad alium exceptis his, quos decanos diximus, ut, si cogitationibus forte quis fluctuat, illius consoletur alloquiis. Post horam nonam in commune concurritur, psalmi resonant, scripturae ex more recitantur et conpletis orationibus cunctisque residentibus medius, quem patrem vocant, incipit disputare. Quo loquente tantum silentium fit, ut nemo ad alium respicere, nemo audeat excreare. Dicentis laus in fletu est audientum. Tacite volvuntur per ora lacrimae et ne in singultus quidem erumpit dolor. Cum vero de regno Christi, de futura beatitudine, de gloria coeperit adnuntiare ventura, videas cunctos moderato suspirio et oculis ad caelum levatis intra se dicere: ' Quis dabit mihi pinnas sicut columbae, et volabo et requiescam?'[1]

Post hoc concilium solvitur et unaquaeque decuria cum suo parente pergit ad mensas, quibus per singulas ebdomadas vicissim ministrant. Nullus in cibo strepitus, nemo comedens loquitur. Vivuntur pane, leguminibus et olere, quae sale et oleo condiuntur. Vinum tantum senes accipiunt, quibus et parvulis saepe fit prandium, ut aliorum fessa sustentetur aetas, aliorum non frangatur incipiens. Dehinc consurgunt pariter et hymno dicto ad praesepia redeunt. Ibi usque ad vesperam cum suis unusquisque loquitur et dicit: ' Vidistis illum et illum,

---

[1] Psalm lv. 6.

in adjoining cells. No monk may visit another before three o'clock in the afternoon, except only the deans or leaders of ten, whose business it is to comfort with soothing words any one disturbed by restless thoughts: until then, there is a cessation of all business. After three o'clock they meet together to sing psalms and duly read the Scriptures. When the prayers have ended and all have sat down, one, whom they call Father, stands up in their midst and discourses; a silence so complete being observed while he is speaking that no one dares to look at his neighbour or to clear his throat. The highest praise that can be given to the preacher is the weeping of his audience. But the tears that run down their cheeks are silent, and not even a sob reveals their emotion. But when he begins to announce the kingdom of Christ, the future happiness, and the coming glory you may see everyone with a gentle sigh and lifted gaze saying to himself: ' Oh, that I had the wings of a dove. For then would I fly away and be at rest.' [1]

After the discourse the meeting breaks up, and each set of ten goes with its Father to its own table; taking turns to serve, each man for a week at a time. No noise is made over the food; no one talks while eating. The fare consists of bread, pulse and greens, and salt and oil is their only condiment. The old men alone receive wine, they often having a special meal prepared in company with the children, so that the weariness of age is refreshed and the weakness of childhood is not impaired. They then rise from table together and after singing a hymn return to their quarters. There each one talks till evening with his friends thus: ' Have you noticed So-and-

quanta in ipso sit gratia, quantum silentium, quam
moderatus incessus?' Si infirmum viderint, consolantur; si in Deo amore ferventem, cohortantur ad
studium. Et quia nocte extra orationes publicas ni
suo cubili unusquisque vigilat, circumeunt cellulas
singulorum et aure adposita, quid faciant, diligenter
explorant. Quem tardiorem deprehenderint, non
increpant, sed dissimulato, quod norunt, eum saepius
visitant et prius incipientes provocant magis orare,
quam cogunt. Opus diei statutum est, quod decano
redditum fertur ad oeconomicum, qui et ipse per
singulos menses patri omnium cum magno reddit
tremore rationem. A quo etiam cibi, cum facti
fuerint, degustantur et, quia non licet dicere cui-
quam: 'Tunicam et sagum textaque iuncis strata
non habeo,' ille ita universa moderatur, ut nemo quid
postulet, nemo dehabeat. Si vero quis coeperit
aegrotare, transfertur ad exedram latiorem et tanto
senum ministerio confovetur, ut nec delicias urbium
nec matris quaerat affectum. Dominicis diebus
orationi tantum et lectionibus vacant; quod quidem
et omni tempore conpletis opusculis faciunt. Cotidie
de scripturis aliquid discitur. Ieiunium totius anni
aequale est excepta quadragesima, in qua sola
conceditur restrictius vivere. Pentecoste cenae
mutantur in prandia, quo et traditioni ecclesiasticae
satisfiat et ventrem cibo non onerent duplicato.
Tales Philo, Platonici sermonis imitator, tales Iose-

so? What grace he has and what powers of silence! How soberly he walks!' If they see that any one is weak, they comfort him: if he is fervent in love for God, they encourage his zeal. At night, besides the common prayers, each man keeps vigil in his own chamber; and so the deans go round to each cell, and putting their ears to the doors carefully ascertain what the inmates are doing. If they catch a monk in slothfulness, they do not upbraid him: but, hiding what they know, they visit him more frequently, and by beginning themselves to pray exhort rather than drive him to his devotions. Every day has its allotted task: the work done is handed to a dean and by him brought to the bursar, who once a month with fear and trembling gives an account to the Community Father. The bursar also tastes the dishes when they are cooked, and as no one is allowed to say: 'I am without a tunic or a cloak or a rush mattress,' he so arranges their entire store that none need ask and none go without. If any one is taken ill, he is moved to a larger room, and is there so sedulously tended by the older monks, that he misses neither the luxuries of cities nor a mother's loving care. Every Lord's day they give their whole time to prayer and reading: which indeed are their usual occupations on ordinary days when work is over. Every day they learn by heart a passage of Scripture. Fasting is regular throughout the year, but in Lent alone an increase of strictness is permitted. After Whitsuntide a midday meal takes the place of the evening repast, and thus the tradition of the Church is satisfied and they avoid overloading their stomachs with a double quantity of food. The Essenes also follow these rules, as we learn from

phus, Graecus Livius, in secunda Iudaicae captivitatis historia Essenos refert.

36. Verum quia nunc de virginibus scribens paene superflue de monachis disputavi, ad tertium genus veniam, quos anchoretas vocant et qui de coenobiis exeuntes excepto pane et sale amplius ad deserta nil perferunt. Huius vitae auctor Paulus, inlustrator Antonius et, ut ad superiora conscendam, princeps Iohannes baptista fuit. Talem virum Hieremias quoque propheta descripsit dicens: ' Bonum est viro, cum portaverit iugum ab adulescentia sua. Sedebit solus et tacebit, quoniam sustulit super se iugum, dabit percutienti se maxillam, saturabitur inproperiis, quia non in sempiternum abiciet dominus.' Horum laborem et conversationem in carne, non carnis, alio tempore, si volueris, explicabo. Nunc ad propositum redeam, quia de avaritia disserens ad monachos verteram. Quorum tibi exempla proponens, non dicam aurum et argentum et ceteras opes, sed ipsam terram caelumque despicies et Christo copulata cantabis: ' Pars mea dominus.'

37. Post haec, quamquam apostolus semper orare nos iubeat et sanctis etiam ipse somnus oratio sit, tamen divisas orandi horas habere debemus, ut si forte aliquo fuerimus opere detenti, ipsum nos ad officium tempus admoneat: horam tertiam, sextam, nonam, diluculum quoque et vesperam nemo qui nesciat. Nec cibus a te sumatur nisi oratione praemissa nec recedatur a mensa, nisi referantur

---

[1] Cf. Josephus, *Jewish War*, II. 8.
[2] Paul the hermit, whose life Jerome wrote.
[3] Cf. index.
[4] Lamentations, iii. 27.
[5] Psalm lxxiii. 26.

Philo, Plato's imitator, and from Josephus,[1] the Greek
Livy, in the second book of his *Jewish Captivity*.

However, as I am writing now about virgins, all
these details about monks may seem rather superfluous. I will proceed to the third class, who are
called anchorites. They go out from a monastery
and live in the desert, taking nothing with them but
bread and salt. The founder of the system was
Paul,[2] and Antony[3] made it famous: going back, the
first example was given by John the Baptist. The
prophet Jeremiah also describes such a solitary:
'It is good for a man that he bear the yoke from his
youth. He sitteth alone and keepeth silence,
because he hath borne it upon him. He giveth his
cheek to him that smiteth him, he is filled full of
reproach. For the Lord will not cast off for ever.'[4]
The struggles of the anchorites and their life, in
the flesh but not of the flesh, I will unfold to you
on some other occasion, if you wish. Let me now
return to my subject, for I was speaking of love of
money when I digressed to the monks. With them
as examples before you, you will look down not only
on gold and silver and worldly possessions, but even
on earth itself and the sky. United to Christ, you
will sing: 'The Lord is my portion.'[5]

Moreover, although the apostle bids us to pray
without ceasing and although to the saints their
very sleep is an orison, yet we ought to have fixed
hours for prayer, so that if perchance we are occupied
with any business the time itself may remind us of
our duty. Every one knows that the set times are
the third, the sixth, and the ninth hours, at dawn
and at evening. No food should be taken except
after prayer, and before leaving the table thanks

gratiae creatori. Noctibus bis terque surgendum, revolvenda de scripturis, quae memoriter tenemus. Egredientes hospitium armet oratio, regredientibus de platea oratio occurrat ante, quam sessio, nec prius corpusculum requiescat, quam anima pascatur. Ad omnem actum, ad omnem incessum manus pingat crucem. Nulli detrahas nec adversus filium matris tuae ponas scandalum. 'Tu quae es, ut alienum servum judices? Suo domino stat aut cadit. Stabit autem; potens est enim Deus statuere illum.'[1] Nec, si biduo ieiunaveris, putes te non ieiunante meliorem. Tu ieiunas et irasceris, ille comedit et forte blanditur; tu vexationem mentis et ventris esuriem rixando digeris, ille moderatius alitur et Deo gratias refert. Unde cotidie clamat Esaias: 'Non tale ieiunium elegi, dicit dominus,'[2] et iterum: 'In diebus enim ieiuniorum invenientur voluntates vestrae et omnes, qui sub potestate vestra eunt, stimulatis. ⟨Si⟩ in iudiciis et litibus ieiunatis et percutitis pugnis humilem, ut quid mihi ieiunatis?'[3] Quale illud potest esse ieiunium, cuius iram, non dicam nox occupat, sed luna integra derelinquit? Te ipsam considerans noli in alterius ruina, sed in tuo opere gloriari.

38. Nec illarum tibi exempla proponas, quae carnis curam facientes possessionum reditus et cotidianas domus impensas subputant. Neque enim undecim apostoli Iudae proditione sunt fracti nec

---

[1] Romans, xiv. 4.   [2] Isaiah, lviii. 5.
[3] Isaiah, lviii. 3.

should be rendered to our Creator. We should rise
from our bed two or three times in the night, and
go over those passages of Scripture which we know
by heart. Let prayer arm us when we leave our
lodging: when we return from the streets let us
pray before we sit down, nor give our miserable body
rest until our soul is fed. In everything we do, in
every step we take let our hand trace the sign of
the Lord's cross. Speak against no one, and slander
not thy mother's son. ' Who art thou that judgest
the servant of another ? To his own lord he standeth
or falleth ; yea, he shall be made to stand, for the
Lord hath power to make him stand.' [1] If you have
fasted for the space of two days, do not think that
you are better than those who have not fasted.
You fast and are angry ; another eats and wears a
smiling face. You work off your irritation and
hunger by quarrelling with others ; your neighbour feeds in moderation and gives thanks to God.
Therefore Isaiah proclaims to us every day : ' Is it
such a fast, that I have chosen, saith the Lord ? ' [2]
And again : ' In the day of your fast ye find your
own pleasure and oppress all your labourers. If
ye fast for strife and contention and smite the lowly
with your fist, the fist of wickedness, how fast ye
unto me ? ' [3] What sort of fast can that be when
not only does the night fall upon a man's wrath,
but even the full moon leaves it unchanged ? Look
to yourself and glory not in the fall of others, but
only in your own works.

Neither take pattern by those women who have
thought for the flesh, and are always reckoning up
their income and their daily household expenditure.
For the eleven apostles did not weaken by Judas'

Phygelo et Alexandro faciente naufragium ceteri a cursu fidei substiterunt. Nec dicas: ' Illa et illa suis rebus fruitur; honoratur ab omnibus; fratres ad eam conveniunt et sorores: numquid ideo virgo esse desivit?' Primum dubium, an virgo sit talis. ' Non enim, quomodo videt homo, videbit Deus. Homo videt in facie, Deus videt in corde.' Dehinc, etiam si corpore virgo est, an spiritu virgo sit, nescio. Apostolus autem ita virginem definivit: ' Ut sit sancta et corpore et spiritu.' Ad extremum habeat sibi gloriam suam; vincat Pauli sententiam, deliciis fruatur et vivat! Nos meliora exempla sectemur.

Propone tibi beatam Mariam, quae tantae extitit puritatis, ut mater esse domini mereretur. Ad quam cum angelus Gabriel in viri specie descendisset dicens: ' Ave, gratia plena, dominus tecum,' consternata respondere non potuit; nunquam enim a viro fuit salutata. Denique nuntium discit et loquitur et, quae hominem formidarat, cum angelo fabulatur intrepida. Potes et tu esse mater domini. ' Accipe tibi tomum magnum, novum et scribe in eo stilo hominis velociter spolia detrahentis,' et, cum accesseris ad prophetissam et conceperis in utero et pepereris filium, dic: ' A timore tuo, domine, concepimus et doluimus et peperimus; spiritum salvationis tuae fecimus super terram.' Tunc et filius tuus

---

[1] 2 Timothy, i. 15. [2] 1 Timothy, i. 19, 20.
[3] 1 Samuel, xvi. 7. [4] 1 Corinthians, vii. 34.
[5] Isaiah, viii. 1.
[6] Isaiah, viii. 3, 'and I went unto the prophetess and she conceived and bare a son.' Jerome, however, puts his own interpretation on the Hebrew, and 'prophetess' should here be 'prophet.' 'As it stands the quotation is meaningless' (Fremantle). [7] Isaiah, xxvi. 18. (Vulgate.)

treachery; and though Phygellus[1] and Alexander[2] made shipwreck the rest did not falter in the race of faith. Nor say: ' So-and-so enjoys her own property; she is honoured by all; the brethren and the sisters assemble at her house. Has she ceased to be a virgin for that?' In the first place, it is doubtful if such an one is a virgin. ' For the Lord will not see as man seeth; for man looketh upon the outward appearance, but the Lord looketh upon the heart.'[3] Furthermore, even if she is a virgin in body, I am not sure that she is a virgin in spirit. The apostle has defined a virgin thus: ' She must be holy both in body and in spirit.'[4] In fine, let her keep her own glory to the last. Let her over-ride Paul's judgment; let her enjoy her good things and live! Let us follow better examples.

Set before your eyes the blessed Mary, whose purity was such that she earned the reward of being the mother of the Lord. When the angel Gabriel came down to her in man's form, and said: ' Hail, thou that art highly favoured; the Lord is with thee,' she was filled with terror and consternation and could not reply; for she had never been greeted by a man before. Soon, however, she learned who the messenger was, and spoke to him: she who had been afraid of a man conversed fearlessly with an angel. You too may be perhaps the Lord's mother. ' Take thee a great new roll and write in it with the pen of a man who is swiftly carrying off the spoils,'[5] and when you have gone to the prophetess, and conceived in your womb and brought forth a son,[6] say: ' Lord, we have been with child by thy fear, we have been in pain, we have brought forth thy spirit of thy salvation which we have wrought upon the earth.'[7]

tibi respondebit et dicet: ' Ecce mater mea et fratres mei.' Et mirum in modum ille, quem in latitudine pectoris tui paulo ante descripseras, quem in novitate cordis stilo volante signaveras, postquam spolia ex hostibus ceperit, postquam denudaverit principatus et potestates et adfixerit eas cruci, conceptus adolescit et maior effectus sponsam te incipit habere de matre. Grandis labor, sed grande praemium esse, quod martyras, esse, quod apostolos, esse, quod Christus est.

Quae quidem universa tunc prosunt, cum in ecclesia fiunt, cum in una domo pascha celebramus, si arcam ingredimur cum Noe, si pereunte Hierico Raab iustificata nos continet. Ceterum virgines, quales apud diversas hereses et quales apud inpurissimum Manicheum esse dicuntur, scorta sunt aestimanda, non virgines. Si enim corporis earum auctor est diabolus, quomodo possunt honorare plasticam hostis sui? Sed quia sciunt virginale vocabulum gloriosum, sub ovium pellibus lupos tegunt. Christum mentitur antichristus et turpitudinem vitae falso nominis honore convestiunt. Gaude, soror, gaude, filia, gaude, mi virgo: quod aliae simulant, tu vere esse coepisti.

39. Haec omnia, quae digessimus, dura videbuntur ei, qui non amat Christum. Qui autem omnem saeculi pompam pro purgamento habuerit et vana duxerit universa sub sole, ut Christum lucrifaciat, qui conmortuus est domino suo et conresurrexit et crucifixit carnem cum vitiis et concupiscentiis, libere

---

[1] St. Matthew, xii. 49.

[2] Founder of the sect of the Manicheans, who believed that matter as such is essentially evil.

Then shall your son reply: 'Behold my mother and
my brethren.'[1] And He whose name just before
you had inscribed upon the tablet of your heart, and
had written with speedy pen upon its new surface,
after He has recovered the spoils from the enemies
and has stripped principalities and powers, nailing
them to His cross, He having been conceived grows to
manhood, and as He becomes older regards you
not as His mother but as His bride. To be as the
martyrs, or as the apostles, or as Christ, is a great
struggle, but for that struggle there is a great reward.

All such efforts are only of avail when they are
made within the Church; when we celebrate the
passover in one house; if we enter the ark with
Noah; if, while Jericho is falling, we shelter beneath
the roof of the justified harlot Rahab. Such virgins
as there are said to be among the different kinds of
heretics, or with the followers of the filthy Manes,[2]
must be considered, not virgins, but prostitutes. If
the devil is the author of their body, how can they
honour a thing fashioned by their foe? It is because
they know that the name of virgin brings glory with
it that they go about as wolves in sheep's clothing.
Antichrist pretends to be Christ: and even so they
falsely cloak their shameful lives under an honourable title. Rejoice, my sister; rejoice, my daughter;
rejoice, my virgin; you have begun to be in truth
that which these others only feign to be.

All the things that I have set out in this letter
will seem hard to her who loves not Christ. But
one who regards all the pomp of this world as dross,
and holds everything under the sun as vain, if only
he may win Christ; one who has died with his Lord
and risen again and crucified the flesh with its weak-

proclamabit: ' Quis nos separabit a caritate Christi?
tribulatio? an angustia? an persecutio? an famis?
an nuditas? an periculum? an gladius?' Et
iterum: ' Certus autem sum, quia neque mors neque
vita neque angelus neque principatus neque instantia
neque futura neque fortitudo neque excelsum neque
profundum neque alia creatura poterit nos separare a
caritate Dei, quae est in Christo Iesu domino nostro.'

Dei filius pro nostra salute hominis factus est filius,
decem mensibus in utero, ut nascatur, expectat,
fastidia sustinet, cruentus egeritur, involvitur pannis,
blanditiis delenitur et ille, cuius pugillo mundus
includitur, praesepis continetur angustiis. Taceo,
quod usque ad tricesimum annum ignobilis parentum
paupertate contentus est: verberabatur et tacet;
crucifigitur et pro crucifigentibus deprecatur. ' Quid,'
igitur,' retribuam domino pro omnibus, quae retribuit
mihi? Calicem salutaris accipiam et nomen domini
invocabo. Pretiosa in conspectu domini mors sanctorum eius.' Haec est sola digna retributio, cum
sanguis sanguine compensatur et redempti cruore
Christi pro redemptore libenter obcumbimus. Quis
sanctorum sine certamine coronatus est? Abel iustus
occiditur; Abraham uxorem periclitatur amittere et,
ne in inmensum volumen extendam, quaere et in-
venies singulos adversa perpessos. Solus in deliciis
Salomon fuit, et forsitan ideo corruit. ' Quem enim
diligit dominus, corripit; castigat autem omnem

---

nesses and lusts; he will freely cry: ' Who shall separate us from the love of Christ? Shall tribulation, or distress, or persecution, or famine, or nakedness, or peril, or sword? ' [1] And again: ' I am persuaded that neither death, nor life, nor angels, nor principalities nor powers, nor things present, nor things to come, nor height, nor depth, nor any other creature shall be able to separate us from the love of God which is in Jesus Christ, our Lord.'

For our salvation the Son of God became the Son of Man. Ten months He awaits birth in the womb, He endures distress, He comes forth covered with blood, He is swathed in napkins, He is comforted with caresses. Though He holds the world in His closed hand, He is contained by the narrow space of a manger. I say nothing of the thirty years He lived in obscurity, content with His parents' poverty. He was scourged and says not a word. He is crucified and prays for His crucifiers. ' What then shall I render unto the Lord for all His benefits towards me? I will take the cup of salvation and call upon the name of the Lord. Precious in the sight of the Lord is the death of His saints.' [2] The only fitting return we can make Him is to pay for blood with blood; and as we are redeemed by the blood of Christ, to die willingly for our Redeemer. What saint was ever crowned without a contest? Righteous Abel is murdered. Abraham runs the risk of losing his wife. And, not to enlarge my screed beyond all measure, look for yourself and you will find that all the saints have suffered adversity. Solomon alone lived in luxury, and that is perhaps the reason why he fell. ' For whom the Lord loveth He chasteneth, and scourgeth every son whom He

filium quem recipit.' Nonne melius est brevi tempore
dimicare, ferre vallum, arma, cibaria, lassescere sub
lorica et postea gaudere victorem, quam inpatientia
unius horae servire perpetuo?

40. Nihil amantibus durum est, nullus difficilis
cupienti labor. Respice, quanta Iacob pro Rachel
pacta uxore sustineat. ' Et servivit,' inquit scriptura,
' Iacob pro Rachel annis septem. Et erant in conspectu eius quasi pauci dies, quia amabat illam.'
Unde et ipse postea memorat: ' In die urebar aestu
et gelu nocte.' Amemus et nos Christum, semper
eius quaeramus amplexus, et facile videbitur omne
difficile. Brevia putabimus universa, quae longa
sunt, et iaculo illius vulnerati per horarum momenta
dicimus: ' Heu me, quia peregrinatio mea pro-
longata est.' ' Non sunt,' enim, ' condignae passiones
huius mundi ad futuram gloriam, quae revelabitur in
nobis'; ' quia tribulatio patientiam operatur, patientia
probationem, probatio autem spem, spes vero non
confundit.' Quando tibi grave videtur esse, quod
sustines, Pauli secundam ad Corinthios lege: ' In
laboribus plurimis, in carceribus abundantius, in
plagis supra modum, in mortibus frequenter—a
Iudaeis quinquies quadragenas una minus accepi, ter
virgis caesus sum, semel lapidatus sum, ter naufragium feci—nocte et die in profundo maris fui, in
itineribus saepius, periculis fluminum, periculis
latronum, periculis ex genere, periculis ex gentibus,
periculis in civitate, periculis in deserto, periculis in

---

[1] Hebrews, xii. 6.

[2] A Roman soldier carried a stake, which he fixed in the
ground at the end of the day's march as part of the rampart
round the camp.

[3] Genesis, xxix. 20.

LETTER XXII

receiveth.'¹ Is it not better to fight for a short
space, to carry a camp-stake,² weapons, rations, to
faint beneath a breastplate, and then to know the
joy of victory, rather than to become slaves for ever
because we could not hold out for a single hour?

Love finds nothing hard: no task is difficult if you
wish to do it. Consider all that Jacob bore to win
Rachel, his promised bride. The Scripture tells us:
' Jacob served seven years for Rachel. And they
seemed to him but a few days for the love he had
to her.'³ So he himself afterwards says: ' In the
day the drought consumed me and the frost by
night.'⁴ Let us also love Christ and ever seek His
embraces. Then everything difficult will seem easy;
all things long we shall think to be short; and
smitten with His javelin we shall say as each hour
passes: ' Woe is me that I have prolonged my
pilgrimage.'⁵ ' For the sufferings of this present
time are not worthy to be compared with the glory
that shall be revealed in us.'⁶ ' Tribulation worketh
patience, and patience experience, and experience
hope; and hope maketh not ashamed.'⁷ Whenever your lot seems hard, read Paul's second epistle
to the Corinthians: ' In labours more abundant;
in stripes above measure; in prisons more frequent;
in deaths oft. Of the Jews five times received I
forty stripes save one; thrice was I beaten with rods;
once was I stoned; thrice I suffered shipwreck; a
night and a day have I been in the deep; in journey-
ings often, in perils of robbers, of torrents, in perils
by my countrymen, in perils by the heathen, in
perils in the city, in perils in the wilderness, in

⁴ Genesis, xxxi. 40.   ⁵ Psalm cxix. 5.   (Vulgate.)
⁶ Romans, viii. 18.   ⁷ Romans, v. 3.

153

mare, periculis in falsis fratribus, in laboribus, in
miseriis, in vigiliis multis, in fame et siti, in ieiuniis
plurimis, in frigore et nuditate.' Quis nostrum
saltim minimam portionem de catalogo harum sibi
potest vindicare virtutum? Utique ille postea confidenter aiebat : ' Cursum consummavi, fidem servavi.
Superest mihi corona iustitiae, quam retribuet mihi
dominus.'

Si cibus insulsior fuerit, contristamur et putamus
nos Deo praestare beneficium, cum aquatius bibimus :
calix frangitur, mensa subvertitur, verbera sonant et
aqua tepidior sanguine vindicatur. ' Regnum caelorum vim patitur et violenti diripiunt illud.' Nisi
vim feceris, caelorum regna non capies. Nisi pul-
saveris inportune, panem non accipies sacramenti.
An non tibi videtur esse violenti, cum caro cupit esse,
quod Deus est, et illuc, unde angeli corruerunt,
angelos iudicatura conscendere ?

41. Egredere, quaeso, paulisper e corpore et
praesentis laboris ante oculos tuos pinge mercedem,
quam ' nec oculus vidit nec auris audivit nec in cor
hominis ascendit.' Qualis erit illa dies, cum tibi
Maria, mater domini, choris occurret comitata vir-
gineis, cum post Rubrum Mare et submersum cum
suo exercitu Pharaonem tympanum tenens praecinet

---

[1] 2 Corinthians, xi. 23.   [2] 2 Timothy, iv. 7.
[3] St. Matthew, xi. 12.   [4] 1 Corinthians, vi. 3.
[5] 1 Corinthians, ii. 9.

perils in the sea, in perils among false brethren, in weariness, and painfulness, in watchings often, in hunger and thirst, in fastings often, in cold and nakedness.' [1] Who of us can claim for himself even the smallest part of this catalogue of virtues? Certainly he could afterwards boldly say: ' I have finished my course, I have kept the faith. Henceforth there is laid up for me a crown of righteousness which the Lord shall give me as a reward.' [2]

And yet we frown if our food seems to lack savour, and fancy that we are doing God a favour when we put more water in our drink. If that water is a trifle too warm, the servant must pay for it with his blood: we smash the cup, knock the table over, and the whip whistles in the air. ' The kingdom of heaven suffereth violence and the violent take it by force.' [3] Unless you use violence you will never seize the kingdom of heaven. Unless you knock importunately you will never receive the sacramental bread. Does it not seem to you to be truly violence when the flesh desires to be as God and to ascend to the place whence angels fell that it may judge angels? [4]

Come out, I pray you, awhile from your prison-house, and picture before your eyes the reward of your present labours, a reward ' which eye hath not seen, nor ear heard, neither hath it entered into the heart of man.' [5] What will be the splendour of that day, when Mary, the mother of the Lord, shall come to meet you, attended by her bands of virgins: when, the Red Sea past and Pharaoh with his hosts drowned beneath its waves, one, with timbrel in her hand, shall chant to her responsive

responsuris: 'Cantemus domino; gloriose enim magnificatus est. Equum et ascensorem proiecit in mare.'[1] Tunc Thecla[2] in tuos laeta volabit amplexus. Tunc et ipse sponsus occurret et dicet: 'Surge, veni, proxima mea, speciosa mea, columba mea, quia ecce hiemps transiit, pluvia abiit sibi.'[3] Tunc angeli mirabuntur et dicent: 'Quae est ista prospiciens quasi diluculum, speciosa ut luna, electa ut sol?'[4] Videbunt te filiae et laudabunt te reginae et concubinae te praedicabunt. Tunc et alius castitatis chorus occurret: Sarra cum nuptis veniet, filia Phanuelis Anna cum viduis. Erunt ut in diversis gregibus, carnis et spiritus, matres tuae.[5] Laetabitur illa, quod genuit; exultabit ista, quod docuit. Tunc vere super asinam dominus ascendet et caelestem ingredietur Hierusalem. Tunc parvuli, de quibus in Esaia salvator effatur: 'Ecce ego et pueri, quos mihi dedit dominus,'[7] palmas victoriae sublevantes consono ore cantabunt: 'Osanna in excelsis; benedictus, qui venit in nomine domini, osanna in excelsis.'[8] Tunc centum quadraginta quattuor milia in conspectu throni et seniorum tenebunt citharas et cantabunt canticum novum et nemo poterit scire canticum illud, nisi numerus definitus: 'Hi sunt, qui se cum mulieribus non coinquinaverunt—virgines enim permanserunt; hi sunt, qui secuntur agnum, quocumque vadit.'[9] Quotienscumque te vana saeculi delectarit ambitio, quo-

---

[1] Exodus, xv. 21.
[2] A virgin of Iconium said to have been converted by Paul.
[3] Song of Solomon, ii. 10.
[4] Song of Solomon, vi. 9 (slightly altered), 10.
[5] Cf. St. Luke, ii. 36.
[6] *I.e.* Paula and Marcella. Cf. Appendix, p. 487.
[7] Isaiah, viii. 18.
[8] St. Matthew, xxi. 9.   [9] Revelation, xiv. 4.

choir: 'Let us sing unto the Lord, for he hath triumphed gloriously; the horse and his rider he hath thrown into the sea.'[1]   Then shall Thecla[2] fly rejoicing to your arms. Then shall your Spouse Himself come to meet you and say: 'Rise up, my love, my fair one, my dove, and come, for lo, the winter is past, the rain is over and gone.'[3]   Then shall the angels gaze in wonder and cry: 'Who is she that looketh forth as the morning, fair as the moon, clear as the sun?'[4]   The daughters shall see you and bless you; yea, the queens shall proclaim and the concubines shall praise you.

And then another chaste band will be there to green you. Sarah will come with the wedded; Anna,[5] the daughter of Phanuel, with the widows. In the one company you will see your natural, and in the other your spiritual mother.[6] The one will rejoice in having borne you, the other will exult in having taught you.   Then truly will the Lord mount upon His ass and enter the heavenly Jerusalem. Then the little ones—of whom in Isaiah the Saviour says: 'Behold I and the children whom the Lord hath given me'[7]—shall lift up palms of victory and with one accord shall sing: 'Hosanna in the highest, blessed is he that cometh in the name of the Lord, hosanna in the highest.'[8]   Then shall the hundred and forty and four thousand hold their harps before the throne and before the elders and sing the new song. And no man shall be able to sing that song save the appointed company: 'These are they which were not defiled with women—for they are virgins; these are they which follow the Lamb whithersoever he goeth.'[9]   As often as this world's vain display delights you; as often as you see in

tiens in mundo aliquid videris gloriosum, ad paradisum mente transgredere; esse incipe, quod futura
es, et audies ab sponso tuo: ' Pone me sicut signaculum in corde tuo, sicut signaculum in brachio tuo,'
et opere pariter ac mente munita clamabis: ' Aqua
multa non poterit extinguere caritatem et flumina
non cooperient eam.'

XXXVIII

AD MARCELLAM

1. ABRAHAM temptatur in filio et fidelior invenitur;
Ioseph in Aegypto venditur, ut patrem pascat et
fratres; Ezechias vicina morte terretur, ut fusus in
lacrimis quindecim annorum spatio proteletur ad
vitam; Petrus apostolus domini passione concutitur,
ut amare flens audiat: ' Pasce oves meas '; Paulus,
lupus rapax et Beniamin adulescentior, in extasi
caecatur, ut videat, et repentino tenebrarum horrore
circumdatus dominum vocat, quem dudum ut hominem persequebatur.

2. Ita et nunc, mi Marcella, Blesillam nostram
vidimus ardore febrium per triginta ferme dies iugiter

---

[1] Song of Solomon, viii. 6.   [2] Song of Solomon, viii. 7.

[3] For Marcella and Blesilla, cf. Introduction, p. viii, and
Appendix I.

[4] Paul belonged to the tribe of Benjamin and Benjamin is
described as a ravening wolf: cf. Genesis, xlix. 27. Paul, a
Benjamite, acted like a wolf in persecuting the Church: cf.
p. 279.

life some empty glory, transport yourself in thought
to Paradise and begin to be now what you will be
hereafter. Then will you hear your Spouse say:
' Set me as a seal in thine heart and as a seal
upon thine arm.' [1] And then, fortified alike in mind
and body, you will cry : ' Many waters cannot quench
love, neither can the floods drown it.' [2]

LETTER XXXVIII

To Marcella [3]

A good woman

Written A.D. 384

ABRAHAM is tempted in the matter of his son, and
is found to be of greater faith. Joseph is sold in
Egypt, and is thereby able to maintain his father
and brothers. Hezekiah is terrified by the near
approach of death, but he bursts into tears and his
life is extended by the space of fifteen years. If the
faith of the apostle Peter is shaken by Our Lord's
passion, it is that amid his bitter tears he may hear
the words : ' Feed my sheep.' Paul, that ravening
wolf, that little Benjamin,[4] is blinded in a trance,
but as the result he gains clear vision, and from
the sudden horror of darkness around him calls upon
Him as Lord whom in the past he persecuted as
man.

So now, my dear Marcella, has it been with our
beloved Blesilla. For nearly thirty days we have
seen her tossing continually in a burning fever, that

159

aestuasse, ut sciret reiciendas delicias corporis, quod
paulo post vermibus exarandum sit. Venit et ad
hanc dominus Iesus tetigitque manum eius et surgens
ministrat ei. Redolebat aliquid neglegentiae et
divitiarum fasciis conligata in saeculi iacebat sepulchro, sed confremuit Iesus et conturbatus in spiritu
clamavit dicens: 'Blesilla, exi foras.' Quae vocata
surrexit et egressa cum domino vescitur. Iudaei
minentur et tumeant, quaerant occidere suscitatam,
soli apostoli glorientur; scit se vitam suam ei debere,
cui credidit; scit se eius amplexare pedes, cuius
paulo ante iudicium pertimescebat. Corpus paene
iacebat exanime et anhelos artus mors vicina quatiebat. Ubi tunc erant auxilia propinquorum, ubi
verba omni inaniora fumo? Nihil tibi debet, o in-
grata cognatio, quae mundo periit et Christo revixit.
Qui Christianus est, gaudeat; qui irascitur, non esse
se indicat Christianum.

3. Vidua, quae soluta est vinculo maritali, nihil
necesse habet nisi perseverare. At scandalizat
quempiam vestis fuscior: scandalizet Iohannes, quo
inter natos mulierum maior nullus fuit, qui angelus
dictus ipsum quoque dominum baptizavit, qui came-
lorum vestitus tegumine zona pellicia cingebatur.

thereby she might learn to cast away all those pamperings of that body into which worms will soon burrow their way. To her also the Lord Jesus came, and He touched her hand, and behold she rises and ministers unto Him. Once there was some suspicion of indifference in her conduct: she was bound fast in the close wrappings of riches, and lay inactive in this world tomb. But Jesus was troubled in spirit, and raised His voice and cried aloud, saying: 'Blesilla, come forth.' At His bidding she arose and came out, and now she feasts with the Lord. The Jews may swell with threats, and seek to slay her who has been roused to life, while the apostles alone give glory: Blesilla knows that she owes her life to Him to whom she entrusted it: she knows that she now embraces the feet of Him before whose judgment just lately she trembled. Life had almost forsaken her prostrate body, and the near approach of death shook her panting frame. Of what avail at that hour was the help that relatives could give, or their words of comfort, emptier than smoke? She owes nothing to you, thankless kinsmen: she is dead to the world and lives again to Christ. Let those who are Christians rejoice: those who feel resentment show thereby that they are not Christians.

A widow who is freed from the marital bond has but one duty laid upon her, and that is to continue as a widow. It may be that some people are offended by her sombre garb: they would be offended also by John the Baptist, and yet among those born of women there has not been a greater than he. He was called God's messenger and baptized the Lord Himself, but he was clothed in camel's-hair raiment and girded with a girdle of skins. It may be that

Cibi displicent viliores; nihil vilius est locustis. Illae Christianos oculos potius scandalizent, quae purpurisso et quibusdam fucis ora oculosque depingunt, quarum facies gypseae et nimio candore deformes idola mentiuntur, quibus si forte inprovidens lacrimarum stilla eruperit, sulco defluit, quas nec numerus annorum potest docere, quod vetulae sunt, quae capillis alienis verticem instruunt et praeteritam iuventutem in rugis anilibus poliunt, quae denique ante nepotum gregem trementes virgunculae conponuntur. Erubescat mulier Christiana, si naturae cogit decorem, si carnis curam facit ad concupiscentiam, in qua qui sunt, secundum apostolum Christo placere non possunt.[1]

4. Vidua nostra ante monilibus ornabatur et die tota, quid sibi deesset, quaerebat ad speculum; nunc loquitur confidenter: ' Nos autem omnes revelata facie gloriam domini speculantes in eandem imaginem transformamur a gloria in gloriam, quasi a domini spiritu.'[2] Tunc crines ancillulae disponebant et mitellis crispantibus vertex artabatur innoxius; nunc neglectum caput scit sibi tantum sufficere, quod velatur. Illo tempore plumarum quoque dura mollities videbatur et in extructis toris iacere vix poterat; nunc ad orandum festina consurgit et modulata voce ceteris ' alleluia ' praecipiens prior incipit

---

some are displeased by a widow's simple food:
nothing can be more simple than locusts. Those
women rather should offend a Christian's eyes, who
paint their cheeks with rouge and their eyes with
belladonna; whose faces are covered with powder
and so disfigured by excessive whiteness that they
look like idols; who find a wet furrow on their skin
if perchance a careless tear escape them; whom no
amount of years can convince that they are old; who
heap their heads with borrowed tresses; who polish
up past youthfulness in spite of the wrinkles of age;
who, in fine, behave like trembling schoolgirls before
a company of their own grandsons. A Christian
woman should blush to win by force what should
be natural beauty, or to rouse men's desires by
bestowing care upon the flesh. As the apostle says:
' Those that are in the flesh cannot be pleasing to
Christ.' [1]

In the past our dear widow used to deck herself
with jewels, and spent whole days before her glass
looking for anything wrong in her appearance.
Now she boldly says: ' We all with unveiled face,
beholding as in a glass the glory of the Lord, are
changed into the same image, from glory to glory,
even as by the spirit of the Lord.' [2] In those days
lady's maids used to arrange her hair, and her poor
head, which had done no harm, was imprisoned in a
head-dress crammed with curls. Now it is left alone,
and knows that it is sufficiently cared for when it is
covered by a veil. At that time the softest down
seemed hard to her limbs, and she could scarcely rest
upon a pile of cushions. Now she rises in haste from
her bed to pray, and with tuneful voice forestalls her
comrades' ' Alleluia,' herself ever the first to praise her

laudare dominum suum. Flectuntur genua super nudam humum et crebris lacrimis facies psimithio ante sordidata purgatur. Post orationem psalmi concrepant et lassa cervix, poplites vacillantes in somnumque vergentes oculi nimio mentis ardore vix impetrant, ut quiescant. Pulla est tunica: minus, cum humi iacuerit, sordidatur. Soccus vilior: auratorum pretium calceorum egentibus largietur. Cingulum non auro gemmisque distinctum est, sed laneum et tota simplicitate purissimum et quod possit adstringere magis vestimenta quam scindere. Si huic proposito invidet scorpius et sermone blando de indebita rursum arbore comedere persuadet, inlidatur ei pro solea anathema et in suo morienti pulvere dicatur: 'Vade retro, Satanas,' quod interpretatur 'adverse'; adversarius quippe Christi est antichristus, cui praecepta displicent Christi.

5. Oro te, quid tale umquam, quale apostoli, fecimus, ut merito scandalizentur; patrem senem cum navicula et rete dimittunt; publicanus a teloneo surgit et sequitur salvatorem; volens discipulus reverti domum et suis ante renuntiare magistri voce prohibetur; sepultura non datur patri et pietatis genus est inpium esse pro domino. Nos, quia serica veste non utimur, monachi iudicamur, quia ebrii non sumus nec cachinno ora dissolvimus, continentes vocamur et tristes. Si tunica non canduerit, statim illud e trivio: 'Inpostor et Graecus est.' Cavil-

Lord. She kneels on the bare ground, and with frequent tears cleanses the face that was once defiled with white lead. After prayer comes the singing of psalms; her neck grows weary, her knees totter, her eyes drop off to sleep; but her ardent spirit will hardly give them leave to rest. Her dress is of dark stuff; therefore it is scarcely soiled by lying on the ground. Her slippers are of a cheap sort; the price of gilded boots will be given as alms to the needy. Her girdle is not adorned with jewels or gold; it is made of wool, perfectly simple and clean, and it is intended to keep her dress close rather than to cut her figure into two halves. If the scorpion, jealous of her resolute purpose, with soft words persuades her to eat again of the forbidden tree, let a curse crush him instead of a boot, and let her say, as he lies dying in the dust that is his due: 'Get thee behind me, Satan.' The word Satan means 'adversary,' since Christ's adversary is the Antichrist, who finds Christ's precepts displeasing.

Pray, have we ever done anything such as the apostles did that men should have reason to be offended with us? The apostles left their boat and their net and their aged father. The publican got up from the receipt of custom and followed the Saviour. When a disciple wished to go back home and give a message first to his people, the Master's voice forbade him. A father even was refused burial; for it is a form of duty to be undutiful for the Lord's sake. We on the other hand are called monks merely because we do not dress in silk. We are dubbed 'sour puritans,' because we do not get drunk or burst into loud guffaws. If our tunic is not spotlessly white, the cry goes up from the street: 'Greek charlatan.'

lentur vafriora licet et pingui aqualiculo farsos cir-
cumferant homines: Blesilla nostra ridebit nec
dignabitur loquacium ranarum audire convicia, cum
dominus eius dictus sit Beelzebub.

XL

AD MARCELLAM DE ONASO

1. MEDICI, quos vocant chirurgicos, crudeles putantur et miseri sunt. An non est miseria alienis
dolere vulneribus et mortuas carnes clementi secare
ferro? Non horrere curantem, quod horret ipse, qui
patitur, et inimicum putari? Ita se natura habet,
ut amara sit veritas, blanda vitia aestimentur.
Esaias in exemplum captivitatis futurae nudus non
erubescit incedere; Heremias de media Hierusalem
ad Eufraten, fluvium Mesopotamiae, mittitur, ut
inter inimicas gentes, ubi est Assyrius et castra sunt
Chaldaeorum, ponat περίζωμα corrumpendum: Hie-
zechiel stercore primum humano, dein bubulo panem
de omni semente conspersum edere iubetur et uxoris
interitum siccis oculis videt; Amos de Samaria
pellitur: cur quaeso? Nempe ideo, quia chirurgici
spiritales secantes vitia peccatorum ad paenitentiam

---

¹ Matthew, x. 25.
² This letter is superscribed ' To Marcella concerning
Onasus,' but most of the fierce invective is addressed personally
to Onasus himself, of whom nothing else is known.
³ Isaiah, xx. 2.   ⁴ Jeremiah, xiii. 7.
⁵ Ezekiel, iv. 9 ff. and xxiv. 15 ff.   ⁶ Amos, vii. 12.

Let men indulge in even sharper witticisms, if they
please, and parade before us their fat-paunched
friends. Our dear Blesilla will laugh at them, and
will not deign to listen to the abuse of noisy frogs.
She knows that her Lord was called by men
Beelzebub.[1]

LETTER XL

To Marcella

Onasus the windbag [2]

Written a.d. 385

Those medical men whom folk call surgeons are
thought to be cruel and really are pitiful. Is it not
a pitiful business to feel the pain of another's wounds,
and to cut dead flesh with the merciful knife? Is it
not pitiful to show no horror at treating a malady
which seems horrible even to the patient, and to be
considered the sufferer's enemy? Man's nature is
such that truth tastes bitter and pleasant vices are
esteemed. Isaiah in token of the coming captivity
does not blush to go abroad naked.[3] Jeremiah is
sent from mid-Jerusalem to Euphrates, the river of
Mesopotamia, among hostile nations, the Assyrians
and the camp of the Chaldaeans, and bidden there
to hide his girdle and let it be marred.[4] Ezekiel is
ordered to eat bread made of every kind of grain
and mingled first with man's and then with cow's
dung, and he looks on at his wife's death with dry
eyes.[5] Amos is driven forth from Samaria.[6] Why
was all this, pray? It was because our spiritual
surgeons by cutting into the faults of sinners exhorted

cohortabantur. Paulus apostolus: 'Inimicus,' inquit, 'vobis factus sum vera dicens.' Et quia salvatoris dura videbantur eloquia, plurimi discipulorum retrorsum abierunt.

2. Unde non mirum est, si et nos vitiis detrahentes offendimus plurimos. Disposui nasum secare fetentem: timeat, qui strumosus est. Volo corniculae detrahere garrienti: rancidulam se intellegat cornix. Numquid unus in orbe Romano est, qui habeat 'truncas inhonesto vulnere nares'? Numquid solus Onasus Segestanus cava verba et in vesicarum modum tumentia buccis trutinatur inflatis? Dico quosdam scelere, periurio, falsitate ad dignitatem nescio quam pervenisse: quid ad te, qui te intellegis innocentem? Rideo advocatum, qui patrono egeat: quadrante dignam eloquentiam nare subsanno: quid ad te, qui disertus es? Volo in nummarios invehi sacerdotes: tu, qui dives es, quid irasceris? Claudum cupio suis ignibus ardere Vulcanum: numquid hospes eius es aut vicinus, quod a delubris idoli niteris incendium submovere? Placet mihi de larvis, de noctua, de bubone, de Niliacis ridere portentis: quicquid dictum fuerit, in te dictum putas. In quodcumque vitium stili mei mucro contorquetur, te clamitas designari, conserta manu in ius vocas et satiricum scriptorem in prosa stulte arguis. An ideo bellus videris, quia fausto vocaris nomine? Quasi

---

[1] Galatians, iv. 16.
[2] Virgil, *Aeneid*, VI. 497, of Deiphobus. Nasus = nose. Onasus = Onesimus = 'the helpful.'

men to repentance. The apostle Paul says: ' I have become your enemy because I tell you the truth.' [1] And because the Saviour's words seemed hard, very many of His disciples went away.

So it is not surprising if we too offend very many when we try to strip away their vices. I am prepared to cut a foul-smelling nose: those who suffer from a wen may well shake in their shoes. I intend to rebuke a chattering crow: the fellow-bird may well see that he too is offensive. But is there only one man in the whole Roman world who has ' a nose lopped short with shameful wound'? [2] Is Onasus of Segesta the only person who puffs his cheeks and weighs out words with nothing in them like a bladder full of wind? I say that certain people have reached a certain position by crime, perjury, and false pretences. What is that to you, who know yourself to be innocent? I laugh at the advocate who himself needs a defender; I sneer scornfully at his eloquence which would be dear at a farthing. What is that to you, who are a good speaker? It is my pleasure to attack those priests who think only of money. Why do you, who are a rich man, become angry? I would fain burn limping Vulcan in his own furnace. Are you a friend or a neighbour of his, that you strive to save the idol's shrine from the flames? I like to laugh at ghosts, night-birds, hooting owls, and all the portents of Egypt: anything I say you think is aimed at yourself. Against whatever vice my pen's sword-point turns, you cry out loudly that you are its mark, you join issue and call me into court, and foolishly try to prove that I am a writer of satire in prose. Do you seem to yourself a fine fellow, because you bear the lucky name of Onasus,

non et lucus ideo dicatur, quod minime luceat, et Parcae ab eo, quod nequaquam parcant, et Eumenides Furiae, et vulgo Aethiopes vocentur argentei. Quodsi in descriptione foedorum semper irasceris, iam te cum Persio cantabo formosum:

' Te optent generum rex et regina, puellae
Te rapiant: quicquid calcaveris tu, rosa fiat.'

3. Dabo tamen consilium, quibus absconditis possis pulchrior apparere: nasus non videatur in facie, sermo non sonet ad loquendum, atque ita et formosus videri potes et disertus.

XLIII

AD MARCELLAM

1. AMBROSIUS, quo chartas, sumptus, notarios ministrante tam innumerabiles libros vere Adamantius et noster Χαλκέντερος explicavit, in quadam epistula,

---

[1] Persius, *Satires*, II. 37, altered.

[2] Not the great Bishop of Milan who lived a century after Origen, but a friend of Origen.

[3] ' Chalkenteros,' ' the man with entrails of brass,' an epithet usually applied to the Alexandrian scholar Didymus, because of his unwearied industry, is here transferred to

170

' the Helpful '? Have you never heard the saying:
Lucus a non lucendo? Are not the Fates called the
Sparers, because they spare no man? Are not the
Furies called Angels of Mercy? Do not common
people often use the name ' silver boys ' for negroes?
Still, if my pictures of ugliness make you angry,
to-day I will call you beautiful and sing with
Persius:[1]

> ' May kings and queens their daughters to you lead
> And for your favours as a bridegroom plead.
> May girls their eager hands upon you lay
> And where you walk red roses deck the way.'

I will give you, however, one piece of advice.
There are some things you must hide, if you are to
appear handsome. Let your nose not be seen upon
your face and let your tongue never be heard in
conversation. Then you may possibly be thought
both good-looking and eloquent.

LETTER XLIII

To Marcella

The country life

Written A.D. 385

AMBROSE,[2] who supplied Origen with parchment,
money, and copyists, and thus enabled our man of
brass[3] and adamant to bring out his innumerable

Origen, who was sometimes called 'Adamantius,' probably
for the same reason.

quam ad eundem de Athenis scripserat, refert
numquam se cibos Origene praesente sine lectione
sumpsisse, nunquam venisse somnum, nisi e fratribus
aliquis sacris litteris personaret, hoc diebus egisse
vel noctibus, ut et lectio orationem susciperet et
oratio lectionem.

2. Quid nos, ventris animalia, tale umquam fecimus? Quos si secunda hora legentes invenerit,
oscitamus, manu faciem defricantes continemus
stomachum et quasi post multum laborem mundiali-
bus rursum negotiis occupamur. Praetermitto
prandia, quibus onerata mens premitur. Pudet
dicere de frequentia salutandi, qua aut ipsi cotidie
ad alios pergimus aut ad nos venientes ceteros
expectamus. Deinceps itur in verba, sermo teritur,
lacerantur absentes, vita aliena describitur et mordentes invicem consumimur ab invicem. Talis nos
cibus et occupat et dimittit. Cum vero amici
recesserint, ratiocinia subputamus. Nunc ira personam nobis leonis inponit, nunc cura superflua in
annos multos duratura praecogitat, nec recordamur
evangelii dicens: ' Stulte, hac nocte repetunt animum
tuam a te; quae autem praeparasti, cuius erunt?'
Vestes non ad usum tantum, sed ad delicias conqui-
runtur. Ubicumque conpendium est, velocior pes,
citus sermo, auris adtentior; si damnum, ut saepe
in re familiari accidere solet, fuerit nuntiatum, vultus
maerore deprimitur. Laetamur ad nummum. obolo

---

[1] St. Luke, xii. 20.

books, in a letter written to his friend from Athens,
declares that he never took a meal in Origen's company without something being read, and that he
never fell asleep save to the sound of some brother's
voice reciting the Scriptures aloud. Day and night
it was their habit to make reading follow upon
prayer, and prayer upon reading, without a break.

Do we, poor creatures of the belly, ever behave
like this ? If we spend more than an hour in reading,
you will find us yawning and trying to restrain our
boredom by rubbing our eyes; then, as though we
had been hard at work, we plunge once more into
worldly affairs. I say nothing of the heavy meals
which crush such mental faculties as we possess. I
am ashamed to speak of our numerous calls, going
ourselves every day to other people's houses, or
waiting for others to come to us. The guests arrive
and talk begins: a brisk conversation is engaged:
we tear to pieces those who are not there: other
people's lives are described in detail: we bite and
are ourselves bitten in turn. With this fare the
company is kept busy, and so at last it disperses.
When our friends have left us, we reckon up our
accounts, now frowning over them like angry lions,
now with useless care planning schemes for the
distant future. We remember not the words of the
Gospel: ' Thou fool, this night thy soul shall be
required of thee: then whose shall those things be
which thou hast provided ? ' [1] We buy clothes, not
solely for use, but for display. When we see a
chance of making money, we quicken our steps, we
talk fast, we strain our ears. If we are told that
we have lost, as often must happen in business, our
face is clouded with sorrow. A penny makes us

contristamur. Unde, cum in uno homine animorum tam diversa sit facies, propheta dominum deprecatur dicens: ' Domine, in civitate tua imaginem eorum dissipa.' Cum enim ad imaginem et similitudinem Dei conditi sumus, ex vitio nostro et personas nobis plurimas superinducimus, et quomodo in theatralibus scaenis unus atque idem histrio nunc Herculem robustus ostentat, nunc mollis in Venerem frangitur, nunc tremulus in Cybelen, ita et nos, qui, si mundi non essemus, odiremur a mundo, tot habemus personarum similitudines, quot peccata.

3. Quapropter, quia vitae multum iam spatium transivimus fluctuando et navis nostra nunc procellarum concussa turbine, nunc scopulorum inlisionibus perforata est, quam primum licet, quasi quemdam portum secreta ruris intremus. Ibi cibarius panis et holus nostris manibus inrigatum, lac, deliciae rusticanae, viles quidem, sed innocentes cibos praebeant. Ita viventes non ab oratione somnus, non saturitas a lectione revocabit. Si aestas est, secretum arboris umbra praebebit; si autumnus, ipsa aeris temperies et strata subter folia locum quietis ostendit. Vere ager floribus depingitur et inter querulas aves psalmi dulcius decantabuntur. Si frigus fuerit et brumales nives, ligna non coemam: calidius vigilabo vel dormiam, certe, quod sciam, vilius non algebo. Habeat sibi Roma suos tumultos, harena saeviat, circus insaniat, theatra luxurient, et

---

[1] Psalm lxxiii. 20. A.V. has 'when thou awakest,' but R.V. gives 'in the city' in margin = *in civitate tua* of Vulgate. (Psalm lxxii. 20.)

merry: a halfpenny makes us sad. Therefore, as
the phases of one man's mind are so conflicting, the
prophet prays to the Lord, saying: ' O Lord, in thy
city scatter their image.'[1] For while we were created
in God's image and likeness, by reason of our own
perversity we hide ourselves behind changing masks,
and as on the stage one and the same actor now
figures as a brawny Hercules, and now relaxes into the
softness of a Venus or the quivering tone of a Cybele,
so we who, if we were not of the world, would be
hated by the world, have a counterfeit mask for
every sin to which we are inclined.

Therefore, as to-day we have traversed a great
part of life's journey through rough seas, and as our
barque has been now shaken by tempestuous winds,
now holed upon rugged rocks, let us take this first
chance and make for the haven of a rural retreat.
Let us live there on coarse bread and on the green-
stuff that we water with our own hands, and on milk,
country delicacies, cheap and harmless. If thus we
spend our days, sleep will not call us away from
prayer, nor overfeeding from study. In summer
the shade of a tree will give us privacy. In autumn
the mild air and the leaves beneath our feet point
out a place for rest. In spring the fields are gay
with flowers, and the birds' plaintive notes will
make our psalms sound all the sweeter. When
the cold weather comes with winter's snows, I shall
not need to buy wood: whether I keep vigil or lie
asleep, I shall be warmer there, and certainly as far
as I know, I shall escape the cold at a cheaper rate.
Let Rome keep her bustle for herself, the fury of the
arena, the madness of the circus, the profligacy of
the theatre, and—for I must not forget our Christian

quia de nostris dicendum est, matronarum cotidie
visitetur senatus: nobis adhaerere Deo bonum est,
ponere in domino spem nostram, ut, cum paupertatem istam caelorum regna mutaverint, erumpamus
in vocem: ' Quid enim mihi restat in caelo et a te
quid volui super terram?' Quo scilicet, cum tanta
reppererimus in caelo, parva et caduca quaesisse nos
doleamus in terra.

XLIV

AD MARCELLAM

UT absentiam corporum spiritus confabulatione
solemur, faciat unusquisque, quod praevalet. Vos
dona transmittitis, nos epistulas remittimus gratiarum, ita tamen, ut, quia velatarum virginum munus
est, aliqua in ipsis munusculis esse mysteria demon-
stremus. Saccus orationis signum atque ieiunii est;
sellae, ut foras pedes virgo non moveat; cerei, ut
accenso lumine sponsi expectetur adventus; calices
mortificationem carnis ostendunt et semper animum
ad martyrium praeparatum—' Calix ' quippe ' domini inebrians perquam optimus '—quod autem et
matronis offertis muscaria parvis animalibus venti-
landa, procul ab illis abesse debere luxurias, quae
cito cum isto interiturae mundo oleum vitae suavioris

---

[1] Psalm lxxiii. 25.
[2] Psalm xxiii. 5. Gallican psalter.

friends—the daily meetings of the matrons' senate.
For us it is good to cleave to God, and to put our
hopes in the Lord, so that, when we have exchanged
this poor life for the kingdom of heaven, we may
cry aloud: 'Whom have I in heaven but thee?
There is none upon earth that I desire beside thee.' [1]
Assuredly, when we have found such wealth in
heaven, we may well grieve to have sought after poor
passing pleasures here on earth.

LETTER XLIV

To Marcella

A letter of thanks

Written A.D. 385

Let us comfort ourselves for bodily absence by
spiritual conversation, each and every one of us doing
what we can do best. You send us gifts, we send you
back letters of thanks; with this addition, as it is an
offering to virgins who have taken the veil, that we
point out to you that there are certain mysteries
hidden in those dear presents of yours. Sackcloth
is a sign of prayer and fasting; chairs warn us that
a virgin does not go abroad; tapers are a reminder
to have our lights burning as we await the Bridegroom's coming; cups signify mortification of the flesh
and readiness for martyrdom—'How excellent is
the Lord's cup that maketh drunk those who partake
thereof!' [2] Furthermore, when you offer matrons
fans to keep off flies, you show them that they must
drive away all those wanton pleasures, which with
this world so quickly perish and corrupt the oil of our

177

exterminant. Hic typus virginum, haec figura sit
matronarum. Nobis autem, in perversum licet,
munera vestra conveniunt : sedere aptum est otiosis,
in sacco iacere paenitentibus, calices habere potanti-
bus, licet et propter nocturnos metus et animo
semper malo conscientiae formidante cereos quoque
accendisse sit gratum.

XLV

AD ASELLAM

1. Si tibi putem a me gratias referri posse, non
sapiam. Potens est Deus super personam meam
sanctae animae tuae restituere, quod meretur. Ego
enim indignus nec aestimare umquam potui nec
optare, ut mihi tantum in Christo largireris adfectum.
Et licet me sceleratum quidam putent et omnibus
flagitiis obrutum et pro peccatis meis etiam haec
parva sint, tamen tu bene facis, quod ex tua mente
etiam malos bonos putas. Periculosum quippe est
de servo alterius iudicare, et non facilis venia prava
dixisse de rectis. Veniet, veniet illa dies, et mecum
dolebis ardere non paucos.

2. Ego probosus, ego versipellis et lubricus, ego

---

[1] This letter was written at Ostia in August A.D. 385, just
before Jerome in company with his brother Paulinian and
the priest Vincentius left Rome for the East. Paula and
Eustochium followed him soon afterwards, and they all three
settled at Bethlehem for the rest of their lives. For Asella,
cf. Appendix, p. 485.

sweeter life. These are the types and figures that virgins and matrons may find in your gifts. To myself also they have an application; although in my case they go by the rule of contrary. Sitting on chairs is suitable for those who have no work to do, lying on sackcloth for those who repent of the past, holding cups for those who drink deep. It may be, however, that I shall be glad to light your tapers, both to banish the terrors of the night and also to appease the constant fears of a guilty conscience.

LETTER XLV

To Asella [1]

Innocent friendships

Were I to think that I could ever repay you for your kindness, I should indeed be lacking in wisdom. God alone is able to give the reward due to your pure spirit. For I am so unworthy of your great love that I have never been able to estimate its extent, or even to hope that you would bestow it upon me in Christ's name. And even though some people regard me as a villain loaded with iniquity, and even though such words are inadequate to my sins, yet you do well who in your own mind think that there is goodness even in bad men. Indeed it is dangerous to pass sentence on another's servant, and to speak evil of the upright is a thing not lightly to be excused. Soon, soon the day of judgment will be coming; and you and I then will see with grief that many are burning in the fire.

I a scandal, I a slippery turncoat, I a liar using

mendax et Satanae arte decipiens! Quid est astu-
tius, haec vel credidisse vel finxisse de insontibus,
an etiam de noxiis credere noluisse? Osculabantur
mihi quidam manus et ore vipereo detrahebant; dole-
bant labiis, corde gaudebant: videbat dominus et
subsannabat eos, et miserum servum suum futuro
cum eis iudicio reservabat. Alius incessum meum
calumniabatur et risum, ille vultui detrahebat, haec
in simplicitate aliud suspicetur. Paene certe triennio
cum eis vixi; multa me virginum crebro turba circumdedit; divinos libros, ut potui, nonnullis saepe
disserui; lectio adsiduitatem, adsiduitas familiaritatem, familiaritas fiduciam fecerat. Dicant, quid
umquam in me aliter senserint, quam Christianum
decebat? Pecuniam cuius accepi? Munera vel
parva vel magna non sprevi? In manu mea aes
alicuius insonuit? Obliquus sermo, oculus petulans
fuit? Nihil mihi aliud obicitur nisi sexus meus, et
hoc numquam obicitur, nisi cum Hierosolyma Paula
proficiscitur. Esto: crediderunt mentienti; cur non
credunt neganti? Idem est homo ipse, qui fuerat:
fatetur insontem, qui dudum noxium loquebatur;
et certe veritatem magis exprimunt tormenta quam
risus, nisi quod facilius creditur, quod aut fictum
libenter auditur aut non fictum, ut fingatur, inpellitur.

---

[1] Cf. Appendix, p. 492.

Satan's art to deceive! Which shows the greater subtlety, I wonder, to believe these charges (perhaps even to invent them about an innocent man), or to say : ' I do not wish to believe them even though he is guilty '? There were some who kissed my hands and maligned me with snakish tongue : their lips lamented, their hearts rejoiced. The Lord saw them and held them in derision, reserving them and His poor servant for common judgment in the future. One man cavilled at my manner of walking and laughing ; another found in my expression something to dislike ; a third lady would suspect something else in my simplicity. With such people I have been living for almost three years : frequently I was surrounded by a throng of virgins : to some of them I often discoursed on the Scriptures to the best of my ability : study brought about familiarity, familiarity friendship, friendship confidence. Let them say if they have ever noticed in my conduct anything unbefitting a Christian. Have I taken anyone's money ? Have I not disdained all gifts great or small ? Has the chink of anyone's coin ever been heard in my hand ? Has my conversation ever been ambiguous, or my eye wanton ? Nothing is laid to my charge except my sex, and that only when Paula is likely to set out for Jerusalem. Well, then ; they believed him when he lied ; why do they not believe him when he retracts ? He is the very same man as before : he confesses I am innocent, though in the past he said I was guilty ; and surely torture is more effective than laughter in forcing out the truth, except indeed that people are more ready to believe a tale which, though false, they hear with pleasure, and urge others to invent it if they have not done so already.[1]

3. Antequam domum sanctae Paulae nossem, totius in me urbis studia consonabant. Omnium paene iudicio dignus summo sacerdotio decernebar; beatae memoriae Damasi os meus sermo erat; dicebar sanctus, dicebar humilis et disertus. Numquid domum alicuius lascivioris ingressus sum? Numquid me vestes sericae, nitentes gemmae, picta facies, auri rapuit ambitio? Nulla fuit Romae alia matronarum, quae meam posset domare mentem, nisi lugens atque ieiunans, squalens sordibus, fletibus paene caecata, quam continuis noctibus domini misericordiam deprecantem sol saepe deprehendit, cuius canticum psalmi sunt, sermo evangelium, deliciae continentia, vita ieiunium. Nulla me alia potuit delectare, nisi illa, quam manducantem numquam vidi; postquam eam pro suae merito sanctitatis venerari, colere, suspicere coepi, omnes me ilico deseruere virtutes.

4. O invidia primum mordax tui! O Satanae calliditas semper sancta persequens. Nullae aliae Romanae urbi fabulam praebuerunt, nisi Paula et Melanium, quae contemptis facultatibus pignoribusque desertis crucem domini quasi quoddam pietatis levavere vexillum. Baias peterent, unguenta eligerent, divitias et viduitatem haberent, materias luxuriae et libertatis, domnae vocarentur et sanctae: nunc in sacco et cinere formonsae volunt videri et in gehennae ignis cum ieiuniis et pedore descendere.

---

[1] Cf. Appendix, pp. 493, 494.

Before I became acquainted with the household of the saintly Paula, all Rome was enthusiastic about me. Almost everyone concurred in judging me worthy of the highest office in the Church. My words were always on the lips of Damasus of blessed memory. Men called me saintly; men called me humble and eloquent. Did I ever enter the house of any woman who was inclined to wantonness? Was I ever attracted by silk dresses, flashing jewels, painted faces, display of gold? No other matron in Rome could dominate my mind but one who mourned and fasted, who was squalid with dirt, almost blinded by weeping. All night long she would beg the Lord for mercy, and often the sun found her still praying. The psalms were her music, the Gospels her conversation; continence was her luxury, her life a fast. No other could give me pleasure but one whom I never saw eating food. But when, recognizing the holiness of her life, I began to revere, respect, and venerate her, all my good qualities at once forsook me.

O tooth of envy, that dost ever first attack thyself! O cunning of Satan, that dost always persecute holy things! The only women to give Rome an opportunity for scandal were Paula and Melanium,[1] who, scorning their wealth and deserting their children, lifted up the Lord's cross and took it as the standard of their faith. Had they frequented fashionable watering-places and used their own particular scent, had they employed their wealth and widow's freedom as opportunities for extravagance and self-indulgence, they would have been called 'Madam,' and 'saint.' As it is they wish to appear beautiful in sackcloth and ashes, and to go down to the fires of hell with fastings

Videlicet non licet eis adplaudente populo perire
cum turbis. Si gentiles hanc vitam carperent, si
Iudaei, haberem solacium non placendi eis, quibus
displicet Christus; nunc vero—pro nefas!—nomine
Christianae praetermissa domum suarum cura et
proprii oculi trabe neglecta in alieno festucam quaerunt. Lacerant sanctum propositum et remedium
poenae suae arbitrantur, si nemo sit sanctus, si
omnibus detrahatur, si turba sit pereuntium, multitudo peccantium.

5. Tibi placet lavare cotidie, alius has munditias
sordes putat; tu attagenam ructuas et de comeso
acipensere gloriaris, ego faba ventrem inpleo; te
delectant cachinnantium greges, Paulam Melani-
umque plangentium; tu aliena desideras, illae contemnunt sua; te delibuta melle vina delectant, illae
potant aquam frigidam suaviorem; tu te perdere
aestimas, quidquid in praesenti non hauseris, come-
deris, devoraris, et illae futura desiderant et credunt
vera esse, quae scripta sunt. Esto: inepte et ani-
liter, quibus resurrectio persuasit corporum; quid ad
te? Nobis e contrario tua vita displicet. Bono tuo
crassus sis, me macies delectat et pallor; tu tales
miseros arbitraris, nos te miseriorem putamus:
invicem nobis videmur insani.

and filth. Oh, plainly they are not allowed to perish amid the mob's applause along with the multitude! If it were Gentiles or Jews who attacked this mode of life, I should have the consolation of not pleasing those to whom Christ Himself is distasteful. But, as it is, shame upon them, women, nominally Christian, neglecting their own households and disregarding the beam in their own eye look for a mote in their neighbour's. They tear religion to shreds, and think they have found a palliative for their own fate, if they can show that no one is a saint and that everyone has weaknesses, that great is the multitude of the sinners, and mighty the host of those that perish.

It is your pleasure to take a bath every day; another man thinks such refinement rubbish. You belch after a meal of wild duck and boast of the sturgeon you devour; I fill my belly with beans. You take delight in troops of jesters; Paula and Melanium prefer those who weep. You want other people's goods; they despise their own. You like wine flavoured with honey; they have a sweeter drink, cold water. You consider that you are losing all that you have not at once drained dry, gobbled up, and devoured; they believe that the Scriptures are true and fix their desires on what is to come. Well, they are foolish old women to be persuaded of the resurrection of the body! But what is that to you? We for our part are not satisfied with your mode of life. Fatten yourself to your heart's content: I prefer a lean body and a pale face. You think people like us miserable: we regard you as more miserable still. Our opinion of you is like your opinion of us, and each in turn thinks the other insane.

6. Haec, mi domina Asella, cum iam navem conscenderem, raptim flens dolensque conscripsi, et gratias ago Deo meo, quod dignus sum, quem mundus oderit. Ora autem, ut de Babylone Hierosolyma regrediar nec mihi dominetur Nabuchodonosor, sed Iesus, filius Iosedech; veniat Hesdras, qui interpretatur ' adiutor,' et reducat me in patriam meam. Stultus ego, qui volebam canticum domini in terra aliena et deserto monte Sion Aegypti auxilium flagitabam. Non recordabar evangelii, quod, qui Hierusalem egreditur, statim incidit in latrones, spoliatur, vulneratur, occiditur. Sed licet sacerdos decipiat atque levites, Samaritanus ille misericors est, cui cum diceretur: ' Samarites es et daemonium habes,' daemonem rennuens Samariten non se negavit, quia, quem nos ' custodem,' Hebraei ' samariten ' vocant. Maleficum me quidam garriunt: titulum fidei servus agnosco; magum vocabant et Iudaei dominum meum, seductor et apostolus dictus est. ' Temptatio ' me ' non adprehendit nisi humana.' Quotam partem angustiarum perpessus sum, qui cruci milito? Infamiam falsi criminis inportarunt, sed scio per bonam et malam famam perveniri ad regna caelorum.

7. Saluta Paulam et Eustochium—velit nolit mundus, in Christo meae sunt—saluta matrem Albinam sororesque Marcellas, Marcellinam quoque et sanctam Felicitatem, et dic eis: ' " Ante tribunal

---

[1] Cf. Haggai, i. 1, etc. It means that however ill the Jews had treated him, he would prefer the rule of Jerusalem to that of Babylon.

[2] Psalm cxxxvii. 4.

[3] St. Luke, x, 30 ff. Cf. St. John, viii. 48.

I write this in haste, dear lady Asella, as I go on board ship, grieving and in tears; and I thank my God that I am held worthy of the world's hate. Pray for me that from Babylon I may return to Jerusalem, and that Joshua, son of Josedech, may have dominion over me rather than Nebuchadnezzar,[1] and that Ezra, whose name means 'helper,' may come and bring me back to my own country. Foolish was I, who wished to sing the Lord's song in a strange land,[2] and left Mount Sion to seek the help of Egypt. I forgot the Gospel story,[3] how that he who goes out from Jerusalem immediately falls among robbers, is stripped, wounded, and left for dead. But though priest and Levite pay no heed, there is the good Samaritan, who, when he was told, 'Thou art a Samaritan and hast a devil,' denied having a devil, but did not deny that he was a Samaritan, that name in Hebrew being equivalent to our 'guardian.' There are some men who style me a sorcerer: I, who am but a servant, recognize the word as a title of faith. The Jews called my master a magician, and the great apostle was spoken of as a deceiver. 'There hath no temptation taken me but such as is common to man.'[4] How few troubles have I endured, I who am a soldier of the cross? Men have laid upon me the disgrace of a false charge, but I know that the road to the kingdom of heaven leads alike through good report and through evil.

Greet Paula and Eustochium for me—whether the world wills it or no, they are mine in Christ—also your mother Albina and your sisters the two Marcellas, together with Marcellina and the saintly Felicitas. Tell them this: ' " We shall stand together

[4] 1 Corinthians, x. 13.

Christi stabimus "; ibi parebit, qua mente quis
vixerit.' Memento mei, exemplum pudicitiae et
virginitatis insigne, fluctusque maris tuis precibus
mitiga.

LII

Ad Nepotianum Presbyterum

1. Petis, Nepotiane carissime, litteris transmarinis et
crebro petis, ut tibi brevi volumine digeram praecepta vivendi et, qua ratione is, qui saeculi militia
derelicta vel monachus coeperit esse vel clericus,
rectum Christi tramitem teneat, ne ad diversa vitiorum diverticula rapiatur. Dum essem adulescens,
immo paene puer, et primos impetus lascivientis
aetatis heremi duritia refrenarem, scripsi ad avunculum tuum, sanctum Heliodorum, exhortatoriam
epistulam plenam lacrimis querimoniisque et quae
deserti sodalis monstraret affectum. Sed in illo
opere pro aetate tunc lusimus et calentibus adhuc
rhetorum studiis atque doctrinis quaedam scolastico
flore depinximus. Nunc iam cano capite et fronte, ad
instar boum pendentibus a mento palearibus :

' Frigidus obsistit circum praecordia sanguis ' ;

---

¹ Romans, xiv. 10.
² This letter, addressed to Nepotian and written in A.D. 394,
is really a treatise on the duties of the clergy. Nepotian was
the nephew of Heliodorus, a life-long friend of Jerome (cf.
Letter XIV), who had become Bishop of Altinum. Both

before Christ's judgment seat ",[1] and there the thoughts of each man's life shall be revealed.' Remember me, my glorious pattern of chastity and virginity, and by your prayers appease the sea waves.

LETTER LII[2]

To Nepotian

A clergyman's duties

You ask me, my dearest Nepotian, in your letters from across the sea, and you ask me often, to set out for you in a brief digest some rules of life, showing how one who has renounced service in the world's army to become a monk or a clergyman may keep to the straight path of Christ and not be led astray into the haunts of vice. When I was a young man, scarcely more than a boy, and was trying to curb the first tides of youthful wantonness by the hardships of the desert, I wrote a letter of exhortation to your reverend uncle Heliodorus, to show him the feelings of the friend he had deserted by the tears and remonstrances with which it was filled. In that production I indulged my youthful fancy, and being still fired with enthusiasm for the teaching of the rhetoricians, I decked out some parts of it with the flowery language of the schools. To-day, however, my hair is grey, my forehead furrowed and dewlaps, like those of an ox, hang from my chin. As the poet says:

' The cold blood round my heart now hinders me ' ;[3]

Nepotian and Heliodorus had been soldiers before joining the Church.

[3] Virgil, *Georgics*, II. 484.

unde et in alio loco idem poeta canit:

> ' Omnia fert aetas, animum quoque¹ ';

et post modicum:

> ' Nunc oblita mihi tot carmina, vox quoque Moerim
> Iam fugit.'²

2. Quod ne de gentili tantum litteratura proferre
videamur, divinorum voluminum sacramenta cog-
nosce. David annos natus septuaginta, bellicosus
quondam vir, senectute frigente non poterat cale-
fieri. Quaeritur itaque puella de universis finibus
Israhel Abisag Somanitis, quae cum rege dormiret et
senile corpus calefaceret. Nonne tibi videtur, si
occidentem sequaris litteram, vel figmentum esse de
mimo vel Atellanarum ludicra³? Frigidus senex
obvolvitur vestimentis et nisi conplexu adulescentulae non tepescit. Vivebat adhuc Betsabee, super-
erat Abigea et reliquae uxores eius et concubinae,
quas scriptura commemorat: omnes quasi frigidae
repudiantur, in unius tantum grandaevus calescit
amplexibus. Abraham multo David senior fuit et
tamen vivente Sarra aliam non quaesivit uxorem;
Isaac duplices David annos habuit et cum Rebecca
iam vetula numquam refrixit; taceo de prioribus
ante diluvium viris, qui post annos nongentos non
dico senilibus, sed paene iam cariosis artubus nequaquam puellares quaesiere conplexus; certe Moyses,
dux Israhelitici populi, centum viginti annos habebat
et Sephoram non mutavit.

---

¹ Virgil, *Bucolics*, IX. 51.   ² Virgil, *Bucolics*, IX. 53.
³ The Atellan plays were broad farces popular on the
Roman stage.

and in another passage:

   ' Age carries all things, e'en the mind, away '; [1]

and a little later:

   ' Those songs are all forgotten, and his voice
     Has left poor Moeris.' [2]

But that I may not seem to quote only from heathen literature, listen to the sacred teaching of God's Book. David once had been a man of war, but in his seventieth year old age had chilled him and he could never get warm. Accordingly they looked for a girl in all the land of Israel and brought in Abishag the Shunamite to sleep with the king and warm his aged limbs. If you were to follow the letter that killeth, does not this seem to you an incident invented for a farce or a broad jest from an Atellan play? [3] The old man's cold body is wrapped in blankets, but nothing save a young girl's embrace can warm him. Bathsheba was still alive and Abigail was also at his service, together with all his other wives and concubines of whom Scripture tells us. But they are all rejected as lacking heat, and it is in the arms of one girl only that the ancient grows warm again. Abraham was far older than David, but while Sarah was still living he did not seek another wife. Isaac had twice David's years, and yet never felt cold with Rebecca, even when she was an old woman. I say nothing of the men before the flood, who after nine hundred years must have found their limbs not merely aged but almost rotten with time and still never sought a young girl's embraces. Certainly Moses, the leader of the people of Israel, lived to be a hundred and twenty without changing his Sephora.

3. Quae est igitur ista Somanitis uxor et virgo tam fervens, ut frigidum calefaceret, tam sancta, ut calentem ad libidinem non provocaret? Exponat sapientissimus Salomon patris sui delicias et pacificus bellatoris viri narret amplexus: ' Posside sapientiam, posside intelligentiam. Ne obliviscaris, et ne declinaveris a verbis oris mei, et ne dereliqueris eam, et adprehendet te; ama illam et servabit te. Principium sapientiae: posside sapientiam et in omni possessione tua posside intelligentiam; circumda illam et exaltabit te; honora illam et amplexabitur te, ut det capiti tuo coronam gratiarum, corona quoque deliciarum protegat te.'

Omnes paene virtutes corporis mutantur in senibus et increscente sola sapientia decrescunt ceterae: ieiunia, chameuniae, huc illucque discursus, peregrinorum susceptio, defensio pauperum, standi in oratione perseverantia, visitatio languentium, labor manuum, unde praebeantur elemosynae, et, ne sermonem longius traham, cuncta, quae per corpus exercentur, fracto corpore minora fiunt. Nec hoc dico, quod in iuvenibus et adhuc solidioris aetatis, his dumtaxat, qui labore et ardentissimo studio, vitae quoque sanctimonia et orationis ad Deum frequentia scientiam secuti sunt, frigeat sapientia, quae in plerisque senibus aetate marcescit, sed quod adulescentia multa corporis bella sustineat et inter incentiva vitiorum et carnis titillationes quasi ignis in lignis viridioribus suffocetur et suum non possit explicare fulgorem. Senectus vero—rursus admoneo —eorum, qui adulescentiam suam honestis artibus

---

[1] Jerome takes the story of the Shunamite (1 Kings, i) as an allegory.

[2] Proverbs, iv. 5.

Who then is this Shunamite, this wife and virgin,
so fervid as to give heat to the cold, so holy as not to
excite to lust the man she had warmed?[1] Let
Solomon, wisest of men, tell us of his father's darling,
and let the man of peace recount the embraces of
the man of war. ' Get wisdom, get understanding:
forget it not; neither decline from the words of my
mouth. Forsake her not and she shall preserve thee:
love her and she shall keep thee. Wisdom is the
principal thing, therefore get wisdom, and with all
thy getting get understanding. Exalt her and she
shall promote thee. She shall bring thee to honour
when thou dost embrace her. She shall give to thine
head an ornament of grace: a crown of glory shall
she deliver to thee.'[2]

In the case of old men, almost all bodily excellences
are changed, and while wisdom alone increases they
decrease. Fasting, sleeping on the ground, moving
to and fro, hospitality to strangers, the defence of
the poor, perseverance in standing at prayer, visiting
the sick, manual labour to supply money for almsgiving, in fact, not to be tedious, all actions that
depend on the body's agency become less as the body
decays. I do not say that young men or even those
of riper vigour—provided that by labour and ardent
study, by a holy life and frequent prayer to God they
have attained knowledge—lack the warmth of
wisdom which in many old men is withered by age;
but I do say that youth has to endure many conflicts
with the body, and amid incentives to vice and
titillations of the flesh, it is stifled, as a fire is when it
is fed with green wood and cannot display its proper
brightness. Old age, however—I repeat my warning
—if men have trained their youth in honourable

instruxerunt et in lege domine meditati sunt die ac
nocte, aetate fit doctior, usu tritior, processu temporis
sapientior et veterum studiorum dulcissimos fructos
metit.

Unde et sapiens ille Graeciae, cum expletis centum
et septem annis se mori cerneret, dixisse fertur
dolere, quod tunc egrederetur e vita, quando sapere
coepisset; Plato octogesimo et uno anno scribens
est mortuus; Isocrates nonaginta et novem annos
in docendi scribendique labore conplevit; taceo
ceteros philosophos, Pythagoram, Democritum, Xeno-
cratem, Zenonem, Cleanthem, qui iam aetate lon-
gaeva in sapientiae studiis floruerunt: ad poetas
venio, Homerum, Hesiodum, Simonidem, Stesichorum,
qui grandes natu cygneum nescio quid et solito
dulcius vicina morte cecinerunt. Sophocles, cum
propter nimiam senectutem et rei familiaris negle-
gentiam a filiis accusaretur amentiae, Oedipi fabulam, quam nuper scripserat, recitavit iudicibus et
tantum sapientiae in aetate iam fracta specimen
dedit, ut severitatem tribunalium in theatri favorem
verteret. Nec mirum, cum etiam Cato, Romani
generis disertissimus, censorius iam et senex, Graecas
litteras nec erubuerit nec desperaverit discere.
Certe Homerus refert, quod de lingua Nestoris iam
vetuli et paene decrepiti dulcior melle oratio fluxerit.

Sed et ipsius 'Abisag' nominis sacramentum
sapientiam senum indicat ampliorem. Interpretatur

---

[1] Theophrastus. Cf. Cicero, *Tusc. Disp.* III. 69.

[2] Hom. *Il.* i. 248: ἡδυεπής . . . τοῦ καὶ ἀπὸ γλώσσης μέλιτος
γλυκίων ῥέεν αὐδή.

accomplishments and day and night have meditated on the Lord's law, becomes more learned by time, more subtle by experience, more wise by lapse of years and reaps the sweet fruit of its ancient studies.

Therefore it was that the Greek sage,[1] when he had reached his hundred and seventh year and saw himself near to death, is said to have expressed his grief at passing away from life just at the moment when he was beginning to have wisdom. Plato died in his eighty-first year with the pen in his hand; Isocrates filled ninety-nine years with the labour of teaching and writing. I say nothing of the other philosophers, Pythagoras, Democritus, Xenocrates, Zeno, Cleanthes, whose long life flourished ever in studies of wisdom. I come to the poets, Homer, Hesiod, Simonides, Stesichorus, who in their old age. when death drew near, sang a swan's song sweeter even than their wont. Sophocles in extreme old age neglected his affairs and was accused by his sons of mental incapacity. But when he read to the court his recently composed play, *Oedipus*, and in spite of bodily weakness gave so signal a proof of wisdom, he turned the strict judgment of a tribunal into the enthusiastic applause of a theatre. Nor need we wonder, seeing that Cato, the most eloquent of the Romans, after he had been censor and was now an old man, did not blush to learn Greek nor despair of acquiring knowledge of that language. Homer certainly tells us that when Nestor was very old and almost decrepit, speech that was sweeter than honey flowed from his tongue.[2]

Even the name Abishag in its mystical interpretation points to the greater wisdom that old men possess. It can be explained as meaning ' my

enim ' pater meus superfluus ' vel ' patris mei rugitus.' Verbum ' superfluum ' ambiguum est et in praesenti loco virtutem sonat, quod amplior sit in senibus et redundans ac larga sapientia, in alio autem loco ' superfluus ' quasi ' non necessarius ' ponitur. ' Sag ' autem, id est ' rugitus,' proprie nuncupatur, cum maris fluctus resonant et, ut ita dicam, de pelago veniens fremitus auditur. Ex quo ostenditur abundantissimum et ultra humanam vocem divini sermonis in senibus tonitruum commorari. Porro ' Somanitis ' in lingua nostra ' coccinea ' dicitur, ut significet calere sapientiam et divina lectione fervere; quod, licet dominici sanguinis indicet sacramentum, tamen et fervorem ostendit sapientiae. Unde et obstetrix illa in Genesi coccinum ligat in manu Phares, qui ab eo, quod parietem diviserat duos ante populos separantem, ' divisoris,' id est ' Phares,' sortitus est nomen. Et Raab meretrix in typo ecclesiae resticulam mysteria sanguinis continentem, ut Hiericho pereunte salvaretur, adpendit. Et in alio loco de viris sanctis scriptura commemorat: ' Hi sunt, Cinaei qui venerunt de calore domus Rechab.' Et dominus noster in evangelio: ' Ignem,' inquit, ' veni mittere in terram et quam volo, ut ardeat!' Qui in discipulorum corde succensus cogebat eos dicere: ' Nonne cor nostrum erat ardens in nobis, dum loqueretur in via et aperiret nobis scripturas?'

4. Quorsum haec tam longo repetita principio? Ne a me quaeras pueriles declamationes, sententiarum flosculos, verborum lenocinia et per fines

---

[1] Cf. Genesis, xxxviii. 27.
[2] 1 Chronicles, ii. 55—in Vulgate.

father's superfluity ' or ' my father's roaring.' The word ' superfluity ' is ambiguous, and in the present case means ' excellence,' inasmuch as in old men wisdom is more copious, redundant, and plentiful. In other cases, however, superfluous means unnecessary. As for ' shag,' that is, ' roaring,' the word is properly used of the sound of sea waves, when, so to speak, we hear the ocean murmuring. Thereby we see that the thunder of God's speech lingers in the ears of old men and is more excellent than human voice. Furthermore, ' Shunamite' in our language means scarlet, signifying the warmth of wisdom when it is fired by reading in God's Book: it contains a mystical reference to Our Lord's blood, but it also indicates the fervour of wisdom. So the midwife [1] in Genesis ties a scarlet thread to Phares' hand, Phares ' the divider,' because he divided the wall which till then kept the two peoples apart. The harlot Rahab also, who typifies the Church, fastened a scarlet cord to her window in mystical reference to His bloodshedding, so that she might be saved from Jericho's downfall. In another passage again the Scripture says of holy men: ' These are the Kenites who came from the warmth of the house of Rechab.' [2] Finally, Our Lord says in the Gospel: ' I am come to cast fire upon the earth, and fain am I to see it kindled.' [3] That fire, when kindled in the disciples' hearts, forced them to say : ' Did not our heart burn within us while He talked with us by the way, and while He opened to us the Scriptures ? ' [4]

Why all these far-fetched references, you may ask. I want you not to expect from me any boyish declamation or flowery sentiment. Here there will

---

[3] St. Luke, xii. 49 (slightly altered).   [4] St. Luke, xxiv. 32.

capitum singulorum acuta quaedam breviterque
conclusa, quae plausus et clamores excitent audientum. Amplexetur me modo sapientia et Abisag
nostra, quae numquam senescit, in meo requiescat
sinu. Inpolluta est virginitatisque perpetuae et in
similitudinem Mariae, cum cotidie generet semperque
parturiat, incorrupta est. Hinc reor dixisse et apostolum ' spiritu ferventes ' et in evangelio dominum
praedicasse, quod in fine mundi, quando iuxta prophetam Zachariam stultus pastor esse coeperit,
sapientia decrescente ' refrigescet caritas multorum.'
Audi igitur, ut beatus Cyprianus ait, ' non diserta,
sed fortia.' Audi fratrem collegio, patrem senio,
qui te ab incunabulis fidei usque ad perfectam ducat
aetatem et per singulos gradus vivendi praecepta
constituens in te ceteros erudiat. Scio quidem ab
avunculo tuo, beato Heliodoro, qui nunc pontifex
Christi est, te et didicisse, quae sancta sunt, et cotidie discere normamque vitae eius exemplum habere
virtutum ; sed et nostra, qualiacumque sunt, suscipe
et libellum hunc libello illius copulato, ut, cum ille
te monachum erudierit, hic clericum doceat esse
perfectum.

5. Igitur clericus, qui Christi servit ecclesiae,
interpretetur primum vocabulum suum et nominis
definitione praelata nitatur esse, quod dicitur. Si
enim κλῆρος Graece ' sors ' Latine appellatur,
propterea vocantur clerici, vel quia de sorte sunt
domini vel quia dominus ipse sors, id est pars,
clericorum est. Qui autem vel ipse pars domini
est vel dominum partem habet, talem se exhibere

---

[1] Romans, xii. 11. [2] Zech. xi. 16. [3] St. Matthew, xxiv. 12.
[4] Or else because they administer the κλῆρος, the Church
estates. Cf. *Fathers of the Church*, p. 12.

be no meretricious writing, no terse pointed epigrams
at the end of each paragraph, put in to excite my
audience to loud applause. Let wisdom alone
embrace me; let my Abishag who never grows old
nestle in my arms. She is undefiled and ever virgin :
like Mary every day she brings forth and is always
in labour, but still she is stainless. Hence, methinks,
the apostle said : ' Be fervent in spirit ' ; [1] hence also
Our Lord in the Gospel declared that at the end of
the world—when, according to the prophet Zechariah, [2]
the shepherd shall begin to grow foolish—with the
decay of wisdom, ' the love of many shall wax cold.' [3]
Listen then, as the blessed Cyprian says, to words
that are weighty rather than eloquent : listen to one
who is your brother in orders and your father in years,
one who can guide you from faith's cradle to perfect
manhood, and by setting forth precepts of life step
by step may instruct others in instructing you.
I know that from your uncle, the reverend Heliodorus
who is now one of Christ's bishops, you have already
learned and are still daily learning all that is holy
and that you have the rule of his life as an example
of virtue set before you. Take then this letter of
mine for what it is worth and join my precepts to his,
so that the one may train you in a monk's duties, the
other may teach you to be a perfect clergyman.

A clergyman then, who is a servant in Christ's
Church, should first know the meaning of his name ;
and when he has that accurately defined, he should
then strive to be what he is called. For since the
Greek κλῆρος means ' lot ' or ' portion,' the clergy
are so named, either because they are the Lord's
portion, or else because the Lord is theirs.[4] Now he
who himself is the Lord's portion, or has the Lord for

debet, ut et possideat dominum et ipse possideatur a domino. Qui dominum possidet et cum propheta dicit: ' Pars mea dominus,' nihil extra dominum habere potest, quod, si quippiam aliud habuerit praeter dominum, pars eius non erit dominus. Verbi gratia, si aurum, si argentum, si possessiones, si variam supellectilem, cum his partibus dominus pars eius fieri non dignatur. Si autem ego pars domini sum et funiculus hereditatis eius, nec accipio partem inter ceteras tribus, sed quasi levita et sacerdos vivo de decimis et altari serviens altaris oblatione sustentor, habens victum et vestitum his contentus ero et nudam crucem nudus sequar. Obsecro itaque te, ' et repetens iterum iterumque monebo,' ne officium clericatus genus antiquae militiae putes, id est, ne lucra saeculi in Christi quaeras militia, ne plus habeas, quam quando clericus esse coepisti, et dicatur tibi: ' Cleri eorum non proderunt eis.' Mensulam tuam pauperes et peregrini et cum illis Christus conviva noverit; negotiatorem clericum et ex inope divitem et ex ignobili gloriosum quasi quandem pestem fuge. ' Corrumpunt mores bonos confabulationes pessimae.' Tu aurum contemnis, alius diligit; tu calcas opes, ille sectatur; tibi cordi est silentium, mansuetudo, secretum, illi verbositas, adtrita frons, fora placent et plateae ac medicorum tabernae: in tanta morum discordia quae potest esse concordia?

---

[1] Psalm lxxiii. 26.   [2] Virgil, *Aeneid*, III. 436.

[3] Jeremiah, xii. 13 :—οἱ κληροι αὐτῶν οὐκ ὠφελήσουσιν αὐτούς· The LXX which Jerome quotes differs from the Vulgate and A.V. There is a play on the two meanings of κλῆροι— portions and clergy.

[4] 1 Corinthians, xv. 33.

his portion, must so bear himself as to possess the
Lord and be possessed by Him. He who possesses
the Lord and says with the prophet:[1] ' The Lord is
my portion,' can have nothing outside the Lord;
for if he has anything except the Lord, the Lord will
not be his portion. For example, if he has gold and
silver, land and inlaid furniture, with portions such
as these the Lord will not deign to be his portion.
If I am the Lord's portion and in the line of His
inheritance, I receive no portion among the other
tribes, but like the Priest and the Levite I live on
tithes, and serving the altar am supported by the
altar offerings. Having food and raiment I shall be
satisfied with them, and naked shall follow the naked
cross. So I beseech you and ' again and yet again
my words repeat,'[2] do not think that clerical orders
are but a variety of your old military service; that
is, do not look for worldly gain when you are fighting
in Christ's army, lest, having more than when you
first became a clergyman, you hear it said of you:
' Their portions ($\kappa\lambda\hat{\eta}\rho\omega$) shall not profit them.'[3] Let
poor men and strangers be acquainted with your
modest table, and with them Christ shall be your
guest. Avoid, as you would the plague, a clergyman
who is also a man of business, one who has risen
from poverty to wealth, from obscurity to a high position. ' Evil communications corrupt good manners.'[4]
You despise gold; the other loves it. You trample
money underfoot; he pursues it. You delight in
silence, peacefulness, solitude; he prefers talking
and effrontery, the markets and the streets and the
apothecaries' shops. When your ways are so
diverse, what unity of heart can there be between
you?

SELECT LETTERS OF ST. JEROME

Hospitiolum tuum aut raro aut numquam mulierum
pedes terant. Omnes puellas et virgines Christi aut
aequaliter ignora aut aequaliter dilige. Ne sub
eodem tecto manseris; ne in praeterita castitate
confidas. Nec David sanctior nec Salomone potes
esse sapientior; memento semper, quod paradisi
colonum de possessione sua mulier eiecerit. Aegrotanti tibi sanctus quilibet frater adsistat et germana
vel mater aut probatae quaelibet apud omnes fidei.
Quod si huiusce modi non fuerint consanguinitatis
castimoniaeque personae, multas anus nutrit ecclesia,
quae et officium praebeant et beneficium accipiant
ministrando, ut infirmitas quoque tua fructum habeat
elemosynae. Scio quosdam convaluisse corpore et
animo aegrotare coepisse. Periculose tibi ministrat,
cuius vultum frequenter adtendis. Si propter officium clericatus aut vidua tibi visitatur aut virgo,
numquam domum solus introeas talesque habeto
socios, quorum contubernio non infameris. Si lector,
si acolythus, si psaltes te sequitur, non ornentur
vestibus, sed moribus, nec calamistro crispent comas,
sed pudicitiam habitu polliceantur. Solus cum sola
secreto et absque arbitro non sedeas. Si familiarius
est aliquid loquendum, habet nutricem, maiorem
domus virginem, viduam, maritatam; non est tam
inhumana, ut nullum praeter te habeat, cui se
audeat credere. Caveto omnes suspiciones et, quid-

A woman's foot should seldom or never cross the threshold of your humble lodging. To all maidens and to all Christ's virgins show the same disregard or the same affection. Do not remain under the same roof with them; do not trust your chastity in the past. You cannot be a man more saintly than David, or more wise than Solomon. Remember always that a woman drove the tiller of Paradise from the garden that had been given him. If you are ill let one of the brethren attend you, or else your sister or your mother or some woman of universally approved faith. If there are no persons marked out by ties of kinship, or reputation for chastity, the Church maintains many elderly women who by their services can both help you and benefit themselves, so that even your sickness may bear fruit in almsgiving. I know of some whose bodily recovery coincided with spiritual sickness. There is danger for you in the ministrations of one whose face you are continually watching. If in the course of your clerical duties you have to visit a widow or a virgin, never enter the house alone, and let your associates be men whose fellowship brings no disgrace. If a reader or acolyte or psalm-singer comes with you, let their character, not their dress, be their adornment; let them not wave their hair with curling tongs but let their outward looks be a guarantee of their chastity. Never sit alone and without witnesses with a woman in a quiet place. If there is anything intimate she wants to say, she has a nurse or some elderly virgin at home, some widow or married woman. She cannot be so cut off from human society as to have no one but yourself to whom she can trust her secret. Beware of men's suspicious

quid probabiliter fingi potest, ne fingatur, ante
devita. Crebra munuscula et orariola et fasciolas,
et vestes ori adplicatas, et degustatos cibos blandasque
et dulces litterulas sanctus amor non habet. ' Mel
meum, lumen meum meumque desiderium ' et
ceteras ineptias amatorum, omnes delicias et lepores
et risu dignas urbanitates in comoediis erubescimus,
in saeculi hominibus detestamur: quanto magis in
clericis et in clericis monachis, quorum et sacerdotium proposito et propositum ornatur sacerdotio!
Nec hoc dico, quod aut in te aut in sanctis viris ista
formidem, sed quod in omni proposito, in omni gradu
et sexu et boni et mali repperiantur malorumque
condemnatio laus bonorum sit.

6. Pudet dicere: sacerdotes idolorum, mimi et
aurigae et scorta hereditates capiunt; solis clericis
et monachis hoc lege prohibetur et prohibetur non
a persecutoribus, sed a principibus Christianis. Nec
de lege conqueror, sed doleo, cur meruerimus hanc
legem. Cauterium bonum est, sed quo mihi vulnus,
ut indigeam cauterio? Provida severaque legis
cautio, et tamen nec sic refrenatur avaritia. Per
fidei commissa legibus inludimus, et quasi maiora
sint imperatorum scita quam Christi, leges timemus,
evangelia contemnimus. Sit heres, sed mater filiorum, id est gregis sui, ecclesia, quae illos genuit,
nutrivit et pavit. Quid nos inserimus inter matrem

---

[1] By Valentinian, A.D. 368.

thoughts, and if a tale can be invented with some probability avoid giving the scandalmonger his opportunity. Frequent gifts of handkerchiefs and ties, pressing a woman's dress to your lips, tasting her food beforehand, writing her fond and flattering *billets-doux*, of all this a holy love knows nothing. ' My honey, my light, my darling '—lover's nonsense like this, and all such wanton playfulness and ridiculous courtesy, makes us blush when we hear it on the stage, and seems detestable even on the lips of worldlings. How much more loathsome is it then in the case of monks and clergymen who adorn the priesthood with their vows and their vows with the priesthood! I say this not because I fear such errors in you or in any holy man, but because in every order, in every rank and sex, both good and bad people are to be found, and to condemn the bad is to praise the good.

I am ashamed to say it, but priests who serve idols, actors, charioteers, and harlots can all inherit property: clergymen and monks alone are by law debarred, a law passed not by persecutors but by Christian emperors.[1] I do not complain of the enactment, but it grieves me to think that we deserved it. A cautery is a good thing, but how is it I have a wound that needs a cautery? The law's precaution is stern and prudent; yet even so greed is not checked. By a fiction of trusteeship we elude its provisions, and, as though imperial enactments were of more importance than Christ's commands, we fear the laws and despise the Gospels. If there must be an heir, let the Church inherit from the children who are her flock, the Church who bore reared and fed them. Why do we thrust ourselves

et liberos? Gloria episcopi est pauperum opibus providere, ignominia omnium sacerdotum est propriis studere divitiis. Natus in paupere domo et in tugurio rusticano, qui vix milio et cibario pane rugientem saturare ventrem poteram, nunc similam et mella fastidio, novi et genera et nomina piscium, in quo litore conca lecta sit calleo, saporibus avium discerno provincias et ciborum me raritas ac novissime damna ipsa delectant.

Audio praeterea in senes et anus absque liberis[1] quorundam turpe servitium. Ipsi apponunt mattulam, obsident lectum, et purulentias stomachi et phlegmata pulmonis manu propria suscipiunt. Pavent ad introitum medici trementibusque labiis, an commodius habeant, sciscitantur et, si paululum senex vegetior fuerit, periclitantur ac simulata laetitia mens intrinsecus avara torquetur. Timent enim, ne perdant ministerium, et vivacem senem Mathusalae annis conparant. O quanta apud dominum merces, si in praesenti pretium non speraret! Quantis sudoribus hereditas cassa expetitur! Minori labore margaritum Christi emi poterat.

7. Divinas scripturas saepius lege, immo numquam de manibus tuis sacra lectio deponatur. Disce, quod doceas; obtine eum, qui secundum doctrinam est,

---

[1] Cf. Juv. iv. 140.
[2] The *orbi* and *orbae* constantly referred to in Latin literature; cf. especially Horace, *Sat.* II. v. and Juv. vi. 39, xii. 99.

in between mother and children? It is the glory of a bishop to provide means for the poor, but it is a disgrace for any priest to think of wealth for himself. Though I was born in a humble home beneath the roof of a country cottage and once could scarcely get enough millet and coarse bread to satisfy the howlings of my stomach, yet now I turn up my nose at wheaten flour and honey cakes, I know the various kinds of fish and their different names, I can tell for certain on what coast an oyster has been picked,[1] I can distinguish by the taste from what province a bird comes, and it is the rarity of a dish and, in the last stage, the money that is wasted on it that gives me pleasure.

I have been told that in some cases disgraceful court is paid to old men and women who have no children.[2] These servile flatterers fetch the basin, sit by the bed, and catch in their own hands ordure and spittle. They tremble at the doctor's appearance, and with quivering lips inquire if his patient is better. If for a little while the old fellow plucks up some strength, they are at their wits' end, and while they pretend to be glad their greedy soul suffers torments within. For they are afraid that they may have wasted their attentions, and they compare an old man with a good hold on life to Methuselah. How great would be their reward with the Lord, if they did not hope for immediate profit. With what labour do they seek an empty inheritance! At less trouble they could have bought for themselves the pearl of Christ.

Read God's Book continually; nay, never let the sacred volume be out of your hand. Learn, so that you may teach. Hold fast to the words of faith

fidelem sermonem, ut possis exhortari in doctrina sana et contradicentes revincere. ' Permane in his, quae didicisti et credita sunt tibi, sciens, a quo didiceris,' ' paratus semper ad satisfactionem omni poscenti te rationem de ea, quae in te est, spe.' Non confundant opera sermonem tuum, ne, cum in ecclesia loqueris, tacitus quilibet respondeat: ' Cur ergo haec ipse non facis? ' Delicatus magister est, qui pleno ventre de ieiuniis disputat; accusare avaritiam et latro potest; sacerdotis Christi mens osque concordent.

Esto subiectus pontifici tuo et quasi animae parentem suspice: amare filiorum, timere servorum est: ' Et si pater sum,' inquit, ' ubi est honor meus? et si dominus ego sum, ubi est timor meus? ' Plura tibi in eodem viro observanda sunt nomina: monachus, pontifex, avunculus. Sed et episcopi sacerdotes se sciant esse, non dominos: honorent clericos quasi clericos, ut et ipsis a clericis quasi episcopis deferatur. Scitum illud est oratoris Domitii: ' Ego te,' inquit, ' habeam ut principem, cum tu me non habeas ut senatorem? ' Quod Aaron et filios eius, hoc episcopum et presbyteros noverimus: unus dominus, unum templum, unum sit etiam ministerium. Recordemur semper, quid apostolus Petrus praecipiat sacerdotibus: ' Pascite eum, qui in vobis est, gregem domini providentes non coacto, sed

---

[1] Titus, i. 9; 2 Timothy, iii. 14. [2] 1 Peter, iii. 15.
[3] Malachi, i. 6.
[4] Cf. Cicero, *De Oratore*, III. 1 : *cum sibi illum consulem esse negaret, cui senator ipse non esset.*

according to sound doctrine, so that you may be able
thereby to exhort and refute the gainsayers. ' Continue thou in the things that thou hast learned and
hast been assured of, knowing of whom thou hast
learned them ';[1] and ' Be ready always to give an
answer to every man that asketh you a reason of the
hope and faith that are in you.'[2] Your deeds must
not belie your words, lest, when you are speaking
in church, some one may say to himself: ' Why do
you not practise what you preach?' A teacher
fond of good living may fill his own stomach and
then discourse on the benefits of fasting; even a
robber can possibly accuse others of greed; but
in a priest of Christ mind and mouth should be in
harmony.

Be obedient to your bishop, and respect him as
your spiritual father. Sons love, slaves fear. ' If I
be a father,' says the Scripture, ' where is mine
honour? and if I am a master, where is my fear?'[3]
In your case one and the same man has many titles
to your respect: he is monk, bishop, uncle. But
even bishops should realize they are priests, not
lords; they should give to clergymen the honour
that is their due, so that the clergy may offer them
the respect proper to bishops. The orator Domitius
spoke to the point when he said: ' Why should I
treat you as leader of the Senate, when you do not
treat me as a senator?'[4] We should recognize that
a bishop and his presbyters are like Aaron and his
sons. There is but one Lord and one Temple; there
should be also but one ministry. Let us always
remember the charge which the apostle Peter gives
to priests: ' Feed the flock of God which is among
you, taking the oversight thereof not by constraint

spontanee secundum Deum, neque turpilucri gratia,
sed voluntarie, neque ut dominantes in cleris, sed
forma facti gregi et ex animo, ut, cum apparuerit
princeps pastorum, percipiatis inmarcescibilem gloriae
coronam.' Pessimae consuetudinis est in quibusdam ecclesiis tacere presbyteros et praesentibus
episcopis non loqui, quasi aut invideant aut non
dignentur audire. ' Et si alii,' inquit Paulus apostolus, ' fuerit revelatum sedenti, prior taceat. Potestis
enim per singulos prophetare, ut omnes discant et
omnes consolentur. Et spiritus prophetarum pro-
phetis subiectus est : non enim est dissensionis Deus,
sed pacis.' Gloria patris est filius sapiens ; gaudeat
episcopus iudicio suo, cum tales Christo elegerit
sacerdotes.

8. Dicente te in ecclesia non clamor populi, sed
gemitus suscitetur ; lacrimae auditorum laudes tuae
sint ; sermo presbyteri scripturarum lectione conditus
sit. Nolo te declamatorem esse et rabulam garru-
lumque, sed mysterii peritum et sacramentorum Dei
tui eruditissimum. Verba volvere et celeritate
dicendi apud inperitum vulgus admirationem sui
facere indoctorum hominum est. Adtrita frons interpretatur saepe, quod nescit, et, cum aliis suaserit,
sibi quoque usurpat scientiam. Praeceptor quondam
meus Gregorius Nazianzenus rogatus a me, ut expo-
neret, quid sibi vellet in Luca sabbatum δευτερόπρωτον,
id est ' secundoprimum,' eleganter lusit : ' Docebo

---

[1] 1 Peter, v. 2.   [2] 1 Corinthians, xiv. 30.
[3] The great Cappadocian preacher, born A.D. 330.
[4] St. Luke, vi. 1 ; cf. Leviticus, xxiii. 15.

but willingly as God would have you; not for filthy
lucre but of a ready mind; neither as being lords
over God's heritage but being examples to the flock,
and that gladly, that when the chief shepherd shall
appear ye may receive a crown of glory that fadeth
not away.'[1]   It is a very bad custom in some
churches for presbyters to be silent and to refrain
from speech in the presence of bishops, on the
ground that these latter would either be jealous of
them or think it unbecoming to be listeners.   The
apostle Paul says: 'If anything be revealed to
another that sitteth by, let the first hold his peace.
For ye may all prophesy one by one that all may
learn and all may be comforted; and the spirits of
the prophets are subject to the prophets.   For God
is not the author of confusion but of peace.'[2]   A
wise son is a glory to his father; and a bishop should
rejoice in his own good judgment, when he chooses
such to be priests of Christ.

When you are preaching in church try to evoke
not applause but lamentation.   Let the tears of your
audience be your glory.   A presbyter's discourse
should be seasoned by his reading of Scripture.   Be
not a declaimer nor a ranter nor a gabbler, but show
yourself skilled in God's mysteries and well acquainted
with the secret meaning of His words.   Only ignorant
men like to roll out phrases and to excite the admiration of the unlettered crowd by the quickness of
their utterance.   Effrontery often tries to explain
things of which it knows nothing, and having persuaded others claims knowledge for itself.   My
former teacher, Gregory of Nazianzus,[3] when I asked
him to explain the meaning of St. Luke's phrase
δευτερόπρωτον,[4] that is, 'second first' sabbath, wittily

te,' inquiens, ' super hac re in ecclesia, in qua omni
mihi populo acclamante cogeris invitus scire, quod
nescis, aut certe, si solus tacueris, solus ab omnibus
stultitiae condemnaberis.' Nihil tam facile, quam
vilem plebiculam et indoctam contionem linguae
volubilitate decipere, quae, quidquid non intellegit,
plus miratur. Marcus Tullius, ad quem pulcherri-
mum illud elogium est : ' Demosthenes tibi praeri-
puit, ne esses primus orator, tu illi, ne solus,' in
oratione pro Quinto Gallio quid de favore vulgi et de
inperitis contionatoribus loquatur, adtende : ' His
autem ludis—loquor enim, quae sunt ipse nuper
expertus—unus quidam poeta dominatur, homo per-
litteratus, cuius sunt illa convivia poetarum ac philo-
sophorum, cum facit Euripiden et Menandrum inter
se et alio loco Socraten atque Epicurum disserentes,
quorum aetates non annis, sed saeculis scimus fuisse
disiunctas. Atque his quantos plausus et clamores
movet! Multos enim condiscipulos habet in theatro,
qui simul litteras non didicerunt.'

9. Vestes pullas aeque vita ut candidas ; ornatus
et sordes pari modo fugiendae, quia alterum delicias,
alterum gloriam redolet. Non absque amictu lineo
incedere, sed pretium vestium linearum non habere
laudabile est ; alioquin ridiculum et plenum dedecoris
referto marsuppio, quod sudarium orariumque non
habeas, gloriari. Sunt, qui pauperibus parum tri-

---

[1] This speech is not extant.

evaded my request. ' I will tell you about that in church,' he said, ' and there, when all the people applaud me, you will be compelled against your wish to know what you do not know, or else, if you alone remain silent, you will undoubtedly be put down by every one as a fool.' There is nothing so easy as to deceive a cheap mob or an ignorant congregation by voluble talk; anything such people do not understand they admire all the more. Listen to Cicero, the man to whom that glorious eulogy was addressed: ' Demosthenes snatched from you the glory of being the first of orators; you have prevented him from being the only one.' In his speech for Quintus Gallius,[1] this is what Cicero says about vulgar enthusiasm and ignorant mob orators: ' At these games—I am telling you of something within my own recent experience—one gentleman, a poet, has been cock of the walk. He is a very literary fellow and he has written a book *Conversations of Poets and Philosophers*. In it he makes Euripides and Menander talk together, and in another passage Socrates and Epicurus, men whose lives we know to be separated not by years but by centuries. And yet what applause and cheers this stuff evokes! He has many fellow pupils in the theatre, schoolfellows who went to the same school and learnt nothing.'

Avoid sombre garments as much as bright ones. Showiness and slovenliness are alike to be shunned: the one savours of vanity, the other of boastfulness. To walk abroad without a linen vest is not praiseworthy: the good thing is not to have money to buy one. In any case it is absurd and scandalous to boast of having neither napkin nor handkerchief, while all the time your purse is well filled. There

buunt, ut amplius accipiant, et sub praetextu elemosynae quaerunt divitias; quae magis venatio
appellanda est quam elemosyna. Sic bestiae, sic
aves, sic capiuntur et pisces: modica in hamo esca
ponitur, ut matronarum in eo sacculi protrahantur.
Scit episcopus, cui commissa est ecclesia, quem dis-
pensationi pauperum curaeque praeficiat. Melius
est non habere, quod tribuam, quam impudenter
petere. Sed et genus adrogantiae est clementiorem
te videri velle, quam pontifex Christi est. 'Non
omnia possumus omnes.' Alius in ecclesia oculus
est, alius lingua, alius manus, alius pes, alius auris,
venter et cetera. Lege Pauli ad Corinthios: diversa
membra unum corpus efficiunt. Nec rusticus et
tantum simplex frater ideo se sanctum putet, si nihil
noverit, nec peritus et eloquens in lingua aestimet
sanctitatem. Multoque melius est e duobus inper-
fectis rusticitatem sanctam habere quam eloquentiam
peccatricem.

10. Multi aedificant parietes et columnas ecclesiae
subtrahunt:[1] marmora nitent, auro splendent lacu-
naria, gemmis altare distinguitur et ministrorum
Christi nulla electio est. Neque vero mihi aliquis
opponat dives in Iudaea templum, mensam, lucernas,
turibula, patellas, scyphos, mortariola et cetera ex
auro fabre facta. Tunc haec probabantur a domino,
quando sacerdotes hostias immolabant et sanguis
pecudum erat redemptio peccatorum—quamquam
haec omnia praecesserint in figura. 'Scripta sunt

---

[1] subtrahunt, *Hilberg*: substernunt.

---

[1] Virgil, *Bucolics*, VIII. 63.
[2] If the text is right Jerome apparently means that a
church should consist of *one* plain room, with no party walls
for separate shrines and no columns.

are some who give a trifle to the poor that they may themselves receive a larger sum, under the cloak of almsgiving seeking their own personal gain. Such conduct should be called almshunting rather than almsgiving. Thus it is that birds, beasts, and fishes are caught. A small piece of bait is put on the hook; and lo! they draw up a fine lady's purse. The bishop, to whose care the church is entrusted, knows whom he should appoint as almoner to the poor. It is better for me not to have anything to give than to be shameless in begging. It is a kind of arrogance also to wish to seem more generous than he who is Christ's bishop. ' We cannot all do all things.'[1] In the Church one man is the eye, another the tongue, another the hand, another the foot, another the ear, the belly, and so on. Read Paul's epistle to the Corinthians, and see how one body is made up of different members. A rough simple brother should not think himself saintly just because he knows nothing; he who is well educated and eloquent must not imagine that holiness consists in a ready tongue. Of the two imperfections a holy clumsiness is much better than a sinful eloquence.

Many people build churches now with party walls not pillars to support them:[2] slabs of marble shine brightly in them, the ceilings are gay with gold, the altar is adorned with jewels, and no care is shown in choosing Christ's ministers. Let no one object against me the richness of the Temple in Judaea, its table, lamps, censers, dishes, cups, spoons, and the rest of its golden ware. These things were approved by the Lord in the days when priests sacrificed victims, and when the blood of sheep was the redemption of sins. They were but a figure ' written for

autem' propter nos, 'in quos fines saeculorum decurrerunt'—nunc vero, cum paupertatem domus suae pauper dominus dedicarit, cogitemus crucem et divitias lutum putabimus. Quid miramur, quod Christus vocat iniquum mammonam? Quid suspicimus et amamus, quod Petrus se non habere testatur? Alioquin, si tantum litteram sequimur et in auro atque divitiis simplex nos delectat historia, cum auro observemus et cetera: ducant pontifices Christi uxores virgines; quamvis bonae mentis sit, qui cicatricem habuerit et deformis est, privetur sacerdotio; lepra corporis animae vitiis praeferatur; crescamus et multiplicemur et repleamus terram; nec immolemus agnum nec mysticum pascha celebremus, quia haec absque templo fieri lege prohibentur; figamus septimo mense tabernaculum et sollemne ieiunium bucina concrepemus. Quodsi haec omnia spiritalibus spiritalia conparantes scientesque cum Paulo, quod lex spiritalis est, et David verba cantantes: 'Revela oculos meas et considerabo mirabilia de lege tua' sic intellegamus, ut dominus quoque noster intellexit et interpretatus est sabbatum, aut aurum repudiemus cum ceteris superstitionibus Iudaeorum aut, si aurum placet, placeant et Iudaei, quos cum auro aut probare nobis necesse est aut damnare.

11. Convivia tibi vitanda sunt saecularium, et maxime eorum, qui honoribus tument. Turpe est ante fores sacerdotis domini crucifixi et pauperis et

---

[1] 1 Corinthians, x. 11.   [2] St. Luke, xvi. 9.
[3] Acts, iii. 6.   [4] Leviticus, xxi. 17.
[5] Psalm cxix. 18.

our admonition upon whom the ends of the world are come.' [1]   But to-day, when Our Lord by his poverty has consecrated the poverty of his house, we should think rather of his cross and count riches to be but dirt. Why do we admire that which Christ calls the Mammon of unrighteousness? [2] Why do we respect and love that which Peter proclaims he does not possess? [3] Moreover, if we follow only the letter and find pleasure in the bare lists of riches and gold, let us keep to everything else together with the gold: let Christ's priests take virgins as wives; let a man be deprived of his priesthood, however honest he be, if he is scarred or disfigured in any way; [4] let bodily leprosy be counted worse than spiritual faults; let us increase and multiply and replenish the earth; let us slay no lamb and celebrate no mystic passover, for the law forbids these things where there is no temple; let us pitch a tent in the seventh month and with a trumpet noise abroad the solemn fast. But if all these things are spiritual, and we compare them with things spiritual, and know with Paul that the Law is spiritual, and chant David's words: ' Open thou mine eyes that I may behold wondrous things out of thy law,' [5] understanding them as Our Lord understood them when He thus explained the Sabbath; then we should reject the gold together with the rest of Jewish superstition, or, if we approve of the gold, we should approve of the Jews as well. The Jews must go with the gold whether we approve or condemn.

Avoid entertaining the worldly at your table, especially those who are swollen with office. You are the priest of a crucified Lord, one who lived in poverty and on the bread of strangers, and it is a

qui cibo quoque vescebatur alieno lictores consulum et milites excubare iudicemque provinciae melius apud te prandere quam in palatio. Quodsi obtenderis facere te haec, ut roges pro miseris atque subiectis, iudex saeculi plus defert clerico continenti quam diviti et magis sanctitatem tuam veneratur quam opes; aut si talis est, qui non audiat clericos nisi inter fialas, libenter carebo huiusce modi beneficio et Christum rogabo pro iudice, qui magis subvenire potest; melius est enim confidere in domino quam confidere in homine, melius est sperare in domino quam sperare in principibus.

Numquam vinum redoleas, ne audias illud philosophi: 'Hoc non est osculum porrigere, sed propinare.' Vinolentos sacerdotes et apostolus damnat et vetus lex prohibet. Qui altari serviunt, vinum et siceram non bibant. Sicera Hebraeo sermone omnis potio nuncupatur, quae inebriare potest, sive illa fermento conficitur sive pomorum suco aut favi decoquuntur in dulcem et barbaram potionem aut palmarum fructus exprimantur in liquorem coctisque frugibus aqua pinguior colatur. Quidquid inebriat et statum mentis evertit, fuge similiter ut vinum. Nec hoc dico, quod Dei a nobis creatura damnetur, siquidem et dominus vini potator appellatur et Timotheo dolenti stomachum modica vini sorbitio relaxata est, sed modum et aetatis et valetudinis et corporum qualitates exigimus in potando. Quodsi absque vino ardeo et ardeo adulescentia et inflammor

---

[1] Psalm cxviii. 9.

[2] Cf. Leviticus, x. 9 and St. Luke, i. 15: οἶνον καὶ σίκερα οὐ μὴ πίῃ.

[3] St. Matthew, xi. 19; 1 Timothy, v. 23.

shameful thing for a consul's attendants and body-
guard to keep watch before your door, and for a
provincial judge to have a better luncheon with you
than he would get in his palace. If you urge that
you do this in order that you may plead for the
unhappy and the oppressed, a worldly judge pays
more regard to a self-denying cleric than to a rich
one, he respects your sanctity more than your wealth.
Or if he is the sort of man who only listens to clergymen over the wine bowl, I will gladly forgo any
benefit from him, and will address my prayer to
Christ who is more able to help than any judge. For
it is better to trust in the Lord than to put your
confidence in men; it is better to fix your hopes in the
Lord than to expect anything from princes.[1]

Never smell of wine, lest the philosopher's words
be said of you: ' This is not a kiss but a wine sip.'
Priests who reek of wine are condemned by the
apostle and forbidden by the old Law. Those who
serve the altar must not drink either wine or shechar,
the Law says;[2] the word shechar in Hebrew means
any intoxicating drink, whether it is made from
barley, or from fruit juice, or from honey boiled down
into a rough sweet liquor, or from pressed dates, or
from the thick syrup strained from a decoction of
corn. Anything that intoxicates and disturbs the
mind's balance you must avoid as you avoid wine.
I do not say that we should condemn a thing that God
made, since indeed Our Lord was called a wine-bibber,
and Timothy was allowed wine in moderation because
of his weak stomach;[3] but I claim that those who
drink wine should have some reason of age or health
or some peculiarity of constitution. If even without
wine I am all aglow, if I feel the fire of youth and am

calore sanguinis et suculento validoque sum corpore, libenter carebo poculo, in quo suspicio veneni est. Pulchre dicitur apud Graecos, sed nescio utrum apud nos aeque resonet: ' Pinguis venter non gignit sensum tenuem.'[1]

12. Tantum tibi ieiuniorum inpone, quantum ferre potes. Sint pura, casta, simplicia, moderata, non superstitiosa ieiunia. Quid prodest oleo non vesci et molestias quasdam difficultatesque ciborum quaerere? Caricae, piper, nuces, palmarum fructus, simila, mel, pistatia, tota hortorum cultura vexatur, ut cibario non vescamur pane. Audio praeterea quosdam contra rerum hominumque naturam aquam non bibere nec vesci pane, sed sorbitiunculas delicatas et contrita holera betarumque sucum non calice sorbere, sed conca. Pro pudor, non erubescimus istiusmodi ineptiis nec taedet superstitionis! Insuper etiam famam abstinentiae in deliciis quaerimus. Fortissimum ieiunium est aqua et panis; sed quia gloriam non habet et omnes pane et aqua vivimus, quasi publicum et commune ieiunium non putatur.

13. Cave, ne hominum rumusculos aucuperis, ne offensam Dei populorum laude commutes. ' Si adhuc,' inquit apostolus, ' hominibus placerem, Christi servus non essem '[2]; desivit placere hominibus et servus factus est Christi. Per bonam et malam famam a dextris et a sinistris Christi miles graditur, nec laude extollitur, nec vituperatione frangitur, non divitiis tumet, non contrahitur paupertate, et laeta contemnit et tristia. Per diem sol non uret eum

---

[1] παχεῖα γαστὴρ λεπτὸν οὐ τίκτει νόον.
[2] Galatians, i. 10.

inflamed by hot blood, if I am of a strong and lusty habit of body, then I will readily forgo the wine cup, in which I may well suspect that poison lurks. The Greeks have a pretty proverb [1] which perhaps in our language loses some of its force: ' A fat paunch never breeds fine thoughts.'

Impose upon yourself such fasting as you are able to bear. Let your fasts be pure, chaste, simple, moderate, and free from superstition. What good is it to abstain from oil and then to seek after food that is troublesome to prepare and difficult to get, dried figs, pepper, nuts, dates, wheaten flour, honey, pistachios? All the resources of the garden are laid under contribution to avoid eating ordinary bread. I have heard that some people outrage nature, and neither drink water nor eat bread, but imbibe fancy decoctions of pounded herbs and beet juice, using a shell to drink from, in place of a cup. Shame on us! We do not blush at such silliness and we feel no disgust at such superstition. Moreover, by such fancifulness we seek a reputation for abstinence. The strictest fast is bread and water: but as that brings no glory with it and bread and water are our usual food, it is reckoned not a fast but an ordinary and common matter.

Beware of angling for compliments, lest you lose God's favour in exchange for the people's praise. ' If I yet pleased men,' says the apostle, ' I should not be the servant of Christ.' [2] He ceased to please men and became Christ's servant. Through good and bad report on right hand and on left Christ's soldier marches; he is not elated by praise nor crushed by abuse; he is not puffed up by riches nor depressed by poverty; he despises joy and sorrow alike. The

neque luna per noctem. Nolo te orare in angulis
platearum, ne rectum iter precum tuarum frangat
aura popularis; nolo te dilatare fimbrias et ostentui
habere φυλακτήρια et conscientia repugnante phari-
saeica ambitione circumdari. Melius est haec in
corde portare quam in corpore, Deum habere
fautorem, non aspectus hominum. Vis scire, quales
dominus quaerat ornatus? Habeto prudentiam,
iustitiam, temperantiam, fortitudinem. His plagis
caeli includere, haec te quadriga velut aurigam Christi
ad metam concitum ferat. Nihil hoc monili pre-
tiosius, nihil hac gemmarum varietate distinctius.
Ex omni parte decoraris, cingeris atque protegeris;
et ornamento tibi sunt et tutamini: gemmae
vertuntur in scuta.

14. Cave quoque, ne aut linguam aut aures habeas
prurientes, id est, ne aut ipse aliis detrahas aut alios
audias detrahentes. 'Sedens,' inquit, 'adversus
fratrem tuum loquebaris et adversus filium matris
tuae ponebas scandalum; haec fecisti et tacui.
Existimasti iniquitatem, quod ero tibi similis;
arguam te et statuam contra faciem tuam.' Subau-
ditur: 'Sermones tuos et cuncta, quae de aliis es
locutus, ut tua sententia iudiceris in his ipse depre-
hensus, quae in aliis arguebas.' Neque vero illa
iusta est excusatio: 'Referentibus aliis iniuriam
facere non possum.' Nemo invito auditori libenter
refert. Sagitta in lapide numquam figitur, interdum

---

[1] Psalm cxxi. 6.   [2] Matt. vi. 5 and xxiii. 5.
[3] Psalm l. 20.

sun will not burn him by day nor the moon by night.[1]
Do not pray at the corners of a square, lest the breeze
of popular favour interrupt the straight course of
your prayers. Do not broaden your fringes and wear
phylacteries for show, or wrap yourself in despite of
conscience in Pharisaic ostentation.[2] It is better to
carry all this in the heart, rather than on the body,
to have God's approval rather than to please the
eyes of men. Would you know what kind of ornaments the Lord requires? Have prudence, justice,
temperance, fortitude. Let these be your four
cardinal points, let them be your four-in-hand to
carry you, Christ's charioteer, at full speed to your
goal. No necklace can be more precious than
these, no jewels can make a brighter galaxy. On
every side they form a decoration, a girdle, a defence;
they are both an ornament and a protection; their
jewels are turned into shields.

Beware also of an itching tongue and ears: in
other words, do not detract from others or listen to
detractors. 'Thou sittest,' says the Scripture,
'and speakest against thy brother; thou slanderest
thine own mother's son. These things hast thou
done and I kept silence; thou thoughtest wickedly
that I was such an one as thyself, but I will reprove
thee, and set the matter before thine eyes.'[3] The
meaning of the passage is this—'Watch over your
talk and over every word you say about others;
by your own sentence you will be judged, and you
will yourself be caught committing the faults you
blamed in other men.' It is not a proper excuse to
say: 'If other people report something to me I
cannot be rude to them.' No one likes to bring
reports to an unwilling listener. An arrow never

resiliens percutit dirigentem. Discat detractor, dum te viderit non libenter audire, non facile detrahere. 'Cum detractoribus,' ait Salomon, 'ne miscearis, quoniam repente veniet perditio eorum, et ruinam utriusque quis novit?'[1] Tam videlicet eius, qui detrahit, quam illius, qui aurem accommodat detrahenti.

15. Officii tui est visitare languentes, nosse domos, matronas ac liberos earum et nobilium virorum non ignorare secreta. Officii ergo tui sit non solum oculos castos servare, sed et linguam. Numquam de formis mulierum disputes, nec alia domus, quid agatur in alia, per te noverit. Hippocrates adiurat discipulos, antequam doceat, et in verba sua iurare conpellit; extorquetque sacramento silentium; sermonem, incessum, habitum moresque describit:[2] quanto magis nos, quibus animarum medicina commissa est, omnium Christianorum domos debemus amare quasi proprias. Consolatores potius nos in maeroribus suis quam convivas in prosperis noverint. Facile contemnitur clericus, qui saepe vocatus ad prandium non recusat.

16. Numquam petentes raro accipiamus rogati. Nescio quo enim modo etiam ipse, qui deprecatur, ut tribuat, cum acceperis, viliorem te iudicat et mirum in modum, si rogantem contempseris, plus

---

[1] Proverbs, xxiv. 21. Vulgate.
[2] See *Hippocrates* (L.C.L. i. 291 ff.): 'To hold my teacher in this art equal to my own parents . . . I will keep pure and holy both my life and my art. . . . Whatsoever I shall see

lodges in a stone, but it sometimes recoils and wounds the shooter. Let detractors, seeing your reluctance to listen, learn not to be so ready to detract. Solomon says: 'Meddle not with them that are given to detraction: for their calamity shall rise suddenly; and who knoweth the destruction of them both?'[1]— the destruction, that is, both of the detractor and of the person who lends ear to him.

It is part of your duty to visit the sick, to be acquainted with people's households, with matrons, and with their children, and to be entrusted with the secrets of the great. Let it therefore be your duty to keep your tongue chaste as well as your eyes. Never discuss a woman's looks, nor let one house know what is going on in another. Hippocrates,[2] before he will instruct his pupils, makes them take an oath and compels them to swear obedience to him. That oath exacts from them silence, and prescribes for them their language, gait, dress, and manners. How much greater an obligation is laid on us who have been entrusted with the healing of souls! We ought to love every Christian household as though it were our own. Let them know us as comforters in their sorrows rather than as guests in their days of prosperity. A clergyman soon becomes an object of contempt, if, however often he is invited to dinner, he does not refuse.

We should never ask for gifts, and seldom accept them even when begged to do so. Somehow or other the very man who entreats leave to offer you a present holds you the cheaper for accepting it; if you refuse, it is strange how much more admiration

and hear in the course of my profession . . . I will never divulge' (p. 299).

miratur. Praedicator continentiae, nuptias ne con-
ciliet. Qui apostolum legit: ' Superest, ut et qui
habent uxores, sic sint, quasi non habentes,' cur
virginem cogit, ut nubat? Qui de monogamia
sacerdos est, quare viduam hortatur, ut δίγαμος sit?
Procuratores et dispensatores domorum alienarum
atque villarum quomodo esse possunt, qui proprias
iubentur contemnere facultates? Amico quippiam
rapere furtum est, ecclesiam fraudare sacrilegium
est. Accepisse pauperibus erogandum et esurienti-
bus plurimis vel cautum esse vel timidum aut—quod
apertissimi sceleris est—aliquid inde subtrahere
omnium praedonum crudelitatem superat. Ego
fame torqueor et tu iudicas, quantum ventri meo
satis sit? Aut divide statim, quod acceperis, aut, si
timidus dispensator es, dimitte largitorem, ut sua
ipse distribuat. Nolo sub occasione mea sacculus
tuus plenus sit. Nemo me melius mea servare
potest. Optimus dispensator est, qui sibi nihil
reservat.

17. Coegisti me, Nepotiane carissime, lapidato iam
virginitatis libello, quem sanctae Eustochiae Romae
scripseram, post annos decem rursus Bethleem ora
reserare et confodiendum me linguis omnium prodere.
Aut enim nihil scribendum fuit, ne hominum iudicium
subiremus, quod tu facere prohibuisti, aut scribentes
nosse cunctorum adversum nos maledicorum tela
torquenda. Quos obsecro, quiescant et desinant
maledicere; non enim ut adversarii, sed ut amici

---

[1] 1 Corinthians, vii. 29.
[2] A ' bigamist ' in the early Church was one who remarried.
[3] Cf. Letter XXII.

for you he feels. The preacher of continence must not try to arrange marriages. The apostle says: ' It remaineth that they who have wives be as though they had none.'[1] Why then should a man who reads those words force a virgin into marriage? A priest is a monogamist: why should he urge a widow to be a bigamist?[2] How can clergymen be agents and stewards of other men's households in town or country, when they are bidden to disregard even their own interests? To rob a friend is theft, but to defraud the Church is sacrilege. When you have received money to be spent on the poor, to be cautious and timid with it while crowds are hungry, or—what is most manifest villainy—to take any of it for yourself, is to surpass the cruelty of the worst robber. While I am racked with hunger, are you to judge how much will satisfy my cravings? Either distribute immediately what you have received, or, if you are a timid almoner, dismiss the donor to hand out his own gifts. I do not wish your purse to be full by taking advantage of me. No one can look after what is mine better than I can. The best almoner is he who keeps back nothing for himself.

The treatise on virginity which I wrote at Rome to the saintly Eustochium[3] was greeted with showers of stones, and you, my dearest Nepotian, have compelled me now ten years later to open my mouth again at Bethlehem, and to expose myself to the stabs of every tongue. If I were to escape criticism either I had to refrain from writing altogether—which you rendered impossible—or if I wrote I knew that all the shafts of calumny would be hurled against me. I beg my opponents now to hold their peace and cease from abuse. I have written not as an adversary

scripsimus, nec invecti sumus in eos, qui peccant,
sed, ne peccent, monuimus.   Neque in illos tantum,
sed et in nos ipsos severi iudices fuimus volentesque
festucam de oculo alterius tollere nostram prius
trabem eiecimus.   Nullum laesi, nullus saltim
descriptione signatus est, neminem specialiter meus
sermo pulsavit: generalis de vitiis disputatio est.
Qui mihi irasci voluerit, prius ipse de se, quod talis
sit, confitetur.

LIV

AD FURIAM DE VIDUITATE SERVANDA

1. OBSECRAS litteris et suppliciter deprecaris, ut
tibi scribam, immo rescribam,[1] quomodo vivere
debeas et viduitatis coronam inlaeso pudicitiae
nomine conservare. Gaudet animus, exultant viscera,
gestit affectus hoc te cupere esse post virum, quod
sanctae memoriae mater tua Titiana multo fuit
tempore sub marito. Exauditae sunt preces et
orationes eius. Inpetravit in unica filia, quod vivens
ipsa possederat. Habes praeterea generis tui grande
privilegium, quod exinde a Camillo vel nulla vel rara
vestrae familiae scribitur secundos nosse concubitus,
ut non tam laudanda sis, si vidua perseveres, quam

---

[1] rescribam, immo scribam: *Hilberg.*

---

[1] Furia was one of the many rich and noble ladies who
gathered round Jerome while he was living in Rome. After
her first husband's death she had thought of a second
marriage, but abandoned the idea and devoted herself to the
care of her young children and aged father. In this letter,
written A.D. 394, Jerome lays down rules for her conduct in
widowhood, and commends her to the care of the presbyter
Exuperius, who afterwards became Bishop of Toulouse. Cf.
p. 436, note 3.

but as a friend. I have not inveighed against sinners, I have only counselled men not to sin. I have judged myself as strictly as I judge them, and have cast out the beam from my own eye before I tried to remove a mote from my neighbour's. I have hurt no one; at least no one has been marked out for special mention, and my discourse has not attacked individuals but has been a general criticism of weaknesses. If any one insists on being angry with me, he confesses thereby that in his case the cap fits.

LETTER LIV

To Furia [1] on the duty of remaining a widow

Written A.D. 394

In your letter you beg and beseech me to write—or rather to write by return—and tell you how you ought to live, keeping the crown of widowhood in unsullied chastity. My heart rejoices, my bowels exult, my every fibre thrills to know that you desire to be after marriage what your mother Titiana of saintly memory was for many a year in marriage. Her prayers and entreaties have been heard. In her only daughter she has been granted that which she herself possessed in her lifetime. Moreover, it is the peculiar glory of your family that from the days of Camillus [2] few or none of your women are recorded as having known a second husband's bed. Therefore you will not be so much deserving of praise if you persist in widowhood, as you would be worthy of

[2] Furius Camillus, *fl.* 400 B.C.

execranda, si id Christiana non serves, quod per tanta saecula gentiles feminae custodierunt.

2. Taceo de Paula et Eustochio, stirpis vestrae floribus, ne per occasionem exhortationis tuae illas laudare videar, Blesillamque praetereo, quae maritum suum, tuum secuta germanum, in brevi vitae spatio tempora virtutum multa complevit. Atque utinam praeconia feminarum imitarentur viri et rugosa senectus redderet, quod sponte offert adulescentia! Sciens et videns in flammam mitto manum: adducentur supercilia, extendetur brachium 'iratusque Chremes tumido desaeviet ore.' Consurgunt proceres et adversum epistolam meam turba patricia detonabit me magum, me seductorem clamitans in terras ultimas asportandum. Addant, si volunt, et Samariten, ut domini mei titulum recognoscam. Certe filiam a parente non divido nec dico illud de evangelio: 'Sine mortui sepeliant mortuos suos.' Vivit enim, qui credit in Christo, et, qui in illum credit, debet utique, 'quomodo ille ambulavit, et ipse ambulare.'

3. Facessat invidia, quam nomine Christiano malidicorum semper genuinus infigit, ut, dum probra metuunt, ad virtutes non provocent. Exceptis epistulis ignoramus alterutrum, solaque causa pietatis est, ubi carnis nulla notitia est. 'Honora patrem tuum,' sed, si te a vero patre non separat. Tam diu

---

[1] Cf. table on p. 482.

[2] Horace, *Ars Poetica*, 94; the Chremes of Terence, *Heauton Timoroumenos*, Act 5, is angry with his son because of a degrading love affair.

[3] St. John, viii. 48.

[4] St. Matthew, viii. 22.

[5] 1 John, ii. 6.

[6] Exodus, xx. 12.

execration if you, a Christian, failed to keep a custom
which heathen women observed for so many
generations.

I say nothing of Paula and Eustochium, those fair
flowers of your stock, lest I should use the opportunity
of exhorting you to praise them. I pass over
Blesilla also, who following your brother her husband
to the grave fulfilled in her life's brief span many
years of virtue.[1] I only wish that men would follow
the example that women have publicly given them,
and that wrinkled age would render that which youth
offers of its own free will. I am thrusting my hand
into the fire knowingly and with my eyes open.
Brows will be knitted, fists shaken against me and
' with swelling voice will angry Chremes rage.'[2]
Our great men rise from their chairs, and in
answer to this letter of mine the patrician mob will
thunder out: ' Magician, seducer; transport him to
the ends of the earth.' If they like, they may call
me ' Samaritan ' as well; for then I shall recognize a
name that was given to my Lord.[3] Assuredly I do
not separate the daughter from her mother nor do I
use the words of the Gospel: ' Let the dead bury
their dead.'[4] For he is alive who believes in Christ,
and he who believes in Him ought in any case
' himself also so to walk even as He walked.'[5]

A truce to the envious attack which the tooth of
calumny is always making upon the name of Christian,
hoping to dissuade men from virtue by fear of abuse.
Except by letter we know nothing of one another,
and where there is no knowledge in the flesh the only
motive for friendship is one of piety. ' Honour thy
father,'[6] but only if he does not separate you from
your true Father. Acknowledge the tie of blood,

scito sanguinis copulam, quam diu ille suum noverit creatorem: alioquin David tibi protinus canet: ' Audi, filia, et vide et inclina aurem tuam et obliviscere populum tuum et domum patris tui; et concupiscet res decorem tuum, quia ipse est dominus Deus tuus.' Grande praemium parentis obliti: ' Concupiscet rex decorem tuum.' Quia audisti, quia vidisti, quia inclinasti aurem tuam et populi tui domusque patris oblita es, idcirco ' concupiscet rex decorem tuum ' et dicet tibi: ' Tota pulchra es, proxima mea, et macula non est in te.' Quid pulchrius anima, quae Dei filia nuncupatur et nullos extrinsecus quaerit ornatus? Credit in Christum et hac ambitione ditata pergit ad sponsum eundem habens dominum, quem et virum.

4. Quid angustiarum habeant nuptiae, didicisti in ipsis nuptiis et quasi coturnicum carnibus usque ad nausiam saturata es. Amarissimam choleram tuae sensere fauces, egessisti acescentes et morbidos cibos, relevasti aestuantem stomachum: quid vis rursus ingerere, quod tibi noxium fuit? ' Canis revertens ad vomitum suum et sus ad volutabrum luti.' Bruta quoque animalia et vagae aves in easdem pedicas retiaque non incidunt. An vereris, ne proles Furiana deficiat et ex te parens tuus non habeat pusionem, qui reptet in pectore et cervices eius stercore linat? Quippini? Omnes habent filios, quae habuere matrimonia, et, quibus nati sunt liberi, suo generi responderunt! Exhibuit Ciceronis filius patrem in eloquentia? Cornelia vestra, pudici-

---

[1] Psalm xlv. 10. [2] Song of Solomon, iv. 7.
[3] Numbers, xi. 31 ff. [4] 2 Peter, ii. 22.
[5] Fremantle thinks this refers to the connection between Furia and Paula's family, who traced their descent from the Gracchi, cf section 13, p. 253, where Eustochium is referred to as Furia's sister.

but only so long as he recognizes his Creator. Otherwise David at once will sing to you: ' Hearken, O daughter, and consider, and incline thine ear; forget also thine own people and thy father's house. So shall the king greatly desire thy beauty for he is thy Lord.' [1] Great is the reward for forgetting a parent: ' the king shall desire thy beauty.' Because you have heard, considered, inclined your ear, and forgotten your people and your father's house, ' the king will desire your beauty ' and will say to you: ' Thou art all fair, my love; there is no spot in thee.' [2] What can be fairer than a soul which is called daughter of God and seeks no outward adorning? She believes in Christ and enriched by this ambition she goes to her Spouse, having her Lord for Bridegroom.

The trials of marriage you have learned in the married state: you have been surfeited to nausea as though with the flesh of quails.[3] Your mouth has tasted the bitterest of gall, you have voided the sour unwholesome food, you have relieved a heaving stomach. Why would you put into it again something which has already proved harmful to you? ' The dog is turned to his own vomit again and the sow that was washed to her wallowing in the mire.' [4] Even brute beasts and roving birds do not fall into the same snares or nets twice. Are you afraid that the line of Camillus will cease to exist and that your father will not have a brat of yours to crawl upon his breast and soil his neck with nastiness? Well, do all those who marry have children, and when children are born do they always answer to their family's fame? Did Cicero's son show his father's eloquence? Had your own Cornelia,[5] pattern

tiae simul et fecunditatis exemplar, Gracchos suos se
genuisse laetata est? Ridiculum sperare pro certo,
quod multos et non habere videas et, cum habuerint,
perdidisse. Cui dimittis tantas divitias? Christo,
qui mori non potest. Quem habebis heredem?
Ipsum, quem et dominum. Contristabitur pater,
sed laetabitur Christus; lugebit familia, sed angeli
gratulabuntur. Faciat pater, quod vult, de substantia
sua: non es eius, cui nata es, sed cui renata, et qui
te grandi pretio redemit, sanguine suo.

5. Cave nutrices et gerulas et istius modi vinosa
animalia, quae de corio tuo saturare ventrem suum
cupiunt. Non suadent, quod tibi, sed, quod sibi
prosit, et saepe illud obganniunt:

> ' Solane perpetua maerens carpere iuventa
> Nec dulces natos Veneris nec praemia noris? '

Ubi pudicitia et sanctitas, ibi frugalitas est; ubi
frugalitas, ibi damna servorum. Quidquid non
tulerint, sibi ablatum putant, nec considerant, de
quanto, sed quantum accipiant; ubicumque viderint
Christianum, statim illud e trivio: ὁ Γραικός, ὁ ἐπιθέ-
της. Hi rumores turpissimos serunt et, quod ab ipsis
egressum est, ab aliis audisse se simulant, idem
auctores et exaggeratores. Exin fama de mendacio,
quae, cum ad matrones pervenerit et earum linguis

---

[1] Virgil, *Aeneid*, IV. 32.

alike of chastity and fruitfulness, cause to rejoice in being mother of the Gracchi? It is absurd to expect as certain the children, which you see many fail to obtain, and many lose after they have got them. To whom are you going to leave your great wealth? To Christ who cannot die. Whom shall you make your heir? The same who is already your Lord. Your father will look sad, but Christ will rejoice: your family will grieve, but the angels will give you their congratulations. Your father may do what he likes with his own estates: you are not his to whom you have been born, but His to whom you have been born again, and who has ransomed you at a great price, even with His own blood.

Beware of foster-mothers and nurses and other drunken creatures of their kind, who desire to fill their bellies at the expense of your skin. They advise you for their own benefit, not yours, continually dinning the poet's lines into your ears:

' And will you ever waste your youth in grief,
    Nor children know and the sweet gifts of love? '[1]

Where there is holiness and chastity, there also is frugality. And where there is frugality, there is the servants' loss. What they do not get they think is taken from them, and they consider only their wages, not your income. Whenever they see a Christian they at once raise the street-cry—' The Greek! The impostor!' They spread abroad the foulest scandals, pretending they have heard from others what really emanates from themselves and exaggerating the stories which they originate. Their lies give rise to talk which soon reaches our matrons' ears, and fanned by their tongues spreads

fuerit ventilata, provincias penetrat. Videas plerasque rabido ore saevire et tincta facie, viperinis
orbibus, dentibus pumicatis carpere Christianos.
Hic aliqua,

> ' Cui circa humeros hyacinthina laena est,
> Rancidulum quiddam balba de nare locuta
> Perstrepit ac tenero supplantat verba palato.'

Omnis consonat chorus et latrant universa subsellia.
Iunguntur nostri ordinis, qui et roduntur et rodunt
adversum nos loquaces, pro se muti; quasi et ipsi
aliud sint quam monachi, et non, quidquid in monachos dicitur, redundet in clericos, qui patres sunt
monachorum.   Detrimentum pecoris pastoris ignominia est, sicut e regione illius monachi vita laudatur,
qui venerationi habet sacerdotes Christi et non
detrahit gradui, per quem factus est Christianus.

6. Haec locutus sum, in Christo filia, non dubitans
de proposito tuo—numquam enim exhortatorias
litteras postulares, si ambigeres de bono mono-
gamiae—sed ut nequitiam servulorum, qui te venalem
portant, et insidias adfinium ac pium parentis errorem
intellegeres, cui, ut amorem in te tribuam, amoris
scientiam non concedo dicens aliquid cum apostolo:
' Confiteor, zelum Dei habent, sed non secundum

---

[1] Persius, I. 32.

through every province. You may see many such
ladies with painted faces, their eyes like those of
vipers and their teeth rubbed with pumice stone,
who when they are girding at Christians actually
foam at the mouth with mad rage. One of them,

> ' A violet mantle round her shoulders thrown,
>   Drawls out some mawkish stuff, speaks through
>   her nose,
>   And minces half her words with tripping tongue.' [1]

At that the rest of the band chime in, and the
whole company falls a-snarling. They are backed
up by men of my own order, who being themselves
a mark for scandal spread scandal about others;
they are fluent enough in attacking me, but in their
own defence they are dumb. As though, forsooth,
they were not monks themselves, and as though
all that is said against monks does not reflect on the
clergy who are their spiritual fathers! To hurt the
flock is to shame the shepherd. On the other hand,
we must praise the life of a monk who holds Christ's
priests in veneration, and does not carp at the order
by whose offices he became a Christian.

I have said all this, my daughter in Christ, not
because I doubt your steadfastness in your vows,
for you would never have requested a letter of
advice if you had been uncertain that monogamy
was a good thing, but that you may understand the
rascality of servants who hold you as something to
be sold, the snares laid for you by relatives, and
your father's mistaken kindness. I allow that your
father loves you, but I do not admit that his love
is according to knowledge, and I say with the apostle:
' I confess that they have a zeal of God, but not

scientiam.' Imitare potius—crebro enim id repetam
—sanctam matrem tuam, cuius ego quotiens recordor,
venit in mentem ardor eius in Christum, pallor ex
ieiuniis, elemosyna in pauperes, obsequium in
servos Dei, humilitas et cordis et vestium atque in
cunctis sermo moderatus. Pater tuus, quem ego
honoris causa nomino—non quia consularis et
patricius, sed quia Christianus est—inpleat nomen
suum et laetetur filiam Christo se genuisse, non
saeculo; quin potius doleat, quod et virginitatem
frustra amiseris et fructus perdideris nuptiarum.
Ubi est maritus, quem tibi dedit? Etiamsi amabilis,
etiamsi bonus fuisset, mors finisset omnia et copulam
carnis solvisset interitus. Arripe, quaeso, occasionem
et fac de necessitate virtutem. Non quaeruntur in
Christianis initia, sed finis: Paulus male coepit, sed
bene finivit; Iudae laudantur exordia, sed finis
proditione damnatur. Lege Ezechiel: 'Iustitia
iusti non liberabit eum, in quacumque die peccaverit,
et inpietas inpii non nocebit ei, in quacumque die
conversus fuerit ab inpietate sua.' Ista est scala
Iacob, per quam angeli conscendunt et descendunt,
cui dominus innititur lapsis[1] porrigens manum et
fessos ascendentium gressus sui contemplatione
sustentans. Sed, sicut non vult mortem peccatoris,

---

[1] lassis: *Hilberg*.

---

[1] Romans, x. 2.   [2] Ezekiel, xxxiii. 12.

according to knowledge!'[1] Take rather for model
—I cannot repeat it too often—your saintly
mother; whose ardent love for Christ comes into
my mind whenever I remember her, and with it
the pallor caused by fasting, the alms she gave to
the poor, the respect she showed to God's servants,
the humility of her heart and dress, and the constant
restraint she put upon her tongue. As for your
father—I speak of him with all respect, not because
he is a patrician and of consular rank, but because
he is a Christian—let him fulfil his Christian obligations and rejoice that he has begotten a daughter
for Christ and not for the world. Nay, rather let
him grieve that you have lost your virginity in vain,
and have failed to reap any of the fruits of marriage.
Where now is the husband whom he gave you?
Even if he had been lovable and good, death would
have ended everything and this decease would have
broken the fleshly bond. Seize the opportunity,
I beg, and make a virtue of necessity. In the case
of Christians, we look not to their beginnings but
to their end. Paul began badly but ended well.
Judas is praised in his early days; his end is condemned by reason of his treachery. Read Ezekiel:
' The righteousness of the righteous shall not deliver
him in the day of his transgression; as for the wickedness of the wicked, he shall not fall thereby in the
day that he turneth from his wickedness.'[2] Ours
is that Jacob's ladder, on which the angels go up
and down, while the Lord leans over holding out
His hand to those who slip and sustaining by the
vision of Himself the weary steps of those who
ascend. But even as He wishes not the death of
a sinner, but only that he should turn again and

tantum ut revertatur et vivat, ita tepidos odit et cito ei nausiam faciunt. Cui plus dimittitur, plus diligit.

7. Meretrix illa in evangelio baptizata lacrimis suis et crine, quo multos ante deceperat, pedes domini tergente servata est. Non habuit crispantes mitras nec stridentes calceolos nec orbes stibio fuliginatos, quanto foedior, tanto pulchrior. Quid facit in facie Christianae purpurissus et cerussa? Quorum alterum ruborem genarum labiorumque mentitur, alterum candorem oris et colli: ignes iuvenum, fomenta libidinum, inpudicae mentis indicia. Quomodo flere potest pro peccatis suis, quae lacrimis cutem nudat et sulcos ducit in facie? Ornatus iste non domini est, velamen istud antichristi est. Qua fiducia erigit ad caelum vultus, quos conditor non agnoscat? Frustra obtenditur adulescentia et aetas puellaris adseritur: vidua, quae marito placere desivit et iuxta apostolum vere vidua est, nihil habet necessarium nisi perseverantiam. Meminit pristinae voluptatis, scit, quid amiserit, quo delectata sit: ardentes diaboli sagittae ieiuniorum et vigiliarum frigore restinguendae sunt. Aut loquendum nobis est, ut vestiti sumus, aut vestiendum, ut loquimur. Quid aliud pollicemur et aliud ostendimus? Lingua personat castitatem et totum corpus praefert inpudicitiam.

8. Hoc quantum ad habitum pertinet et ornatum. Ceterum vidua, ' quae in deliciis est '—non est meum, sed apostoli—' vivens mortua est.' Quid sibi vult

---

[1] 1 Timothy, v. 5.   [2] 1 Timothy, v. 6.

live, so He hates the lukewarm and they inspire
loathing. To whom more is forgiven, the same
loveth more.

The harlot in the Gospel found salvation, baptized
in her own tears and wiping the Lord's feet with
the hair which had before lured many a lover. She
wore no waving head-dress, no creaking shoes, nor
did she darken her eyes with antimony: the more
squalid she was, the more lovely she seemed. What
have rouge and white lead to do on a Christian
woman's face? The one simulates the natural red
of cheeks and lips, the other the whiteness of the
face and neck. They are fires to inflame young
men, stimulants of lustful desire, plain evidence of
an unchaste mind. How can a woman weep for
her sins when tears lay her skin bare and make
furrows on her face? Such adorning is not of the
Lord, it is the mask of Antichrist. With what
confidence can a woman lift to heaven features
which her Creator cannot recognize? It is in vain
to make youth an excuse for all this, or to put in the
plea of girlish folly. A widow who has no husband
to please, and in the apostle's words is a widow in
deed, needs nothing but perseverance.[1] She still
remembers the pleasures of the past, she knows the
delights that she has lost, and she must quench the
fire of the devil's shafts with the cold streams of
fast and vigil. Either we must speak as we dress,
or dress as we speak. Why do we profess one thing
and display another? The tongue talks of chastity,
but the whole body reveals incontinence.

So much for dress and adornment. But a widow
' that liveth in pleasure '—the words are not mine,
but the apostle's—' is dead while she liveth.'[2] What

241

hoc, quod ait: ' vivens mortua est'? Vivere
quidem videtur ignorantibus et non esse peccato
mortua, sed Christo, quem secreta non fallunt,
mortua est. ' Anima,' enim, ' quae peccaverit, ipsa
morietur.'[1] ' Quorundam hominum peccata manifesta
sunt praecedentia ad iudicium, quosdam autem et
subsequuntur. Similiter et facta bona manifesta
sunt, et quae aliter se habent, abscondi non possunt.'[2]
Quod dicit, istius modi est: quidam tam libere et
palam peccant, ut, postquam eos videris, statim
intellegas peccatores; alios autem, qui callide
occultant vitia sua, ex sequenti conversatione
cognoscimus. Similiter et bona apud alios in propatulo sunt, in aliis longo usu discimus. Quid ergo
necesse est nos iactare pudicitiam, quae sine comiti-
bus et adpendiculis suis, continentia et parcitate,
fidem sui facere non potest? Apostolus macerat
corpus suum et animae subicit imperio, ne, quod aliis
praecipit, ipse non servet: et adulescentula fervente
cibis corpore de castitate secura est?

9. Neque vero haec dicens condemno cibos, ' quos
Deus creavit ad utendum cum gratiarum actione,'[3]
sed iuvenibus et puellis incentiva esse adsero voluptatum. Non Aetnaei ignes, non Vulcania tellus,
non Vesevus et Olympus tantis ardoribus aestuant,
ut iuveniles medullae vino plenae, dapibus inflam-
matae. Avaritia calcatur a plerisque et cum marsuppio deponitur; maledicam linguam indictum
emendat silentium; cultus corporis et habitus

---

[1] Ezekiel, xviii. 20.
[2] 1 Timothy, v. 24.
[3] 1 Timothy, iv. 4.

does it mean, 'is dead while she liveth'? Why, to those who know not the truth she seems to be alive and not to be dead in sin, but to Christ from whom no secrets are hid she is a dead woman. 'For the soul that sinneth, it shall die.' [1] 'Some men's sins are manifest, going before unto judgment, and some men also they follow after. Likewise also good works are manifest, and they that are otherwise cannot be hid.' [2] The words mean this—some men sin with such lack of restraint and concealment that you know them at first sight to be sinners. But there are others who cunningly conceal their vices, and we only learn of them by subsequent intercourse. In the same way the good deeds of some men are openly displayed, in the case of others we only become acquainted with them after long intimacy. Why then must we make a boast of chastity, which cannot be regarded as genuine unless it is supported by its two handmaids and assistants, continence and frugality? The apostle macerates his body and subjects it to the soul's control, lest he himself should fail to keep the precept he has given to others. How then can a young girl be confident of her chastity if her body is all on fire with rich food?

In saying this I do not condemn food 'which God created to be enjoyed with thanksgiving,' [3] but I assert that for young men and girls some food is an incentive to sensuality. Neither Etna's fire, nor Vulcan's isle, nor Vesuvius and Olympus, seethe with such burning heat as does the youthful marrow when it is flushed with wine and inflamed by feasting. Many men trample avarice underfoot and lay it down as easily as their purses. An enforced silence serves as corrective to a slanderous tongue. One

vestium unius horae spatio commutatur; omnia alia
peccata extrinsecus sunt, et, quod a foris est, facile
abicitur: sola libido insita a Deo ob liberorum
creationem, si fines suos egressa fuerit, redundat in
vitium et quadam lege naturae in coitum gestit
erumpere. Grandis ergo virtutis est et sollicitae
diligentiae superare, quod natus sis in carne, non
carnaliter vivere, tecum pugnare cottidie et inclusum
hostem Argi, ut fabulae ferunt, centum oculis
observare. Hoc est, quod apostolus verbis aliis
loquebatur: 'Omne peccatum, quod fecerit homo,
extra corpus est; qui autem fornicatur, in corpus
suum peccat.' Aiunt medici et qui de humanorum
corporum scripsere naturis praecipueque Galenus in
libris, quorum titulus est περὶ ὑγιεινῶν, puerorum
et iuvenum ac perfectae aetatis virorum mulierumque
corpora insito calore fervere et noxios esse his
aetatibus cibos, qui calorem augeant, sanitatique
conducere frigida quaeque in esu et potu sumere,
sicut e contrario senibus, qui pituita laborent et frigore, calidos cibos et vetera vina prodesse. Unde
et salvator: 'Adtendite,' inquit, 'vobis, ne forte
adgraventur corda vestra in crapula et ebrietate
et curis huius vitae.' Et apostolus: 'Vino, in quo
est luxuria.' Nec mirum hoc figulum sensisse de
vasculo, quod ipse fabricatus est, cum etiam comicus

---

[1] Corinthians, vi. 18.   [2] St. Luke, xxi. 34.
[3] Ephesians, v. 18.

single hour can change a man's fashion of dress and outward appearance. All other sins are outside ourselves, and what is external can easily be cast away. Carnal desire alone, implanted in men by God for the procreation of children, if it oversteps its due limits, becomes a sin, and by a law of nature burns to force its way to carnal intercourse. It is a task for pre-eminent virtue and the most watchful care, seeing that you were born in the flesh, not to live the life of the flesh. You must fight against yourself every day and keep guard against the enemy within you with the hundred eyes of the fabled Argus. This is what the apostle said in other words: 'Every sin that a man doeth is without the body; but he that committeth fornication sinneth against his own body.'[1] Physicians and those who have written on the nature of the human frame, especially Galen in his treatise *On Health*, say that the bodies of young men and of full-grown men and women glow with an innate warmth, and that for persons of these ages all food is harmful which tends to increase that heat, while it is conducive to health for them to eat and drink anything that is cold. On the other hand they say that for old people who suffer from humours and from chilliness, warm food and old wine are beneficial. Hence the Saviour says: 'Take heed to yourselves lest at any time your hearts be overcharged with surfeiting and drunkenness, and cares of this life.'[2] So too the apostle: 'Be not drunk with wine, wherein is excess.'[3] No wonder that the potter felt thus about the frail vessel which He had made,[4] seeing

[4] Romans, ix. 21. 'Hath not the potter power over the clay, of the same lump to make one vessel unto honour, and another unto dishonour?'

cuius finis est humanos mores nosse atque describere, dixit: ' Sine Cerere et Libero friget Venus.'

10. Primum igitur, si tamen stomachi firmitas patitur, donec puellares annos transeas, aquam in potum sume, quae natura frigidissima est, aut, si hoc inbecillitas prohibet, audi cum Timotheo : ' Vino modico utere propter stomachum et frequentes tuas infirmitates.' Deinde in ipsis cibis calida quaeque devita; non solum de carnibus loquor, super quibus vas electionis profert sententiam : ' Bonum est vinum non bibere et carnem non manducare,' sed etiam in ipsis leguminibus inflantia quaeque et gravia declinanda sunt—nihilque ita scias conducere Christianis adulescentibus ut esum holerum, unde et in alio loco : ' Qui infirmus est,' ait, ' holera manducet '—ardorque corporum frigidioribus epulis temperandus est. Si autem tres pueri et Daniel leguminibus vescebantur, pueri erant, necdum ad sartiginem venerant in qua rex Babylonius senes iudices frixit. Nobis non corporum cultus, qui in illis—excepto privilegio gratiae Dei—ex huiusce modi cibis enituerat, sed animae vigor quaeritur, quae carnis infirmitate fit fortior. Inde est, quod nonnulli vitam pudicam adpetentium in medio itinere corruunt, dum solam abstinentiam carnium putant et leguminibus onerant stomachum, quae moderate parceque sumpta innoxia sunt. Et ut, quod sentio, loquar,

---

[1] Terence, *Eunuchus*, 732.
[2] 1 Timothy, v. 23.
[3] Romans, xiv. 21.
[4] Romans, xiv. 2.
[5] Daniel, i. 8.
[6] There is a tradition that the elders who tempted Susannah were thus burned.

that even the comic dramatist, whose aim is to know and to describe the ways of men, says :—

> ' Venus grows cold if Ceres be not there
> And Bacchus with her.' [1]

In the first place then, if your stomach is strong enough, until you pass out of girlhood drink only water, by nature the coolest of all beverages. If your health renders this impossible, listen to the advice given to Timothy : ' Use a little wine for thy stomach's sake and thine often infirmities.' [2] Secondly, in the way of food avoid all heating dishes. I do not speak of meat only—although on it the chosen vessel delivers this judgment : ' It is good neither to eat flesh nor to drink wine ' [3]—but with vegetables also anything that creates wind or lies heavy on the stomach should be rejected. You should know that nothing is so good for young Christians as a diet of herbs. So in another place Paul says : ' Let him who is weak eat herbs.' [4] By cold food the heat of the body should be tempered. Though Daniel and the three children lived on vegetables,[5] they were only children and had not reached that frying pan in which the king of Babylon cooked the elders who were judges.[6] We do not seek for the physical strength which by a special privilege of God's grace they gained from this diet; we aim rather at vigour of soul, which becomes stronger as the flesh grows weaker. This is the reason why some of those who aspire to a life of chastity fall midway on the road. They think that they need merely abstain from meat, and they load their stomach with vegetables which are only harmless when taken sparingly and in moderation. To give you my real opinion, I

nihil sic inflammat corpora et titillat membra genitalia nisi indigestus cibus ructusque convulsus. Malo apud te, filia, verecundia parumper quam causa periclitari. Quidquid seminarium voluptatum est, venenum puta. Parcus cibus et semper venter esuriens triduanis ieiuniis praeferatur, et multo melius est cottidie parum quam raro satis sumere. Pluvia illa optima est, quae sensim descendit in terras; subitus et nimius imber praeceps arva subvertit.

11. Quando comedis, cogita, quod statim tibi orandum, ilico legendum sit. De scripturis sanctis habeto fixum versuum numerum; istud pensum domino tuo redde nec ante quieti membra concedas, quam calathum pectoris tui hoc subtegmine impleveris. Post scripturas sanctas doctorum hominum tractatus lege, eorum dumtaxat, quorum fides nota est. Non necesse habes aurum in luto quaerere : multis margaritis unam redime margaritam. Sta iuxta Hieremiam in viis pluribus, ut ad illam viam, quae ad patrem ducit, pervenias. Amorem monilium atque gemmarum sericarumque vestium transfer ad scientiam scripturarum. Ingredere terram repromissionis lacte et melle manantem, comede similam et oleum, vestire cum Ioseph variis indumentis, perforentur aures tuae cum Hierusalem sermone Dei, ut pretiosa ex illis novarum segetum grana dependeant. Habes sanctum Exuperium probatae aetatis et fidei, qui te monitis suis frequenter instituat.

---

[1] *Pensum,* properly the weight of wool allotted to a servant to be made into yarn; the day's task.

[2] Cf. Jeremiah, vi. 16.

[3] Cf. Ezekiel, xvi. 12.   [4] Cf. p. 436, note 3.

think that nothing so inflames the body and titillates the organs of generation as undigested food, and convulsive belching. With you, my daughter, I would rather risk offending your modesty than understate my case. Regard as poison anything that has within it the seeds of sensual pleasure. A frugal diet which leaves you always hungry is to be preferred to a three days' fast, and it is much better to go short every day than occasionally to satisfy your appetite to the full. That rain is best which falls slowly to earth: a sudden and excessive shower which comes tumbling down washes away the soil.

When you are eating, remember that immediately afterwards you will have to pray and read. Take a fixed number of lines from the Holy Scripture and show them up as your task [1] to your Lord; and do not lie down to rest until you have filled your heart's basket with this precious yarn. After the Holy Scriptures, read the treatises that have been written by learned men, provided, of course, that they are persons of known faith. You need not seek for gold amid the mire: with many pearls buy the one pearl of price. As Jeremiah [2] says, stand in more ways than one, so that you may come to the way that leads to the Father. Change your love of necklaces and jewels and silk dresses to a desire for scriptural knowledge. Enter the land of promise that flows with milk and honey. Eat wheaten flour and oil, dress like Joseph in coats of many colours, let your ears, like Jerusalem's,[3] be pierced by the word of God, so that the precious grains of new corn may hang from them. You have in the saintly Exuperius [4] a man of tried years and faith, who can give you constant support with his advice.

12. Fac tibi amicos de iniquo mammona, qui te recipiant in aeterna tabernacula. Illis tribue divitias tuas, qui non Phasides aves, sed cibarium panem coemant, qui famem expellant, qui non augeant luxuriam. Intellege super egenum et pauperem. ' Omni petenti te da,' sed ' maxime domesticis fidei ' : nudum vesti, esurientem ciba, aegrotantem visita ; quotienscumque manum extendis, Christum cogita, cave ne mendicante domino tuo alienas divitias augeas.

13. Iuvenum fuge consortia. Comatulos, comptos atque lascivos domus tuae tecta non videant. Cantor pellatur ut noxius ; fidicinas et psaltrias et istius modi chorum diaboli quasi mortifera sirenarum carmina proturba ex aedibus tuis. Noli ad publicum subinde procedere et spadonum exercitu praeeunte viduarum circumferri libertate. Pessimae consuetudinis est, cum fragilis sexus et inbecilla aetas suo arbitrio abutitur et putat licere, quod libet. ' Omnia ' quidem ' licent, sed non omnia expediunt.' Nec procurator calamistratus nec formosus conlactaneus nec candidulus et rubicundus adsecula adhaereant lateri tuo : interdum animus dominarum ex ancillarum habitu iudicatur. Sanctarum virginum et viduarum societatem adpete, et si sermocinandi cum viris incumbit necessitas, arbitros ne devites tantaque confabulandi fiducia sit, ut intrante alio nec paveas nec erubescas. Speculum mentis est facies et taciti

---

¹ St. Luke, vi. 30, and Galatians, vi. 10.
² 1 Corinthians, vi. 12.

Make to yourself friends of the mammon of unrighteousness that they may receive you into everlasting habitations. Give your wealth to those who purchase not pheasants but coarse bread, staying their hunger, not stimulating wantonness. Consider the poor and needy. ' Give to everyone that asketh of thee,' but ' especially unto them that are of the household of faith ';[1] clothe the naked, feed the hungry, visit the sick ; every time you hold out your hand, think of Christ ; beware lest, when your Lord asks alms, you increase other people's riches.

Avoid the society of young men. Let your house never see beneath its roof wanton long-haired dandies. Repel a singer like the plague. Drive from your dwelling all women who live by playing and singing, the devil's choir whose songs are as deadly as those of the sirens. Do not constantly claim a widow's liberty and appear in the streets with a host of eunuchs walking before your chair. It is a very bad habit for weak young persons of the frailer sex to abuse their freedom from restraint, and to think that they are allowed to do anything they please. ' All things are lawful but all things are not expedient.'[2] Let no curled steward or handsome foster-brother or fair ruddy footman stand continually by your side. Sometimes the character of the mistress is inferred from the dress of her maids. Seek the company of holy virgins and widows, and if you are obliged to talk with men, do not refuse to have other people present. Let your conversation be so sure of itself that the entry of a third person will neither make you start nor blush. The face is the mirror of the mind, and eyes without

oculi cordis fatentur arcana. Vidimus nuper ignominiosum per totum orientem volitasse: et aetas et
cultus et habitus et incessus, indiscreta societas,
exquisitae epulae, regius apparatus Neronis et Sarda-
napalli nuptias loquebantur. Aliorum vulnus nostra
sit cautio; 'Pestilente flagellato stultus sapientior
erit.'

Sanctus amor inpatientiam non habet; falsus
rumor cito opprimitur et vita posterior iudicat de
priori. Fieri quidem non potest, ut absque morsu
hominum vitae huius curricula quis pertranseat,
malorumque solacium est bonos carpere, dum
peccantium multitudine putant culpam minui peccatorum; sed tamen cito ignis stipulae conquiescit et
exundans flamma deficientibus nutrimentis paulatim
emoritur. Si anno praeterito fama mentita est aut,
si certe verum dixit, cesset[1] vitium, cessabit et
rumor. Haec dico, non quo de te sinistrum quid
metuam, sed quo pietatis affectu etiam, quae tuta
sunt, pertimescam. O si videres sororem tuam et
illud sacri oris eloquium coram audire contingeret,
cerneres in parvo corpusculo ingentes animos, audires
totam veteris et novi testamenti supellectilem ex
illius corde fervere! Ieiunia pro ludo habet, orationem pro deliciis. Tenet tympanum in exemplum
Mariae et Pharaone submerso virginum choro
praecinit: 'Cantemus domino: gloriose enim magnificatus est, equum et ascensorem deiecit in mare.'

<hr>

[1] cesset, *Hilberg*: cessavit.

<hr>

[1] Proverbs, xix. 25. Vulgate.   [2] Cf. p. 232, note 5.
[3] Exodus, xv. 21.

speaking confess the secrets of the heart. I have lately seen a scandalous object flitting this way and that through the East. Her age, her style, her dress, her mien, the indiscriminate company she kept, and the regal pomp of her elaborate dinners, all proclaimed her a fitting bride for Nero or Sardanapallus. Let us take warning from another's wound: ' When he that causeth trouble is scourged the fool will be wiser.' [1]

A holy love is never impatient: a false rumour is quickly stifled, and the after life passes judgment on that which has gone before. It is not possible, indeed, that any one should reach the end of life's race without suffering from the tooth of calumny: it is a consolation for the wicked to gird at the good, and they think that a multitude of sinners lessens the guilt of sin. But, nevertheless, a fire of straw soon dies down, and a spreading flame gradually expires if it has nothing to feed on. If last year's rumour was a lie, or if, though it was true, the sin shall now cease, then the scandal will cease also. I say this, not that I fear anything wrong in your case, but because my fatherly love for you is so great that even safety makes me afraid. Oh, if you could see your sister,[2] and be allowed to listen to the eloquence of her holy lips, and behold the mighty spirit that dwells within her small body! Oh, if you could hear the whole contents of the Old and New Testament come bubbling from her heart! Fasting is her sport, prayer her favourite pastime. Like Miriam after the drowning of Pharaoh, she takes up her timbrel and leads the virgin choir: ' Let us sing to the Lord, for He hath triumphed gloriously; the horse and his rider He hath thrown into the sea.' [3] She

Has docet psaltrias Christo, has fidicinas erudit salvatori. Sic dies, sic nox ducitur et oleo ad lampadas praeparato sponsi expectatur adventus. Imitare ergo et tu consanguineam tuam: habeat Roma, quod angustior urbe Romana possidet Bethleem.

14. Habes opes, facile tibi est indigentibus victus subsidia ministrare. Quod luxuriae parabatur, virtus insumat; nulla nuptias contemptura timeat egestatem. Redime virgines, quas in cubiculum salvatoris inducas, suscipe viduas, quas inter virginum lilia et martyrum rosas quasi quasdam violas misceas; pro corona spinea, in qua mundi Christus delicta portavit, talia serta compone. Laetetur et adiuvet vir nobilissimus, pater tuus; discat a filia, quod didicerat ab uxore. Iam incanuit caput, tremunt genua, dentes cadunt et frontem obscenam rugis arat, vicina est mors in foribus, designatur rogus prope: velimus nolimus, senes sumus. Paret sibi viaticum, quos longo itinere necessarium est. Secum portet, quod invitus dimissurus est, immo praemittat in caelum, quod, ni caruerit, terra sumptura est.

15. Solent adulescentulae viduae, quarum nonnullae ' abierunt retro Satanam, cum luxuriatae fuerint in Christo,' subantes dicere: ' Patrimoniolum meum cottidie perit, maiorum hereditas dissipatur, servus contumeliose locutus est, imperium ancilla

---

[1] At this time many Romans were being taken captive by invading barbarians and held to ransom.

[2] 1 Timothy, v. 15, 11.

teaches her companions to be music-girls for Christ, and trains them as lute-players for the Saviour. Thus she passes her days and nights, and with oil ready in her lamp awaits the coming of the Bridegroom. Take pattern then by your kinswoman. Let Rome have what Bethlehem, a smaller place than Rome, already possesses.

You have money, and can easily supply food to those who want it. Let virtue take what was meant for extravagance: no woman who means to scorn marriage need fear poverty. Ransom [1] virgins and lead them into the Saviour's chamber. Support widows and mingle them like violets with the virgins' lilies and the martyrs' roses. These are the garlands you must make for Christ in place of the crown of thorns in which He bore the sins of the world. Let your noble father rejoice to help you; let him learn from his daughter as he once learned from his wife. His hair is grey, his knees shake, his teeth are falling out, his forehead is disfigured by wrinkles, death stands near at his door, and the pyre is being marked out for him close by. Whether we like it or not, we are old men now. Let him provide for himself the provision he needs for his long journey. Let him take with him that which otherwise he must reluctantly leave behind; nay, let him send before him to heaven what, if he does not take care, will be appropriated by earth.

Young widows, of whom some 'are already turned aside after Satan, when they have begun to wax wanton against Christ,' [2] in their lustful moments are wont to say: 'My little estate is wasting every day, the property I have inherited is being scattered, my footman has spoken insultingly to me, my maid

neglexit. Quis procedet ad publicum? Quis
respondebit pro agrorum tributis? Parvulos meos
quis erudiet? Vernulas quis educabit?' Et hanc—
pro nefas!—causam opponunt matrimonii, quae vel
sola debuit nuptias inpedire. Superducit mater
filiis non vitricum, sed hostem, non parentem, sed
tyrannum. Inflammata libidine obliviscitur uteri
sui, et inter parvulos suas miserias nescientes lugens
dudum nova nupta conponitur. Quid obtendis
patrimonium, quid superbiam servulorum? Con-
fitere turpitudinem. Nulla idcirco ducit maritum,
ut cum marito non dormiat. Aut si certe libido non
stimulat, quae tanta insania est in morem scortorum
prostituere castitatem, ut augeantur divitiae, et
propter rem vilem atque perituram pudicitia, quae
et pretiosa et aeterna est, polluatur? Si habes
liberos, nuptias quid requiris? Si non habes, quare
expertam non metuis sterilitatem et rem incertam
certo praefers pudori? Scribuntur tibi nunc sponsales
tabulae, ut post paululum testamentum facere
conpellaris. Simulabitur mariti infirmitas et, quod
te morituram facere volet, ipse victurus faciet. Aut
si evenerit, ut de secundo marito habeas filios,
domestica pugna, intestinum proelium. Non licebit
tibi amare liberos nec aequis aspicere oculis, quos
genuisti. Clam porriges cibos, invidebit mortuo,

pays no attention to my orders. Who will appear
for me in public? Who will be responsible for my
land-tax? Who will educate my little children and
bring up my house-slaves?' Shame on them!
They bring forward as a reason for marriage the
very thing which should in itself render marriage
impossible. A mother sets over her children not
a stepfather but an enemy, not a parent but a tyrant.
Inflamed by lustfulness she forgets her own offspring, and in the midst of the little ones who know
nothing of their sad fate the lately weeping widow
arrays herself afresh as a bride. Why these pre-
texts of property and arrogant servants? Confess
your vileness. No woman marries with the idea
of not sleeping with a husband. If you are not
spurred on by lust, surely it is the height of madness
to prostitute yourself like a harlot merely to increase
your wealth, and for a paltry and passing gain to
pollute that precious chastity which might endure
for ever. If you have children, why do you want
to marry? If you have none, why do you not fear
the barrenness you have already known? Why do
you put an uncertain gain before a certain loss of
modesty? A marriage settlement is made in your
favour to-day, but soon you will be induced to make
your will. Your husband will feign illness, and
will do for you what he wants you to do for him:
but he means to go on living, and you are destined
for an early grave. Or if it should happen that you
have sons by your second husband, domestic war-
fare and intestine feuds will be the result. You
will not be allowed to love your own children, or
to look kindly on those to whom you gave birth.
You will hand them their food secretly; for *he* will

et nisi oderis filios, adhuc eorum amare videberis patrem. Quodsi de priori uxore habens sobolem te domum introduxerit, etiam si clementissima fueris, omnes comoediae et mimographi et communes rhetorum loci in novercam saevissimam declamabunt. Si privignus languerit et condoluerit caput, infamaberis ut venefica. Si non dederis cibos, crudelis, si dederis, malefica diceris. Oro te, quid habent tantum boni secundae nuptiae, ut haec mala valeant conpensare?

16. Volumus scire, quales esse debeant viduae? Legamus evangelium secundum Lucam: ' Et erat,' inquit, ' Anna prophetissa, filia Phanuel de tribu Aser.'¹ Anna interpretatur ' gratia,' Phanuel in lingua nostra resonat ' vultum Dei,' Aser vel in ' beatitudinem ' vel in ' divitias ' vertitur. Quia ergo ab adulescentia usque ad octoginta quattuor annos viduitatis onus sustinuerat et non recedebat de templo Dei diebus ac noctibus insistens ieiuniis et obsecrationibus, idcirco meruit gratiam spiritalem et nuncupatur filia vultus Dei et atavis beatitudine divitiisque censetur. Recordemur viduae Sareptenae, quae et suae et filiorum saluti Heliae praetulit famem et ipsa nocte moritura cum filio superstitem hospitem relinquebat malens vitam perdere quam elemosynam et in pugillo farris seminarium sibi messis dominicae preparavit. Farina seritur et olei capsaces nascitur.²

---

¹ St. Luke, ii. 36.　　² 1 Kings, xvii. 10 ff.

be jealous of your dead husband, and unless you hate your sons he will think you still in love with their father. If he, for his part, has issue by a former wife, when he brings you into his house, then, even though you have a heart of gold, you will be the cruel stepmother, against whom every comedy, every mime-writer, and every dealer in rhetorical commonplaces raises his voice. If your stepson falls sick or has a headache, you will be maligned as a poisoner. If you refuse him food, you will be cruel; if you give it, you will be said to have bewitched him. What benefit, I pray you, can a second marriage confer sufficient to compensate for these disadvantages?

Do we wish to know how widows ought to behave? Let us read the Gospel according to Luke: ' There was one Anna,' he says,' a prophetess, the daughter of Phanuel of the tribe of Aser.'[1] Anna means ' grace,' Phanuel in our language is the ' face of God,' Aser is translated either as ' blessedness ' or ' wealth.' As then she had borne the burden of widowhood from her youth up to the age of fourscore and four years, and never left the temple day or night, giving herself to fasting and prayer, therefore she earned spiritual grace and is called daughter of the face of God, and in blessedness and wealth is reckoned with her ancestors. Let us remember the widow of Zarephath,[2] who considered the satisfaction of Elijah's hunger more important than her own and her children's lives. Though she thought that she and her son that very night would die, she meant her guest to survive, preferring to lose life rather than her name for charity. In her handful of meal she found the seed of the Lord's harvest. She sows her meal

In Iudaea frumenti penuria—granum enim tritici ibi mortuum fuerat—et in gentium viduae olei fluenta manabant. Legimus Iudith—si cui tamen placet volumen recipere—viduam confectam ieiuniis et habitu lugubri sordidatam, quae non lugebat mortuum virum, sed squalore corporis sponsi quaerebat adventum. Video armatam gladio manum, cruentam dexteram, recognosco caput Holofernae de mediis hostibus reportatum. Vincit viros femina et castitas truncat libidinem habituque repente mutato ad victrices sordes redit omnibus saeculi cultibus mundiores.

17. Quidam inperite et Debboram inter viduas numerant ducemque Barac arbitrantur Debborae filium, cum aliud scriptura commemoret. Nobis ad hoc nominabitur, quod prophetissa fuerit et in ordine iudicum supputetur. Et quia dicere poterat: ' Quam dulcia gutturi meo eloquia tua, super mel et favum ori meo,' apis nomen accepit scripturarum floribus pasta, Spiritus Sancti odore perfusa et dulces ambrosiae sucos prophetali ore conponens. Noomin, quae nobiscum sonat παρακεκλημένη, quam interpretari possumus ' consolatam,' marito et liberis peregre mortuis pudicitiam reportavit in patriam et hoc sustentata viatico nurum Moabitidem tenuit, ut illud Esaiae vaticinium conplerentur: ' Emitte agnum, domine, dominatorem terrae, de petra

---

[1] Psalm cxix. 103.   [2] Ruth, i. 6, 16.

and, lo! a cruse of oil appears. In Judaea there was
a scarcity of corn, for the grain of wheat had died;
but in the house of a heathen widow streams of oil
gushed forth. We read in the book of Judith, if
we may accept that record, of a widow spent with
fasting and unkempt in mourner's dress, who was
not so much grieving for her dead husband but in
squalor awaiting the advent of the Bridegroom.
I see her hand armed with a sword and stained with
blood, I recognize the head of Holofernes carried
in triumph from the midst of the enemy. A woman
conquers men, chastity beheads lust, and then
suddenly changing her dress she returns again to
her victorious squalor, a squalor finer than all the
pomp of this world.

Some people ignorantly count Deborah among
the widows, and think that Barak, the leader of the
army, was her son. The Scripture gives a different
account. I will mention her now because she was
a prophetess and is reckoned as one of the judges,
and also because she could say: ' How sweet are
thy words unto my taste! Yea, sweeter than honey
to my mouth.' [1] Rightly was she called ' the bee,'
for she fed on the flowers of the Scriptures, she was
steeped in the fragrance of the Holy Spirit, and
with prophetic lips she gathered the sweet juices
of the nectar. Naomi, in our language παρακεκλημένη,
' she who is consoled,' when her husband and children
died in a foreign land, carried her chastity back to
her native country, and supported by that provision for her journey, kept with her the Moabite
woman who was her son's wife,[2] that in her the
prophecy of Isaiah might be fulfilled: ' Send out
the lamb, O Lord, to rule over the land from

deserti.' Venio ad viduam de evangelio, viduam pauperculam, omni Israhelitico populo ditiorem, quae accipiens granum sinapis et mittens fermentum in farinae satis tribus Patris et Filii confessionem Spiritus Sancti gratia temperavit et duo minuta misit in gazophylacium quidquid habere poterat in substantia sua universasque divitias in utroque fidei suae obtulit testamento. Haec sunt duo seraphin ter glorificantia Trinitatem et in thesauro ecclesiae condita, unde et forcipe utriusque instrumenti ardens carbo conprehensus purgat labia peccatoris.

18. Quid vetera repetam et virtutes feminarum de libris proferam, cum possis multas tibi ante oculos proponere in urbe, qua vivis, quarum imitari exemplum debeas? Et ne videar adulatione per singulas currere, sufficit tibi sancta Marcella, quae respondens generi suo aliquid nobis de evangelio retulit. Anna septem annis a virginitate sua vixerat cum marito, ista septem mensibus; illa Christi expectabat adventum, ista tenet, quem illa susceperat; illa vagientem canebat; ista praedicat triumphantem; illa loquebatur de eo omnibus, qui expectabant redemptionem Hierusalem, haec cum redemptis gentibus clamitat: 'Frater non redimit, redimet homo,' et de alio psalmo: 'Homo natus est in ea et ipse fundavit eam altissimus.' Scio me ante hoc

---

[1] Isaiah. xvi. 1. [2] Isaiah, vi. 2, 3.
[3] Psalm xlix. 7. [4] Psalm lxxxvii. 5.

the rock of the desert.'[1] I come now to the widow in the Gospel, that poor humble widow who was richer than all the people of Israel. She had but a grain of mustard seed, but she put her leaven into three measures of flour, and tempering her confession of the Father and Son with the grace of the Holy Spirit, she cast her two mites into the treasury. All her substance and her entire wealth she offered in the double testament of her faith. These are the two seraphim which glorify the Trinity with triple song, and are stored among the treasures of the Church.[2] Hence, also, the double pincers wherewith the live coal is gripped to purge the sinner's lips.

But why should I go back to ancient times and quote instances of female virtue from books? Before your own eyes in Rome, where you are living now, you have many women whom you might well choose for your model. I will not take them individually lest I should seem to flatter: you may be content with one, the saintly Marcella, who while she maintains the glory of her family has given us an example of the Gospel life. Anna lived with a husband seven years from her virginity; Marcella lived seven months. Anna looked for the coming of Christ; Marcella holds fast to the Lord whom Anna welcomed. Anna sang of Him, when He was still a puling infant; Marcella proclaims His triumph. Anna spoke of Him to all those who were awaiting the redemption of Jerusalem; Marcella cries aloud with the nations of the redeemed: 'A brother redeemeth not, yet a man shall redeem,'[3] and from another psalm: 'A man was born in her and the Highest Himself hath established her.'[4] About two years ago

ferme biennium edidisse libros contra Iovinianum,
quibus venientes e contrario quaestiones, ubi apostolus
concedit secunda matrimonia, scripturarum auctoritate contrivi. Et non necesse est eadem ex
integro scribere, cum possis inde, quae scripta sunt,
mutuari. Hoc tantum, ne modum egrediar epistulae,
admonitam volo: cogita te cottidie esse morituram,
et numquam de secundis nuptiis cogitabis.

LX

Ad Heliodorum Epitaphium Nepotiani

1. Grandes materias ingenia parva non sufferunt
et in ipso conatu ultra vires ausa succumbunt;
quantoque maius fuerit, quod dicendum est, tanto
magis obruitur, qui magnitudinem rerum verbis non
potest explicare. Nepotianus meus, tuus, noster,
immo Christi, et quia Christi, idcirco plus noster,
reliquit senes et desiderii sui iaculo vulneratos
intolerabili dolore confecit. Quem heredem puta-
vimus, funus tenemus. Cui iam meum sudabit
ingenium? Cui litterulae placere gestient? Ubi est
ille ἐργοδιώκτης noster et cygneo canore vox dulcior?
Stupet animus, manus tremit, caligant oculi, lingua
balbutit. Quidquid dixero, quia ille non audiet,

---

¹ At one time a monk, later an opponent of Christian
asceticism. Pammachius sent a copy of his work to Jerome
at Bethlehem and Jerome's answer to it was written in 393.

I know that I published a treatise against Jovinian,[1] in which I refuted by the authority of the Scriptures the objections based on the apostle's concession of second marriages. It is unnecessary to repeat my arguments afresh, for you can borrow them from that book. That I may not exceed the limits of a letter, I will give you this final piece of advice. Think every day that you must die, and then you will never think of a second marriage.

LETTER LX

To HELIODORUS

A Letter of Consolation for the death of Nepotianus

Written A.D. 396

SMALL minds cannot deal adequately with great subjects; if they venture beyond their strength they fail in the attempt; and the greater the theme, the more completely is he overwhelmed who cannot find words to express its grandeur. Nepotian who was mine and yours and ours—nay rather, who was Christ's and because Christ's therefore the more ours—has left us in our old age overwhelmed with a grief that is past bearing, our hearts all sore with longing for him still. We thought of him as our heir, but now we only have his dead body. For whom now shall my mind exert itself? Whom shall my poor writings strive to please? Where is he, the inspirer of my labours, whose voice was sweeter than a swan's song? My heart is numbed, my hand trembles, my eyes are misty, my tongue stammers. All that I say seems voiceless, for he no

mutum videtur. Stilus ipse quasi sentiens et cera subtristior vel rubigine vel situ obducitur. Quotienscumque nitor in verba prorumpere et super tumulum eius epitaphii huius flores spargere, totiens conplentur oculi et renovato dolore totus in funere sum. Moris quondam fuit, ut super cadavera defunctorum in contione pro rostris laudes liberi dicerent et instar lugubrium carminum ad fletus et gemitus audientium pectora concitarent : en rerum in nobis ordo mutatus est et in calamitatem nostram perdidit sua iura natura : quod exhibere senibus iuvenis debuit, hoc iuveni exhibemus senes.

2. Quid igitur faciam? Iungam tecum lacrimas? Sed apostolus prohibet Christianorum mortuos dormientes vocans et dominus in evangelio : ' Non est,' inquit, ' mortua puella, sed dormit.' Lazarus quoque, quia dormierat, suscitatus est. Laeter et gaudeam, quod ' raptus sit, ne malitia inmutaret mentem eius,' quia placeret Deo anima illius? Sed invito et repugnanti per genas lacrimae fluunt et inter praecepta virtutum resurrectionisque spem credulam mentem desiderii frangit affectus. O mors, quae fratres dividis et amore sociatos crudelis ac dura dissocias! ' Adduxit urentem ventum dominus de deserto ascendentem, qui siccavit venas tuas et desolavit fontem tuum.' Devorasti quidem Ionam,

---

[1] Cf. Virgil, *Aeneid*, V. 79, *purpureosque iacit flores* (on the tomb of Anchises).

[2] Thessalonians, iv. 13.   [3] St. Mark, v. 39.

[4] Wisdom, iv. 11.   [5] Hosea, xiii. 15.

longer hears. My very pen is rusty as though it felt his loss, my wax tablet looks dull and is covered over with mould. Whenever I try to give vent to speech and to scatter the flowers [1] of this funeral panegyric on his tomb, my eyes fill with tears, my pain begins again to rankle, and I can think of nothing but his death. It was the ancient custom for children over the dead bodies of their parents to recite their praises on the platform of a public meeting, and as though by the singing of dirges to stir their audience to sobs and lamentations. Behold, with us the order of things is changed, and nature has lost her rights in bringing this disaster upon us. What the young man should have done for his elders, we his elders are doing now for him.

What shall I do then? Shall I join my tears to yours? The apostle forbids, for he calls dead Christians 'them which are asleep,' [2] and the Lord in the Gospel says: 'The damsel is not dead but sleepeth.' [3] Lazarus also, inasmuch as he had but fallen asleep, was raised back to life. Shall I rather rejoice and be glad, that ' speedily he was taken away lest that wickedness should alter his understanding,' [4] for his soul was pleasing to the Lord? Nay, though I struggle and try to fight against them, the tears still run down my cheeks, and in spite of virtue's teaching and our hope of the resurrection a passion of regret is breaking my fond heart. O death that partest brothers and dost unknit the close bonds of love, how cruel art thou and how stern! 'The Lord hath fetched a burning wind that cometh up from the wilderness: which hath dried thy veins and hath made thy fountain desolate.' [5] Thou didst swallow our Jonah, O death, but even in thy belly He

sed et in utero tuo vivus fuit. Portasti quasi mortuum, ut tempestas mundi conquiesceret et Nineve nostra illius praeconio salvaretur. Ille, ille te vicit, ille iugulavit fugitivus propheta, qui reliquit domum suam, dimisit hereditatem suam, dedit dilectam animam suam in manus quaerentium eam. Qui per Osee quondam tibi rigidus minabatur: ' Ero mors tua, o mors; ero morsus tuus, inferne,' illius morte tu mortua es, illius morte nos vivimus. Devorasti et devorata es, dumque adsumpti corporis sollicitaris inlecebra et avidis faucibus praedam putas, interiora tua adunco dente confossa sunt.

3. Gratias tibi, Christe salvator, tua agimus creatura, quod tam potentem adversarium nostrum, dum occideris, occidisti. Quis ante miserior homine, qui aeterno mortis terrore prostratus vivendi sensum ad hoc tantum acceperat, ut periret? ' Regnavit,' enim, ' mors ab Adam usque ad Moysen etiam super eos, qui non peccaverunt in similitudinem praevaricationis Adam.' Si Abraham, Isaac et Iacob in inferno, quis in caelorum regno? Si amici tui sub poena offendentis Adam et, qui non peccaverant, alienis peccatis tenebantur obnoxii, quid de his credendum est, qui dixerunt in cordibus suis: ' non est Deus,' qui ' corrupti et abominabiles facti sunt in voluntatibus suis,' qui ' declinaverunt, simul inutiles facti sunt; non est, qui faciat bonum, non est usque ad unum '? Quodsi Lazarus videtur in sinu Abraham locoque refrigerii, quid simile infernus et regna

---

[1] Hosea, xiii. 14.   [2] Romans, v. 14.
[3] Psalm xiv. 1.   [4] Psalm xiv. 3.

lived. Thou didst carry Him as one dead, that the
storms of this world might be appeased and our
Nineveh saved by His preaching. He, He was thy
conqueror, He it was who slew thee, the fugitive
prophet who left His home, gave up His inheritance,
and surrendered His dear life into the hands of those
that sought it. He it was who once by the mouth
of Hosea uttered against thee the stern threat:
' O death, I will be thy death ; O grave, I will be thy
destruction.' [1] By His death thou art dead ; by His
death we live. Thou hast swallowed and thou art
swallowed up, and while thou wert tempted by the
lure of the body they had seized and thought it a
prey for thy greedy jaws, lo ! thy inward parts are
pierced with the hook's carved teeth.

We Thy creatures render thanks to Thee, O Saviour
Christ, for that whilst Thou wert slain Thou didst
slay our so mighty adversary. Before Thy coming
was there anything more miserable than man, who
cowering in eternal fear of death had but received
the sense of life that he might perish ? ' Death
reigned from Adam to Moses even over them that
had not sinned after the similitude of Adam's transgression.' [2] If Abraham, Isaac, and Jacob be in
the tomb, who can be in the kingdom of heaven ?
If thy friends who had not sinned were for the sins
of another held liable to the punishment of offending
Adam, what must be believed of those who said
in their hearts : ' There is no God,' [3] men ' corrupt
and abominable in their self-will, who are gone out of
the way, they are become unprofitable ; there is none
that doeth good, no, not one ' ? [4] Even if Lazarus is
seen in Abraham's bosom and in a place of refreshment, what likeness can there be between the lower

caelorum? Ante Christum Abraham apud inferos;
post Christum latro in paradiso. Et idcirco in
resurrectione eius multa dormientium corpora surrexerunt et visa sunt in caelesti Hierusalem.
Tuncque conpletum est illud eloquium: ' Surge, qui
dormis, et elevare et inluminabit te Christus.'
Iohannes Baptista in heremo personat: ' Paenitentiam agite; adpropinquavit enim regnum caelorum.' A diebus enim Iohannis Baptistae regnum
caelorum vim passum est et violenti diripuerunt
illud. Flamma illa rumphea, custos paradisi, et
praesidentia foribus cherubin Christi restincta et
reserata sunt sanguine. Nec mirum hoc nobis in
resurrectione promitti, cum omnes, qui in carne non
secundum carnem vivimus, municipatum habeamus
in caelo et hic adhuc positis dicatur in terra: ' Regnum
Dei intra vos est.'

4. Adde quod ante resurrectionem Christi ' notus '
tantum erat ' in Iudaea Deus, in Israhel magnum
nomen eius,' et ipsi, qui noverant eum, tamen ad
inferos trahebantur. Ubi tunc totius orbis homines
ab India usque ad Britanniam, a rigida septentrionis
plaga usque ad fervores Atlantici oceani, tam innumerabiles populi et tantarum gentium multitudines
' quam variae linguis, habitu tam vestis et armis '?
Piscium ritu ac lucustarum et velut muscae et culices
conterebantur; absque notitia enim creatoris sui
omnis homo pecus est. Nunc vero passionem
Christi et resurrectionem eius cunctarum gentium

---

[1] Ephesians, v. 14. [2] St. Matthew, iii. 2.
[3] St. Luke, xvii. 21. [4] Psalm lxxvi. 1.
[5] Virgil, *Aeneid*, VIII. 723.

regions and the kingdom of heaven? Before Christ
Abraham was in the ground beneath; after Christ
the robber is in Paradise. And therefore at His
resurrection many bodies of those that slept arose
and were seen in the heavenly Jerusalem. Then was
fulfilled the saying: 'Awake thou that sleepest,
and arise from the dead, and Christ shall give thee
light.'[1] John the Baptist cries in the desert: 'Repent ye; for the kingdom of heaven is at hand.'[2]
For from the days of John the Baptist the kingdom
of heaven suffered violence and the violent took
it by force. The flaming sword that guarded Paradise, and the cherubim that kept its doors, were
alike quenched and unloosed by the blood of Christ.
Nor is it surprising that this is promised us at the
resurrection, seeing that all of us, who now in the
flesh live not after the manner of the flesh, have our
citizenship in heaven, and while we are still here
on earth we are told 'the kingdom of heaven is
within you.'[3]

Moreover, before the resurrection of Christ God
was only 'known in Judah and his name was great
in Israel,'[4] and even those who knew Him were still
dragged down to the nether world. Where at that
time were the inhabitants of the whole world from
India to Britain, from the ice-bound northern zone
to the burning heat of the Atlantic Ocean? Where
were its countless peoples, its thronging tribes

'In dress and arms as varied as in speech'?[5]

They were but packed together like fishes and
locusts, flies and gnats; for without knowledge of
his Creator every man is but a brute. But to-day
the voices and the writings of all nations proclaim

271

voces et litterae sonant. Taceo de Hebraeis, Graecis
et Latinis, quas nationes fidei suae in crucis titulo
dominus dedicavit. Immortalem animam et post
dissolutionem corporis subsistentem, quod Pythagoras somniavit, Democritus non credidit, in consola-
tionem damnationis suae Socrates disputavit in
carcere, Indus, Persa, Gothus, Aegyptius philoso-
phantur. Bessorum feritas et pellitorum turba
populorum, qui mortuorum quondam inferiis homines
immolabant, stridorem suum in dulce crucis fregerunt
melos et totius mundi una vox Christus est.

5. Quid agimus, anima? Quo nos vertimus?
Quid primum adsumimus? Quid tacemus? Exci-
derunt tibi praecepta rhetorum et occupata luctu,
oppressa lacrimis, praepedita singultibus dicendi
ordinem non tenes! Ubi illud ab infantia studium
litterarum et Anaxagorae ac Telamonis semper
laudata sententia: ' Sciebam me genuisse mortalem '? Legimus Crantorem, cuius volumen ad
confovendum dolorem suum secutus est Cicero,
Platonis, Diogenis, Clitomachi, Carneadis, Posidonii
ad sedandos luctus opuscula percurrimus, qui diversis
aetatibus diversorum lamenta vel libris vel epistulis
minuere sunt conati, ut, etiamsi nostrum areret
ingenium, de illorum posset fontibus inrigari: pro-
ponunt innumerabiles viros et maxime Periclen et
Xenophontem Socraticum, quorum alter amissis

---

[1] A Thracian tribe.

the passion and the resurrection of Christ. I say
nothing of the Hebrews, the Greeks, and the Latins,
peoples whom the Lord dedicated to His faith by
the inscription on His cross. That immortality of
the soul, and its existence after the dissolution of the
body, which Pythagoras dreamed, Democritus would
not believe, and Socrates discussed in prison to
console himself for his conviction, that is now the
common philosophy of Indian and Persian, Egyptian
and Goth. The savage Bessians [1] and their host of
skin-clad tribes, who used to offer human sacrifice to
the dead, have now dissolved their rough discord
into the sweet music of the Cross, and the whole
world with one voice cries out, ' Christ.'

What shall we do, O my soul? Whither shall we
turn? What theme shall we choose first? What
shall we omit? Have you forgotten the precepts
of the rhetoricians, and are you so preoccupied with
grief, oppressed with tears, and hindered by sobs
that you cannot keep to any ordered narrative?
Where now is that love of literature which you have
cherished from childhood? Where is the saying
of Anaxagoras and Telamon which you always used
to praise: ' I knew that I was born a mortal '? I
have read Crantor, whose treatise written to comfort his own grief Cicero imitated. I have perused
those works of Plato, Diogenes, Clitomachus,
Carneades, and Posidonius, in which by book or
letter they have tried at different times to lessen
the sorrow of various persons and to console their
grief. Therefore, even if my own wits were dry,
I could water them from these fountains. They
set before us men without number as examples,
and particularly Pericles and Socrates' pupil Xeno-

duobus filiis coronatus in contione disseruit, alter,
cum sacrificans filium in bello audisset occisum,
deposuisse coronam dicitur et eandem capiti repo-
suisse, postquam fortiter in acie dimicantem repperit
concidisse. Quid memorem Romanos duces, quorum
virtutibus quasi quibusdam stellis Latinae micant
historiae? Pulvillus Capitolium dedicans mortuum,
ut nuntiabatur, subito filium se iussit absente
sepeliri; Lucius Paulus septem diebus inter duorum
exequias filiorum triumphans urbem ingressus est.
Praetermitto Maximos, Catones, Gallos, Pisones,
Brutos, Scaevolas, Metellos, Scauros, Marios, Crassos,
Marcellos atque Aufidios, quorum non minor in luctu
quam in bellis virtus fuit et quorum orbitates in
Consolationis libro Tullius explicavit, ne videar
aliena potius quam nostra quaesisse; quamquam et
haec in suggilationem nostri breviter dicta sint, si
non praestet fides, quod exhibuit infidelitas.

6. Igitur ad nostra veniamus. Non plangam cum
Iacob et David filios in lege morientes, sed cum
Christo in evangelio suscipiam resurgentes. Iudaeorum luctus Christianorum gaudium est. ' Ad
vesperum demorabitur fletus et ad matutinum
laetitia.'[1] ' Nox praecessit, dies autem adpropinquavit.'[2] Unde et Moyses moriens plangitur, Iesus
absque funere et lacrimis in monte sepelitur. Quidquid de scripturis super lamentatione dici potest, in

---

[1] Psalm xxx. 5. [2] Romans, xiii. 12.

phon. The first, after the loss of his two sons, put
on a garland and addressed a public meeting. The
second was offering sacrifice when news came that
his son had been killed in battle; thereupon, we are
told, he took off his sacrificial garland, but replaced it
when he heard that he had fallen fighting bravely.
Why should I speak of those Roman leaders whose
virtues glitter like stars in the pages of Latin history?
Pulvillus was dedicating the Capitol when he was
told that his son had suddenly died. ' Bury him,'
he said, ' without me.' Lucius Paulus in the week
that intervened between the funerals of his two
sons entered Rome in triumphal procession. I pass
over the Maximi, the Catos, the Galli, the Pisos,
the Bruti, the Scaevolas, the Metelli, the Scauri,
the Marii, the Crassi, the Marcelli and the Aufidii,
men whose courage was as conspicuous in their sorrows
as in their wars. Cicero has dealt with their bereave-
ments in his book *On Consolation*, and of them I will
say no more, lest I should seem to seek examples
from strangers rather than from our own community.
Not but what even this brief reference might serve
as a mortification to us, if faith were not to give us
what unbelief afforded them.

Let us come then to our people. I will not weep
with Jacob and David for sons who died under the
Law, but with Christ I will welcome those who rise
again under the Gospel dispensation. The Jew's
mourning is the Christian's joy. ' Weeping may
endure for a night but joy cometh in the morning.' [1]
' The night is far spent, the day is at hand.' [2] Wherefore even Moses is lamented when he dies;
Joshua is buried on a mountain-top without funeral
or tears. All that can be drawn from the Scriptures

275

eo libro, quo Paulam Romae consolati sumus, breviter explicavimus. Nunc nobis per aliam semitam ad eundem locum perveniendum est, ne videamur praeterita et obsoleta quondam calcare vestigia.

7. Scimus quidem Nepotianum nostrum esse cum Christo et sanctorum mixtum choris, quod nobiscum eminus rimabatur in terris et aestimatione quaerebat, ibi videntem comminus dicere: ' Sicut audivimus, ita et vidimus in civitate domini virtutum, in civitate Dei nostri,'[1] sed desiderium absentiae eius ferre non possumus, non illius, sed nostram vicem dolentes. Quanto ille felicior, tanto nos amplius in dolore, quod tali caremus bono. Flebant et sorores Lazarum, quem resurrecturum noverant, et, ut veros hominis exprimeret affectus, ipse salvator ploravit, quem suscitaturus erat. Apostolus quoque eius, qui dixerat: ' Cupio dissolvi et esse cum Christo '[2] et alibi: ' Mihi vivere Christus est et mori lucrum,'[3] gratias agit, quod Epaphras de mortis sibi vicinia redditus sit, ne haberet tristitiam super tristitiam, non incredulitatis metu, sed desiderio caritatis. Quanto magis tu, et avunculus et episcopus, hoc est in carne et in spiritu pater, aves viscera tua et quasi a te divulsa suspiras! Sed obsecro, ut modum adhibeas in dolore memor illius sententiae: ' Ne quid nimis '[4] obligatoque parumper vulnere audias laudes eius, cuius semper virtute laetatus es, nec doleas,

---

[1] Psalm xlviii. 8.   [2] Philippians, i. 23.
[3] Philippians, i. 21.   [4] The Greek proverb μηδὲν ἄγαν

on the subject of lamentation I have briefly set out in the letter of consolation which I wrote to Paula at Rome. Now I must traverse another path to arrive at the same goal, for I would not have people see me treading again an old and used-up track.

We know, indeed, that our dear Nepotian is with Christ, and that he has joined the choirs of the saints. We know that what here with us on earth he groped after at a distance and sought by guess-work, there he sees face to face and can say: 'As we have heard so we have seen in the city of the Lord of hosts, in the city of our God.'[1] But we cannot bear our regret at his absence, and we grieve not on his account but for ourselves. The greater his happiness, the deeper our pain in lacking the blessings that he enjoys. The sisters of Lazarus wept for their brother, although they knew that he would rise again, and the Saviour Himself, to show that He possessed true human feelings, mourned for the man He was going to raise. His apostle also who said: 'I desire to depart and be with Christ,'[2] and in another place: 'To me to live in Christ and to die is gain,'[3] thanks God that Epaphras has been given back to him when he was nigh to death, that he might not have sorrow upon sorrow. His words were spoken not in unbelieving fear but in loving regret, and how much more keenly must you who were both uncle and bishop, a father both in the flesh and the spirit, deplore a death that meant the rending asunder of your own body. I beg you, however, to set a limit to your grief and to remember the saying: 'Nothing too much.'[4] Bind up your wound for a little while, and listen to the praises of him in whose virtue you always delighted. Do not

quod talem amiseris, sed gaudeas, quod talem
habueris, et sicut hi, qui in brevi tabella terrarum
situs pingunt, ita in parvo isto volumine cernas
adumbrata, non expressa signa virtutum, suscipias-
que a nobis non vires, sed voluntatem.

8. Praecepta sunt rhetorum, ut maiores eius, qui
laudandus est, et eorum altius gesta repetantur
sicque ad ipsum per gradus sermo perveniat, quo
videlicet avitis paternisque virtutibus inlustrior fiat
et aut non degenerasse a bonis aut mediocres ipse
ornasse videatur. Ego carnis bona, quae semper et
ipse contempsit, in animae laudibus non requiram
nec me iactabo de genere, id est de alienis bonis, cum
et Abraham et Isaac, sancti viri, Ismahelem et Esau
peccatores genuerint et a regione Iephte in catalogo
iustorum apostoli voce numeratus de meretrice sit
natus. 'Anima,' inquit, 'quae peccaverit, ipsa
morietur'; ergo et, quae non peccaverit, ipsa vivet.
Nec virtutes nec vitia parentum liberis inputantur;
ab eo tempore censemur, ex quo in Christo renasci-
mur. Paulus, persecutor ecclesiae et mane lupus
rapax Beniamin, ad vesperam dedit escam Ananiae
ovi submittens caput. Igitur et Nepotianus noster
quasi infantulus vagiens et rudis puer subito nobis
de Iordane nascatur.

---

[1] Ezekiel, xviii. 4.
[2] Cf. p. 158, note 4.
[3] Who baptized Paul, cf. Acts, ix. 10 ff.

grieve that you have lost such a paragon, but rather rejoice that he once was yours. As men draw a map of the world on one small tablet, so in this little scroll of mine you may see his virtues, not indeed fully delineated but sketched in outline, and will recognize that my will is good even if my strength be lacking.

The rhetoricians' rule is that you should go back to the ancestors of the man you have to praise, and first recount their glorious deeds. Then gradually you will come to your hero, making him the more illustrious by the virtues of his forefathers, and showing either that he has not degenerated from a worthy stock or that he has brought honour to mediocrity. I for my part in praising Nepotian's soul shall not trouble about the fleshly advantages which he himself always despised, nor shall I boast of his family, that is, of other people's merits. Even such holy men as Abraham and Isaac were the fathers of sinners like Ishmael and Esau, while Jephthah, on the other hand, who is reckoned by the apostle in the roll of the righteous, was the son of a harlot. The Scripture says: 'The soul that sinneth, it shall die.'[1] Therefore, also, the soul that hath not sinned shall live. Neither the virtues nor the vices of parents are set to the children's account. That reckoning begins with the hour when we are born again in Christ. Paul, the persecutor of the Church, who in the morning was Benjamin,[2] a ravening wolf, in the evening bowed his head and gave food to the sheep Ananias.[3] We then also should think of our dear Nepotian as a crying babe or as an innocent child fresh born to us from the waters of Jordan.

9. Alius forsitan scriberet, quod ob salutem illius orientem heremumque dimiseris et me, carissimum sodalem tuum, redeundi spe lactaveris, ut primum, si fieri posset, sororem cum parvulo viduam, dein, si consilium illa respueret, saltem nepotem dulcissimum conservares. Hic est enim ille, de quo tibi quondam vaticinatus sum: 'Licet parvulus ex collo pendeat nepos.'[1] Referret, inquam, alius, quod in palatii militia sub chlamyde et candenti lino corpus eius cilicio tritum sit, quod stans ante saeculi potestates lurida ieiuniis ora portaverit, quod adhuc sub alterius indumentis alteri militarit et ad hoc habuerit cingulum, ut viduis, pupillis, oppressis, miseris subveniret: mihi non placent dilationes istae inperfectae servitutis Dei et centurionem Cornelium, ut lego iustum, statim audio baptizatum.

10. Verumtamen velut incunabula quaedam nascentis fidei conprobemus, ut, qui sub alienis signis devotus miles fuit, donandus laurea sit, postquam suo regi coeperit militare. Balteo posito habituque mutato, quidquid castrensis peculii fuit, in pauperes erogavit. Legerat enim: 'Qui vult perfectus esse, vendat omnia, quae habet, et det pauperibus et sequatur me,'[2] et iterum: 'Non potestis duobus dominis servire, Deo et mammonae.'[3] Excepta vili tunica et operimento pari, quod tecto tantum corpore frigus excluderet, nihil sibi amplius reservavit. Cultus ipse provinciae morem sequens nec munditiis

---

[1] Cf. Letter XIV, p. 31.
[2] St. Matthew, xix. 21.   [3] St. Matthew, vi. 24.

Another might perhaps describe how for his
salvation you left the East and the desert, and how
you fed me, your dearest comrade, with hopes of
your return; desiring in the first place, if it were
possible, to save your widowed sister and her little
son, or, if she rejected your counsels, at least to
preserve your dear little nephew. He is the child
of whom I once used the prophetic words, ' though
your little nephew cling to your neck.' [1] Another,
I repeat, might tell how, while he was a soldier at
court, beneath his military cloak and white linen
tunic his skin was chafed by sackcloth; how, while
he stood before the powers of this world, his lips
were pale with fasting; how, while he wore one
master's uniform, he served another; and how he
only wore a sword-belt that he might succour the
widow and the fatherless, the wretched and the
oppressed. For my own part I do not like an in-
complete or a deferred dedication to God's service,
and when I read of the centurion Cornelius that he
was a just man I immediately hear of him as being
baptized.

Still, we may approve of all this as being the
cradlings of a new-born faith. He who has been
a loyal soldier under a foreign banner is sure to
deserve the laurel when he begins to serve his own
king. When Nepotian laid aside his soldier's belt
and changed his dress, he gave all his army savings
to the poor. For he had read the words: ' If thou
wilt be perfect, sell that thou hast, and give to the poor
and follow me,' [2] and again: ' Ye cannot serve two
masters, God and Mammon.' [3] He kept nothing for
himself except a coarse tunic and cloak to protect
him from the cold. His dress was of provincial cut,

nec sordibus notabilis erat. Cumque arderet cotidie
aut ad Aegypti monasteria pergere aut Mesopotamiae
invisere choros vel certe insularum Dalmatiae, quae
Altino tantum freto distant, solitudines occupare,
avunculum pontificem deserere non audebat tota in
illo cernens exempla virtutum domique habens, unde
disceret. In uno atque eodem et imitabatur monachum et episcopum venerabatur. Non, ut in plerisque accidere solet, adsiduitas familiaritatem, familiaritas contemptum illius fecerat, sed ita eum colebat,
quasi parentem, ita admirabatur, quasi cotidie novum
cerneret.

Quid multa? Fit clericus et per solitos gradus
presbyter ordinatur. Iesu bone, qui gemitus, qui
heiulatus, quae cibi interdictio, quae fuga oculorum
omnium! Tum primum et solum avunculo iratus
est. Querebatur se ferre non posse, et iuvenalem
aetatem incongruam sacerdotio causabatur. Sed
quanto plus repugnabat, tanto magis omnium in se
studia concitabat et merebatur negando, quod esse
nolebat, eoque dignior erat, quod se clamabat
indignum. Vidimus Timotheum nostri temporis et
canos in Sapientia electumque a Moysi presbyterum,
quem ipse sciret esse presbyterum. Igitur cleri-
catum non honorem intellegens sed onus primam
curam habuit, ut humilitate superaret invidiam,
deinde, ut nullam obsceni in se rumoris fabulam daret,

---

[1] Altinum, in Venetia, on the border of the lagoons, and
opposite Torcello island, to which the episcopal see was
transferred in A.D. 635.

[2] Cf. p. 412, note 1.

[3] Wisdom, iv. 9. 'But wisdom is the grey hair unto man,
and an unspotted life is old age.'

not noticeable either for elegance or for shabbiness. Every day he burned either to go to the monasteries of Egypt, or to visit the saintly companies of Mesopotamia, or at least to take up his dwelling in the lonely spaces of the Dalmatian islands, separated from Altinum only by a strait.[1] But he could not bring himself to desert his episcopal uncle, in whom he saw a pattern of every virtue and from whose lessons he could profit at home. In one and the same person he had a monk to imitate and a bishop to revere. With him it was not as so often with many; intimacy did not breed familiarity, nor familiarity contempt. He honoured his bishop as though he had been his father; he admired him as though every day he saw in him a new man.

To be brief, Nepotian became a clergyman, and passing through the usual stages was ordained as presbyter.[2] Good Jesus! how he sobbed and groaned! how he forbade himself food and fled from the eyes of all! For the first and only time he was angry with his uncle, complaining that he could not bear his burden and alleging that his youth unfitted him for the priesthood. But the more he resisted, the more he drew to himself the love of all; his refusal showed him worthy of the rank he did not wish to take; all the more worthy indeed because he proclaimed his unworthiness. We too in our day have had a Timothy before our eyes; we too have seen the grey hairs of which the Book of Wisdom speaks;[3] our Moses has chosen a presbyter whom he knew to be a presbyter indeed. Nepotian regarded the clerical office not as an honour but as a burden. He made it his first care to silence envy by humility, his second to give no ground for scandal against him

283

ut, qui mordebantur ad aetatem eius, stuperent
ad continentiam. Subvenire pauperibus, visitare
languentes, provocare hospitio, lenire blanditiis,
' gaudere cum gaudentibus, flere cum flentibus ';
caecorum baculus, esurientium cibus, spes miserorum,
solamen lugentium fuit. Ita in singulis virtutibus
eminebat, quasi ceteras non haberet. Inter presbyteros et coaequales primus in opere, extremus in
ordine. Quidquid boni fecerat, ad avunculum
referebat; si quid forte aliter evenerat, quam
putarat, illum nescire, se errasse dicebat. In
publico episcopum, domi patrem noverat. Gravi-
tatem morum hilaritate frontis temperabat.
Gaudium risu, non cachinno, intellegeres. Viduas et
virgines Christi honorare ut matres, hortari ut
sorores cum omni castitate. Iam vero, postquam
domum se contulerat et relicto foris clerico duritiae
se tradiderat monachorum, creber in orationibus,
vigilans in precando lacrimas Deo, non hominibus,
offerebat; ieiunia in aurigae modum pro lassitudine
et viribus corporis moderabatur. Mensae avunculi
intererat et sic adposita quaeque libabat, ut et
superstitionem fugeret et continentiam reservaret.
Sermo eius et omne convivium de scripturis aliquid
proponere, libenter audire, respondere verecunde,
recta suscipere, prava non acriter confutare, dispu-

---

[1] Rom. xii. 15.

and by continence to dumbfound those who railed against his youth. He helped the poor, visited the sick, challenged others to acts of hospitality, soothed men's anger with soft words, 'rejoiced with those who rejoiced and wept with those who wept.'[1] He was a staff to the blind, food to the hungry, hope to the wretched, a consolation to the sorrowful. Each single virtue was as conspicuous in him as if he possessed no others. Among his fellow-presbyters and equals in age, he was first in industry, last in rank. Any good that he did he ascribed to his uncle; if the result was different from what he had expected, he would say that his uncle knew nothing of the matter and that it was his own mistake. In public he recognized him as a bishop, at home he treated him as a father. The gravity of his character was tempered by the cheerfulness of his looks. A smile, not a guffaw, was the sign that he felt glad. Widows and Christ's virgins he honoured as mothers, and exhorted as sisters, with all chastity. On his return home he left the clergyman outside, and submitted himself to the hard rule of a monk. Frequent in supplication, wakeful in prayer, he offered his tears not to men but to God. His fasts he regulated, as a charioteer does his pace, by the weariness or the vigour of his body. He would sit at his uncle's table and just taste the dishes set before him, thus both avoiding superstition and yet keeping to his rule of self-restraint. His chief topic of conversation and his favourite form of entertainment was to bring forward some passage from the Scriptures for discussion; then he would listen modestly, answer diffidently, support the right, and mildly refute the wrong, instructing his opponent

tantem contra se magis docere quam vincere et ingenuo pudore, qui ornabat aetatem, quid cuius esset, simpliciter confiteri; atque in hunc modum eruditionis gloriam declinando eruditissimus habebatur. ' Illud,' aiebat, ' Tertulliani, istud Cypriani, hoc Lactantii, illud Hilarii est. Sic Minucius Felix, ita Victorinus, in hunc modum est locutus Arnobius.' Me quoque, quia pro sodalitate avunculi diligebat, interdum proferebat in medium. Lectione quoque adsidua et meditatione diuturna pectus suum bibliothecam fecerat Christi.

11. Quotiens ille transmarinis epistulis deprecatus est, ut aliquid ad se scriberem! Quotiens nocturnum de evangelio petitorem et interpellatricem duri iudicis mihi viduam exhibuit! Cumque ego silentio magis quam litteris denegarem et pudore reticentis pudorem suffunderem postulantis, avunculum mihi opposuit precatorem, qui et liberius pro alio peteret et pro reverentia sacerdotii facilius inpetraret. Feci ergo, quod voluit, et brevi libello amicitias nostras aeternae memoriae consecravi; quo suscepto Croesi opes et Darii divitias se vicisse iactabat. Illum oculis, illum sinu, illum manibus, illum ore retinebat; cumque in strato frequenter evolveret, super pectus soporati dulcis pagina decidebat. Si vero peregri-

---

[1] Letter LII.

rather than vanquishing him. With the ingenuous modesty which was one of his youthful charms he would frankly confess the source of each argument he used, and in this way by disclaiming any reputation for learning he gradually came to be considered the most learned of us all. 'This,' he would say, 'is Tertullian's view and this is Cyprian's; this is the opinion of Lactantius and this of Hilary; such is the doctrine of Minucius Felix, so Victorinus teaches, in this fashion Arnobius speaks.' Myself too he sometimes quoted, for he loved me because of my association with his uncle. Indeed, by constant reading and long meditation he had made his mind a library of Christ.

How often did he beg me in his letters from across the sea to write something for him! How often did he remind me of the man in the Gospel who sought help by night, and of the widow who importuned the harsh judge! When he found that I did not write and saw himself checked by my silence, the modesty of his request being matched by the modesty of my refusal, he made another move. He got his uncle to ask on his behalf, knowing that a request for another could be more freely made and that my respect for a bishop would ensure him an easier success. Accordingly I did what he wished, and in a short treatise [1] dedicated our friendships to eternal remembrance, while he on receiving it boasted that he surpassed the wealth of Croesus and the treasures of Darius. He would always hold my book in his hands, devour it with his eyes, fondle it in his breast, and repeat it with his lips. In bed he would frequently undo the roll and fall asleep with the dear page upon his heart. If a stranger or a friend came

norum, si amicorum quispiam venerat, laetabatur
super se nostro testimonio et, quidquid minus in
opusculo erat, distinctione moderata et pronunti-
ationis varietate pensabat, ut in recitando illo ipse [1]
vel placere vel displicere cotidie videretur. Unde
his fervor, nisi ex amore Dei? Unde legis Christi
indefessa meditatio, nisi ex desiderio eius, qui legem
dedit? Alii nummum addant nummo et marsup-
pium suffocantes matronarum opes venentur obsequiis,
sint ditiores monachi, quam fuerant saeculares,
possideant opes sub Christo paupere, quas sub
locuplete diabolo non habuerant, et suspiret eos
ecclesia divites, quos tenuit mundus ante mendicos:
Nepotianus noster aurum calcans scedulas con-
sectatur, sed, sicut sui in carne contemptor est et
paupertate incedit ornatior, ita totum ecclesiae
investigat ornatum.

12. Ad conparationem quidem superiorum modica
sunt, quae dicturi sumus, sed et in parvis idem animus
ostenditur. Ut enim creatorem non in caelo tantum
miramur et terra, sole et oceano, elefantis, camelis,
equis, bubus, pardis, ursis, leonibus, sed et in minutis
quoque animalibus, formica, culice, muscis, vermi-
culis et istius modi genere, quorum magis corpora
scimus quam nomina, eandemque in cunctis vene-
ramur sollertiam, ita mens Christo dedita aeque et
in maioribus et in minoribus intenta est sciens etiam
pro otioso verbo reddendam esse rationem. Erat
ergo sollicitus, si niteret altare, si parietes absque

---

[1] ipso: *Hilberg.*

in, he rejoiced to show him the evidence of my regard; and anything lacking in my poor work was compensated for by careful modulation and varied emphasis, so that, when it was read aloud, it was he, not I, who seemed to please or to displease. Whence could this fervour come save from love of God? Whence this tireless meditation on the law of Christ save from longing for Him who gave that law? Let others add shilling to shilling, fastening their claws on married ladies' purses and hunting wealth by flattering attentions; let them be richer as monks than they were as men of the world; let them possess wealth in the service of a poor Christ such as they never had in the service of a rich devil; let the Church sigh over the opulence of men who in the world were beggars. Our dear Nepotian tramples gold underfoot, books are the only things he desires. But while he despises himself in the flesh and walks abroad in splendid poverty, he yet seeks out everything that may adorn his church.

In comparison with what I have already said the following details are trivial; but even in small things the same spirit is revealed. We admire the Creator, not only as the framer of heaven and earth, of sun and ocean, of elephants, camels, horses, oxen, leopards, bears and lions, but also as the maker of tiny creatures, ants, gnats, flies, worms, and the like, things whose shapes we know better than their names. And as in all creation we reverence His skill, so the mind that is given to Christ is equally earnest in small things as in great, knowing that an account must be given even for an idle word. Nepotian therefore took anxious pains to keep the altar bright, to have the walls free from soot and the

fuligine, si pavimenta tersa, si ianitor creber in porta, vela semper in ostiis, si sacrarium mundum, si vasa lucentia; et in omnes caerimonias pia sollicitudo disposita non minus, non maius neglegebat officium. Ubicumque eum in ecclesia quaereres, invenires.

Nobilem virum Quintum Fabium miratur antiquitas, qui etiam Romanae scriptor historiae est, sed magis ex pictura quam litteris nomen invenit; et Beselehel nostrum plenum sapientia et spiritu Dei scriptura testatur, Hiram quoque, filium mulieris Tyriae, quod alter tabernaculi, alter templi supellectilem fabricati sunt. Quomodo enim laetae segetes et uberes agri interdum culmis aristisque luxuriant, ita praeclara ingenia et mens plena virtutibus in variarum artium redundat elegantiam. Unde apud Graecos philosophus ille laudatur, qui omne, quod uteretur, usque ad pallium et anulum manu sua factum gloriatus est. Hoc idem possumus et de isto dicere, qui basilicas ecclesiae et martyrum conciliabula diversis floribus et arborum comis vitiumque pampinis adumbraret, ut, quidquid placebat in ecclesia tam dispositione quam visu, laborem presbyteri et studium testaretur.

13. Macte virtute. Cuius talia principia, qualis finis erit? O miserabilis humana condicio et sine Christo vanum omne, quod vivimus. Quid te sub-

---

[1] Jerome here confuses C. Fabius Pictor the painter (fl. 300) with his grandson Quintus the historian.

[2] Exodus, xxxi. 2, 3; 1 Kings, vii. 14.

[3] Hippias of Elis.

pavement duly swept. He saw to it that the door-keeper was constantly at his post, that the curtains were hanging at the entrance, that the sanctuary was neat, and the church-vessels brightly polished. His careful reverence extended to every form of ceremonial, and no duty, small or great, was neglected. Whenever you looked for him in his church, there you found him.

In Quintus Fabius [1] antiquity admired a man of rank, who not only wrote a history of Rome but won even greater fame from his paintings than from his books. Our own Bezaleel also and Hiram, [2] the son of a Tyrian woman, are spoken of in Scripture as men filled with wisdom and the spirit of God, because one made the furniture of the tabernacle, the other that of the temple. As rich crops and fertile fields are at times one great luxuriance of stalk and ear, so great talents and minds that are filled with virtue overflow into a variety of elegant accomplishments. So among the Greeks the great philosopher [3] was praised, who boasted that he had made with his own hands everything which he used, including his cloak and his finger-ring. We can say the same about Nepotian, for he adorned the church-buildings and the halls of the martyrs with different kinds of flowers and with the foliage of trees and clusters of vine leaves. Indeed, every-thing in his church that pleased by its arrangement or its appearance bore witness to the labour and the zeal of its presbyter.

A blessing on such virtue! After such a beginning what sort of ending should we expect? How miser-able is the condition of man, how vain is all our life without Christ! Why do you shrink, O my words,

trahis, quid tergiversaris, oratio? Quasi enim mortem illius differe possimus et vitam facere longiorem, sic timemus ad ultimum pervenire. ' Omnis caro faenum et omnis gloria eius quasi flos faeni.'[1] Ubi nunc decora illa facies, ubi totius corporis dignitas, quo veluti pulchro indumento pulchritudo animae vestiebatur? Marcescebat, pro dolor, flante austro lilium et purpura violae in pallorem sensim migrabat. Cumque aestuaret febribus et venarum fontes hauriret calor, lasso anhelitu tristem avunculum consolabatur. Laetus erat vultus et universis circa plorantibus solus ipse ridebat. Proicere pallium, manus extendere, videre, quod alii non videbant, et quasi in occursum se erigens salutare venientes: intellegeres illum non emori, sed migrare, et mutare amicos, non relinquere. Volvuntur per ora lacrimae et obfirmato animo non queo dolorem dissimulare, quem patior. Quis crederet in tali illum tempore nostrae necessitudinis recordari et luctante anima studiorum scire dulcedinem?[2] Adprehensa avunculi manu: ' Hanc,' inquit, ' tunicam, qua utebar in ministerio Christi, mitte dilectissimo mihi, aetate patri, fratri collegio, et, quidquid a te nepoti debebatur affectus, in illum transfer, quem mecum pariter diligebas.' Atque in talia verba defecit avunculum manu, me recordatione contrectans.

14. Scio, quod nolueris amorem in te civium sic probare, et affectum patriae magis quaesisse in

---

why do you hesitate? I fear to come to the end, as though I could put off his death and make his life longer. 'All flesh is as grass and all the glory of man as the flower of grass.' [1] Where now is that comely face, where is that dignified figure, which clothed his fair soul as with a fair garment? O grief! the lily withered when the south wind blew, and the violet's purple slowly faded into paleness. He burned with fever, and all the moisture in his veins was dried up with heat, but gasping and weary he still tried to comfort his uncle's grief. His face was bright, and while all around him wept, he alone smiled. [2] Suddenly he flung off his cloak and stretched out his hands, seeing something that was not revealed to others' eyes, and raising himself up as though to meet them he greeted those that were coming to him. You would have thought that he was starting on a journey, not dying, and that he was exchanging friends, not leaving friends behind. The tears roll down my face, and though I steel my courage I cannot hide the pain which I suffer. Who would believe that in such an hour he still remembered our friendship, and that while he was struggling for life he still recalled the delights of study? Grasping his uncle's hand he said: 'Send this tunic which I wore in the service of Christ to my beloved friend, my father in age and my brother in office, and any affection due to your nephew transfer to him, who is as dear to you as he is to me.' With these words he passed away, his uncle's hand in his, and thoughts of me in his heart.

I know that you were reluctant to prove your people's love at such a cost, and that you would have preferred to win your country's affection under

prosperis. Sed huiusce modi officium in bonis
iucundius est, in malis gratius. Tota hunc civitas,
tota planxit Italia. Corpus terra suscepit, anima
Christo reddita est. Tu nepotem quaerebas, ecclesia
sacerdotem. Praecessit te successor tuus. Quod tu
eras, ille post te iudicio omnium merebatur. Atque
ita ex una domo duplex pontificatus egressa est
dignitas : dum in altero gratulatio est, quod tenuerit,
in altero maeror, quod raptus sit, ne teneret. Platonis sententia est omnem sapienti vitam meditationem esse mortis. Laudant hoc philosophi et in
caelum ferunt, sed multo fortius apostolus : ' Cotidie,'
inquit, ' morior per vestram gloriam.' Aliud est
conari, aliud agere; aliud vivere moriturum, aliud
mori victurum. Ille moriturus ex gloria est; iste
moritur semper ad gloriam.

Debemus igitur et nos animo praemeditari, quod
aliquando futuri sumus et quod—velimus nolimus—
abesse longius non potest. Nam si nongentos vitae
excederemus annos, ut ante diluvium vivebat
humanum genus, et Mathusalae nobis tempora
donarentur, tamen nihil esset praeterita longitudo,
quae esse desisset. Etenim inter eum, qui decem
vixit annos, et illum, qui mille, postquam idem vitae
finis advenerit et inrecusabilis mortis necessitas,

---

[1] Plato, *Phaedo*, 81A, says of the philosophic life : ἦ οὐ τοῦτ'
ἂν εἴη μελετὴ θανάτου;

[2] 1 Corinthians, xv. 31 : νὴ τὴν ὑμετέραν καύχησιν ἣν ἔχω ἐν

happier circumstances. But such dutiful attentions as were shown you then, while more pleasant in prosperity, are especially grateful in times of grief. All Altinum, all Italy wept for your nephew. The earth received his body, his soul was given back to Christ. You lost a nephew, the Church a priest. He who should have followed you went before you. What you were, he in all men's judgment deserved to be. One household has had the honour of producing two bishops, the first congratulated on having held office, the second lamented on being taken away before he could hold it. There is a saying of Plato that a wise man's whole life should be a preparation for death.[1] Philosophers praise the sentiment and laud it to the skies, but the apostle speaks with a higher courage when he says: 'By my glory in you I die daily.'[2] It is one thing to attempt, another to do; one thing to live so as to die, another to die so as to live. The sage passes from glory when death comes, the Christian proceeds to glory when he dies.

Therefore we too ought to meditate beforehand, and to consider the fate which must one day come upon us, a fate which, whether we wish it or not, cannot be very far distant. Even if we lived for nine hundred years and more, as men did before the flood, even if the age of Methuselah were granted to us, that length of time once passed would be nothing when it had ceased to be. Between the man who has lived for ten years and the man who has lived for a thousand, there is no difference when once the end of life has come to both alike and death's inexorable necessity. The only point is that

ὑμῖν. But Jerome takes advantage of the Vulgate version to play on the phrases *per gloriam, ex gloria, ad gloriam.*

transactum omne tantundem est, nisi quod magis senex onustus peccatorum fasce proficiscitur.

' Optima quaeque dies miseris mortalibus aevi
Prima fugit, subeunt morbi tristisque senectus
Et labor et durae rapit inclementia mortis.'

Naevius poeta ' Pati,' inquit, ' necesse est multa mortalem mala.' Unde et Niobam, qui multum fleverit in lapidem et in diversas bestias ⟨conversas alias et Hecubam in canem⟩ commutatam finxit antiquitas, et. Hesiodus natales hominum plangens gaudet in funere, prudenterque Ennius:

' Plebes,' ait, ' in hoc regio [1] antistat loco: licet
Lacrimare plebi, regi honeste non licet.'

Ut regi, sic episcopo, immo minus regi quam episcopo. Ille enim nolentibus praeest, hic volentibus; ille terrore subicit, hic servitute dominatur; ille corpora custodit ad mortem, hic animas servat ad vitam. In te omnium oculi diriguntur, domus tua et conversatio quasi in specula constituta magistra est publicae disciplinae. Quidquid feceris, id sibi omnes faciendum putant. Cave ne committas, quod aut, qui reprehendere volunt, digne lacerasse videantur aut, qui imitari, cogantur delinquere. Vince quantum potes, immo plus quam potes, mollitiem animi tui et ubertim fluentes lacrimas reprime, ne grandis pietas in nepotem apud incredulas mentes desperatio putetur in Deum. Desiderandus tibi est quasi

---

[1] The best reading is *regi*.

---

[1] Virgil, *Georgics*, III. 66.
[2] Ennius, *Iphigenia*, fr. 7.

the older a man is, the heavier is the load of sin he
takes with him on his journey.

> ' O hapless men! the brightest years are first
>   To fly: disease and age come on us soon
>   And trouble and the ruthlessness of death.' [1]

So the poet Naevius says: ' Mortals perforce must
many ills endure.' Therefore antiquity feigned
that Niobe, because of her long weeping, was turned
into stone, and that other women were changed into
various kinds of animals, Hecuba, for example, into
a dog. Hesiod too bewails men's birthdays and
rejoices at their death, and Ennius wisely says:

> ' The mob in this outvies the kingly state,
>   For they may weep; tears to a king are shame.' [2]

As with a king, so with a bishop: or rather a
bishop has less licence than a king. The king rules
over the unwilling, the bishop over the willing. The
king subdues by inspiring fear, the bishop is master
because he is servant. The king guards bodies for
future death, the bishop saves souls for eternal life.
The eyes of all men are turned upon you, your
house is set as it were upon a watch-tower, and your
life gives to all a lesson of public discipline. Whatever you do, everyone thinks that he may do also.
Take care not to commit any act which those who
wish to blame you may seem right in censuring, or
which would force those who wish to imitate you to
do wrong. Use all your strength, and even more,
to overcome the softness of your heart, and check
the copious flood of your tears lest your great love
for your nephew be taken by unbelievers as showing
despair of God. You must regret him not as one

absens, non quasi mortuus, ut illum expectare, non amisisse videaris.

15. Verum quid ago medens dolori, quem iam reor et tempore et ratione sedatum, ac non potius replico tibi vicinas regum miserias et nostri temporis calamitates, ut non tam plangendus sit, qui hac luce caruerit, quam congratulandum ei, quod de tantis malis evaserit? Constantius, Arrianae fautor hereseos, dum contra inimicum paratur et concitus fertur ad pugnam, in Mopsi viculo moriens magno dolore hosti reliquit imperium. Iulianus, perditor animae suae et Christiani iugulator exercitus, Christum sensit in Media, quem primum in Gallia denegarat; dumque Romanos propagare vult fines, perdidit propagatos. Iovianus gustatis tantum regalibus bonis fetore prunarum suffocatus interiit ostendens omnibus, quid sit humana potentia. Valentinianus vastato genitali solo et inultam patriam dereliquens vomitu sanguinis extinctus est. Huius germanus Valens Gothico bello victus in Thracia eundem locum et mortis habuit et sepulchri. Gratianus ab exercitu suo proditus et ab obviis urbibus non receptus ludibrio hosti fuit cruentaeque manus vestigia parietes tui, Lugdune, testantur. Adulescens Valentinianus et paene puer post fugam, post exilia, post recuperatum multo sanguine imperium haut procul ab urbe

---

[1] The Emperors here mentioned followed one another in quick succession. Constantius died in 361 while marching to Constantinople to resist Julian. Julian was killed fighting the Persians in 363, and was succeeded by Jovian who only reigned a few months. His place was taken in the West by Valentinian (364–375), and in the East by Valens (364–378), while Gratian, who came next, was murdered at Lyons in 383. Procopius, Maximus and Eugenius were usurpers of short duration, overthrown by Theodosius the Great (379–395).

who is dead, but as one who has gone away. Let men see that you have not lost him, but are waiting to see him again.

But what am I doing in thus seeking to heal a pain which I imagine has already been assuaged by time and philosophy? Why do I not rather unfold to you the miseries of kings [1] in our near neighbourhood and the disasters that have come upon our age? He who has escaped from this world's light is not so much to be lamented as he is to be congratulated on having been saved from such great evils. Constantius, the patron of the Arian heresy, was making preparations against his enemy and advancing in haste to give him battle, when he died at the village of Mopsus, and to his great grief left the empire to the foe. Julian, the betrayer of his own soul, the assassin of a Christian army, felt in Media the power of that Christ whom in Gaul he had denied, and while he was trying to extend the territories of Rome he lost the annexations which had already been made. Jovian had but just tasted the sweets of kingship when he was suffocated by a coal fire, revealing to all men the true nature of human power. Valentinian died of a broken blood-vessel, leaving his country unavenged and his native soil devastated. His brother Valens was defeated in the Gothic war, and in Thrace was buried where he fell. Gratian, betrayed by his own army and refused admittance by all the cities which he approached, became the laughing-stock of the enemy: your walls, O Lyons, still bear the mark of that bloody hand. Valentinian was but a youth, hardly more than a boy, when, after flight and exile and the recovery of his throne amid streams of blood, he was murdered not far

fraternae mortis conscia necatus est et cadaver
exanimis infamatum suspendio. Quid loquar de
Procopio, Maximo, Eugenio, qui utique, dum rerum
potirentur, terrori gentibus erant? Omnes capti
steterunt ante ora victorum et, quod potentissimis
quondam miserrimum est, prius ignominia servitutis
quam hostili mucrone confossi sunt.

16. Dicat aliquis: ' Regum talis condicio est,
" feriuntque summos fulgura montes." ' Ad privatas
veniam dignitates nec de his loquar, qui excedunt
biennium; atque, ut ceteros praetermittam, sufficit
nobis trium nuper consularium diversos exitus
scribere. Abundantius egens Pityunte exulat;
Rufini caput pilo Constantinopolin gestatum est et
abscissa manus dextera ad dedecus insatiabilis
avaritiae ostiatim stipes mendicavit; Timasius
praecipitatus repente de altissimo dignitatis gradu
evasisse se putat, quod Assae [1] vivit inglorius. Non
calamitates miserorum, sed fragilem humanae condicionis narro statum—horret animus temporum
nostrorum ruinas prosequi—viginti et eo amplius anni
sunt, quod inter Constantinopolin et Alpes Iulias
cotidie Romanus sanguis effunditur. Scythiam,
Thraciam, Macedoniam, Thessaliam, Dardaniam,
Daciam, Epiros, Dalmatiam, cunctasque Pannonias
Gothus, Sarmata, Quadus, Alanus, Huni, Vandali,
Marcomanni vastant, trahunt, rapiunt. Quot ma-

---

[1] in Oase: *Hilberg*.

---

[1] Horace, *Odes*, II. x. 11.
[2] Banished *c.* 396 to Pityus on the Black Sea by Eutropius,
whom he had helped to raise to power.
[3] Prime Minister of Theodosius I, assassinated by Gainas
in the reign of Arcadius.
[4] A general of Theodosius banished by Eutropius.

from the city which had witnessed his brother's death, and suffered the shame of having his corpse hung from a gibbet. Why speak of Procopius, Maximus, and Eugenius, who, while they ruled at any rate, were a terror to the nations? They all stood as prisoners in the presence of their conquerors, and—fate most wretched for those who had once been supreme!—felt their hearts stabbed by the shame of slavery before they perished by the enemy's sword.

Some one may say : ' Such is the lot of kings, " the lightnings strike the mountain tops." '[1] I will come, then, to persons of private rank, and even in their case I will not go back for more than two years. Omitting any others, it is sufficient for me to record the diverse ends of three men recently of consular position. Abundantius[2] is now a beggar and lives in exile at Pityus. The head of Rufinus[3] was carried on a pike to Constantinople, and to shame his insatiable greed his severed hand begged for pence from door to door. Timasius[4] was hurled down suddenly from a post of the highest dignity, and thinks it an escape that he now lives in obscurity at Assa. I will say no more of the calamities of individuals; I come now to the frail fortunes of human life, and my soul shudders to recount the downfall of our age.

For twenty years and more the blood of Romans has every day been shed between Constantinople and the Julian Alps. Scythia, Thrace, Macedonia, Thessaly, Dardania, Dacia, Epirus, Dalmatia, and all the provinces of Pannonia, have been sacked, pillaged and plundered by Goths and Sarmatians, Quadians and Alans, Huns and Vandals and Mar-

tronae, quot virgines Dei et ingenua nobiliaque
corpora his beluis fuere ludibrio! Capti episcopi,
interfecti presbyteri et diversorum officia clericorum,
subversae ecclesiae, ad altaria Christi stabulati
equi, martyrum effossae reliquae: ubique luctus,
ubique gemitus ' et plurima mortis imago.' Romanus
orbis ruit et tamen cervix nostra erecta non flectitur.
Quid putas nunc animi habere Corinthios, Atheni-
enses, Lacedaemonios, Arcadas cunctamque Grae-
ciam, quibus imperant barbari? Et certe paucas
urbes nominavi, in quibus olim fuere regna non
modica. Inmunis ab his malis videbatur oriens et
tantum nuntiis consternatus: ecce tibi anno praeterito ex ultimis Caucasi rupibus inmissi in nos non
Arabiae, sed septentrionis lupi tantas brevi provincias percucurrerunt. Quot monasteria capta,
quantae fluviorum aquae humano cruore mutatae
sunt! Obsessa Antiochia et urbes reliquae, quas
Halys, Cydnus, Orontes Eufratesque praeterfluunt.
Tracti greges captivorum; Arabia, Phoenix, Palae-
stina, Aegyptus timore captivae.

' Non mihi si linguae centum sint oraque centum,
Ferrea vox,
Omnia poenarum percurrere nomina possim.'

---

[1] Virgil, *Aeneid*, II. 369.   [2] A.D. 395.
[3] Virgil, *Aeneid*, VI. 625.

comanni. How many matrons, how many of God's virgins, ladies of gentle birth and high position, have been made the sport of these beasts! Bishops have been taken prisoners, presbyters and other clergymen of different orders murdered. Churches have been overthrown, horses stabled at Christ's altar, the relics of martyrs dug up.

> 'Sorrow and grief on every side we see
> And death in many a shape.' [1]

The Roman world is falling, and yet we hold our heads erect instead of bowing our necks. What, think you, are the feelings of the Corinthians, the Athenians, the Lacedaemonians, the Arcadians, and all the other Greeks over whom barbarians now are ruling? I have only mentioned a few cities certainly, but they were once the seats of no small powers. The East seemed to be immune from these dangers and was only dismayed by the news that reached her. But lo! last year [2] the wolves—not of Arabia, but from the far north—were let loose upon us from the distant crags of Caucasus, and in a short time overran whole provinces. How many monasteries did they capture, how many rivers were reddened with men's blood! They besieged Antioch and all the other cities on the Halys, Cydnus, Orontes, and Euphrates. They carried off troops of captives. Arabia, Phoenicia, Palestine and Egypt in their terror felt themselves already enslaved.

> ' Had I a hundred tongues, a hundred mouths,
>   A voice of brass, I could not tell the names
>   Of all those punishments.' [3]

Neque enim historiam proposui scribere, sed nostras breviter flere miserias. Alioquin ad haec merito explicanda et Thucydides et Sallustius muti sunt.

17. Felix Nepotianus, qui haec non videt; felix, qui ista non audit. Nos miseri, qui aut patimur aut patientes fratres nostros tanta perspicimus; et tamen vivere volumus eosque, qui his carent, flendos potius quam beandos putamus. Olim offensum sentimus nec placamus Deum. Nostris peccatis barbari fortes sunt, nostris vitiis Romanus superatur exercitus; et quasi non hoc sufficeret cladibus plus paene bella civilia quam hostilis mucro consumpsit. Miseri Israhelitae, ad quorum conparationem Nabuchodonosor servus Dei scribitur[1]; infelices nos, qui tantum displicemus Deo, ut per rabiem barbarorum illius in nos ira desaeviat. Ezechias egit paenitentiam, et centum octoginta quinque milia Assyriorum ab uno angelo una nocte deleta sunt[2]; Iosaphat laudes domino concinebat, et dominus pro laudante superabat[3]; Moyses contra Amalech non gladio sed oratione pugnavit[4]. Si erigi volumus, prosternamur. Pro pudor et stolida usque ad incredulitatem mens! Romanus exercitus, victor orbis et dominus, ab his[5] vincitur, hos pavet, horum terretur aspectu, qui ingredi non valent, qui, si terram tetigerint, se mortuos arbitrantur, et non intellegimus prophetarum voces: ' fugient mille uno persequente ' nec ampu-

---

[1] Jeremiah, xxvii. 6.   [2] 2 Kings, xix. 35.
[3] 2 Chron., xx. 5 ff.   [4] Exodus, xvii, 11.
[5] *l.e.* the Huns.

But I did not propose to write a history: I only wished briefly to lament our miseries. In any case, if it came to telling this tale adequately, even Thucydides and Sallust would have no voice.

Happy is Nepotian, for he does not see these sights nor hear those cries. We are the unhappy. who either suffer ourselves or see our brothers suffer so much. And yet we wish to go on living, and think that those who have escaped from these evils are to be lamented rather than counted happy. For a long time now we have felt that God is offended with us, but we do not try to appease Him. It is by reason of our sins that the barbarians are strong, it is our vices that bring defeat to the armies of Rome; and as if this were not enough of carnage, civil wars have spilt almost more blood than the enemy's sword. Miserable were the Israelites, in comparison with whom Nebuchadnezzar is called the servant of God:[1] unhappy are we, who have so displeased God that His anger vents its fury on us by the barbarians' mad attacks. Hezekiah repented, and one hundred and eighty-five thousand Assyrians were destroyed by one angel in a night.[2] Jehosaphat sang the praises of the Lord, and the Lord gave his worshipper the victory.[3] Moses fought against Amalek, not with the sword, but with prayer.[4] If we wish to be lifted up, let us first prostrate ourselves. Shame on us who are too stupid for belief! The soldiers of Rome, who once subdued and ruled the world, now are conquered by these men, tremble and shrink in fear from these who cannot walk on foot and think themselves as good as dead if once they are unhorsed.[5] We do not understand the prophet's words: ' One thousand shall flee at the rebuke of

tamus causas morbi, ut morbus pariter auferatur, statimque cernamus [1] sagittas pilis, tiaras galeis, caballos equis cedere?

18. Excessimus consolandi modum, et, dum unius mortem flere prohibemus, totius orbis mortuos planximus. Xerxes, ille rex potentissimus, qui subvertit montes, maria constravit, cum de sublimi loco infinitam hominum multitudinem et innumerabilem vidisset exercitum, flesse dicitur, quod post centum annos nullus eorum, quos tunc cernebat, superfuturus esset. O si possemus in talem ascendere speculam, de qua universam terram sub nostris pedibus cerneremus! Iam tibi ostenderem totius mundi ruinas, gentes gentibus et regnis regna conlisa; alios torqueri, alios necari, alios obrui fluctibus, alios ad servitutem trahi; hic nuptias, ibi planctum; illos nasci, istos mori; alios affluere divitiis, alios mendicare; et non Xerxis tantum exercitum, sed totius mundi homines, qui nunc vivunt, in brevi spatio defuturos. Vincitur sermo rei magnitudine et minus est omne quod dicimus.

19. Redeamus igitur ad nos et quasi e caelo descendentes paulisper nostra videamus. Sentisne, obsecro te, quando infans, quando puer, quando iuvenis, quando robustae aetatis, quando senex factus sis? Cotidie morimur, cotidie commutamur et tamen aeternos esse nos credimus. Hoc ipsum, quod dicto, quod scribitur, quod relego, quod emendo,

---

[1] cernimus: *Hilberg*.

---

[1] Isaiah, xxx. 17.
[2] That is to say, the enemy weapons would give way to the Roman.
[3] Herodotus, VII. 45.

one.'[1] We do not cut away the causes of our malady, and thereby remove the malady itself. Then we should see arrows give way to javelins, caps to helmets, and nags to chargers.[2]

I have passed beyond the limits of consolation, and in forbidding you to weep for one man's death I have mourned for the dead of the whole world. That mighty king Xerxes, who overthrew mountains and turned the sea into solid ground, when from his high place he looked upon his infinite multitudes and his countless host of men, is said to have wept at the thought that not one of those whom he saw would in a hundred years be alive.[3] Oh, if we could ascend into such a watch-tower as would give us a view of the whole world spread beneath our feet! Then I would show you a universe in ruins, peoples warring against peoples, and kingdoms shattered on kingdoms. You would see some men being tortured, some killed, others drowned at sea, others dragged off to slavery; here a wedding, there lamentation; some being born, others dying; some living in affluence, others begging their bread; not merely Xerxes' army, but the inhabitants of the whole world now alive destined soon to pass away. Words fail; for language is inadequate to the greatness of this theme.

Let us return then to ourselves, and coming down from the skies consider for a moment our own position. Are you conscious now, pray, of the time when you were an infant, or of the stages you have passed from boyhood to manhood, from maturity to old age? Every day we die, every day we are changed, and yet we believe ourselves to be eternal. This very act of dictation, writing, revising and

de vita mea trahitur. Quot puncta notarii, tot meorum damna sunt temporum. Scribimus atque rescribimus, transeunt maria epistulae et fidente sulcos carina per singulos fluctus aetatis nostrae momenta minuuntur. Solum habemus lucri, quod Christi nobis amore sociamur. ' Caritas patiens est, benigna est; caritas non zelatur, non agit perperam, non inflatur, omnia sustinet, omnia credit, omnia sperat, omnia patitur; caritas numquam excidit.'[1] Haec semper vivit in pectore; ob hanc Nepotianus noster absens praesens est et per tanta terrarum spatia divisos utraque conplectitur manu. Habemus mutuae obsidem caritatis. Iungamur spiritu, stringamur affectu et fortitudinem mentis, quam beatus papa Chromatius[2] ostendit in dormitione germani, nos imitemur in filio. Illum nostra pagella decantet, illum cunctae litterae sonent. Quem corpore non valemus, recordatione teneamus et, cum quo loqui non possumus, de eo numquam loqui desinamus.

LXXVII

AD OCEANUM DE MORTE FABIOLAE[3]

1. PLURES anni sunt, quod super dormitione Blesillae Paulam, venerabilem feminam, recenti

---

[1] 1 Corinthians, xiii. 4, 7.

[2] Bishop of Aquileia, *d. c.* 407 : his brother Eusebius was also a bishop. Cf. Letter VII. The title " Pope," at first applied to the " spiritual father," who was the means of a man's conversion, later became restricted first to bishops and abbots, then to the Bishop of Rome and the patriarchs of Alexandria, Antioch, Jerusalem and Constantinople, and finally after 1073 was claimed exclusively for the Bishop of Rome.

[3] This letter, addressed to Oceanus, and written in A.D. 399, gives an account of the life of Fabiola, one of the rich Roman matrons who took Jerome as their spiritual guide. She

correction is something taken from my span. Every stroke of my secretary's pen is so much loss of life for me. We write letters and send replies, our messages cross the seas, and as the ship cleaves a furrow through the waves the moments that we have to live grow less. We have but one profit: we are joined together by the love of Christ. ' Charity suffereth long and is kind; charity envieth not; charity vaunteth not itself, is not puffed up; beareth all things, believeth all things, hopeth all things, endureth all things. Charity never faileth.' [1] It lives ever in the heart, and by it our Nepotian is present though absent, and grasps us each by a hand, severed as we are in distant lands. We have in him a pledge of our mutual love. Let us join in spirit, let us bind ourselves together in affection's chains, and let us who have lost a son take pattern by the courage that the blessed Pope Chromatius [2] showed when his brother fell asleep. Let our pages chant his praise, let every letter echo his name. We cannot have him in the body, but let us hold him fast in remembrance. We cannot speak with him, but let u never cease to speak of him.

LETTER LXXVII

To Oceanus [3] on the Death of Fabiola

MANY years have passed since I consoled the venerated Paula, while her wound was still fresh,

divorced her first husband and then married again, but did penance for this error and visited the Holy Land, where she was staying with Jerome when the Huns invaded Palestine. She then returned to Rome, and in conjunction with Pammachius, the widowed husband of the rich Paulina, established a hostel for travellers at Ostia just before her death. Cf. App., p. 486.

adhuc vulnere consolatus sum. Quartae aestatis circulus volvitur, ex quo ad Heliodorum episcopum Nepotiani scribens epitaphium, quidquid habere virium potui, in illo tunc dolore consumpsi. Ante hoc ferme biennium Pammachio meo pro subita peregrinatione Paulinae brevem epistulam dedi erubescens ad disertissimum virum plura loqui et ei sua ingerere, ne non tam consolari amicum viderer, quam stulta iactantia docere perfectum. Nunc mihi, fili Oceane, volenti et ultro adpetenti debitum munus inponis, quod pro novitate virtutum veterem materiam novam faciam. In illis enim vel parentis affectus vel maeror avunculi vel desiderium mariti temperandum fuit et pro diversitate personarum diversa de scripturis adhibenda medicina.

2. In praesentiarum tradis mihi Fabiolam, laudem Christianorum, miraculum gentilium, luctum pauperum, solacium monachorum. Quidquid primum adripuero, sequentium conparatione vilescit. Ieiunium praedicem? Praevertunt elemosynae. Humilitatem laudem? Maior est ardor fidei. Dicam adpetitas sordes et in condemnationem vestium sericarum plebeium cultum et servilia indumenta quaesita? Plus est animum deposuisse quam cultum. Difficilius adrogantia quam auro caremus et gemmis. His enim abiectis interdum gloriosis tumemus sordibus et vendibilem paupertatem populari aurae

---

[1] Letter XXXIX.   [2] Letter LX.
[3] Letter LXVI.

for the falling asleep of Blesilla.[1] Four summers
have rolled by since I wrote to Bishop Heliodorus a
funeral panegyric on Nepotian,[2] spending all the
strength that I possessed in giving expression to
my grief. About two years have elapsed since I
sent a brief letter to my dear Pammachius on the
sudden passing of his Paulina,[3] for I blushed to say
more to so learned a man or to repeat to him his
own thoughts, lest I should seem, not so much to
be comforting a friend, as in foolish ostentation to
be instructing one already perfect. To-day, my
son Oceanus, the task of duty you impose upon me
is one that I gladly accept and would even seek
unasked; for dealing with new virtues I shall make
an old subject fresh. In those other cases I had
to assuage a mother's love, an uncle's grief, and a
husband's yearning; and as the persons differed
I had to apply from the Scriptures a different remedy.

On this occasion you give me as my subject Fabiola,
the glory of the Christians, the wonder of the Gentiles,
the sorrow of the poor, and the consolation of the
monks. Whatever point I take first pales in comparison with what is to come. Shall I tell of her
fastings? Her alms are greater still. Shall I
praise her humility? It is outstripped by the
ardour of her faith. Shall I mention her studied
squalor, her plebeian dress, and the slave's garb
she choose in condemnation of silken robes? It is
a greater thing to change one's disposition than to
change one's dress. We part with arrogance less
easily than with gold and jewels. Even when these
are thrown away, we sometimes pride ourselves on
our ostentatious shabbiness and make a bid for
popular favour by offering poverty as its price. A

offerimus. Celata virtus et in conscientiae fota secreto Deum solum iudicem respicit. Unde novis mihi est efferenda praeconiis et ordine rhetorum praetermisso tota de conversionis ac paenitentiae incunabulis adsumenda. Alius forsitan scholae memor Quintum Maximum,

' Unus qui nobis cunctando restituit rem,'

et totam Fabiorum gentem proferret in medium, diceret pugnas, describeret proelia et per tantae nobilitatis gradus Fabiolam venisse iactaret, ut, quod in virga non poterat, in radicibus demonstraret. Ego, diversorii Bethlemitici et praesepis dominici amator, in quo virgo puerpera Deum fudit infantem, ancillam Christi non de nobilitate veteris historiae, sed de ecclesiae humilitate producam.

3. Et quia statim in principio quasi scopulus quidam et procella mihi obtrectatorum eius opponitur, quod secundum sortita matrimonium prius reliquerit, non laudabo conversam, nisi ream absolvero. Tanta prior maritus vitia habuisse narratur, ut ne scortum quidem et vile mancipium ea sustinere posset. Quae si voluero dicere, perdam virtutem feminae, quae maluit culpam subire discidii quam quandam corporis sui infamare partem et maculas eius detegere. Hoc solum proferam, quod verecundae matronae et Christianae satis est. Praecepit dominus uxorem non debere dimitti excepta causa

---

[1] Ennius and Virgil, *Aeneid*, VI. 846.

virtue that is concealed and cherished in the inner consciousness looks to God alone as judge. So the eulogy I bestow upon her must be altogether new: I must neglect all the rules of rhetoric and begin my story at the cradle of her conversion and penitence. Others perhaps might remember their school-days and bring forward Quintus Maximus:

'The man who by delaying saved the state,'[1]

and with him the whole Fabian family. They might tell of their conflicts and describe their battles, and boast that Fabiola had come of so noble a line, showing in the root a glory which they could not find in the branch. I for my part, who am a lover of the inn at Bethlehem, and the Lord's stable where the Virgin in childbirth brought forth an infant God, I will bring forward a handmaid of Christ who shall rely not on the fame of ancient history but on the humility of the Church.

As at the very outset there is a rock in the path, and I am faced by the storm of censure that was directed against her for having taken a second husband and abandoned her first, I shall not praise her for her conversion until I have cleared her from this charge. We are told that her first husband was a man of such heinous vices that even a prostitute or a common slave could not have put up with them. If I describe them, I shall mar the heroism of the woman, who preferred to bear the blame of separation rather than to expose to shame the man who was one body with her, and thus reveal the stains upon his character. This only I will say, and it is a plea sufficient to excuse a chaste matron and a Christian wife. The Lord ordained that a wife

fornicationis et, si dimissa fuerit, manere innuptam. Quidquid viris iubetur, hoc consequenter redundat ad feminas. Neque enim adultera uxor dimittenda est et vir moechus tenendus. Si ʻ qui meretrici iungitur, unum corpus facit,ʼ ergo et, quae scortatori inpuroque sociatur, unum cum eo corpus efficitur. Aliae sunt leges Caesarum, aliae Christi; aliud Papinianus, aliud Paulus noster praecipit. Apud illos in viris pudicitiae frena laxantur et solo stupro atque adulterio condemnato passim per lupanaria et ancillulas libido permittitur, quasi culpam dignitas faciat, non voluptas. Apud nos, quod non licet feminis, aeque non licet viris et eadem servitus pari condicione censetur. Dimisit ergo, ut aiunt, vitiosum; dimisit illius et illius criminis noxium; dimisit—paene dixi, quod clamante vicinia uxor non sola prodidit. Sin autem arguitur, quare repudiato marito non innupta permanserit, facile culpam fatebor, dum tamen referam necessitatem. ʻ Melius est,ʼ inquit apostolus, ʻ nubere quam uri.ʼ Adulescentula erat, viduitatem suam servare non poterat. Videbat aliam legem in membris suis repugnantem legi mentis suae et se vinctam atque captivam ad coitum trahi. Melius arbitrata est aperte confiteri inbecillitatem suam et umbram quandam miserabilis subire coniugii quam

---

[1] 1 Corinthians, vi. 16.
[2] The great Roman jurist, put to death by Caracalla.
[3] 1 Corinthians, vii. 9.

must not be put away except for fornication, and
that, if she was put away, she must remain unmarried. A command that is given to men applies
logically also to women. It cannot be that an
adulterous wife should be put away and an unfaithful
husband retained. If ' he which is joined to a harlot
is one body,' [1] she who is joined to a filthy whoremonger is one body with him also. The laws of
Caesar are different from the laws of Christ: Papinian [2]
commands one thing, our Paul another. Among
the Romans men's unchastity goes unchecked;
seduction and adultery are condemned, but free
permission is given to lust to range the brothels and
to have slave girls, as though it were a person's
rank and not the sensual pleasure that constituted
the offence. With us what is unlawful for women is
equally unlawful for men, and as both sexes serve
God they are bound by the same conditions. Fabiola,
as men say, put away a vicious husband; she put
away a man who was guilty of this and that crime;
she put him away because—I almost mentioned
the scandal which the whole neighbourhood proclaimed but which his wife alone refused to reveal.
If she is blamed because after repudiating her husband she did not remain unmarried, I will readily
admit her fault, provided that I may put in the
plea of necessity. ' It is better,' says the apostle,
' to marry than to burn.' [3] She was a very young
woman and she could not remain a widow. She
saw another law in her members warring against the
law of her mind, and she felt herself dragged like
a chained captive into carnal intercourse. She
thought it better to confess her weakness openly
and to accept the dark stain that such a lamentable

315

sub gloria univirae exercere meretricium. Idem apostolus vult viduas ' adulescentulas nubere, filios procreare, nullam dare occasionem maledicti gratia.' Et protinus, cur hoc velit, exponit: ' Iam enim quaedam abierunt retro Satanan.' Igitur et Fabia, quia persuaserat sibi et putabat virum iure a se dimissum nec evangelii rigorem[1] noverat, in quo nubendi universa causatio viventibus viris feminis Christianis amputatur, dum multa diaboli vitat vulnera, unum incauta vulnus accepit.

4. Sed quid ego in abolitis et antiquis moror quaerens excusare culpam, cuius paenitentiam ipsa confessa est? Quis hoc crederet, ut post mortem secundi viri in semet reversa, quo tempore solent viduae neglegentes iugo servitutis excusso agere se liberius, adire balneas, volitare per plateas, vultus circumferre meretricios, saccum indueret, errorem publice fateretur, et tota urbe spectante Romana ante diem paschae in basilica quondam Laterani, qui Caesariano truncatus est gladio, staret in ordine paenitentum, episcopo et presbyteris et omni populo conlacrimanti sparsum crinem, ora lurida, squalidas manus, sordida colla submitteret? Quae peccata fletus iste non purget? Quas inveteratas maculas haec lamenta non abluant? Petrus trinam nega-

---

[1] Rigorem *Engelbrecht* : vigorem.

[1] 1 Timothy, v. 14, 15.
[2] A Roman senator who conspired against Nero : the basilica was perhaps S. John Lateran.

marriage would bring, rather than to claim to be the wife of one husband and under that disguise to ply the harlot's trade. The same apostle expresses his wish that 'young widows should marry, bear children, and give no handle to calumny.' And then at once he gives his reason: 'For some are already turned aside after Satan.'[1] Fabiola therefore had convinced herself, and thought that she was justified in putting away her husband. She did not know the Gospel's strict ordinance, which precludes Christian women from marrying again in their first husband's lifetime, whatever their case may be. Thus she evaded the other assaults of the devil, but this one wound from him she unwittingly received.

But why do I linger over the forgotten past, seeking to excuse a fault for which she herself confessed her penitence? Who would believe that after the death of her second husband, at a time when widows, having shaken off the yoke of slavery, are wont to grow careless and indulge in licence, frequenting the public baths, flitting to and fro in the squares, showing their harlot faces everywhere— who, I say, would believe that it was then that she came to herself, put on sackcloth and made public confession of error. On the eve of passover, in the presence of all Rome, she took her stand among the other penitents in the church of that Lateranus who perished formerly by Caesar's sword.[2] There before bishop, presbyters, and weeping populace she exposed to view her dishevelled hair, wan face, soiled hands, and dust-stained neck. What sins would not such lamentation purge away? What stains so deep that these tears would not wash them out? By a threefold confession Peter annulled his three-

SELECT LETTERS OF ST. JEROME

tionem trina confessione delevit. Aaron sacrilegium
et conflatum ex auro vituli caput fraternae correxere
preces. David, sancti et mansuetissimi viri, homicidium pariter et adulterium septem dierum emenda-
vit fames. Iacebat in terra, volutabatur in cinere et
oblitus regiae potestatis lumen quaerebat in tenebris
illumque tantum respiciens, quem offenderat, lacri-
mabili voce dicebat: ' Tibi soli peccavi et malum
coram te feci,' et: ' Redde mihi laetitiam salutaris
tui et spiritu principali confirma me.' Atque ita
factum est, ut, qui me prius docuerat virtutibus suis,
quomodo stans non caderem, doceret per paenitentiam, quomodo cadens resurgerem. Quid tam
inpium legimus inter reges quam Achab, de quo
scriptura dicit: ' Non fuit alius talis ut Achab, qui
venumdatus est, ut faceret malum in conspectu
domini.' Hic, cum pro sanguine Nabuthae cor-
reptus fuisset ab Helia et audisset iram domini per
prophetam: ' Occidisti, insuper et possedisti,' et:
' Ecce ego inducam super te mala et demetam
posteriora tua,' et reliqua, ' Scidit vestimenta sua et
operuit cilicio carnem suam ieiunavitque in sacco et
ambulabat demisso capite. Tunc factus est sermo
domini ad Heliam Thesbiten dicens: " Nonne vidisti
humilitatem Achab coram me? Quia ergo humili-
tatus est in timore mei, non inducam malum in
diebus eius." ' O felix paenitentia, quae ad se Dei
traxit oculos, quae furentem sententiam domini
confesso errore mutavit! Hoc idem et Manassen in
Paralipomenon et Nineven fecisse legimus in pro-

---

[1] Psalm li. 6. [2] Psalm li. 14.
[3] 1 Kings, xxi. 25 *seq.* [4] 2 Chron., xxxiii. 12.
[5] Jonah, iii. 5–10.

fold denial. Aaron did a sacrilegious act by fashion-
ing a calf's head in gold; but his brother's prayers
made amends. David, that saintly and most merciful
man, committed both murder and adultery; but
he atoned for it by fasting for seven days. He lay
on the ground, he grovelled in the ashes, he forgot
his royal power, he sought for light in the darkness.
He turned his eyes only to Him whom he had offended
and cried with a lamentable voice: ' Against thee,
thee only have I sinned, and done this evil in thy
sight,' [1] and, ' Restore unto me the joy of thy salvation and uphold me with thy free spirit.' [2] So it
came about that he who by his virtues taught me
first how I might stand and not fall, by his penitence
taught me how if I fell I might rise again. Do we
read of any among the kings so wicked as Ahab, of
whom the Scripture says: ' There was none like
unto Ahab which did sell himself to work wickedness
in the sight of the Lord '? [3] But when he was re-
buked by Elijah for shedding Naboth's blood and
heard the prophet threaten him with God's wrath:
' Thou hast killed and taken possession: behold I
will bring evil upon thee and will take away thy
posterity,' and so on, then: ' he rent his clothes,
and put sackcloth upon his flesh and fasted in sackcloth and went softly. Then came the word of the
Lord to Elijah the Tishbite, saying: " Seest thou
how Ahab humbleth himself before me? Because
he humbleth himself before me, I will not bring
the evil in his days." ' O happy penitence, which
drew God's eyes to itself, and by a confession of
error changed the sentence of the Lord's wrath!
The same conduct is attributed to Manasseh in the
Chronicles,[4] to Nineveh [5] in the book of the prophet

pheta, publicanum quoque in evangelio, e quibus primus non solum indulgentiam, sed et regnum recipere meruit, alius inpendentem Dei fregit iram, tertius pectus verberans pugnis oculos non levabat ad caelum et multo iustificatior recessit humili confessione vitiorum quam superba pharisaeus iactatione virtutum. Non est loci huius, ut paenitentiam praedicem et quasi contra Montanum Novatumque scribens dicam illam hostiam domini esse placabilem et sacrificium Deo spiritum contribulatum et : ' Malo paenitentiam peccatoris quam mortem,' et : ' Exsurge, exsurge, Hierusalem,' et multa alia, quae prophetarum clangunt tubae.

5. Hoc unum loquar, quod et legentibus utile sit et praesenti causae conveniat. Non est confusa dominum in terris et ille eam non confundetur in caelo. Aperuit cunctis vulnus suum et decolore in corpore cicatricem flens Roma conspexit. Dissuta habuit latera, nudum caput, clausum os. Non est ingressa ecclesiam domini, sed extra castra cum Maria, sorore Moysi, separata consedit, ut, quam sacerdos eiecerat, ipse revocaret. Descendit de solio deliciarum suarum, accepit molam, fecit farinam et discalciatis pedibus transivit fluenta lacrimarum. Sedit super carbonis ignis ; hi ei fuere in adiutorium. Faciem, per quam secundo viro placuerat, verberabat, oderat gemmas, linteamina videre non poterat, orna-

---

[1] S. Luke, xviii, 13.
[2] Founders of heretical sects in the second and third centuries.
[3] Ezekiel, xviii. 23.   [4] Baruch, v. 5.

Jonah, and to the publican in the Gospel.[1] The first not only earned God's pardon but regained his kingdom; the second broke the force of God's impending anger; the third smiting his breast with his fists would not lift his eyes to heaven, and yet by the humble confession of his faults he went away more justified than the Pharisee with his arrogant boasting of his virtues. This, however, is not the place to preach penitence, or to say of it, as though I were writing against Montanus and Novatus,[2] that it is a victim well pleasing to the Lord and that a broken spirit is God's sacrifice. Nor will I quote the words: ' I prefer the repentance of a sinner rather than his death,'[3] or ' Arise, arise, O Jerusalem,'[4] or any other of the many sayings which are noised abroad by the trumpets of the prophets.

This one thing I will say, for it is both useful to my readers and pertinent to the present case. Fabiola was not ashamed of the Lord on earth, and He will not be ashamed of her in heaven. She laid bare her wound to all, and Rome beheld with tears the scar upon her livid body. She uncovered her limbs, bared her head, and closed her mouth. She did not enter God's church but like Miriam, the sister of Moses, sat apart outside the camp, until the priest who had cast her out should call her back again. She came down from her throne of luxury, she took up the millstone and ground meal, with unshod feet she passed through rivers of tears. She sat upon coals of fire, and these became her aid. She beat the face by which she had won her second husband's love, she abhorred all jewelry, she could not bear even to look upon fine linen, she shrank

menta fugiebat. Sic dolebat, quasi adulterium com-
misisset et multis inpendiis medicaminum unum
vulnus sanare cupiebat.

6. Diu morati sumus in paenitentia, in qua velut in
vadosis locis resedimus, ut maior nobis et absque ullo
inpedimento se laudum eius campus aperiret. Re-
cepta sub oculis omnis ecclesiae communione quid
fecit? Scilicet in die bona malorum oblita est et
post naufragium rursum temptare voluit pericula
navigandi? Quin potius omnem censum, quem
habere poterat—erat autem amplissimus et respondens generi eius—dilapidavit ac vendidit et in pecunia
congregatum usibus pauperum praeparavit. Et
primo omnium νοσοκομεῖον instituit, in quo aegro-
tantes colligeret de plateis et consumpta languoribus
atque inedia miserorum membra refoveret. Describam nunc ego diversas hominum calamitates,
truncas nares, effossos oculos, semiustos pedes,
luridas manus, tumentes alvos, exile femur, crura
turgentia et de exesis ac putridis carnibus vermiculos
bullientes? Quotiens morbo regio et paedore con-
fectos humeris suis portavit? Quotiens lavit puru-
lentam vulnerum saniem, quam alius aspicere non
audebat? Praebebat cibos propria manu et spirans
cadaver sorbitiunculis inrigabat. Scio multos divites
et religiosos ob stomachi angustiam exercere huiusce
modi misericordiam per aliena ministeria et clementes

from all adornment. If she had committed adultery her grief could not have been greater, and she went to the expense of many remedies in her eagerness to cure one wound.

I have lingered long in describing Fabiola's penitence, and my barque has grounded in shallow waters; but I wished to open up a wider and unimpeded field for her praises. When she was restored to communion before the eyes of the whole church, what did she do? Did she forget her sorrows in the midst of happiness, and determine after being shipwrecked to face once more the dangers of the main? Nay, she preferred to break up and sell all that she could lay hands on of her property—it was a large one and suitable to her rank—and when she had turned it into money she disposed of everything for the benefit of the poor. First of all she founded an infirmary and gathered into it sufferers from the streets, giving their poor bodies worn with sickness and hunger all a nurse's care. Need I describe here the diverse troubles from which human beings suffer, the maimed noses, the lost eyes, the scorched feet, the leprous arms, the swollen bellies, the shrunken thighs, the dropsical legs, and the diseased flesh alive with hungry worms? How often did she carry on her own shoulders poor filthy wretches tortured by epilepsy! How often did she wash away the purulent matter from wounds which others could not even endure to look upon! She gave food with her own hand, and even when a man was but a breathing corpse, she would moisten his lips with drops of water. I know that many wealthy and devout persons by reason of their weak stomachs carry on this work of mercy by the agency of others,

esse pecunia, non manu. Quos equidem non reprobo et teneritudinem animi nequaquam interpretor infidelitatem; sed, sicut inbecillitati stomachi veniam tribuo, sic perfectae mentis ardorem in caelum laudibus fero. Magna fides ista contemnit; scit, quid in Lazaro dives purpuratus aliquando non fecerit, quali superba mens retributione damnata sit. Ille, quem despicimus, quem videre non possumus, ad cuius intuitum vomitus nobis erumpit, nostri similis est, de eodem nobiscum formatus luto, isdem conpactus elementis. Quidquid patitur, et nos pati possumus. Vulnera eius aestimemus propria et omnis animi in alterum duritia clementi in nosmet ipsos cogitatione frangetur.

' Non, mihi si linguae centum sint oraque centum,
    Ferrea vox,
  Omnia morborum percurrere nomina possim,'

quae Fabiola in tanta miserorum refrigeria commutavit, ut multi pauperum sani languentibus inviderent. Quamquam illa simili liberalitate erga clericos et monachos ac virgines fuerit—quod monasterium non illius opibus sustentatum est? Quem nudum et clinicum non Fabiolae vestimenta texerunt? In quos se indigentium eius non effudit praeceps et festina largitio? Angusta misericordiae Roma fuit; peragrabat ergo insulas. Etruscum mare Vulscorumque provinciam et reconditos curvorum litorum sinus, in quibus monachorum consistunt chori, vel proprio corpore vel transmissa per fideles ac sanctos viros munificentia circuibat.

7. Unde repente et contra opinionem omnium

---

[1] Virgil, *Aeneid*, VI. 625.

and show mercy with the purse, not with the hand.
I do not blame nor do I by any means construe their
lack of fortitude as lack of faith. But while I excuse
their weakness, I extol to the skies the ardent zeal
that perfect courage possesses. A great faith
makes light of discomfort: it knows the retribution
that fell upon the rich man clothed in purple, who
in his pride refused Lazarus aid. The sufferer
whom we despise and cannot bear to behold, whose
very aspect turns our stomachs, is a man like ourselves, formed of the same clay, made out of the
same elements. Whatever he suffers we may
possibly suffer also. Let us regard his wounds as
our own, and then all our lack of sympathy for others
will be overcome by our pity for ourselves.

> ' Had I a hundred tongues, a hundred mouths
>   With voice of brass, I could not tell the names '[1]

of all the maladies which Fabiola treated. She was,
indeed, such a comforter that many poor people
who were well fell to envying the sick. Not but
what she showed the same generosity to the clergy,
monks, and virgins. What monastery was there
which her purse did not aid? What naked or bed-
ridden sufferer did she not supply with clothes? On
what indigent person did she not pour out her swift
and lavish donations? Rome was not large enough
for her compassionate kindness. She went from
island to island, and travelled round the Etruscan
Sea, and through the Volscian province, with its
lonely curving bays, where bands of monks have
taken up their home, bestowing her bounty either
in person or by the agency of holy men of the faith.
Then suddenly, and to every one's surprise, she

Hierosolymam navigavit, ubi multorum excepta
concursu nostro parumper usa est hospitio; cuius
societatis recordans videor mihi adhuc videre, quam
vidi. Iesu bone, quo illa fervore, quo studio intenta
erat divinis voluminibus et veluti quandam famem
satiare desiderans per prophetas, evangelia psal-
mosque currebat quaestiones proponens et solutas
recondens in scriniolo pectoris sui! Nec vero satiaba-
tur audiendi cupidine, sed addens scientiam addebat
dolorem, et, quasi oleum flammae adiceres, maioris
ardoris fomenta capiebat. Quodam die, cum in
manibus Moysi Numeros teneremus, et me verecunde
rogaret, quid sibi vellet nominum tanta congeries, cur
singulae tribus in aliis atque in aliis locis varie
iungerentur, quomodo Balaam ariolus sic futura
Christi mysteria prophetarit, ut nullus propemodum
prophetarum tam aperte de eo vaticinatus sit,
respondi, ut potui, et visus sum interrogationi eius
satisfacere. Revolvens ergo librum pervenit ad eum
locum, ubi catalogus describitur omnium mansionum,
per quas de Aegypto egrediens populus pervenit
usque ad fluenta Iordanis. Cumque causas et
rationes quaereret singularum, in quibusdam haesi-
tavi, in aliis inoffenso cucurri pede, in plerisque
simpliciter ignorantiam confessus sum. Tunc vero
magis coepit urguere et, quasi mihi non liceret
nescire, quod nescio, expostulare ac se indignam
tantis mysteriis dicere. Quid plura? Extorsit mihi

---

[1] Numbers, xxiv. 17 ff.

sailed to Jerusalem, where she was welcomed by a great concourse of people, and for a short time was my guest. When I remember that meeting, I seem to see her still as I saw her then. Blessed Jesus, with what fervour and zeal did she study the sacred volumes! In her eagerness to satisfy her hunger, she ran through the prophets, the gospels and the psalms; she suggested questions and stored up my answers in her heart's repository. Nor did her eagerness to hear ever bring with it satiety; increasing her knowledge she also increased her sorrow, and as though oil were cast upon fire she supplied fuel ever for a more burning zeal. One day we were occupied with Moses' Numbers, and she modestly questioned me as to the meaning of its mass of names. Why was it, she asked, that individual tribes were grouped in so many different ways in different places, and how did it happen that the soothsayer Balaam in prophesying the future mysteries of Christ foretold His coming more plainly than almost any of the prophets.[1] I replied as best I could, and I think I satisfied her inquiries. So she unrolled the book further, and came to the passage where the list is given of all the halting places by which the people on leaving Egypt made their way to the river Jordan. She asked me the meaning and the origin of each name, and in some cases I hesitated, in others I hurried through without stumbling, in very many I had frankly to confess ignorance. Thereupon she began to press me harder, expostulating with me as though it were not allowed me to be in ignorance of what I do not know, and declaring that she herself was unworthy of understanding such mysteries. Why say more?

negandi verecundia, ut proprium ei opus huiusce
modi disputatiunculae pollicerer, quod usque in
presens tempus, ut nunc intellego, domini voluntate
dilatum redditur memoriae illius, ut sacerdotalibus
prioris ad se voluminis induta vestibus per mundi
huius solitudinem gaudeat se ad terram repromissionis
aliquando venisse.

8. Verum, quod coepimus, persequamur. Quaerentibus nobis dignum tantae feminae habitaculum,
cum ita solitudinem cuperet, ut diversorio Mariae
carere nollet, ecce subito discurrentibus nuntiis
oriens totus intremuit, ab ultima Maeotide inter
glacialem Tanain et Massagetarum immanes populos,
ubi Caucasi rupibus feras gentes Alexandri claustra
cohibent, erupisse Hunorum examina, quae pernicibus
equis huc illucque volitantia caedis pariter ac
terroris cuncta conplerent. Aberat tunc Romanus
exercitus et bellis civilibus in Italia tenebatur.
Hanc gentem Herodotus refert sub Dario, rege
Medorum, viginti annis Orientem tenuisse captivum
et ab Aegyptiis atque Aethiopibus annuum exegisse
vectigal. Avertat Iesus ab orbe Romano tales ultra
bestias! Insperati ubique aderant et famam celeritate vincentes non religioni, non dignitatibus, non
aetati, non vagienti miserebantur infantiae. Coge-
bantur mori, qui dudum vivere coeperant et nesci-

---

[1] The first treatise dedicated to Fabiola was on the vestments worn by the Jewish priests, the second on the places
passed by the chosen people on their journey from Egypt to
the Promised Land.

[2] The Caspian Gates.

[3] Herodotus, I. 104. He calls them Σκύθαι.

I was ashamed to refuse her, and she compelled me to promise a special work on this subject for her use. Up till this moment I have deferred writing it; but my delay, I now see, was God's will, and it is now consecrated to her memory. As a previous treatise addressed to her clothed her in priestly vestments, so now she may rejoice that she has passed through the wilderness of this world and come at last to the land of promise.[1]

But let me continue the task I have begun. While I was seeking a dwelling suitable for so great a lady, whose desire for solitude included an unwillingness not to visit the place where Mary once lodged, suddenly messengers flew this way and that and the whole Eastern world trembled. We were told that swarms of Huns had poured forth from the distant Sea of Azov, midway between the icy river Tanais and the savage tribes of the Massagetae, where the gates of Alexander [2] keep back the barbarians behind the rocky Caucasus. Flying hither and thither on their swift steeds, said our informants, these invaders were filling the whole world with bloodshed and panic. At that time the Roman army was absent, being kept in Italy by reason of civil war. Of this race Herodotus [3] tells us that under Darius, king of the Medes, they held the East captive for twenty years, and exacted a yearly tribute from the Egyptians and the Ethiopians. May Jesus save the Roman world from such wild beasts in the future! Everywhere their approach was unexpected, they outstripped rumour by their speed, and they spared neither religion nor rank nor age; nay, even for wailing infants they had no pity. Children were forced to die, who had only just begun to live, and

entes malum suum inter hostium manus ac tela ridebant. Consonus inter omnes rumor petere eos Hierosolymam et ob nimiam auri cupiditatem ad hanc urbem concurrere. Muri neglecti pacis incuria sarciebantur Antiochiae; Tyrus volens a terra abrumpere insulam quaerebat antiquam. Tunc et nos conpulsi sumus parare naves, esse in litore, adventum hostium praecavere et saevientibus ventis magis barbaros metuere quam naufragium, non tam propriae saluti quam virginum castimoniae providentes. Erat in illo tempore quaedam apud nos dissensio et barbarorum pugnam domestica bella superabant. Nos in Oriente tenuerunt iam fixae sedes et inveteratum locorum sanctorum desiderium; illa, quia tota in sarcinis erat et in omni orbe peregrina, reversa est ad patriam, ut ibi pauper viveret, ubi dives fuerat, manens in alieno, quae multos prius hospites habuit, et—ne sermonem longius traham—in conspectu Romanae urbis pauperibus erogaret, quod illa teste vendiderat.

9. Nos hoc tantum dolemus, quod pretiosissimum de sanctis locis monile perdidimus. Recepit Roma, quod amiserat, ac procax et maledica lingua gentilium oculorum testimonio confutata est. Laudent ceteri misericordiam eius, humilitatem, fidem: ego ardorem animi plus laudabo. Librum, quo Heliodorum quondam iuvenis ad heremum cohortatus sum,

---

[1] Cf. Appendix II, p. 498 ff.
[2] At Bethlehem. Cf. Introd., p. ix.　　　[3] Letter XIV.

in ignorance of their fate smiled amid the brandished
weapons of the foe. The general report was that
they were making for Jerusalem, and that it was
their excessive greed for gold that urged them to
flock to that city. The walls of Antioch, neglected
in the careless days of peace, were hastily repaired.
Tyre, desirous of cutting herself off from the land,
sought again her ancient island. We too were
compelled to prepare ships, and to wait on the sea-
shore as a precaution against the enemy's arrival;
to fear the barbarians more than shipwreck, however fierce the winds might be; for we had to
think not so much of our own lives as of the chastity
of our virgins. At that time also there was a certain
dissension amongst us,[1] and our domestic quarrels
seemed more important than any fighting with
barbarians. I myself clung to my fixed abode in the
East,[2] and could not give up my inveterate longing
for the Holy Land. Fabiola, however, who only
had her travelling baggage and was a stranger in
every land, returned to her native city to live in
poverty where she had been rich, to lodge in the
house of another, she who had once entertained
many guests, and—not to prolong my story unduly—
to pay over to the poor before the eyes of Rome all
that she had sold with Rome for witness.

This only do I grieve for, that we in the Holy
Land lost in her a most precious jewel. Rome
recovered what she had lost, and the shameless
tongue of slander was confuted by the testimony
of the heathens' own eyes. Let others praise her
pity, her humility, her faith: I will rather extol the
ardour of her soul. The treatise [3] in which as a
young man I urged Heliodorus to be a hermit she

tenebat memoriter, et Romana cernens moenia
inclusam se esse plangebat. Oblita sexus, fragili-
tatis inmemor ac solitudinis tantum cupida ibi erat,
ubi animo morabatur. Non poterat teneri consiliis
amicorum: ita ex urbe quasi de vinculis gestiebat
erumpere. Dispensationem pecuniae et cautam
distributionem genus infidelitatis vocabat. Non
aliis elemosynam tribuere, sed suis pariter effusis
ipsa pro Christo stipes optabat accipere. Sic festina-
bat, sic inpatiens erat morarum, ut illam crederes
profecturam. Itaque, dum semper paratur, mors
eam invenire non potuit inparatam.

10. Inter laudes feminae subito mihi Pammachius
meus exoritur. Paulina dormit, ut ipse vigilet;
praecedit maritum, ut Christo famulum derelinquat.
Hic heres uxoris et hereditatis alii possessores.
Certabant vir et femina, quis in portu Abrahae
tabernaculum figeret, et haec erat inter utrumque
contentio, quis humanitate superaret. Vicit uterque
et uterque superatus est. Ambo se victos et victores
fatentur, dum, quod alter cupiebat, uterque perfecit.
Iungunt opes, sociant voluntates, ut, quod aemulatio
dissipatura erat, concordia cresceret. Necdum
dictum, iam factum: emitur hospitium et ad hospitium turba concurrit. 'Non est' enim 'labor in
Iacob nec dolor in Israhel.' Adducunt maria, quos
in gremio suo terra suscipiat. Mittit Roma pro-
perantes, quos navigaturos litus molle confoveat.

---

[1] Numbers, xxiii. 21.

knew by heart, and when she looked upon the walls of Rome she complained that she was their prisoner. Forgetful of her sex, unmindful of her frailty, she craved only for solitude and was in truth where her soul lingered. Her friends' advice could not restrain her, so anxious was she to escape from the fetters of Rome. She said that to weigh out money and distribute it carefully showed a lack of faith. She desired not to hand over the task of almsgiving to others, but to spend all that she possessed, and then herself to receive a dole in Christ's name. In such haste was she, and so impatient of delay, that you might have thought her always on the brink of departure. So, as she was ever making ready, death could not find her unprepared.

As I sing her praises, my dear Pammachius suddenly rises before me. Paulina sleeps that he may keep vigil; she has gone before her husband, that she may leave him behind to serve Christ. He was his wife's heir, but others now possess that inheritance. A man and a woman contended for the privilege of setting up Abraham's tent in the harbour of Rome; and this was the struggle between the two, who should be first in that contest of kindness. Each won and each lost. Both confess themselves victors and vanquished, for what each desired they carried out together. They join purses and combine their plans, that harmony might increase what rivalry would have wasted. Hardly said, the thing was done; a hostel was purchased and a crowd flocked to it for hospitality; for 'There is no more travail in Jacob nor distress in Israel.' [1] The seas brought in travellers for the land to welcome. Rome sent others, who hastened to enjoy the comforts of the mild shore before they

Quod Publius semel fecit in insula Melita erga unum
apostolum et—ne contradictioni locum tribuam—in
una nave, hoc isti et frequenter faciunt et in plures.
Nec solum inopum necessitas sustentatur, sed prona
in omnes munificentia aliquid et habentibus providet.
Xenodochium in portu Romano situm totus pariter
mundus audivit. Sub una aestate didicit Britania,
quod Aegyptus et Parthus agnoverant vere.

11. Quod scriptum est: ' Timentibus dominum
omnia cooperantur in bonum,' in obitu tantae feminae
vidimus conprobatum. Quodam praesagio futurorum
ad multos scripserat monachos, ut venirent et gravi
onore laborantem absolverent faceretque sibi de
iniquo mammona amicos, qui eam reciperent in
aeterna tabernacula. Venerunt, amici facti sunt:
dormivit illa—quod voluit—et deposita tandem
sarcina levior volavit ad caelos. Quantum haberet
viventis Fabiolae Roma miraculum, in mortua
demonstravit. Necdum spiritum exalaverat necdum
debitam Christo reddiderat animam,

' Et iam fama volans, tanti praenuntia luctus,'

totius urbis populos exequias congregabat. Sona-
bant psalmi et aurata tecta templorum reboans in
sublime alleluia quatiebat.

' Hic iuvenum chorus, ille senum, qui carmine laudes
    Femineas et facta ferant.'

---

[1] Acts, xxviii. 7: 'who received us, and lodged us three
days courteously.'
[2] Apparently this means 'that no one may criticize me as
exaggerating.'   [3] The regular name for an inn, ξενοδοχεῖον.
[4] Romans, viii. 28. Jerome substitutes 'fear' for 'love.'
[5] St. Luke, xvi. 9.   [6] Virgil, *Aeneid*, XI. 139.
        [7] Virgil, *Aeneid*, VIII. 287.

set sail. What Publius [1] did once in the island of
Malta for a single apostle and—not to leave room
for contradiction [2]—for a single ship, they did many
times for many men. Not only did they relieve
the wants of the destitute; their generosity was
at every one's service and provided even for those
who possessed something themselves. The whole
world heard that a Home for Strangers [3] had been
founded in the port of Rome, and Britain knew in
the summer what Egypt and the Parthians had
learned in the spring.

It is written: ' All things work together for good
to them that fear God,' [4] and in the death of the
noble lady the words have been proved true. She
had a presentiment of what was to happen, and had
written to several monks, that they might come and
relieve her from the heavy burden under which she
groaned, and that she might make to herself friends
of the mammon of unrighteousness, to receive her
into everlasting habitations. [5] They came, and were
welcomed as friends; she fell asleep, as she had
wished, and having at length rid herself of her
burden, soared more lightly to heaven. How great
had been the wonder of Fabiola's life Rome showed
when she was dead. She had scarcely drawn her
last breath and paid the debt of her soul to Christ,
when

' Flying rumour heralding such woe ' [6]

brought the peoples of the whole city to attend her
funeral. Psalms re-echoed loudly and cries of
' Alleluia ' shook the gilded roofs of the temples.

' Young men and old unite in song to praise
A woman and her fame to heaven raise.' [7]

Non sic Furius de Gallis, non Papirius de Samnitibus, non Scipio de Numantia, non Pompeius de Ponti gentibus triumphavit. Illi corpora vicere, haec spiritales nequitias subiugavit. Audio: praecedentium turmas et catervatim exequias eius multitudinem fluctuantem non plateae, non porticus, non inminentia desuper tecta capere poterant prospectantes. Tunc suos in unum populos Roma conspexit: favebant sibi omnes in gloria paenitentis. Nec mirum, si de eius salute homines exultarent, de cuius conversione angeli laetabantur in caelo.

12. Hoc tibi, Fabiola, ingenii mei senile munus, has officiorum inferias dedi. Laudavimus virgines, viduas ac maritatas, quarum semper fuere candida vestimenta, quae ' sequuntur agnum, quocumque vadit.' Felix praeconium, quod nulla totius vitae sorde maculatur! Procul livor, facessat invidia. Si pater familias bonus est, quare oculus noster malus? Quae inciderat in latrones, Christi humeris reportata est. ' Multae mansiones sunt apud patrem. Ubi abundavit peccatum, superabundavit gratia.' Cui plus dimittitur, plus amat.

---

[1] Letters LXXVII and LXXVIII.   [2] Revelation, xiv. 4.
[3] St. Matthew, xx. 15.   [4] St. Luke x. 30, xv. 5.
[5] St. John, xiv. 2.   [6] Romans, v. 20.
[7] St. Luke, vii. 47.

LETTER LXXVII

Not so gloriously did Furius triumph over the Gauls, Papirius over the Samnites, Scipio over Numantia, or Pompey over the peoples of the Black Sea. They conquered physical strength, she overcame spiritual iniquities. I hear it still: the crowds that went before the bier, the swaying multitude that attended her obsequies in throngs, no streets, no colonnades could contain, no overhanging roofs could hold the eager onlookers. On that day Rome saw all her peoples gathered together. Every one flattered himself that he had a share in the glory of her penitence. No wonder that men exulted in her salvation, seeing that the angels in heaven rejoiced over her conversion.

This,[1] the best gift of my aged powers, I present to you, Fabiola, as a funeral offering of respect. I have praised virgins, widows and married women who have kept their vestments always white, ' who follow the Lamb whithersoever He goeth.' [2] Blessed indeed is the praise of her whose life has been stained by no foulness. Let envy hold aloof, let jealousy be silent. If the father of the house be good, why should our eye be evil ? [3] She who fell among thieves has been carried home upon Christ's shoulders.[4] ' In our father's house there are many mansions.' [5] ' Where sin hath abounded, grace hath much more abounded.' [6] To whom more is forgiven, the same loveth more.[7]

CVII

Ad Laetam de Institutione Filiae

1. Beatus apostolus Paulus scribens ad Corinthios et rudem Christi ecclesiam sacris instruens disciplinis inter cetera mandata hoc quoque posuit dicens: ' Si qua mulier habet virum infidelem et hic consentit habitare cum ea, ne dimittat virum. Sanctificatus est enim vir infidelis in uxore fideli et sanctificata est mulier infidelis in fratre. Alioquin filii vestri inmundi essent, nunc autem sancti sunt.' Si cui forte hactenus videbantur nimium disciplinae vincula laxata et praeceps indulgentia praeceptoris, consideret domum patris tui, clarissimi quidem et eruditissimi viri, sed adhuc ambulantis in tenebris, et intelleget consilium apostoli illuc profecisse, ut radicis amaritudinem dulcedo fructuum conpensaret et vites virgulae balsama pretiosa sudarent. Tu es nata de inpari matrimonio, de te et Toxotio meo Paula generata est. Quis hoc crederet, ut Albini pontificis neptis de repromissione matris nasceretur, ut praesente et gaudente avo parvulae adhuc lingua balbutiens alleluia resonaret et virginem Christi in

---

¹ Laeta, to whom this letter was sent in A.D. 403, married Toxotius, son of Paula and Toxotius, ' in whose veins ran the noble blood of Aeneas' (Letter CVIII, 4). She herself was the daughter of a pagan, the pontiff Albinus, and had written to Jerome concerning the education of her child Paula. The advice given in this letter, that the little girl should be sent to Bethlehem to be educated by her grandmother Paula and her aunt Eustochium, was accepted, and she eventually succeeded Eustochium as head of the nunnery there.

² 1 Corinthians, vii. 13.

LETTER CVII

To Laeta [1]

A Girl's Education

Written A.D. 403

THE blessed apostle Paul, writing to the Corinthians and instructing Christ's novice church in the ways of sacred discipline, among his other precepts laid down also the following rule: ' The woman that hath an husband that believeth not, and if he be pleased to dwell with her, let her not leave him. For the unbelieving husband is sanctified by the believing wife, and the unbelieving wife is sanctified by the believing husband; else were your children unclean, but now they are holy.' [2] If any one up till now has perchance considered that Paul relaxed the bonds of discipline too much, and in his teaching was over-inclined to indulgence, let him consider the household of your father, who is a man of the highest rank and learning, but still walking in darkness, and he will perceive that the apostle's counsel has succeeded in making the sweetness of the fruit compensate for the bitterness of the parent tree, and has induced a common bush to exude precious balsam. You yourself are the child of a mixed marriage; but now you and my dear Toxotius are Paula's parents. Who would ever have believed that the granddaughter of the Roman pontiff Albinus would be born in answer to a mother's vows; that the grandfather would stand by and rejoice while the baby's yet stammering tongue cried ' Alleluia '; and that even the old man would nurse in his arms one of

339

suo gremio nutriret et senex? Bene et feliciter
expectavimus. Sancta et fidelis domus unum sancti-
ficat infidelem. Candidatus est fidei, quem filiorum
et nepotum credens turba circumdat. Ego puto
etiam ipsum Iovem, si habuisset talem cognationem,
potuisse in Christum credere. Despuat licet et
inrideat epistulam meam et me vel stultum vel
insanum clamitet, hoc et gener eius faciebat, antequam crederet. Fiunt, non nascuntur Christiani.
Auratum squalet Capitolium, fuligine et aranearum
telis omnia Romae templa cooperta sunt, movetur
urbs sedibus suis et inundans populus ante delubra
semiruta currit ad martyrum tumulos. Si non
extorquet fidem prudentia, extorqueat saltim verecundia.

2. Hoc Laeta, religiosissima in Christo filia, dictum
sit, ut non desperes parentis salutem et eadem fide,
qua meruisti filiam, et patrem recipias totaque domus
beatitudine perfruaris sciens illud a domino repromis-
sum: ' Quae apud homines inpossibilia, apud Deum
possibilia sunt.'[1] Numquam est sera conversio.
Latro de cruce transiit ad paradisum: Nabuchodonosor, rex Babylonius, post efferationem et cordis et
corporis et beluarum in heremo convictum mentem
recepit humanam. Et, ut omittam vetera, ne apud
incredulos nimis fabulosa videantur, ante paucos
annos propinquus vester Gracchus, nobilitatem
patriciam nomine sonans, cum praefecturam regeret
urbanam, nonne specu Mithrae et omnia portentuosa[2]

---

[1] St. Luke, xviii. 27.   [2] Probably in 378.

Christ's own virgins? We did well to expect this happy issue. The one unbeliever is sanctified by a saintly household of believers. He is a candidate for the faith, who has around him a throng of believing sons and grandsons: (I, for my part, think that even Jove might well have believed in Christ if he had had kinsfolk of this kind). He may spit in scorn upon this letter, and cry out that I am a fool or a madman; but his son-in-law did the same before he became a believer. Christians are not born but made. The gilded Capitol to-day looks dingy, all the temples in Rome are covered with soot and cobwebs, the city is shaken to its foundations, and the people hurry past the ruined shrines and pour out to visit the martyrs' graves. If knowledge does not compel faith, let shame at least do so.

Let this be said, dear Laeta, most dutiful daughter in Christ, so that you may not despair of your father's salvation. I hope that the same faith which has gained you a daughter as its reward may also win you your father, and that you may rejoice over blessings bestowed upon your whole household, knowing God's promise: 'The things which are impossible with men are possible with God.'[1] It is never too late to be converted. The robber passed from the cross to Paradise. Nebuchadnezzar, king of Babylon, recovered his human understanding after he had been made like an animal in body and heart, and had lived with the beasts in the wilderness. To pass over incidents in remote antiquity, which to the sceptical may appear too fabulous for belief, did not your kinsman Gracchus whose name recalls his patrician rank, destroy the cave of Mithras a few years ago when he was Prefect of Rome?[2] Did

341

simulacra, quibus corax, nymphius,[1] miles, leo, Perses,
heliodromus, pater initiantur, subvertit, fregit,
exussit et his quasi obsidibus ante praemissis inpetravit baptismum Christi?

Solitudinem patitur et in urbe gentilitas. Dii
quondam nationum cum bubonibus et noctuis in solis
culminibus remanserunt; vexilla militum crucis
insignia sunt, regum purpuras et ardentes diadema-
tum gemmas patibuli salutaris pictura condecorat.
Iam et Aegyptius Serapis factus est Christianus;
Marnas Gazae luget inclusus et eversionem templi
iugiter pertremescit. De India, Perside et Aethiopia
monachorum cotidie turbas suscipimus; deposuit
faretras Armenius, Huni discunt psalterium, Scythae
fervent calore fidei; Getarum rutulus et flavus
exercitus ecclesiarum circumfert tentoria et ideo
forsitan contra nos aequa pugnat acie, quia pari
religione confidunt.

3. Paene lapsus sum ad aliam materiam et currente
rota, dum urceum facere cogito, amphoram finxit
manus. Propositum enim mihi erat sanctae Marcellae et tuis precibus invitato ad matrem, id est ad
te, sermonem dirigere et docere, quomodo instruere
Paululam nostram debeas, quae prius Christo est
consecrata quam genita, quam ante votis quam utero

[1] cryphius: *Hilberg.*

---

[1] The initiates passed through several grades, of which
these are titles. The Raven and Lion, for example, dressed
in character, and imitated the creatures in their mummery.

[2] In A.D. 389 the temple of Serapis at Alexandria was pulled
down, and a Christian church built on the site.

[3] The chief Syrian god in Gaza. Cf. Jerome's life of
Hilarion, § 20.

he not break and burn all the monstrous images there by which worshippers were initiated as Raven, Bridegroom, Soldier, Lion, Perseus, Sun-runner, and Father?[1] Did he not send them before him as hostages, and gain for himself baptism in Christ?

Even in Rome now heathenism languishes in solitude. Those who once were the gods of the Gentiles are left beneath their deserted pinnacles to the company of owls and night-birds. The army standards bear the emblem of the cross. The purple robes of kings and the jewels that sparkle on their diadems are adorned with the gibbet sign that has brought to us salvation. To-day even the Egyptian Serapis[2] has become a Christian: Marnas[3] mourns in his prison at Gaza, and fears continually that his temple will be overthrown. From India, from Persia and from Ethiopia we welcome crowds of monks every hour. The Armenians have laid aside their quivers, the Huns are learning the psalter, the frosts of Scythia are warmed by the fire of faith. The ruddy, flaxen-haired Getae carry tent-churches about with their armies; and perhaps the reason why they fight with us on equal terms is that they believe in the same religion.

I have almost slipped into another subject, and thinking to make a pitcher on my running wheel my hand has moulded a flagon.[4] It was my intention, in answer to your prayers and those of the saintly Marcella, to direct my discourse to a mother, that is, to you, and to show you how to bring up our little Paula, who was consecrated to Christ before she was born, the child of prayers before the hour of

[4] Horace, *Ars Poetica*, 21: *amphora coepit institui: currente rota | cur urceus exit?*

suscepisti. Vidimus aliquid temporibus nostris de prophetalibus libris: Anna sterilitatem alvi fecunditate mutavit, tu luctuosam fecunditatem vitalibus liberis conmutasti. Fidens loquor accepturam te filios, quae primum foetum domino reddidisti. Ista sunt primogenita, quae offeruntur in lege. Sic natus Samuel, sic ortus est Samson, sic Iohannes propheta ad introitum Mariae exultavit et lusit.[1] Audiebat enim per os virginis verba domini pertonantis et de utero matris in occursum eius gestiebat erumpere. Igitur, quae de repromissione nata est, dignam habeat ortu suo institutionem parentum. Samuel nutritur in templo, Iohannes in solitudine praeparatur. Ille sacro crine venerabilis est, vinum et siceram non bibit, adhuc parvulus cum Deo sermocinatur; hic fugit urbes, zona pellicia cingitur, locustis alitur et melle silvestri et in typum paenitentiae praedicat tortuosissimi animalis[2] vestitus exuviis.

4. Sic erudienda est anima, quae futura est templum domini. Nihil aliud discat audire, nihil loqui, nisi quod ad timorem Dei pertinet. Turpia verba non intellegat, cantica mundi ignoret, adhuc tenera lingua psalmis dulcibus inbuatur. Procul sit aetas lasciva puerorum, ipsae puellae et pedisequae a saecularium consortiis arceantur, ne, quod mali didicerint, peius doceant. Fiant ei litterae vel

---

[1] St. Luke, i. 41.   [2] *I.e.* the camel.

conception. In our own days we have seen something such as we read of in the prophets: Hannah exchanged her barrenness for fruitful motherhood, you have exchanged a fertility bound up with sorrow for children who will live for ever. I tell you confidently that you who have given your first-born to the Lord will receive sons at His hand. The first-born are the offerings due under the Law. Such was the case both with Samuel and with Samson, and so it was that John the Baptist leaped for joy when Mary came in.[1] For he heard the thunder of the Lord's voice on the Virgin's lips, and was eager to break out from his mother's womb to meet Him. Therefore let your child of promise have a training from her parents worthy of her birth. Samuel was nurtured in the Temple, John was trained in the Wilderness. The one inspired veneration with his long hair, took neither wine nor strong drink, and even in his childhood talked with God. The other avoided cities, wore a skin girdle, and fed on locusts and wild honey, clothing himself in the hair of the most twisted of all animals[2] as a symbol of the repentance which he preached.

Thus must a soul be trained which is to be a temple of God. It must learn to hear nothing and to say nothing save what pertains to the fear of the Lord. It must have no comprehension of foul words, no knowledge of worldly songs, and its childish tongue must be imbued with the sweet music of the psalms. Let boys with their wanton frolics be kept far from Paula: let even her maids and attendants hold aloof from association with the worldly, lest they render their evil knowledge worse by teaching it to her. Have a set of letters made for her, of boxwood

345

buxeae vel eburneae et suis nominibus appellentur. Ludat in eis, ut et lusus eius eruditio sit, et non solum ordinem teneat litterarum, ut memoria nominum in canticum transeat, sed ipse inter se crebro ordo turbetur et mediis ultima, primis media misceantur, ut eas non sonu tantum, sed et visu noverit. Cum vero coeperit trementi manu stilum in cera ducere, vel alterius superposita manu teneri regantur articuli vel in tabella sculpantur elementa, ut per eosdem sulcos inclusa marginibus trahantur vestigia et foras non queant evagari. Syllabas iungat ad praemium, et, quibus illa aetas delectari potest, munusculis invitetur. Habeat et in discendo socias, quibus invideat, quarum laudibus mordeatur. Non est obiurganda, si tardior sit, sed laudibus excitandum ingenium; et vicisse se gaudeat et victam doleat. Cavendum in primis, ne oderit studia, ne amaritudo eorum percepta in infantia ultra rudes annos transeat. Ipsa nomina, per quae consuescet verba contexere, non sint fortuita, sed certa et coacervata de industria, prophetarum videlicet atque apostolorum, et omnis ab Adam patriarcharum series de Matheo Lucaque descendat, ut, dum aliud agit, futurae memoriae praeparetur.

Magister probae aetatis et vitae atque eruditionis est eligendus nec, puto, erubescit doctus vir id

or of ivory, and tell her their names. Let her play
with them, making play a road to learning, and
let her not only grasp the right order of the letters
and remember their names in a simple song, but
also frequently upset their order and mix the last
letters with the middle ones, the middle with the
first. Thus she will know them all by sight as well
as by sound. When she begins with uncertain
hand to use the pen, either let another hand be put
over hers to guide her baby fingers, or else have the
letters marked on the tablet so that her writing
may follow their outlines and keep to their limits
without straying away. Offer her prizes for spelling,
tempting her with such trifling gifts as please young
children. Let her have companions too in her
lessons, so that she may seek to rival them and be
stimulated by any praise they win. You must not
scold her if she is somewhat slow; praise is the best
sharpener of wits. Let her be glad when she is
first and sorry when she falls behind. Above all
take care not to make her lessons distasteful; a
childish dislike often lasts longer than childhood.
The very words from which she will get into the
way of forming sentences should not be taken at
haphazard but be definitely chosen and arranged
on purpose. For example, let her have the names
of the prophets and the apostles, and the whole list
of patriarchs from Adam downwards, as Matthew
and Luke give it. She will then be doing two things
at the same time, and will remember them afterwards.

For teacher you must choose a man of approved
years, life and learning. Even a sage is not
ashamed, methinks, to do for a relative or for a

facere vel in propinqua vel in nobili virgine, quod
Aristoteles fecit in Philippi filio, ut ipse libra-
riorum vilitate initia ei traderet litterarum. Non
sunt contemnenda quasi parva, sine quibus magna
constare non possunt. Ipse elementorum sonus et
prima institutio praeceptoris aliter de erudito, aliter
de rustico ore profertur. Unde et tibi est providendum, ne ineptis blanditiis feminarum dimidiata
dicere filiam verba consuescas et in auro atque
purpura ludere, quorum alterum linguae, alterum
moribus officit, ne discat in tenero, quod ei postea
dediscendum est. Gracchorum [1] eloquentiae multum
ab infantia sermo matris scribitur contulisse, Hor-
tensii [2] oratio in paterno sinu coaluit. Difficulter
eraditur, quod rudes animi perbiberunt. Lanarum
conchylia quis in pristinum candorem revocet?
Rudis testa diu et saporem retinet et odorem, quo
primum imbuta est. Graeca narrat historia Alex-
andrum, potentissimum regem orbisque domitorem,
et in moribus et in incessu Leonidis, paedagogi sui,
non potuisse carere vitiis, quibus parvulus adhuc
fuerat infectus. Proclivis est enim malorum aemulatio et, quorum virtutem adsequi nequeas, cito
imitere vitia. Nutrix ipsa non sit temulenta, non
lasciva, non garrula; habeat modestam gerulam,
nutricium gravem. Cum avum viderit, in pectus
eius transiliat, e collo pendeat, nolenti alleluia decantet. Rapiat eam avia, patrem risibus recognoscat,

---

[1] Graccorum : *Hilberg.*   [2] Hortensiae : *Hilberg.*

---

[1] Dyed purple with the juice of the *murex.*
[2] Horace, *Epistles,* I. ii. 70: *quo semel est imbuta recens
servabit | odorem testa diu.*

high-born virgin what Aristotle did for Philip's son, when like some humble clerk he taught him his first letters. Things must not be despised as trifles, if without them great results are impossible. The very letters themselves, and so the first lesson in them, sound quite differently from the mouth of a learned man, and of a rustic. And so you must take care not to let women's silly coaxing get your daughter into the way of cutting her words short, or of disporting herself in gold brocade and fine purple. The first habit ruins talk, the second character; and children should never learn what they will afterwards have to unlearn. We are told that the eloquence of the Gracchi was largely due to the way in which their mother talked to them as children, and it was by sitting on his father's lap that Hortensius became a great orator. The first impression made on a young mind is hard to remove. The shell-dyed wool[1]—who can bring back its pristine whiteness? A new jar keeps for a long time the taste and smell of its original contents.[2] Greek history tells us that the mighty king Alexander, who subdued the whole world, could not rid himself of the tricks of manner and gait which in his childhood he had caught from his governor Leonides. For it is easy to imitate the bad, and you may soon copy the faults of those to whose virtue you can never attain. Let Paula's foster-mother be a person neither drunken nor wanton nor fond of gossip: let her nurse be a modest woman, her foster-father a respectable man. When she sees her grandfather, she must leap into his arms, hang on his neck, and sing 'Alleluia' whether he likes it or not. Let her grandmother snatch her away, let her recog-

sit omnibus amabilis et universa propinquitas rosam ex se natam gaudeat. Discat statim, quam habeat et alteram aviam, quam amitam, cui imperatori, cui exercitui tiruncula nutriatur. Illas desideret, ad illas tibi minitetur abscessum.

5. Ipse habitus et vestitus doceat eam, cui promissa sit. Cave ne aures perfores, ne cerussa et purpurisso consecrata Christo ora depingas, ne collum margaritis et auro premas, ne caput gemmis oneres, ne capillum inrufes et ei aliquid de gehennae ignibus auspiceris. Habeat alias margaritas, quibus postea venditis emptura est pretiosissimum margaritum. Praetextata, nobilissima quondam femina, iubente viro Hymetio, qui patruus Eustochiae virginis fuit, habitum eius cultumque mutavit et neglectum crinem undanti gradu texuit vincere cupiens et virginis propositum et matris desiderium. Et ecce tibi eadem nocte cernit in somnis venisse ad se angelum terribili facie minitantem poenas et haec verba frangentem: ' Tune ausa es viri imperium praeferre Christo? Tu caput virginis Dei sacrilegis adtrectare manibus? Quae iam nunc arescent, ut sentias excruciata, quid feceris, et finito mense quinto ad inferna ducaris. Sin autem perseveraveris in scelere, et marito simul orbaberis et filiis.' Omnia

---

[1] Cf. Appendix, p. 488.

nize her father with a smile, let her endear herself to all, so that the whole family may rejoice that they have such a rosebud among them. Let her learn too at once who is her other grandmother and her aunt, who is her captain and for whose army she is being trained as a recruit. Let her crave their company and threaten you that she will leave you for them.

Her very dress and outward appearance should remind her of Him to whom she is promised. Do not pierce her ears, or paint with white lead and rouge the cheeks that are consecrated to Christ. Do not load her neck with pearls and gold, do not weigh down her head with jewels, do not dye her hair red and thereby presage for her the fires of hell. Let her have other pearls which she will sell hereafter and buy the pearl that is of great price. There was once a lady of rank named Praetextata, who at the bidding of her husband Hymetius, the uncle of Eustochia,[1] altered that virgin's dress and appearance, and had her hair waved, desiring thus to overcome the virgin's resolution and her mother's wishes. But lo! that same night in her dreams she saw an angel, terrible of aspect, standing before her, who threatened her with punishment and broke into speech thus: ‘ Have you dared to put your husband's orders before those of Christ? Have you presumed to lay sacrilegious hands upon the head of God's virgin? Those hands this very hour shall wither, and in torment you shall recognize your guilt, until at the fifth month's end you be carried off to hell. Moreover, if you persist in your wickedness, you shall lose both your husband and your children.’ All this was duly fulfilled, and a swift

per ordinem expleta sunt et seram miserae paenitentiam velox signavit interitus. Sic ulciscitur Christus violatores templi sui, sic gemmas et pretiosissima ornamenta defendit. Et hoc retuli, non quod insultare velim calamitatibus infelicium, sed ut te moneam, cum quanto metu et cautione servare debeas, quod domino spopondisti.

6. Heli sacerdos offendit dominum ob vitia liberorum;[1] episcopus fieri non potest, qui filios habuerit luxuriosos et non subditos. At e contrario de muliere scribitur, quod ' salva fiet per filiorum generationem, si permanserit in fide et caritate et sanctificatione cum pudicitia.'[2] Si perfecta aetas et sui iuris inputatur parentibus, quanto magis lactans et fragilis et quae iuxta sententiam domini ignorat dexteram aut sinistram, id est boni ac mali nescit differentiam! Sollicita provides, ne filia percutiatur a vipera; cur non eadem cura providias, ne feriatur a malleo universae terrae, ne bibat de aureo calice Babylonis,[3] ne egrediatur cum Dina et velit videre filias regionis alienae,[4] ne ludat pedibus, ne trahat tunicas? Venena non dantur nisi melle circumlita et vitia non decipiunt nisi sub specie umbraque virtutum.[5] ' Et quomodo,' inquies, ' peccata patrum filiis non redduntur nec filiorum parentibus, sed " anima quae peccaverit, ipsa morietur "?'[6] Hoc de his dicitur, qui possunt sapere, de quibus in evangelio scriptum

---

[1] 1 Samuel, ii. 30.

[2] 1 Timothy, ii. 15. Jerome substitutes ' chastity ' for ' sobriety.'   [3] *I.e.*, Babylon.   [4] Genesis, xxxiv. 1.

[5] Lucr. I. 936: *veluti pueris absinthia tetra medentes* | *cum dare conantur, prius oras pocula circum* | *contingunt mellis dulci flavoque liquore.*   [6] Ezekiel, xviii. 20.

death marked the unhappy woman's late repentance. So it is that Christ takes vengeance upon the violators of his temple, so he defends his pearls and precious jewels. I have told you this, not with any wish to exult over the downfall of the wretched, but to remind you with what anxiety and carefulness you must watch over that which you have vowed to the Lord.

The priest Eli lost God's favour because of his children's faults;[1] a man cannot be a bishop, if his sons are men of profligate and disorderly life. On the other hand it is written of the woman: ' She shall be saved in childbearing, if they continue in faith and charity and holiness with chastity.'[2] If parents get the credit for their children's deeds, even when they are of ripe age and their own masters, how much more are they responsible for a frail baby girl, who, as the Lord says, cannot discern between right hand and left, that is, does not know the difference between good and evil. You take anxious thought to prevent a viper biting your daughter; why do you not show the same prudent care to save her from the hammer of the whole earth,[3] to guard her from drinking of Babylon's golden cup, from going out with Dinah to see the daughters of a strange land,[4] from sporting in the dance, from trailing her robe at her heels? You smear honey round the cup before you give a drug,[5] and vices only deceive when they wear the mien and semblance of virtue. You will ask: ' how is it that the sins of the fathers are not reckoned against the sons, nor the sins of the sons against the parents, but " the soul that sinneth it shall die " ? '[6] That passage, I answer, refers to those who have reached the age of discre-

est: 'Aetatem habet, pro se loquatur.' Qui autem
parvulus est et sapit ut parvulus, donec ad annos
sapientiae veniat et Pythagorae litterae eum perdu-
cant ad bivium, tam mala eius quam bona parentibus
inputantur, nisi forte aestimas Christianorum filios,
si baptisma non acceperint, ipsos tantum reos esse
peccati et non scelus referri ad eos, qui dare noluerint,
maxime eo tempore, quo contradicere non poterant,
qui accepturi erant, sicut e regione salus infantium
maiorum lucrum est. Offerre necne filiam potestatis
tuae fuit, quamquam alia sit tua condicio, quae prius
eam vovisti, quam conceperis; ut autem oblatam
neglegas, ad periculum tuum pertinet. Qui claudam
et mutilam et qualibet sorde maculatam obtulerit
hostiam, sacrilegii reus est; quanto magis, qui
partem corporis sui et inlibatae animae puritatem
regiis amplexibus parat, si negligens fuerit, punietur!

7. Postquam grandicula esse coeperit et in exemplum sponsi sui crescere sapientia, aetate et gratia
apud Deum et homines, pergat cum parentibus ad
templum veri patris, sed cum illis non egrediatur e
templo. Quaerant eam in itinere saeculi, inter
turbas et frequentiam propinquorum et nusquam
alibi reperiant nisi in adyto scripturarum prophetas
et apostolos de spiritalibus nuptiis sciscitantem.
Imitetur Mariam, quam Gabriel solam in cubiculo

---

[1] St. John, ix. 21.

[2] Pythagoras depicted the Choice of Life under the form
of the Greek letter Υ, which was originally made with one
straight stroke on the right, and half-way up a curved branch
on the left. The lower part represents the period of childhood; the branching ways the time when the choice has to be
made between good and evil. The steep path to the right is
the path of virtue.

tion, of whom the Gospel says: ' He is of age, let
him speak for himself.'[1]   As for the little child
with a child's understanding, until he comes to
years of wisdom and the letter of Pythagoras [2] con-
fronts him with the two roads, his evil deeds as well
as his good are laid to his parents' account; unless
indeed you imagine that the children of Christians,
if they have not received baptism, are themselves
alone responsible for their sins and no guilt attaches
to those who refused it them at the time when the
recipients could not have objected.   The truth is
that baptism means salvation for the child and advantage for the parents.   It rested with you whether
you should offer your daughter or not; although
you scarcely had the option, since you offered her
before she was conceived.   But now that you have
offered her you neglect her at your peril.   He that
offers a victim that is lame or maimed or marked
with any blemish is considered guilty of sacrilege.
How much greater will be the punishment, if one
proves negligent, who makes ready for the King's
embrace a portion of her own body and the purity
of the unmutilated soul!

When Paula begins to be a big girl, and like her
Spouse to increase in wisdom and stature and in
favour with God and man, let her go with her parents
to the temple of her true Father, but let her not
come out from the temple with them.   Let them
seek her upon the world's highway, amid crowds
and the company of their kinsfolk, but let them find
her nowhere save in the shrine of the Scriptures,
inquiring there of the prophets and apostles concerning her spiritual nuptials.   Let her take pattern
by Mary whom Gabriel found alone in her chamber,

suo repperit et ideo forsitan timore perterrita est, quia virum, quem non solebat, aspexit. Aemuletur eam, de qua dicitur: ' Omnis gloria filiae regis ab intus'; loquatur et ipsa electo caritatis iaculo vulnerata: ' Introduxit me rex in cubiculum suum.' Nunquam exeat foras, ne inveniant eam, qui circumeunt civitatem, ne percutiant et vulnerent et auferentes theristrum pudicitiae nudam in sanguine derelinquant; quin potius, cum aliquis ostium eius pulsaverit, dicat: ' Ego murus et ubera mea turris. Lavi pedes meos, non possum inquinare eos.'

8. Non vescatur in publico, id est in parentum convivio, nec videat cibos, quos desideret. Et licet quidam putent maioris esse virtutis praesentem contemnere voluptatem, tamen ego securioris arbitror continentiae nescire, quod quaeras. Legi quondam in scholis puer: 'Aegre reprehendas, quod sinas consuescere.' Discat iam tunc et vinum non bibere, ' in quo est luxuria.' Ante annos robustae aetatis periculosa est teneris gravis abstinentia. Usque ad id tempus, si necessitas postularit, et balneas adeat et vino modico utatur propter stomachum et carnium edulio sustentetur, ne prius deficiant pedes, quam currere incipiant. Et ' haec dico iuxta indulgentiam, non iuxta imperium,' timens debilitatem, non docens luxuriam. Alioquin, quod Iudaica superstitio ex parte facit in eiuratione quorundam animalium atque escarum, quod Indorum Bragmanae et Aegyptiorum

---

[1] Psalm xlv. 13.
[2] Song of Solomon, i. 4.
[3] Song of Solomon, viii. 10 and v. 3.
[4] Publilius Syrus, *Sententiae*, 180. Cf. p. 478.
[5] Ephesians, v. 18.
[6] 1 Timothy, v. 23.   [7] 1 Corinthians, vii. 6.

Mary who perchance was terrified because she saw
a strange man. Let her seek to rival that one of
whom it is said : ' All the glory of the king's
daughter is from within.'[1] Wounded with love's
arrow let her too say to her chosen: ' The king
hath brought me into his chamber.'[2] At no time
let her go out abroad, lest those that go about the
city find her, lest they smite her and wound her and
take away the veil of her chastity and leave her
naked in her blood. Nay rather, when one knocketh
at her door let her say : ' I am a wall and my
breasts are a tower. I have washed my feet; how
can I defile them ? '[3]

She should not take her food in public, that is, at
her parents' guest-table ; for she may there see
dishes that she will crave for. And though some
people think it shows the higher virtue to despise a
pleasure ready to your hand, I for my part judge
it part of the surer self-restraint to remain in ignorance of what you would like. Once when I was a
boy at school I read this line : ' Things that have
become a habit you will find it hard to blame.'[4] Let
her learn even now not to drink wine ' wherein is
excess.'[5] Until they have reached their full strength,
however, strict abstinence is dangerous for young
children : so till then, if needs must, let her visit
the baths, and take a little wine for the stomach's
sake,[6] and have the support of a meat diet, lest her
feet fail before the race begins. ' I say this by way
of indulgence and not by way of command,'[7] fearing
weakness, not teaching wantonness. Moreover, what
the Jewish superstition does in part, solemnly re-
jecting certain animals and certain products as food,
what the Brahmans in India and the Gymnosophists

357

gymnosophistae in polentae et orizae et pomorum
solo observant cibo, cur virgo Christi non faciat in
toto? Si tanti vitrum, quare non maioris sit pretii
margaritum? Quae nata est ex repromissione, sic
vivat, ut illi vixerunt, qui de repromissione generati
sunt. Aequa gratia aequum habeat et laborem.
Surda sit ad organa: tibia, lyra et cithara cur facta
sint, nesciat.

9. Reddat tibi pensum cotidie scripturarum certum.
Ediscat Graecorum versuum numerum. Sequatur
statim et Latina eruditio; quae si non ab initio os
tenerum conposuit, in peregrinum sonum lingua
corrumpitur et externis vitiis sermo patrius sordidatur. Te habeat magistram, te rudis miretur
infantia. Nihil in te et in patre suo videat, quod si
fecerit, peccet. Memento vos parentes virginis et
magis eam exemplis docere posse quam voce. Cito
flores pereunt, cito violas et lilia et crocum pestilens
aura corrumpit. Numquam absque te procedat in
publicum, basilicas martyrum et ecclesias sine matre
non adeat. Nullus ei iuvenis, nullus cincinnatus
adrideat. Vigiliarum dies et sollemnes per-
noctationes sic virguncula nostra celebret, ut ne
transversum quidem unguem a matre discedat.
Nolo de ancillulis suis aliquam plus diligat, cuius
crebro auribus insusurret. Quicquid uni loquitur,
hoc omnes sciant. Placeat ei comes non compta
atque formosa, quae liquido gutture carmen dulce

in Egypt observe on their diet of only porridge, rice, and fruit, why should not Christ's virgin do altogether? If a glass bead is worth so much, surely a pearl must have a higher value. The child of promise must live as those lived before her who were born under the same vow. Let an equal favour bring with it also an equal labour. Paula must be deaf to all musical instruments, and never even know why the flute, the lyre, and the harp came into existence.

Let her every day repeat to you a portion of the Scriptures as her fixed task. A good number of lines she should learn by heart in the Greek, but knowledge of the Latin should follow close after. If the tender lips are not trained from the beginning, the language is spoiled by a foreign accent and our native tongue debased by alien faults. You must be her teacher, to you her childish ignorance must look for a model. Let her never see anything in you or her father which she would do wrong to imitate. Remember that you are a virgin's parents and that you can teach her better by example than by words. Flowers quickly fade; violets, lilies, and saffron are soon withered by a baleful breeze. Let her never appear in public without you, let her never visit the churches and the martyrs' shrines except in your company. Let no youth or curled dandy ogle her. Let our little virgin never stir a finger's breadth from her mother when she attends a vigil or an all-night service. I would not let her have a favourite maid into whose ear she might frequently whisper: what she says to one, all ought to know. Let her choose as companion not a spruce, handsome girl, able to warble sweet songs in liquid

moderetur, sed gravis, pallens, sordidata, subtristis. Praeponatur ei probae fidei et morum ac pudicitiae virgo veterana, quae illam doceat et adsuescat exemplo ad orationem et psalmos nocte consurgere, mane hymnos canere, tertia, sexta, nona hora quasi bellatricem Christi stare in acie accensaque lucernula reddere sacrificium vespertinum. Sic dies transeat, sic nox inveniat laborantem. Orationi lectio, lectioni succedat oratio. Breve videbitur tempus, quod tantis operum varietatibus occupatur.

10. Discat et lanam facere, tenere colum, ponere in gremio calatum, rotare fusum, stamina pollice ducere. Spernat bombycum telas, Serum vellera et aurum in fila lentescens. Talia vestimenta paret, quibus pellatur frigus, non quibus corpora vestita nudentur. Cibus eius holusculum sit et simila raroque pisciculi. Et ne gulae praecepta longius traham, de quibus in alio loco plenius sum locutus, sic comedat, ut semper esuriat, ut statim post cibum possit legere, orare, psallere. Displicent mihi in teneris vel maxime aetatibus longa et inmoderata ieiunia, quibus iunguntur ebdomades et oleum in cibo ac poma vitantur. Experimento didici asellum in via, cum lassus fuerit, diverticula quaerere. Faciant hoc cultores Isidis et Cybelae, qui gulosa abstinentia Fasides aves et fumantes turtures vorant,

notes, but one grave and pale, carelessly dressed and inclined to melancholy. Set before her as a pattern some aged virgin of approved faith, character, and chastity, one who may instruct her by word, and by example accustom her to rise from her bed at night for prayer and psalm singing, to chant hymns in the morning, at the third, sixth, and ninth hour, to take her place in the ranks as one of Christ's amazons, and with kindled lamp to offer the evening sacrifice. So let the day pass, and so let the night find her still labouring. Let reading follow prayer and prayer follow reading. The time will seem short when it is occupied with such a diversity of tasks.

Let her learn also to make wool, to hold the distaff, to put the basket in her lap, to turn the spindle, to shape the thread with her thumb. Let her scorn silk fabrics, Chinese fleeces, and gold brocades. Let her have clothes which keep out the cold, not expose the limbs they pretend to cover. Let her food be vegetables and wheaten bread and occasionally a little fish. I do not wish here to give long rules for eating, since I have treated that subject more fully in another place; but let her meals always leave her hungry and able at once to begin reading or praying or singing the psalms. I disapprove, especially with young people, of long and immoderate fasts, when week is added to week and even oil in food and fruit are banned. I have learned by experience that the ass on the high road makes for an inn when it is weary. Leave such things to the worshippers of Isis and Cybele, who in gluttonous abstinence gobble up pheasants and turtle doves all smoking hot, of course to avoid contaminating

ne scilicet Cerealia dona contaminent. Hoc in perpetuo ieiunio praeceptum sit, ut longo itineri vires perpetes supparentur, ne in prima mansione currentes corruamus in mediis. Ceterum, ut ante scripsi, in quadragesima continentiae vela pandenda sunt et tota aurigae retinacula equis laxanda properantibus, quamquam alia sit condicio saecularium, alia virginum ac monachorum. Saecularis homo in quadragesima ventris ingluviem decoquit et in coclearum morem suo victitans suco futuris dapibus ac saginae aqualiculum parat; virgo et monachus sic in quadragesima suos emittant equos, ut sibi meminerint semper esse currendum. Finitus labor maior, infinitus moderatior est; ibi enim respiramus, hic perpetuo incedimus.

11. Si quando ad suburbana pergis, domi filiam non relinquas; nesciat sine te nec possit vivere; cum sola fuerit, pertremescat. Non habeat conloquia saecularium, non malarum virginum contubernia, non intersit nuptiis servulorum nec familiae perstrepentis lusibus misceatur. Scio praecepisse quosdam, ne virgo Christi cum eunuchis lavet, ne cum maritis feminis, quia alii non deponant animos virorum, aliae tumentibus uteris praeferant foeditatem. Mihi omnino in adulta virgine lavacra displicent, quae se ipsam debet erubescere et nudam videre non posse. Si enim vigiliis et ieiuniis macerat corpus suum et in servitutem redigit, si flammam libidinis et incentiva ferventis aetatis extinguere cupit continentiae

---

[1] Cf. Plautus, *Captivi*, 80.

the gift of Ceres. If you fast without a break, you must so arrange things that your strength lasts out the long journey: we must not run well for the first lap and then fall in the middle of the race. In Lent, however, as I have written previously, the sails of self-denial may be spread wide, and the charioteer may loosen the reins and let his horses go full speed. Not but what there is one rule for worldlings, and another for virgins and monks. The worldling in Lent digests again what remains in his crop, and like a snail lives on his own juice,[1] while he gets his belly fit for the rich food and feasts that are to come. Not so with the monk and virgin: when they give their steeds the rein in Lent, they must remember that their race lasts for ever. Limited efforts are greater, unlimited more moderate: for there we have breathing space, here we never stop.

If ever you visit the country, do not leave your daughter behind at Rome. She should have neither the knowledge nor the power to live without you, and should tremble to be alone. Let her not converse with worldlings, nor associate with virgins who neglect their vows. Let her not be present at slaves' weddings, nor take part in noisy household games. I know that some people have laid down the rule that a Christian virgin should not bathe along with eunuchs or with married women, inasmuch as eunuchs are still men at heart, and women big with child are a revolting sight. For myself I disapprove altogether of baths in the case of a full-grown virgin. She ought to blush at herself and be unable to look at her own nakedness. If she mortifies and enslaves her body by vigils and fasting, if she desires to quench the flame of lust and to

frigore, si adpetitis sordibus turpare festinat naturalem pulchritudinem, cur e contrario balnearum fomentis sopitos ignes suscitat?

12. Pro gemmis aut serico divinos codices amet, in quibus non auri et pellis Babyloniae vermiculata pictura, sed ad fidem placeat emendata et erudita distinctio. Discat primum Psalterium, his se canticis avocet, et in Proverbiis Salomonis erudiatur ad vitam. In Ecclesiaste consuescat calcare, quae mundi sunt; in Iob virtutis et patientiae exempla sectetur. Ad Evangelia transeat numquam ea positura de manibus; Apostolorum Acta et Epistulas tota cordis inbibat voluntate. Cumque pectoris sui cellarium his opibus locupletarit, mandet memoriae Prophetas et Heptateuchum et Regum ac Paralipomenon libros Hesdraeque et Hester volumina, ut ultimum sine periculo discat Canticum Canticorum, ne, si in exordio legerit, sub carnalibus verbis spiritalium nuptiarum epithalamium non intellegens vulneretur. Caveat omnia apocrypha et, si quando ea non ad dogmatum veritatem, sed ad signorum reverentiam legere voluerit, sciat non eorum esse, quorum titulis praenotantur, multaque his admixta vitiosa et grandis esse prudentiae aurum in luto quaerere. Cypriani opuscula semper in manu teneat, Athanasii epistulas et

---

[1] *I.e.*, the Roman, or as we call them "Turkish," baths.

check the hot desires of youth by a cold chastity, if she hastens to spoil her natural beauty by a deliberate squalor, why should she rouse a sleeping fire by the incentive of baths? [1]

Instead of jewels or silk let her love the manuscripts of the Holy Scriptures, and in them let her prefer correctness and accurate punctuation to gilding and Babylonian parchment with elaborate decorations. Let her learn the Psalter first, with these songs let her distract herself, and then let her learn lessons of life in the Proverbs of Solomon. In reading Ecclesiastes let her become accustomed to tread underfoot the things of this world; let her follow the examples of virtue and patience that she will find in Job. Let her then pass on to the Gospels and never again lay them down. Let her drink in the Acts of the Apostles and the Epistles with all the will of her heart. As soon as she has enriched her mind's storehouse with these treasures, let her commit to memory the Prophets, the Heptateuch, the books of Kings and the Chronicles, and the rolls of Ezra and Esther. Then at last she may safely read the Song of Songs: if she were to read it at the beginning, she might be harmed by not perceiving that it was the song of a spiritual bridal expressed in fleshly language. Let her avoid all the apocryphal books, and if she ever wishes to read them, not for the truth of their doctrines but out of respect for their wondrous tales, let her realize that they are not really written by those to whom they are ascribed, that there are many faulty elements in them, and that it requires great skill to look for gold in mud. Let her always keep Cyprian's works by her, and let her peruse the letters of Atha-

Hilarii libros inoffenso decurrat pede. Illorum tractatibus, illorum delectetur ingeniis, in quorum libris pietas fidei non vacillet; ceteros sic legat, ut magis iudicet quam sequatur.

13. Respondebis: ' Quomodo haec omnia mulier saecularis in tanta frequentia hominum Romae custodire potero?' Noli ergo subire onus, quod ferre non potes, sed, postquam ablactaveris eam cum Isaac et vestieris cum Samuhele, mitte aviae et amitae. Redde pretiosissimam gemmam cubiculo Mariae, et cunis Iesu vagientis inpone. Nutriatur in monasterio, sit inter virginum choros, iurare non discat, mentiri sacrilegium putet, nesciat saeculum, vivat angelice, sit in carne sine carne, omne hominum genus sui simile putet et, ut cetera taceam, certe te liberet servandi difficultate et custodiae periculo. Melius est tibi desiderare absentem quam pavere ad singula, cum quo loquatur, quid loquatur, cui adnuat, quem libenter aspiciat. Trade Eustochio parvulam, cuius nunc et ipse vagitus pro te oratio est, trade comitem futuram sanctitatis heredem. Illam videat, illam amet, illam ' primis miretur ab annis,' cuius et sermo et habitus et incessus doctrina virtutum est. Sit in gremio aviae, quae repetat in nepte, quidquid praemisit in filia, quae longo usu didicit nutrire,

---

[1] Virgil, *Aeneid*, VIII. 517.

nasius and the treatises of Hilary without fear of
stumbling. She may take pleasure in the learned
expositions of all such writers as maintain in their
books a steady love of the faith. If she reads others,
let it be as a critic rather than as a disciple.

You will answer : ' How shall I, a woman of the
world living in crowded Rome, be able to keep all
these injunctions? ' Do not then take up a burden
which you cannot bear. When you have weaned
Paula as Isaac was weaned, and when you have
clothed her as Samuel was clothed, send her to her
grandmother and her aunt. Set this most precious
jewel in Mary's chamber, and place her on the
cradle where Jesus cried. Let her be reared in a
monastery amid bands of virgins, where she will learn
never to take an oath, and to regard a lie as sacrilege. Let her know nothing of the world, but live
like the angels ; let her be in the flesh and without
the flesh, thinking all mankind to be like herself.
Thus, to say nothing of other things, she will free
you from the difficult task of watching over her and
from all the responsibility of guardianship. It is
better for you to regret her absence than every
moment to be fearing what she is saying, to whom
she is talking, whom she greets and whom she likes
to see. Give to Eustochium the little child, whose
very wailings are now a prayer on your behalf ; give
her, to be her companion to-day, to be the inheritor
of her sanctity in the years to come. Let her gaze
upon and love, let her ' from her first years admire ' [1]
one whose words and gait and dress are an education
in virtue. Let her grandmother take her on her
lap and repeat to her grandchild the lessons she
once taught her daughter. Long experience has

docere, servare virgines, in cuius corona centenarii
cotidie numeri castitas texitur. Felix virgo, felix
Paula Toxotii, quae per aviae amitaeque virtutes
nobilior est sanctitate quam genere! O si tibi
contingeret videre socrum et cognatam tuam et
in parvis corpusculis ingentes animos intueri! Pro
insita tibi pudicitia non ambigerem, quin praecederes
filiam et primam Dei sententiam secunda evangelii
lege mutares. Ne tu parvi penderes aliorum desideria
liberorum et te ipsa magis offerres Deo! Sed quia
' tempus est amplexandi et tempus longe fieri a
conplexibus ' et ' uxor non habet potestatem corporis
sui ' et ' unusquisque in ea vocatione, qua vocatus est,
in ea permaneat ' in domino, et, qui sub iugo est,
sic debet currere, ne in luto comitem derelinquat,
totum redde in subole, quod in te interim distulisti.
Anna filium, quem Deo voverat, postquam obtulit
tabernaculo, numquam recepit indecens arbitrata,
ut futurus propheta in huius domo cresceret, quae
adhuc alios filios habere cupiebat. Denique, postquam concepit et peperit, non est ausa ad templum
accedere et vacua apparere coram domino, nisi prius
redderet, quod debebat, talique immolato sacrificio
reversa domum quinque liberos sibi genuit, quia
primogenitum Deo peperat. Miraris felicitatem
sanctae mulieris? Imitare fidem. Ipse, si Paulam

---

[1] Cf. *c. Jov.* I. 3, where the respective merits of the estates
of marriage, widowhood and virginity are compared to the
seeds which brought forth thirty, sixty and a hundred fold:
for this association of 100 with virginity, cf. also Letters
XXII, 15 and 19, and LXVI, 2.

[2] Genesis, xxxv. 11 : Be fruitful and multiply.

[3] Ecclesiastes, iii. 5. [4] 1 Corinthians, vii. 4.

[5] 1 Corinthians, vii. 20. [6] 1 Samuel, i. 22.

taught her how to rear, instruct, and watch over virgins, and in her crown every day is woven the mystic hundred of chastity.[1] O happy virgin! O happy Paula, daughter of Toxotius! By the virtues of her grandmother and her aunt she is nobler in sanctity even than in lineage. Oh, if you could only see your mother-in-law and your sister, and know the mighty souls that dwell within their feeble bodies! Then I doubt not that you would obey your innate love of chastity and come to them even before your daughter, exchanging God's first decree[2] for the Gospel's second dispensation. You would surely count as nothing your desire for other children and would rather offer yourself to God. But inasmuch as ' there is a time to embrace and a time to refrain from embracing,'[3] and ' the wife hath not power over her own body,'[4] and ' every man should abide in the same calling wherein he was called '[5] in the Lord, and because he who is under the yoke ought so to run as not to leave his companion in the mire, pay back in your children all that you defer paying in your own person. When Hannah had brought to the tabernacle the son whom she had vowed to God, she never took him back again, thinking it improper that a future prophet should grow up in the house of one who still desired to have other sons.[6] In fine, after she had conceived and borne him, she did not venture to visit the temple and appear before God empty-handed, but first paid her debt, and then after offering her great sacrifice returned home, and having borne her first son for God was then given five children for herself. Do you wonder at the happiness of that holy woman? Then imitate her faith. If you

miseris, balbutientia senex verba formabo multo
gloriosior mundi philosopho, qui non regem Mace-
donum Babylonio periturum veneno, sed ancillam et
sponsam   Christi   erudiam   regnis   caelestibus
offerendam.

CXVII

Ad Matrem et Filiam in Gallia Commorantes

1. Rettulit mihi quidam frater e Gallia se habere
sororem virginem matremque viduam, quae in eadem
urbe divisis habitarent cellulis et vel ob hospitii
solitudinem vel custodiendas facultatulas praesules
sibi quosdam clericos adsumpsissent, ut maiori
dedecore iungerentur alienis, quam a se fuerant
separatae. Cumque ego ingemescerem et multo
plura tacendo quam loquendo significarem : ' Quaeso
te,' inquit, ' corripias eas litteris tuis et ad concordiam revoces, ut mater filiam, filia matrem
agnoscat.' Cui ego: ' Optimam,' inquam, ' mihi
iniungis provinciam, ut alienus conciliem, quas filius
fraterque non potuit, quasi vero episcopalem cathe-
dram teneam et non clausus cellula ac procul a turbis
remotus vel praeterita plangam vitia vel vitare nitar

will send us Paula, I undertake to be both her
tutor and her foster-father. I will carry her on my
shoulders, and my old tongue shall train her stammering lips. And I shall take more pride in my
task than did the worldly philosopher; for I shall
not be teaching a Macedonian king, destined to
die by poison in Babylon, but a handmaid and bride
of Christ who one day shall be presented to the
heavenly throne.

LETTER CXVII

To a Mother and Daughter living in Gaul

Dangerous friendships

Written a.d. 405

A certain brother from Gaul told me the other day
that he had a virgin sister and a widowed mother
who, though living in the same city, had separate
apartments, and had taken to themselves clerical
directors, either to prevent their feeling lonely, or
else to manage their small properties; and that by
this union with strangers they had caused more
scandal even than by living apart. I groaned to
hear his tale, and by silence expressed far more than
I could by words. 'Pray,' he continued, 'rebuke
them in a letter and recall them to harmony, so that
the mother may recognize her daughter, and the
daughter her mother.' 'This is a fine commission,'
I replied, 'that you lay upon me, that I a stranger
should reconcile those with whom a son and brother
has failed. You talk as though I held a bishop's
chair instead of being confined, far from men's
turmoil, in a tiny cell, where I lament past sins and

praesentia. Sed et incongruum est latere corpore et lingua per orbem vagari.' Et ille : ' Nimium,' ait, ' formidolosus ; ubi illa quondam constantia, in qua multo sale urbem defricans Lucilianum quippiam rettulisti ? ' ' Hoc est,' aio, ' quod me fugat et labra dividere non sinit. Postquam ergo arguendo crimina factus sum criminosus et iuxta tritum vulgi sermone proverbium iurantibus et negantibus cunctis me aures nec credo habere nec tango ipsique parietes in me maledicta resonarunt " Et psallebant contra me, qui bibebant vinum," coactus malo tacere didici rectius esse arbitrans ponere custodiam ori meo et ostium munitum labiis meis, quam declinare cor in verba malitiae et, dum carpo vitia, in vitium detractionis incurrere.' Quod cum dixissem : ' Non est,' inquit, ' detrahere verum dicere, nec privata correptio generalem doctrinam facit, cum aut rarus aut nullus sit, qui sub huius culpae reatum cadat. Quaeso ergo te, ne me tanto itinere vexatum frustra venisse patiaris. Scit enim dominus, quod post visionem sanctorum locorum hanc vel maxime causam habui, ut tuis litteris sorori me redderes et matri.' Et ego : ' Iam iam,' inquam, ' quod vis, faciam ; nam et epistulae transmarinae sunt et specialiter sermo dictatus raros potest invenire, quos mordeat. Te autem moneo, ut clam sermonem hunc habeas. Cumque portaveris pro viatico, si auditus fuerit, laetemur pariter ; sin autem contemptus, quod et magis reor, ego verba perdiderim, tu itineris longitudinem.'

---

[1] Horace, *Satires,* I. x. 3: *sale multo urbem defricuit.* Lucilius was a satirist.

[2] This proverb has not been identified nor has any satisfactory explanation of its nature been given.

[3] Psalm lxix. 12.

[4] *I.e.* the journey from Gaul to Palestine.

try to avoid present temptations. It is inconsistent surely to hide one's body, and to allow one's tongue to roam the world.' Thereupon he answered : ' You are too fearful ; where now is the hardihood where-with, like Lucilius of old,[1] you scoured the city with abundant salt ? ' ' It is just that,' said I, ' which deters me and forbids me now to open my lips. Because I tried to convict crime I have myself been made out a criminal. It is like the popular proverb : [2] as all the world declares on oath that I have no ears, I believe it too and do not touch them. The very walls resounded with curses against me and " I was the song of drunkards." [3] I have been taught by painful experience to hold my tongue, and now I think it better to set a guard to my mouth, and keep the door of my lips close fastened, rather than to incline my heart to malicious words, and while censur-ing the faults of others myself to fall into that of detraction.' To that he said : ' Speaking the truth is not detraction, and a special rebuke is not a general lecture. There are few persons or none who are guilty of this particular fault. I beg you therefore not to let me have made this long and painful journey[4] in vain. The Lord knows that after the sight of the holy places my chief motive for coming was to get you to restore me by a letter to my mother and sister.' ' Well, well,' I answered, ' I will do as you wish. My letters will pass across the sea, and a discourse specially composed can seldom offend others. I warn you, however, to keep what I say private. Take it as part of your luggage, and if it is listened to, let us rejoice together. But if it is rejected, as I rather think it will be, I shall have wasted my words and you your long journey.'

373

2. Primum scire vos cupio, soror ac filia, me non idcirco scribere, quia aliquid de vobis suspicer, sed, ne ceteri suspicentur, vestram orare concordiam. Alioquin—quod absit!—si peccati vos aestimarem glutino cohaesisse, numquam scriberem sciremque me surdis narrare fabulam. Deinde hoc obsecro, ut, si mordacius quippiam scripsero, non tam meae austeritatis putetis esse quam morbi. Putridae carnes ferro curantur et cauterio, venena serpentino pelluntur antidoto; quod satis dolet, maiori dolore expellitur. Ad extremum hoc dico, quod, etiam si conscientia vulnus non habeat, habet tamen fama ignominiam. Mater et filia, nomina pietatis, officiorum vocabula, vincula naturae secundaque post Deum foederatio, non est laus, si vos diligitis; scelus est, quod odistis. Dominus Iesus subiectus est parentibus suis: venerabatur matrem, cuius erat ipse pater, colebat nutricium, quem nutrierat, gestatumque se meminerat alterius utero, alterius brachiis. Unde et in cruce pendens commendat parentem discipulo, quam numquam ante crucem dimiserat.

3. Tu vero, filia—iam enim desino ad matrem loqui, quam forsitan aetas et inbecillitas ac solitudo excusabilem faciunt—tu, inquam, filia, eius domum angustam iudicas, cuius non tibi fuit venter angustus? Decem mensibus utero clausa vixisti, et uno die in

LETTER CXVII

The Letter

In the first place, my sister and daughter, I wish
you to know that I am writing not because I suspect
anything evil of you, but that I am begging you to
live in harmony to prevent other people becoming
suspicious. In any case, if I had thought—far be it
from me—that you were caught in the snares of sin,
I should never have written, knowing that my tale
would be addressed to deaf ears. In the second
place, if I write at all sharply, I beg you to attribute
it not to any harshness on my part, but to the malady
which I am treating. When the flesh has mortified,
cautery and the knife are the remedies; for poison
snake's venom is the antidote; serious pain is cured
by greater pain. Lastly I say this: even if your
own conscience is unhurt, scandal brings disgrace.
Mother and daughter! names of affection, titles of
duties, bonds of nature, an alliance second after
God, there is no praise if you love; it is crime that
you hate. Our Lord Jesus was subject to His
parents: He reverenced the mother of whom He
was Himself the parent: He honoured the foster-
father whom He Himself had fostered: He remembered that the one had carried Him in her womb,
and the other in his arms. Wherefore also when He
was hanging on the cross, He commended to a disciple
the mother whom before the cross He had never sent
away.

For the moment I say no more to the mother;
perhaps age, weakness and loneliness make her
excusable. But you, my daughter, you, I say, do
you think that her house is too small for you whose
womb was not too small? You lived for ten months
in the shelter of your mother's body; can you not

375

uno cubiculo cum matre non duras? An oculos eius
ferre non potes et, quia omnes motus tuos illa, quae
genuit, quae aluit et ad hanc perduxit aetatem,
facilius intellegit, testem domesticam fugis? Si
virgo es, quid times diligentem custodiam? Si
corrupta, cur non palam nubis? Secunda post
naufragium tabula est, quod male coeperis, saltim
hoc remedio temperare. Neque vero hoc dico, quo
post peccatum tollam paenitentiam, ut, quod male
coepit, male perseveret, sed quod desperem in istius
modi copula divulsionem. Alioquin, si ad matrem
migraveris post ruinam, facilius poteris cum ea
plangere, quod per illius absentiam perdidisti.
Quodsi adhuc integra es et non perdidisti, serva, ne
perdas. Quid tibi necesse est in ea versari domo, in
qua necesse habeas cotidie aut perire aut vincere?
Quisquamne mortalium iuxta viperam securus
somnos capit? Quae ut non percutiat, certe solli-
citat. Securius est perire non posse quam iuxta
periculum non perisse; in altero tranquillitas est, in
altero gubernatio, ibi gaudemus, hic evadimus.

4. Sed forte respondeas: 'Non bene morata
mater est, res saeculi cupit, amat divitias, ignorat
ieiunium, oculos stibio linit, vult compta procedere
et nocet proposito meo nec possum cum huiusce
modi vivere.' Primum quidem, etiam si talis est, ut
causaris, maius habebis praemium, si talem non

endure to live with her for one day in one room?
Or is it that you cannot bear her eyes? Knowing
that she who bore you, nursed you and reared you
understands all your movements without difficulty, do
you shrink from a witness to your home life? If you
are a virgin, why do you fear careful guardianship?
If you have lost your virginity, why do you not marry
openly? Marriage is a raft for the shipwrecked, a
remedy that may at least cure a bad beginning. Nor
do I say this, because after sin I would abolish repentance, so that what began wrong may go on
wrong; but because with connections of this sort
I despair of a break. In any case, if you return
to your mother after your downfall, you will be
more easily able in her company to lament that
which you lost by separating from her. If, on the
other hand, you are still a pure virgin and have
not lost your chastity, guard it lest you lose it
now. Why must you live in a house where you
must every day win a battle or be ruined? Can
any one sleep soundly by the side of a viper? It may
not attack, but it certainly causes uneasiness. It is
safer to be where you cannot possibly perish, than to
graze the peril and just not to perish. In the first
case, calm water; in the second, skilful steering;
there we are gay, here we just escape.

You may perhaps reply: 'My mother has not a
good character, she desires the things of this world,
she loves riches, she ignores all fasts, she rubs her
eyes with antimony, she likes to go out in fine clothes,
she is a danger to my vows, I cannot live with a person
of her kind.' To begin with, even if she is the sort
of woman you allege, you will have the greater reward
if you refuse to desert her with all her faults. She

deseras. Illa te diu portavit, diu aluit et difficiliores
infantiae mores blanda pietate sustinuit. Lavit
pannorum sordes et inmundo saepe foedata est
stercore. Adsedit aegrotanti et, quae propter te
sua fastidia sustinuerat, tua quoque passa est. Ad
hanc perduxit aetatem; ut Christum amares, docuit.
Non tibi displiceat eius conversatio, quae te sponso
tuo virginem consecravit. Quodsi ferri non potest et
delicias eius fugis atque, ut vulgo soletis dicere,
saecularis est mater, habes alienas virgines, habes
sanctum pudicitiae chorum. Quid matrem deserens
eum eligis, qui suam forsitan sororem reliquit et
matrem? Illa difficilis, sed iste facilis; illa iurgatrix,
iste placabilis. Quem quaero utrum secuta sis an
postea inveneris. Si secuta es, manifestum est, cur
matrem reliqueris; si postea repperisti, ostendis,
quid in matris hospitio non potueris invenire. Durus
doctor et meo mucrone me vulnerans: ' Qui ambulat,'
inquit, ' simpliciter, ambulat confidenter.' Tacerem,
si me remorderet conscientia, et in aliis meum crimen
non reprehenderem nec per trabem oculi mei alterius
festucam viderem. Nunc autem, cum inter fratres
procul habitans eorumque fruens contubernio honeste
sub arbitris et videam raro et videar, inpudentissi-

---

[1] Proverbs, x. 9.

carried you long, and she nursed you for many
months; her gentle love bore with the peevish ways
of your infancy. She washed your soiled napkins and
often dirtied her hands with their nastiness. She sat
by your bed when you were ill and was patient with
your sickness, even as she had before endured the
sickness of maternity which you caused. She
brought you up to womanhood; she taught you to
love Christ. The company of one who consecrated
you as a virgin to your Spouse ought not to be distasteful to you. Still, if you cannot put up with her
and her fashionable ways, if she is really, as people
say, a worldly mother, there are virgins of other
families, a holy company of chaste maidens, with
whom you might live. Why, when you desert your
mother, do you choose a man who perhaps has left
a sister and mother of his own? She is hard to get
on with, you will say, he is easy; she is fond of
quarrels, he is amiable. Well, I have one question
to ask: did you leave your mother to follow this man
or did you come upon him after you had left her?
In the first case, it is plain why you deserted your
parent; in the second, you reveal clearly what it
was that you could not find under your mother's
roof. A stern teacher, who wounds me with my
own scalpel, says: ' He that walketh uprightly
walketh surely.'[1] If I had a guilty conscience I
would hold my tongue, and not blame in others an
offence which I myself commit, nor see the mote in
my neighbour's eye through the beam in my own.
But as it is, since I live far away in a community of
brothers whose society, as witnesses can testify, I
honourably enjoy, rarely seeing or being seen by
other men, it would be the height of shamelessness

mum est eius te verecundiam non sequi, cuius te
sequi testeris exemplum. Quodsi dixeris: ' Et
mihi sufficit conscientia mea; habeo Deum iudicem,
qui meae vitae testis est; non curo, quid loquantur
homines,' audi apostolum scribentem: ' Providentes
bona non solum coram Deo, sed etiam hominibus.'
Si quis te carpit, quod sis Christiana, quod virgo, ne
cures, quod ideo dimiseris matrem, ut in monasterio
inter virgines viveres; talis detractio laus tua est.
Ubi non luxuria in puella Dei, sed duritia carpitur,
crudelitas ista pietas est. Illum enim praefers matri,
quem praeferre iuberis et animae tuae. Quem si et
ipsa praetulerit, et filiam te sentiet et sororem.

5. Quid igitur? Scelus est sancti viri habere
contubernium? Obtorto collo me in ius trahis, ut aut
probem, quod nolo, aut multorum invidiam subeam.
Sanctus vir numquam filiam a matre seiungit; utramque suspicit, utramque veneratur. Sit quamlibet
sancta filia, mater vidua indicium castitatis est. Si
coaevus tuus est ille nescio quis, matrem tuam
honoret et suam; si senior, te ut filiam diligat et
parentis subiciat disciplinae. Non expedit amborum
famae plus te illum amare quam matrem, ne non
videatur affectum in te eligere, sed aetatem. Et

---

[1] Romans, xii. 17.

for you not to adopt the modest life of the man whom
you profess to have taken as your exemplar. You
may reply: ' For me also my own conscience is
sufficient. God is my judge who is witness of my
life. I care not what men may say.' Listen then
to the apostle's words: ' Provide things honest not
only in the sight of God but also in the sight of men.'[1]
Heed it not if anyone criticizes you for being a
Christian and a virgin, and for having left your
mother to live in a monastery with other virgins.
Such censure is your truest praise. When men blame
one of God's maidens, not for self-indulgence, but for
sternness, what they call cruelty is really devotion.
You are preferring to your mother Him whom you
are bidden to prefer to your own soul. And if she
herself should ever also thus prefer Him, she will
find in you both a daughter and a sister.

' What! ' you may say, ' is it a crime to live under
the same roof with a holy man? ' You drag me by
the scruff of the neck into court, and give me choice
either to approve against my will, or else incur
odium from many. A holy man never separates a
daughter from her mother; he respects them both,
he regards both of them with reverence. However
saintly a daughter may be, a widowed mother is a
warranty of her chastity. If this man of yours is of
the same age as you are, he should honour your
mother as his own; if he is your elder, he should
love you as a daughter and submit you to a mother's
discipline. It is not expedient, for your reputation
or for his, that he should love you more than he
loves your mother: so that he may not seem to
make his choice in you not of your affection but
of your youth. And I should still say this, if you

hoc dicerem, si fratrem monachum non haberes, si domesticis careres praesidiis; nunc vero, pro dolor, inter matrem atque germanum—et matrem viduam fratremque monachum—cur se alienus interserit? Bonum quidem est, ut te et filiam noveris et sororem; si autem utrumque non potes et mater quasi dura respuitur, saltim frater placeat. Si frater asperior est, mollior sit illa, quae genuit. Quid palles? Quid aestuas? Quid vultum rubore suffundis et trementibus labiis inpatientiam pectoris contestaris? Non superat amorem matris et fratris nisi solus uxoris affectus.

6. Audio praeterea te suburbana, villarum amoenitates cum adfinibus et cognatis et istius modi genus hominibus circumire. Nec dubito, quin vel consobrina vel soror sit, in quarum solacium novi generis ducaris adsecula—absit quippe, ut, quamvis proximi sint et cognati, virorum te suspicer captare consortia—obsecro ergo te, virgo, ut mihi respondeas: sola vadis in comitatu propinquorum an cum amasio tuo? Quamvis sis inpudens, saecularium oculis eum ingerere non audebis. Si enim hoc feceris, et te et illum familia universa cantabit, vos cunctorum digiti denotabunt, ipsa quoque soror aut adfinis sive cognata, quae in adulationem tui sanctum et nonnum

had no brother who is a monk, if you lacked
protectors at home. But as things stand, why
does a stranger—O grievous thought!—thrust himself in between you and your mother and brother,
your mother a widow and your brother a monk?
It would be a good thing for you to know that you
are both a daughter and a sister. But if you cannot
do both, and if your palate rejects your mother as
being a rough wine, your brother at least should
prove satisfactory. If he should be somewhat
harsh, then she who bore you may seem more mellow.
Why do you turn pale? Why does your bosom heave?
Why do your hot blushes and quivering lips confess
your restlessness? Nothing can overcome a woman's
love for a mother and a brother, except only the
passion of a wife.

I hear, moreover, that you go the round of suburban
retreats and pleasant country houses in company
with your relatives and connections by marriage and
such like intimate friends. Nor do I doubt, that
there is some female cousin or sister, for whose
comfort you may be taken as a new sort of attendant—indeed, far be it from me to suppose, that
although they may be members of your own
family, you angle for the society of men—and
so I pray you, my virgin, tell me this: do you
appear alone in your kinsfolk's society or do you
take your sweetheart with you? However shameless you may be, you will scarcely dare to flaunt
him in the eyes of worldly people. For if you
should do so, your entire family will make a song of
you and him; every finger will be pointed at the pair
of you; even your sister or kinswoman or relative,
who in your presence to flatter you calls him a monk

coram te vocant, cum se paululum converterit, portentosum ridebit maritum. Sin autem sola ieris—quod et magis aestimo—utique inter servos adulescentes, inter maritas feminas atque nupturas, inter lascivas puellas et comatos linteatosque iuvenes furvarum vestium puella gradieris. Dabit tibi barbatulus quilibet manum, sustentabit lassam et pressis digitis aut temptabitur aut temptabit. Erit tibi inter viros matronasque convivium: expectabis aliena oscula, praegustatos cibos et absque scandalo tuo in aliis sericas vestes auratasque miraberis. In ipso quoque convivio, ut vescaris carnibus, quasi invita cogeris, ut vinum bibas, Dei laudabitur creatura, ut laves balneis, sordibus detrahetur; et omnes te, cum aliquid eorum, quae suadent, retractans feceris, puram, simplicem, dominam et vere ingenuam conclamabunt. Personabit interim aliquis cantator ad mensam et inter psalmos dulci modulatione currentes, quoniam alienas non audebit uxores, te, quae custodem non habes, saepius respectabit. Loquetur nutibus et, quidquid metuet dicere, significabit affectibus. Inter has et tantas inlecebras voluptatum etiam ferreas mentes libido domat, quae maiorem in virginibus patitur famem, dum dulcius putat omne, quod nescit. Narrant gentilium fabulae

and a holy man, will laugh behind his back at your
fright of a husband. If, on the other hand, you go
out alone—which I rather suppose—you, a girl in
your dark clothes, will be one of a party of youthful
attendants, married women and women soon to be
brides, pleasure-loving damsels, and young fops with
long hair and close-fitting tunics. Some boy with a
little beard will give you his arm, and hold you up if
you are tired, and as your fingers squeeze he will either
be tempted himself or will tempt you. You will sit
down to table with married men and women; you
will wait till the others have finished kissing and the
dishes have been tasted, and without making any
protest will admire the silk dresses and the gold
brocade that the others are wearing. At the dinner
itself they will pretend you are unwilling and will
force you to partake of the meat; to get you to
drink wine, they will praise it as the gift of the
Creator. To induce you to visit the baths, they will
speak of dirt with disgust. And when you reluctantly
do something of what they would have you do, they
will cry out in chorus: ' What a frank, innocent girl
she is! What a genuine lady! ' Meanwhile some
singer will come into the dining-room, and as he per-
forms a selection of soft flowing airs, he will not
dare to look at other men's wives, but he will very
often glance at you, who have no protector. He will
speak by gestures, and a meaning emphasis in his
voice will convey what he is afraid to put into words.
Amid such strong allurements to pleasure as these
even iron wills are overcome by desire, which in
the case of virgins is the sharper set because it
thinks that anything of which it knows nothing is
especially delightful. Heathen legends tell us that

cantibus sirenarum nautas in saxa praecipites et ad
Orphei citharam arbores bestiasque ac silicum dura
mollita. Difficile inter epulas servatur pudicitia.
Nitens cutis sordidum ostentat animum.

7. Legimus in scolis pueri—et spirantia in plateis
aera conspecimus—aliquem ossibus vix haerentem[1]
inlicitis arsisse amoribus et ante vita caruisse quam
peste. Quid tu facies, puella sani corporis, delicata,
pinguis, rubens, aestuans inter carnes, inter vina et
balneas, iuxta maritas, iuxta adulescentulos? Etsi
rogata non dederis, tamen formae putes testimonium,
si rogeris. Libidinosa mens ardentius honesta persequitur et, quod non licet, dulcius suspicatur. Vestis
ipsa vilis et pulla animi tacentis indicium est, si
rugam non habeat, si per terram, ut altior videaris,
trahatur, si de industria dissuta sit tunica, ut aliquid
intus appareat operiatque, quod foedum est, et
aperiat, quod formosum. Caliga quoque ambulantis
nigella ac nitens stridore iuvenes ad se vocat.
Papillae fasciolis conprimuntur et crispanti cingulo
angustius pectus artatur. Capilli vel in frontem vel
in aures defluunt. Palliolum interdum cadit, ut
candidos nudet umeros, et, quasi videri noluerit,
celat festina, quod volens retraxerat. Et quando in
publico quasi per verecundiam operit faciem, lupa-

---

[1] Virgil, *Eclogues,* III. 102: *vix ossibus haerent.*

the songs of the sirens drew sailors headlong on to
their rocks, and that trees and beasts and hard stones
were all softened by the music of Orpheus' lyre. At
a banquet it is hard to preserve one's chastity. A
sleek skin is the sure sign of a foul mind.

When I was a boy at school I read of a man—and in
the streets I have since seen his living image in
bronze—who burned with unlawful passion even
when his flesh scarcely clung to his bones,[1] and who
passed away from life with his malady still unhealed.
What then will you do, a healthy young girl,
dainty, plump, rosy, all afire amid the fleshpots,
amid the wines and baths, side by side with
married women, with young men? Even if you
refuse to give what they ask for, you may think
that the asking is evidence of your beauty. A
libertine is all the more ardent when he is pursuing
virtue, and thinks that the unlawful is especially
delightful. Your very robe, coarse and sombre
though it be, betrays your unexpressed desires,
if it be without crease, if it be trailed upon the
ground to make you seem taller, if your vest be
slit on purpose to let something be seen within,
hiding that which is unsightly and disclosing that
which is fair. As you walk along, your shiny
black shoes by their creaking give an invitation to
young men. Your breasts are confined in strips of
linen, and your chest is imprisoned close by a tight
girdle. Your hair comes down over your forehead or
over your ears. Your shawl sometimes drops, so as
to leave your white shoulders bare, and then, as
though unwilling to be seen, it hastily hides what
it intentionally revealed. And when in public it
hides the face in a pretence of modesty, with a

narum arte id solum ostendit, quod ostensum magis
placere potest.

8. Respondebis: ' Unde me nosti? et quomodo
tam longe in me iactas oculos tuos?' Fratris hoc
tui mihi narravere lacrimae et intolerabiles per
momenta singultus. Atque utinam ille mentitus sit
et magis timens hoc quam arguens dixerit! Sed
mihi crede, soror: nemo mentiens plorat. Dolet
sibi praelatum iuvenem, non quidem comatum, non
vestium sericarum, sed trossulum et in sordibus
delicatum, qui ipse sacculum signet, textrinum teneat,
pensa distribuat, regat familiam, emat quicquid de
publico necessarium est, dispensator et dominus et
praeveniens officula servulorum, quem omnes rodant
famuli, et quicquid domina non dederit, illum clami-
tent subtraxisse. Querulum servulorum genus est
et, quantumcumque dederis, semper eis minus est.
Non enim considerant de quanto, sed quantum detur,
doloremque suum solis, quod possunt, detractationibus consolantur. Ille parasitum, iste inpostorem,
hic heredipetam, alius novo quolibet appellat vocabulo.
Ipsum iactant adsidere lectulo, obstetrices adhibere
languenti, portare matulam, calefacere lintea, plicare
fasciolas. Facilius mala credunt homines et quodcumque domi fingitur, rumor in publico fit. Nec
mireris, si ancillae et servuli de vobis ista confingant,
cum mater quoque id ipsum queratur et frater.

harlot's skill it shows only those features which give men when shown more pleasure.

You will reply: ' From what source do you know all this about me? How could you ever have set eyes upon me when you live so far away?' Your brother's tears told me this and his scarcely endurable outbursts of sobbing. Would that he may have spoken falsely, would that his words may have been the expression of fears, not of facts! But believe me, sister; no one ever weeps when he is lying. He is indignant that a young man is preferred to himself, not indeed a long-haired fop in silk clothes, but still a coxcomb dainty even in his squalor, a rogue who puts his own seal on your purse, manages the weaving, apportions the wool to be spun, directs the household, and buys all that is needed in the market. He is both steward and master, and anticipates the servants in all their duties, so that the whole household have their teeth in him and protest that he has filched all that their mistress does not give them. Servants are always full of complaints, and, however much you give them, it is always too little. They do not consider how much you have, but only how much they get, and they console their indignation in the only way they can, by finding fault. One calls him a parasite, another an incubus, another a legacy-hunter, another any fresh name he can invent. They put it about that he sits at your bedside, fetches nurses when you feel unwell, removes the slops, makes you warm bandages, and folds compresses. People are only too ready to believe evil, and tales invented within doors soon get noised abroad. Nor need you wonder that your maids and footmen invent such tales about you both, when even your mother and brother make similar complaints.

9. Fac igitur, quod moneo, quod precor, ut primum matri, dehinc, si id fieri non potest, saltim fratri reconcilieris. Aut si ista tam cara nomina hostiliter detestaris, dividere ab eo, quem tuis diceris praetulisse. Si autem et hoc non potes—reverteris enim ad tuos, si illum possis deserere—vel honestius sodali tuo utere. Separentur domus vestrae dividaturque convivium, ne maledici homines sub uno tectulo vos manentes lectulum quoque criminentur habere communem. Potes et ad necessitates tuas, quale voluisti, habere solacium et aliqua ex parte publica carere infamia, quamquam cavenda sit macula, quae nullo nitro secundum Hieremiam, nulla fullonum herba lui potest. Quando vis, ut te videat —et inviset—adhibe arbitros amicos, libertos, servulos. Bona conscientia nullius oculos fugiet. Intret intrepidus, securus exeat. Taciti oculi et sermo silens et totius corporis habitus vel trepidationem interdum vel securitatem loquuntur. Aperi, quaeso, aures tuas et clamorem totius civitatis exaudi. Iam perdidisti vestra vocabula et mutuo ex vobis cognomina suscepistis: tu illius diceris et ille tuus. Hoc mater audit et frater paratique sunt et precantur vos sibi dividere et privatam vestrae coniunctionis infamiam laudem facere communem. Tu esto cum matre, sit ille cum fratre. Audentius diliges [1] sodalem fratris tui: honestius amabit mater amicum filii quam filiae suae. Quodsi nolueris, si mea

---

[1] diligis: *Hilberg.*

---

[1] Jeremiah, ii. 20, 22: 'playing the harlot.'

Do, therefore, what I advise and pray you to do. Be reconciled with your mother: if that is impossible, at least make peace with your brother. Or, if you abominate those dear names, separate yourself from the man whom you are said to have preferred to your own people. If even this you cannot do—for you would return to your own folk if you could bear to leave him—pay more regard to appearances in your dealings with your friend. Live in separate houses and take your meals apart; if you stay under one roof, slanderers will accuse you of sharing one bed together. You can thus have the help you wished for when you need it, and to a certain degree avoid public disgrace. Not but what you must ever beware of that stain which Jeremiah[1] tells us no nitre or fuller's soap can wash out. When you wish him to see you—and he will visit you—have people in the room with you, friends or freedmen or slaves. A good conscience will shrink from no man's gaze. Let him come in without embarrassment and go away without anxiety. Silent looks, unspoken words, a man's whole bearing, at times spell uneasiness, at other times security. Pray, open your ears and listen to the outcry of the whole city. You two have already lost your own names and interchanged them for new ones: he is known as your man and you as his woman. Your mother and your brother have heard this talk, and they are ready each to take one of you, begging you thus to turn a private disgrace into a common glory. You can live with your mother, he with your brother. You may then more boldly show affection for your brother's friend: your mother may with more propriety love her son's comrade than she could her daughter's. But if you

monita rugata fronte contempseris, epistula tibi
haec voce libera proclamabit : ' Quid alienum servum
obsides ? Quid ministrum Christi tuum famulum
facis ? Respice ad populum, singulorum facies
intuere. Ille in ecclesia legit et te aspiciunt universi,
nisi quod paene licentia coniugali de tua infamia gloriaris nec iam secreto dedecore potes esse contenta ;
procacitatem libertatem vocas. " Facies meretricis
facta est tibi, nescis erubescere."'

10. Iterum me malignum, iterum suspiciosum,
iterum rumigerulum clamitas. Egone suspiciosus,
egone malivolus, qui, ut in principio epistulae praefatus sum, ideo scripsi, quia non suspicabar, an tu
negligens, dissoluta, contemptrix, quae annis nata
viginti et quinque adulescentem necdum bene
barbatulum ita brachiis tuis quasi cassibus inclusisti ?
Optimum re vera paedagogum, qui te moneat, qui
asperitate frontis exterreat et, quamquam in nullis
aetatibus libido sit tuta, tamen vel cano capite ab
aperta defendat ignominia! Veniet, veniet tempus
—dies adlabitur, dum ignoras—et iste formosulus
tuus, quia cito senescunt mulieres, maxime quae
iuxta viros sunt, vel ditiorem reperiet vel iuniorem.
Tunc te paenitebit pertinaciae, quando et rem et
famam amiseris, quando, quod male iunctum fuerat,
dividetur bene, nisi forte secura es et coalescente
tanti temporis caritate discidium non vereris.

---

[1] Jeremiah, iii. 3.

still refuse, if with wrinkled brow you reject my warning, then this letter will cry aloud to you with unchecked voice. ' Why,' it will say, ' do you besiege another's servant? Why do you make Christ's minister your slave? Look at the people and regard each individual face. When he is reading in church the whole congregation fix their eyes on you: but you perhaps with almost a wife's recklessness glory in your shame, and secret disgrace no longer satisfies you; you call boldness freedom. " You have a whore's forehead and refuse to be ashamed." ' [1]

Again you cry out that I am a malignant, that I am suspicious, that I am a scandal-monger. Am I truly suspicious or malignant, I who, as I said at the beginning of this letter, only took up my pen because I felt no suspicions of you? Is it not you rather who are careless, loose and scornful, you who at the age of twenty-five have caught in the snare of your arms a youth whose beard has hardly grown? A fine instructor in truth he must be, able to advise, by stern looks to frighten, and even by his grey hair to defend you from open shame! Not but what lust is never safe at any time of life. The day will surely, surely come— for time glides on while you notice it not—when your handsome youngster will find a richer or a more youthful mistress. Women soon grow old, especially when they live with a man at their side. You will be sorry for your decision and regret your obstinacy, on the day when you find property and reputation gone and this unhappy union happily broken—unless perhaps you feel quite at ease, and seeing that your affection has had so long a time to become established, you have no fear of a rupture.

11. Tu quoque, mater, quae propter aetatem
maledicta non metuis, noli sic vindicari, ut pecces.
Magis a te discat filia separari, quam tu ab illa dis-
iungi. Habes filium et filiam et generum, immo
contubernalem filiae tuae; quid quaeris aliena
solacia et ignes iam sopitos suscitas? Honestius
tibi est saltim culpam filiae sustentare quam occasionem tuae quaerere. Sit tecum filius monachus,
pietatis viduitatisque praesidium. Quid tibi alienum
hominem in ea praesertim domo, quae filium et
filiam capere non potuit? Eius iam aetatis es, ut
possis nepotes habere de filia. Invita ad te utrumque.
Revertatur cum viro, quae sola exierat—virum dixi,
non maritum; nemo calumnietur: sexum significare
volui, ne coniugium—aut, si erubescit et retractat et
domum, in qua nata est, arbitratur angustam, vos
ad eius hospitiolum pergite. Quamvis artum sit,
facilius potest matrem et fratrem capere quam
alienum hominem, cum quo certe in uno cubiculo
manere non poterat. Sint in una domo duae feminae,
duo masculi. Sin autem et tertius ille γηροβοσκὸς
tuus abire non vult et seditiones ac turbas concitat,
sit biga, sit triga, frater vester ac filius et sororem
illis exhibebit et matrem. Alii vitricum et generum
vocent, ille nutricium appellet et fratrem.

---

[1] Jerome insists that the brother should live in the house;
preferably with one other man—his sister's mate—but even
if the mother's male friend remains the brother must stay:
thus there are either two men or three men in the
establishment.

LETTER CXVII

As for you, my friend's mother, your age frees
you from any fear of scandal; but do not think that
it gives you liberty to do wrong. Your daughter
should rather learn from you how to separate from a
companion than you be taught by her how to break
away from a paramour. You have a son and a
daughter and a son-in-law, or rather a man who
lives under your daughter's roof. Why seek other
consolations or try to wake sleeping fires? It would
at least be more respectable for you to screen your
daughter's fault than to seek in it an occasion for
wrongdoing on your own part. Let your son who is
a monk live with you and strengthen you in your
natural affection and in your vow of widowhood.
Why do you have a stranger in the house that could
not hold a son and a daughter? You are old enough
now to have grandchildren by your daughter. Invite
the pair to your home. Let her return with her man,
she who went out alone. I say 'man,' not 'husband';
so no one need cavil; I merely refer to his sex and
not to any conjugal relationship. If she is ashamed
and hangs back, and thinks the house where she was
born is too small for her, then let all of you move to
her lodging. However cramped it may be, it can
more easily contain a mother and a brother than it
could a strange man, for surely she could not have
remained in the same bedroom with him. Let there
be two females and two males in the one house.
But if the third male too, that 'nurturer of your
old age,' refuses to leave you and stirs up quarrels
and confusion, be it a team of two, be it a team of
three, he who is both brother and son will offer to
the other men a sister and a mother.[1] Others
may speak of them as step-father and son-in-law:
your son must call them foster-father and brother.

395

12. Haec ad brevem lucubratiunculam celeri sermone dictavi volens desiderio postulantis satisfacere et quasi ad scholasticam materiam me exercens —eadem enim die mane pulsabat ostium, qui profecturus erat—simulque, ut ostenderem obtrectatoribus meis, quod et ego possim, quicquid venerit in buccam, dicere. Unde et de scripturis pauca perstrinxi nec orationem meam, ut in ceteris libris facere solitus sum, illarum floribus texui. Extemporalis est dictio et tanta ad lumen lucernulae facultate perfusa, ut notariorum manus lingua praecurreret et signa ac furta verborum volubilitas sermonis obrueret. Quod idcirco dixi, ut, qui non ignoscit ingenio, ignoscat vel tempori.

CXXV

AD RUSTICUM MONACHUM

1. NIHIL Christiano felicius, cui promittuntur regna caelorum; nihil laboriosius, qui cotidie de vita periclitatur. Nihil fortius, qui vincit diabolum; nihil inbecillius, qui a carne superatur. Utriusque rei exempla sunt plurima. Latro credidit in cruce et

---

[1] Probably Rusticus of Narbonne; following Jerome's advice he entered a monastery, was ordained later and consecrated Bishop of Narbonne 430.

LETTER CXVII AND LETTER CXXV

Note

I dictated this letter, talking quickly, in the space of one short night, wishing to satisfy a friend's earnest request and to try my hand, as it were, upon a scholastic subject—for that same morning my visitor, who was on the point of departure, knocked at my door—and at the same time, wishing to show my detractors that I too can say the first thing that comes into my head. I therefore introduced few quotations from the Scriptures and did not interweave my discourse with its flowers, as I have done in my other books. I extemporized as I went, and by the light of one small lamp poured forth my words in such profusion, that my tongue outstripped my secretaries' pens and my volubility baffled the tricks of their shorthand. I say this that those who make no excuses for lack of ability may make some for lack of time.

LETTER CXXV

To Rusticus [1]

Good and bad monks

Written A.D. 411

NOTHING is happier than the Christian, for to him is promised the kingdom of heaven: nothing is more toil-worn, for every day he goes in danger of his life. Nothing is stronger than he is, for he triumphs over the devil: nothing is weaker, for he is conquered by the flesh. There are many examples of the truth of both statements. The robber on the cross believed, and it was immediately vouchsafed him

statim meretur audire: 'Amen, amen dico tibi: hodie mecum eris in paradiso.' Iudas de apostolatus fastigio in proditionis tartarum labitur et nec familiaritate convivii nec intinctione buccellae nec osculi gratia frangitur, ne quasi hominem tradat, quem filium Dei noverat. Quid Samaritana vilius? Non solum ipsa credidit et post sex viros unum invenit dominum Messiamque cognoscit ad fontem, quem in templo Iudaeorum populus ignorabat, sed auctor fit multorum salutis et apostolis ementibus cibos esurientem reficit lassumque sustentat. Quid Salomone sapientius? Attamen infatuatur amoribus feminarum. 'Bonum est sal' nullumque sacrificium absque huius aspersione suscipitur—unde et apostolus praecipit: 'Sermo vester sit sale conditus'—quod, si infatuetur, foras proicitur in tantumque perdit nominis dignitatem, ut ne in sterquilinio quidem utile sit, quo solent credentium arva condiri et sterile animarum solum pinguescere. Haec dicimus, ut prima te, fili Rustice, fronte doceamus magna coepisse, excelsa sectari et adulescentiae, immo pubertatis, incentiva calcantem perfectae quidem aetatis gradum scandere, sed lubricum iter est, per quod ingrederis, nec tantam sequi gloriam post victoriam, quantam ignominiam post ruinam.

2. Non mihi nunc per virtutum prata ducendus es nec laborandum ut ostendam tibi variorum pulchri-

---

[1] St. Luke, xxiii. 43.　　[2] Colossians, iv. 6.　　[3] Matt. v. 13.

to hear the words: ' Verily I say unto thee, to-day shalt thou be with me in Paradise.' [1] Judas on the other hand fell from his high place as apostle into the traitor's hell, and neither by the close intercourse of the banquet nor by the dipping of the sop nor by the grace of Christ's kiss was he prevented from betraying as man Him whom he had known as the Son of God. What could be of less worth than the woman of Samaria? Yet not only did she herself believe, and after her six husbands find one Lord, not only did she recognize at the well the Messiah whom the Jews failed to recognize in the temple; she brought salvation to many, and while the apostles were buying food she comforted Him who was hungry and weary. What could be wiser than Solomon? Yet he was rendered foolish by his love of women. ' Salt is good,' and no sacrifice is received unless it is sprinkled with it. Therefore it was that the apostle gave command: ' Let your speech be alway with grace, seasoned with salt.' [2] But if salt has lost its savour, it is cast out,[3] and so completely loses its credit that it is not even useful on the dunghill to season believers' fields and enrich the barren soil of their souls. I say all this, my son Rusticus, because in the forefront of this treatise I would teach the greatness of your undertaking and the loftiness of your goal. You must know that only by treading underfoot the allurements of youth and early manhood can you climb to the heights of perfect maturity. The path you tread is slippery, and the glory of success is less than the disgrace of failure.

It is not my task now to lead you through the meadows of virtue, nor need I labour to show you the beauty of their gay blossoms, the purity of the

tudinem florum, quid in se lilia habeant puritatis,
quid rosarum verecundia possideat, quid violae
purpura promittat in regno, quid rutilantium spon-
deat pictura gemmarum. Iam enim propitio domino
stivam tenes, iam in tectum atque solarium cum
Petro apostolo conscendisti, qui esuriens in Iudaeis
Cornelii saturatur fide et famem incredulitatis eorum
gentium conversione restinguit atque in vase evan-
geliorum quadrangulo, quod de caelo descendit ad
terras, docetur et discit omnes homines posse salvari.
Rursumque, quod viderat, in specie candidissimi
linteaminis in superna transfertur et credentium
turbas de terris in caelum rapit, ut pollicitatio domini
conpleatur: ' Beati mundo corde, quoniam ipsi
Deum videbunt.' Totum, quod adprehensa manu
insinuare tibi cupio, quod quasi doctus nauta post
multa naufragia rudem conor instruere vectorem,
illud est, ut, in quo litore pudicitiae pirata sit, noveris,
ubi Charybdis et radix omnium malorum avaritia, ubi
Scyllaei obtrectatorum canes, de quibus apostolus
loquitur: ' Ne mordentes invicem mutuo consu-
mamini,' quomodo in media tranquillitate securi
Libycis interdum vitiorum Syrtibus obruamur, quid
venenatorum animantium desertum huius saeculi
nutriat.

3. Navigantes Rubrum Mare, in quo optandum
nobis est ut verus Pharao cum suo mergatur exercitu,
multis difficultatibus ac periculis ad urbem Abisamam
perveniunt. Utroque litore gentes vagae, immo

---

[1] Acts x. 9–16. [2] St. Matthew, v. 8.
[3] Galatians, v. 15. [4] A city of Arabia Felix.

lilies, the modesty of the roses, and the sure promise
of the kingdom given by the violet's purple and the
jewelled brilliance of each painted flower.   By God's
favour you have already put your hand to the plough,
and have already climbed up to the house-top and the
terrace like the apostle Peter, who when he was
hungry among the Jews was satisfied by the faith of
Cornelius and appeased the cravings caused through
their unbelief by the conversion of the Gentiles, being
taught by the four-cornered vessel of the Gospels let
down from heaven to earth that it was possible for all
men to be saved.[1]   And then, again, the fair white
sheet which he saw in his vision was taken up, carrying hosts of believers from earth to heaven, that the
promise of the Lord might be fulfilled: ' Blessed are
the pure in heart, for they shall see God.'[2]   In all
this I only wish to take you by the hand and convey
to you certain knowledge.   Like an experienced
sailor who has been in many a shipwreck, I seek to
instruct an unskilled steersman, to tell you where to
find the pirates who would rob you of chastity, where
lies the Charybdis of avarice, root of all evils, where
are Scylla's dogs, those calumniators of whom the
apostle says: ' If ye bite and devour one another,
take heed that ye be not consumed one of another.'[3]
I would warn you too that sometimes as we sail at
ease in calm weather we may be sucked down by the
quicksands of vice, and that many venomous creatures
have their home in the desert of this world.

Those who navigate the Red Sea, where we must
hope that the real Pharaoh may be drowned with
all his host, have to face many difficulties and dangers
before they reach the city of Abisama.[4]   Both shores
are infested by nomad tribes and savage beasts.

beluae habitant ferocissimae. Semper solliciti, semper armati totius anni vehunt cibaria. Latentibus saxis vadisque durissimis plena sunt omnia, ita ut speculator et ductor in summa mali arbore sedeat et inde regendae et circumflectendae navis dictata praedicat. Felix cursus est, si post sex menses supra dictae urbis portum teneant, a quo se incipit aperire oceanus, per quem vix anno perpetuo ad Indiam pervenitur et ad Gangem fluvium—quem Phison sancta scriptura cognominat—qui circuit omnem terram Evilat et multa genera pigmentorum de paradisi dicitur fonte evehere. Ibi nascitur carbunculus et zmaragdus et margarita candentia et uniones, quibus nobilium feminarum ardet ambitio, montesque aurei, quos adire propter dracones et gryphas et inmensorum corporum monstra hominibus inpossibile est, ut ostendatur nobis, quales custodes habeat avaritia.

4. Quorsum ista? Perspicuum est. Si negotiatores saeculi tanta sustinent, ut ad incertas perveniant perituras divitias, et servant cum animae discrimine, quae multis periculis quaesierunt, quid Christi negotiatori non faciendum est, qui venditis omnibus quaerit pretiosissimum margaritum, qui totis substantiae suis opibus emit agrum, in quo reperiat thesaurum, quem nec fur effodere nec latro possit auferre?

5. Scio me offensurum esse quam plurimos, qui generalem de vitiis disputationem in suam referant contumeliam et, dum mihi irascuntur, suam indicant conscientiam multoque peius de se quam de me iudicant. Ego enim neminem nominabo nec veteris

---

[1] Genesis, ii. 11.   [2] St. Matthew, xiii. 45 and vi. 19.

Travellers must be always on the alert, always armed, and they must take a year's provisions with them. The sea is full of hidden rocks and dangerous shoals, so that a look-out man on the top of the mast has to call out directions for the ship's course and steering. It is a successful trip if the harbour of the above-named city is reached in six months. At that point begins the ocean, which takes nearly a year to cross before you come to India and the river Ganges—called Phison in the Scriptures—which compasses the whole land of Evilat,[1] and is said to carry down from its source in Paradise many kinds of bright pigments. This land is the home of the carbuncle and the emerald, and those gleaming pearls which our great ladies so ardently desire. There are also in it mountains of gold which men cannot approach because of the dragons and griffins and other huge monsters, set there to show us what sort of guardians avarice employs.

To what end, you ask, do I say this? My reason is plain. If the merchants of this world undergo such pains to arrive at doubtful and passing riches, and after seeking them in the midst of dangers keep them at the risk of their lives, what should not Christ's merchant do who sells all he has to buy the pearl of great price, and with his whole substance buys a field that he may find therein a treasure which neither thief can dig up nor robber carry away?[2]

I know that I shall offend a very large number of people, who think that any general discourse on vice is meant as an attack upon themselves. Their anger against me is evidence of a guilty conscience, and they pass a severer judgment on their own character than on mine. I shall not mention names nor use

comoediae licentia certas personas eligam atque
perstringam. Prudentis viri est ac prudentium
feminarum dissimulare, immo emendare, quod in se
intellegant, et indignari sibi magis quam mihi nec in
monitorem maledicta congerere, qui, ut isdem
teneatur criminibus, certe in eo melior est, quod sua
ei mala non placent.

6. Audio religiosam habere te matrem, multorum
annorum viduam, quae aluit, quae erudivit infantem
et post studia Galliarum, quae vel florentissima sunt,
misit Romam non parcens sumptibus et absentiam
filii spe sustinens futurorum, ut ubertatem Gallici
nitoremque sermonis gravitas Romana condiret nec
calcaribus in te sed frenis uteretur, quod et in diser-
tissimis viris Graeciae legimus, qui Asianum tumorem
Attico siccabat sale et luxuriantes flagellis vineas
falcibus reprimebant, ut eloquentiae torcularia non
verborum pampinis, sed sensuum quasi uvarum
expressionibus redundarent. Hanc tu suscipe ut
parentem, ama ut nutricem, venerare ut sanctam.
Nec aliorum imiteris exemplum, qui relinquunt suas
et alienas appetunt, quorum dedecus in propatulo
est sub nominibus pietatis quaerentium suspecta
consortia. Novi ego quasdam iam maturioris aetatis
et plerasque generis libertini adulescentibus delectari
et filios quaerere spiritales paulatimque pudore
superato per ficta matrum nomina erumpere in
licentiam maritalem. Alii sorores virgines deserunt

the licence of the Old Comedy to pick out definite persons for criticism. A wise man and wise women will either hide or correct any faults they find in themselves, they will be more indignant with themselves than with me, and will not heap curses upon their adviser. Granted that he is liable to the same charges as they are, in his case his faults give him no pleasure; and so far at least he is their superior.

I hear that your mother is a religious woman who for many years has been a widow, and that when you were a child she reared and taught you herself. After you had studied in the flourishing academies of Gaul she sent you to Rome, sparing no expense and consoling herself for her son's absence with bright hopes of his future. Her idea was that Roman gravity would temper the exuberance and glitter of your Gallic eloquence, and in your case would act as a bit rather than as a spur. So we read of the greatest Greek orators, that they seasoned the bombast of Asia with Attic salt and pruned their vines severely when the shoots were too luxuriant. They wished to fill the wine-press of eloquence, not with leaf-clusters of words, but with the rich grape-juice of sound sense. Respect her then as a parent, love her as a mother, venerate her as a saint. Do not imitate those who leave their own relatives and run after strange women. Their infamy is plain; for under pretext of piety they really seek illicit intercourse. I know some women of ripe age who in many cases take their pleasure with young freedmen, calling them their spiritual children, and gradually so far overcoming any sense of shame as to allow themselves under this pretence of motherhood all the licence of marriage. In other cases men

et extraneis viduis copulantur. Sunt, quae oderunt
suos et non suorum palpantur affectu, quarum inpatientia, index animi, nullam recepit excusationem
et cassa inpudicitiae velamenta quasi aranearum fila
disrumpit. Videas nonnullos accinctis renibus, pulla
tunica, barba prolixa a mulieribus non posse discedere, sub eodem conmanere tecto, simul inire
convivia, ancillas iuvenes habere in ministerio et
praeter vocabulum nuptiarum omnia esse matrimonii. Nec culpa est nominis Christiani, si simulator
religionis in vitio sit, quin immo confusio gentilium,
cum ea vident ecclesiis displicere, quae omnibus bonis
non placent.

7. Tu vero, si monachus esse vis, non videri, habeto
curam non rei familiaris, cui renuntiando hoc esse
coepisti, sed animae tuae. Sordes vestium candidae
mentis indicio sint, vilis tunica contemptum saeculi
probet ita dumtaxat, ne animus tumeat, ne habitus
sermoque dissentiat. Balnearum fomenta non
quaeras, qui calorem corporis ieiuniorum cupis
frigore extinguere. Quae et ipsa moderata sint, ne
nimia debilitent stomachum et maiorem refectionem
poscentia erumpant in cruditatem, quae parens libidinum est. Modicus et temperatus cibus et carni
et animae utilis est. Matrem ita vide, ne per
illam alias videre cogaris, quarum vultus cordi tuo

abandon their sisters who are virgins, and unite themselves to widows who are no relations. There are
women who hate their own kin and feel no affection
for their family. Their restlessness reveals their
state of mind, for it disdains excuses and rends asunder
like cobwebs any veils that might conceal their
licentiousness. You may see some men also with
girded loins, sombre tunics and long beards, who yet
can never leave women's society. They live with
them under one roof, they go out to dinner with
them, they have young girls to wait upon them, and,
save that they are not called husbands, they enjoy
all the privileges of marriage. But it is no fault of
Christianity if a hypocrite falls into sin : rather it is
the confusion of the Gentiles when they see that
the churches condemn what is condemned by all
honest folk.

If you wish to be, and not merely seem, a monk,
have regard not for your property—you began your
vows by renouncing it—but for your soul. Let a
squalid garb be the evidence of a clean heart : let a
coarse tunic prove that you despise the world ;
provided only that you do not pride yourself on such
things nor let your dress and language be at variance.
Avoid hot baths : your aim is to quench the heat of
the body by the help of chilling fasts. But let your
fasts be moderate, since if they are carried to excess
they weaken the stomach, and by making more food
necessary to make up for it lead to indigestion,
which is the parent of lust. A frugal, temperate
diet is good both for body and soul.

See your mother often, but do not be forced to see
other women when you visit her. Their faces may
dwell in your heart and so

haereant, ' Et tacitum vivat sub pectore vulnus.'
Ancillulas, quae illi in obsequio sunt, tibi scias esse in
insidiis, quia, quantum vilior earum condicio, tanto
facilior ruina est. Et Iohannes Baptista sanctam
matrem habuit pontificisque filius erat et tamen nec
matris affectu nec patris opibus vincebatur, ut in
domo parentum cum periculo viveret castitatis.
Vivebat in heremo et oculis desiderantibus Christum
nihil aliud dignabatur aspicere. Vestis aspera, zona
pellicia, cibus locustae melque silvestre, omnia
virtuti et continentiae praeparata. Filii prophetarum—quos monachos in veteri legimus testamento
—aedificabant sibi casulas propter fluenta Iordanis et
turbis urbium derelictis polenta et herbis agrestibus
victitabant. Quamdiu in patria tua es, habeto
cellulam pro paradiso, varia scripturarum poma
decerpe, his utere deliciis, harum fruere conplexu.
Si scandalizat te oculus, pes, manus tua, proice ea.
Nulli parcas, ut soli parcas animae. ' Qui viderit
mulierem ad concupiscendum eam, iam moechatus
est eam in corde suo. Quis gloriabitur castum se
habere cor?' Astra non sunt munda in conspectu
domini: quanto magis homines, quorum vita temptatio est! Vae nobis, qui, quotiens concupiscimus,
totiens fornicamur. ' Inebriatus est,' inquit,' gladius
meus in caelo ': multo amplius in terra, quae spinas
et tribulos generat. Vas electionis, in cuius Christus
ore sonabat, macerat corpus suum et subicit servituti
et tamen cernit naturalem carnis ardorem suae

---

[1] Virgil, *Aeneid*, IV. 67.   [2] St. Matthew, xviii. 9.
[3] St. Matthew, v. 28.   [4] Proverbs, xx. 9.
[5] Isaiah, xxxiv. 5.

' A secret wound may fester in your breast.' [1]

You must remember too that the maids who wait upon her are an especial snare; the lower they are in rank, the easier it is to ruin them. John the Baptist had a saintly mother and his father was a priest; but neither his mother's love nor his father's wealth could prevail upon him to live in his parents' house at the risk of his chastity. He took up his abode in the desert, and desiring only to see Christ refused to look at anything else. His rough garb, his skin girdle, his diet of locusts and wild honey were all alike meant to ensure virtue and self-restraint. The sons of the prophets, who are the monks of the Old Testament, built huts for themselves by the stream of Jordan, and leaving the crowded cities lived on porridge and wild herbs. As long as you stay in your native city, regard your cell as Paradise, gather in it the varied fruits of the Scriptures, make them your delight, and rejoice in their embrace. If your eye or your foot or your hand offend you, cast it off. [2] Spare nothing, provided that you spare your soul. 'Whosoever looketh on a woman to lust after her hath committed adultery with her already in his heart.' [3] 'Who can boast " I have made my heart clean "?' [4] The stars are not pure in God's sight: how much less are men, whose life is one long temptation! Woe to us, who commit fornication whenever we have lustful thoughts! 'My sword,' says the Scripture, ' hath drunk its fill in heaven' [5]: much more then will it on earth, which produces thorns and thistles. The chosen vessel, from whose mouth we hear Christ's own words, keeps his body under and brings it into subjection; but still he perceives that the natural

repugnare sententiae, ut, quod non vult, hoc agere
conpellatur, et quasi vim patiens vociferatur et
dicit: ' Miser ego homo, quis me liberabit de corpore
mortis huius?'[1] Et tu te arbitraris absque lapsu et
vulnere posse transire, nisi omni custodia servaveris
cor tuum et cum salvatore dixeris: ' Mater mea et
fratres mei hi sunt, qui faciunt voluntatem patris
mei'?[2] Crudelitas ista pietas est; immo quid tam
pium, quam sanctae matri sanctum filium custodire?
Optat et illa te vivere, non videre ad tempus, ut
semper cum Christo videat. Anna Samuhelem non
sibi, sed tabernaculo genuit.

Filii Ionadab, qui vinum et siceram non bibebant,
qui habitabant in tentoriis et, quas nox conpulerat,
sedes habebant, scribuntur in psalmo, quod primi
captivitatem sustinuerint, quia exercitu Chaldaeorum
vastante Iudaeam urbes introire conpulsi sunt.[3]

8. Viderint, quid alii sentiant—unusquisque enim
suo sensu ducitur—mihi oppidum carcer est et solitudo paradisus. Quid desideramus urbium frequentiam, qui de singularite censemur?[4] Moyses, ut
praeesset populo Iudaeorum, quadraginta annis
eruditur in heremo, pastor ovium hominum factus est
pastor; apostoli de piscatione lacus Genesar ad
piscationem hominum transierunt. Tunc habebant
patrem, rete, naviculam: secuti dominum protinus
omnia reliquerunt portantes cotidie crucem suam et

---

[1] Romans, vii. 24.

[2] St. Luke, viii. 21.

[3] Jeremiah, xxxv. 6.

[4] The reference is to the heading of Psalm lxxi, given in
the Septuagint (70): τῷ Δαυὶδ υἱῶν Ἰωναδάβ, καὶ τῶν πρώτων
αἰχμαλωτισθέντων.

[5] *Monachus* means 'lonely.'

heat of the body fights against his fixed purpose,
and he is compelled to do what he will not. Like
a man suffering violence he cries aloud and says:
' O wretched man that I am, who shall deliver me
from the body of this death?'[1] And do *you* think
then that you can pass through life without a fall and
without a wound, if you do not keep your heart with
all diligence and say with the Saviour: ' My mother
and my brethren are these which hear the word of
God and do it'?[2] Such cruelty as this is really love.
Nay, what greater love can there be than to guard a
holy son for a holy mother? She desires your eternal
life: she is content not to see you for the moment,
provided that she may see you for ever with Christ.
She is like Hannah, who brought forth Samuel, not
for her own comfort, but for the service of the
tabernacle.

The sons of Jonadab drank no wine nor strong
drink and lived in tents which they pitched whenever
night came on.[3] Of them the psalm[4] says that they
were the first to undergo captivity, for when the
Chaldean host was devastating Judaea they were
compelled to enter cities. Let others think as they
will—every one follows his own bent—but to me a
town is a prison, and the wilderness a paradise.
What do we monks want with crowded cities, we
whose very name bespeaks loneliness?[5] Moses was
trained for forty years in the desert to fit him for the
task of leading the Jewish people, and from being a
shepherd of sheep he became a shepherd of men. The
apostles left their fishing on Lake Gennesaret to fish
for human souls. Then they had a father, nets, and
a little boat: but they followed the Lord straightway
and abandoned everything, carrying their cross

ne virgam quidem in manu habentes. Hoc dico, ut,
etiam si clericatus te titillat desiderium, discas, quod
possis docere, et rationabilem hostiam offeras Christo,
ne miles antequam tiro, ne prius magister sis quam
discipulus. Non est humilitatis meae neque men-
surae iudicare de ceteris et de ministris ecclesiarum
sinistrum quippiam dicere. Habeant illi ordinem et
gradum suum, quem si tenueris, quomodo tibi in eo
vivendum sit, editus ad Nepotianum liber docere te
poterit. Nunc monachi incunabula moresque dis-
cutimus et eius monachi, qui liberalibus studiis
eruditus in adulescentia iugum Christi collo suo
inposuit.

9. Primumque tractandum est, utrum solus an
cum aliis in monasterio vivere debeas. Mihi placet,
ut habeas sanctorum contubernium nec ipse te
doceas et absque ductore [1] ingrediaris viam, quam
numquam ingressus es, statimque in partem tibi
alteram declinandum sit et errori pateas plusque aut
minus ambules, quam necesse est, ut currens lasseris,
moram faciens obdormias. In solitudine cito subre-
pit superbia et, si parumper ieiunaverit hominemque
non viderit, putat se alicuius esse momenti oblitusque
sui, unde quo venerit, intus corpore lingua foris
vagatur. Iudicat contra apostoli voluntatem alienos
servos; quod gula poposcerit, porrigit manus; dormit,

[1] doctore: *Hilberg.*

---

[1] A monk—*monachus*—originally was a solitary living in
the desert, but after the time of St. Basil monks were usually
organized in communities under a rule, and devoted their time
to prayer, meditation and useful work. If a monk wished to
enter the ministry of the Church he had to be ordained as
deacon by a bishop. He then normally lived in a city and
had a cure of souls.

[2] Letter LII.   [3] Romans, xiv. 4.

every day, without so much as a stick in their hands.
I say this, so that if you are tickled by a desire to
become a clergyman,[1] you may learn now what you
will then be able to teach others, offering a reasonable sacrifice to Christ. You must not think yourself
an old soldier while you are still a recruit, a master
while you are still a pupil. It would not become my
lowly rank to pass judgment on others, or to say
anything unfavourable about those who serve in
churches. Let them keep their proper place and
station, and if you ever join them, my treatise
written for Nepotian [2] will show you how you ought
to live in that position. For the moment I am
discussing a monk's early training and character, a
monk, moreover, who after a liberal education in his
early manhood placed upon his neck the yoke of
Christ.

The first point with which I must deal is whether
you ought to live alone or in a monastery with
others. I would prefer you to have the society of
holy men and not to be your own teacher. If you
set out on a strange road without a guide you may
easily at the start take a wrong turning and make
a mistake, going too far or not far enough, running
till you weary yourself or delaying your journey for
a sleep. In solitude pride quickly creeps in, and
when a man has fasted for a little while and has seen
no one, he thinks himself a person of some account.
He forgets who he is, whence he comes, and where
he is going, and lets his body run riot within, his
tongue abroad. Contrary to the apostle's [3] wishes, he
judges another man's servants; he stretches out his
hand for anything that his gullet craves; he does
what he pleases and sleeps as long as he pleases; he

quantum voluerit; nullum veretur, omnes se inferiores putat crebriusque in urbibus quam in cellula est et inter fratres simulat verecundiam, qui platearum turbis conliditur. Quid igitur? Solitariam vitam reprehendimus? Minime, quippe quam saepe laudavimus. Sed de ludo monasteriorum huiusce modi volumus egreái milites, quos rudimenta non terreant, qui specimen conversationis suae multo tempore dederint, qui omnium fuerunt minimi, ut primi omnium fierent, quos nec esuries nec saturitas aliquando superavit, qui paupertate laetantur, quorum habitus, sermo, vultus, incessus doctrina virtutum est, qui nesciunt secundum quosdam ineptos homines daemonum obpugnantium contra se portenta confingere, ut apud inperitos et vulgi homines miraculum sui faciant et exinde sectentur lucra.

10. Vidimus nuper et planximus Croesi opes unius morte deprehensas urbisque stipes quasi in usus pauperum congregatas stirpi et posteris derelictas. Tunc ferrum, quod latebat in profundo, supernatavit aquae et inter palmarum arbores Merrae amaritudo monstrata est.[1] Nec mirum: talem et socium habuit et magistrum, qui egentium famem suas fecit esse divitias et miseris derelicta in suam miseriam tenuit. Quorum clamor tandem pervenit ad caelum et patientissimas Dei vicit aures, ut missus angelus pessimo Nabal Carmelio diceret: 'Stulte, hac nocte auferent animam tuam a te; quae autem preparasti, cuius erunt?'[2]

---

[1] Exodus, xv. 23.   [2] St. Luke, xii. 20.

fears no one, he thinks all men his inferiors, spends more time in cities than in his cell, and though among the brethren he makes a pretence of modesty, in the crowded squares he ruffles it with the best. What then, you will say? Do I disapprove of the solitary life? Not at all: I have often commended it. But I wish to see the soldiers who march out from a monastery-school men who have not been frightened by their early training, who have given proof of a holy life for many months, who have made themselves last that they might be first, who have not been overcome by hunger or satiety, who take pleasure in poverty, whose garb, conversation, looks and gait all teach virtue, and who have no skill—as some foolish fellows have—in inventing monstrous stories of their struggles with demons, tales invented to excite the admiration of the ignorant mob and to extract money from their pockets.

Just lately, to my sorrow, I saw the fortune of a Croesus brought to light at one man's death, and beheld a city's alms collected ostensibly for the poor's benefit left by will to his sons and their descendants. Then the iron which was hidden in the depths floated upon the surface, and amid the palm trees the bitter waters of Marah [1] were seen. Nor need we wonder at his avarice: his partner and teacher was a man who turned the hunger of the needy into a source of wealth for himself, and to his own wretchedness kept back the legacies that were left to the wretched. But at last their cries reached heaven and were too much for God's patient ears, so that he sent an angel to say to this villainous Nabal the Carmelite: 'Thou fool, this night thy soul shall be required of thee: then whose shall those things be which thou hast provided?' [2]

11. Volo ergo te et propter causas, quas supra exposui, non habitare cum matre et praecipue, ne offerentem delicatos cibos rennuendo contristes aut, si acceperis, oleum igni adicias et inter frequentiam puellarum per diem videas, quod noctibus cogites. Numquam de manu et oculis tuis recedat liber, psalterium discatur ad verbum, oratio sine intermissione, vigil sensus nec vanis cogitationibus patens. Corpus pariter animusque tendatur ad dominum. Iram vince patientia; ama scientiam scripturarum et carnis vitia non amabis. Nec vacet mens tua variis perturbationibus, quae, si pectori insederint, dominabuntur tui et te deducent ad delictum maximum. Fac et aliquid operis, ut semper te diabolus inveniat occupatum. Si apostoli habentes potestatem de evangelio vivere laborabant manibus suis, ne quem gravarent, et aliis tribuebant refrigeria, quorum pro spiritalibus debebant metere carnalia, cur tu in usus tuos cessura non praepares? Vel fiscellam texe iunco vel canistrum lentis plecte viminibus, sariatur humus, areolae aequo limite dividantur; in quibus cum holerum iacta fuerint semina vel plantae per ordinem positae, aquae ducantur inriguae, ut pulcherrimorum versuum spectator adsistas:

' Ecce supercilio clivosi tramitis undam
    Elicit, illa cadens raucum per levia murmur
    Saxa ciet scatebrisque arentia temperat arva.'

---

[1] 2 Thessalonians, iii. 8.   [2] Virgil, *Georgics*, I. 108.

For the reasons then which I have given above, I wish you not to live with your mother. And there are some further considerations. If she offers you a dainty dish, you would grieve her by refusing it, while if you take it you would be throwing oil on fire. Moreover, in a house that is full of girls you would see things in the day-time that you would think about in the night. Always have a book in your hand and before your eyes; learn the psalms word by word, pray without ceasing, keep your senses on the alert and closed against vain imaginings. Let your mind and body both strain towards the Lord, overcome wrath by patience; love the knowledge of the Scriptures and you will not love the sins of the flesh. Do not let your mind offer a lodging to disturbing thoughts, for if they once find a home in your breast they will become your masters and lead you on into fatal sin. Engage in some occupation, so that the devil may always find you busy. If the apostles who had the power to make the Gospel their livelihood still worked with their hands that they might not be a burden on any man,[1] and gave relief to others whose carnal possessions they had a right to enjoy in return for their spiritual benefits, why should you not provide for your own future wants? Make creels of reeds or weave baskets of pliant osiers. Hoe the ground and mark it out into equal plots, and when you have sown cabbage seed or set out plants in rows, bring water down in channels and stand by like the onlooker in the lovely lines:

' Lo, from the channelled slope he brings the stream,
  Which falls hoarse murmuring o'er the polished
      stones
  And with its bubbling flood allays the heat
  Of sun-scorched fields.' [2]

417

Inserantur infructuosae arbores vel gemmis vel
surculis, et parvo post tempore laboris tui dulcia
poma decerpas. Apum fabricare alvearia, ad quas
te mittunt Proverbia,¹ et monasteriorum ordinem ac
regiam disciplinam in parvis disce corporibus.
Texantur et lina capiendis piscibus, scribantur libri,
ut et manus operetur cibos et anima lectione satu-
retur. ' In desideriis est omnis otiosus.'² Aegyptiorum monasteria hunc morem tenent, ut nullum
absque opere ac labore suscipiant, non tam propter
victus necessaria quam propter animae salutem, ne
vagetur perniciosis cogitationibus, et instar fornicantis
Hierusalem omni transeunti divaricet pedes suos.

12. Dum essem iuvenis et solitudinis me deserta
vallarent, incentiva vitiorum ardoremque naturae
ferre non poteram; quae cum crebris ieiuniis fran-
gerem, mens tamen cogitationibus aestuabat. Ad
quam edomandam cuidam fratri, qui ex Hebraeis
crediderat, me in disciplinam dedi, ut post Quin-
tiliani acumina Ciceronisque fluvios gravitatemque
Frontonis et lenitatem Plinii alphabetum discerem,
stridentia anhelantiaque verba meditarer. Quid ibi
laboris insumpserim, quid sustinuerim difficultatis,
quotiens desperaverim quotiensque cessaverim et
contentione discendi rursus inceperim, testis est
conscientia tam mea, qui passus sum, quam eorum,
qui mecum duxere vitam. Et gratias ago domino,

---

¹ Proverbs, vi. 8, where LXX. adds: ἢ πορεύθητι πρὸς τὴν
μέλισσαν καὶ μάθε ὡς ἐργάτις ἐστι κ.τ.λ.
² Proverbs, xiii. 4. (LXX.)

Graft barren trees with buds or slips, so that you may, after a little time, pluck sweet fruit as a reward for your labours. Make hives for bees, for to them the Proverbs of Solomon send you,[1] and by watching the tiny creatures learn the ordinance of a monastery and the discipline of a kingdom. Twist lines too for catching fish, and copy out manuscripts, so that your hand may earn you food and your soul be satisfied with reading. 'Every one that is idle is a prey to vain desires.'[2] Monasteries in Egypt make it a rule not to take any one who will not work, thinking not so much of the necessities of life as of the safety of men's souls, lest they should be led astray by dangerous imaginings, and be like Jerusalem in her whoredoms, who opened her feet to every chance comer.

When I was a young man, though I was protected by the rampart of the lonely desert, I could not endure against the promptings of sin and the ardent heat of my nature. I tried to crush them by frequent fasting, but my mind was always in a turmoil of imagination. To subdue it I put myself in the hands of one of the brethren who had been a Hebrew before his conversion, and asked him to teach me his language. Thus, after having studied the pointed style of Quintilian, the fluency of Cicero, the weightiness of Fronto, and the gentleness of Pliny, I now began to learn the alphabet again and practise harsh and guttural words. What efforts I spent on that task, what difficulties I had to face, how often I despaired, how often I gave up and then in my eagerness to learn began again, my own knowledge can witness from personal experience and those can testify who were then living with me. I thank the

quod de amaro semine litterarum dulces fructus
capio.

13. Dicam et aliud, quid in Aegyptio viderim.
Graecus adulescens erat in coenobio, qui nulla continentiae, nulla operis magnitudine flammam poterat
carnis extinguere. Hunc periclitantem pater monasterii hac arte servavit. Imperat cuidam viro gravi,
ut iurgiis atque conviciis insectaretur hominem et
post inrogatam iniuriam primus veniret ad queri-
monias. Vocati testes pro eo loquebantur, qui
contumeliam fecerat. Flere ille contra mendacium;
nullus alius credere veritati, solus pater defensionem
suam callide opponere, ne ' abundantiori tristitia
absorberetur frater.'[1] Quid multa? Ita annus ductus
est, quo expleto interrogatus adulescens super cogitationibus pristinis, an adhuc molestiae aliquid
sustineret: ' Papae,' inquit, ' vivere non licet, et
fornicari libet?' Hic si solus fuisset, quo adiutore
superasset?

14. Philosophi saeculi solent amorem veterem
amore novo quasi clavum clavo expellere. Quod et
Asuero septem principes fecere Persarum, ut Vasti
reginae desiderium aliarum puellarum amore con-
pescerent.[2] Illi vitium vitio peccatumque peccato
remediantur, nos amore virtutum vitia superemus.
' Declina,' ait, ' a malo et fac bonum; quaerere
pacem et persequere eam.'[3] Nisi oderimus malum,
bonum amare non possumus. Quin potius faciendum est bonum, ut declinemus a malo; pax
quaerenda, ut bella fugiamus. Nec sufficit eam

---

[1] 2 Corinthians, ii. 7.   [2] Esther, ii. 2.
[3] Psalm xxxiv. 14.

Lord that from a bitter seed of learning I am now plucking sweet fruits.

I will tell you of another thing that I saw in Egypt. There was a young Greek in a community there, who could not quench the fires of the flesh by any continence or any labour however severe. In his danger the father of the monastery saved him by the following device. He instructed a grave elder to pursue the young man with revilings and abuse, and after having thus insulted him to be the first to lay a complaint. When witnesses were called they always spoke in favour of the aggressor. The youth could only weep at the false charge, but no one believed the truth. The father alone would cleverly put in a plea on his behalf, lest ' our brother be swallowed up by overmuch sorrow.' [1] To cut a long tale short, a whole year passed in this way, and at the end the youth was asked about his former imaginings, whether they still troubled him. ' Good heavens,' he replied, ' how can I want to fornicate, when I am not allowed even to live ? ' If he had been alone, by whose help could he have overcome temptation ?

Worldly philosophers are wont to drive out an old passion by a new one, as you drive out an old nail by hammering in another. This is what the seven princes of Persia did to Ahasuerus, when they assuaged his regret for queen Vashti by suggesting an amour with other maidens.[2] They cure fault by fault and sin by sin : we must overcome vice by love of virtue. ' Depart from evil,' says the Scripture, ' and do good ; seek peace and pursue it.' [3] If we do not hate evil we cannot love good. Nay more, we must do good if we are to depart from evil : we must seek peace, if we are to avoid wars. Nor is it

quaerere, nisi inventam fugientemque omni studio
persequamur, 'quae exsuperat omnem sensum,' in
qua habitatio Dei est dicente propheta: 'Et factus
est in pace locus eius,' pulchreque persecutio pacis
dicitur iuxta illud apostoli: 'Hospitalitatem per-
sequentes,' ut non levi citatoque sermone et—ut ita
loquar—summis labiis hospites invitemus, sed toto
mentis ardore teneamus quasi auferentes secum de
lucro nostro atque conpendio.

15. Nulla ars absque magistro discitur. Etiam
muta animalia et ferarum greges ductores sequuntur
suos. In apibus principes sunt; grues unam sequuntur ordine litterato. Imperator unus, iudex
unus provinciae. Roma, ut condita est, duos fratres
simul habere reges non potuit et parricidio dedicatur.
In Rebeccae utero Esau et Iacob bella gesserunt.
Singuli ecclesiarum episcopi, singuli archipresbyteri,
singuli archidiaconi et omnis ordo ecclesiasticus suis
rectoribus nititur. In navi unus gubernator, in domo
unus dominus; in quamvis grandi exercitu unius
signum expectatur. Et ne plura replicando fastidium legenti faciam, per haec omnia ad illud tendit
oratio, ut doceam te non tuo arbitrio dimittendum,
sed vivere debere in monasterio sub unius disciplina
patris consortioque multorum, ut ab alio discas
humilitatem, ab alio patientiam, hic te silentium, ille
doceat mansuetudinem, non facias, quod vis, comedas,

---

[1] Philippians, iv. 7.   [2] Psalm lxxvi. 2. (Septuagint
lxxv. 2.)   [3] Romans, xii. 13.   [4] Genesis, xxv. 22.

enough merely to seek peace; when we have found
it and it flies from us, we must pursue with all our
might. ' Peace passeth all understanding,' [1] and in
it is God's dwelling. As the prophet says: ' In
peace also is His habitation.' [2] The pursuing of peace
is a fine metaphor, and is like the saying of the
apostle, ' pursuing hospitality.' [3] Our invitation to
guests should not be a mere light form of words,
spoken, if I may use the phrase, with the surface of
the lips; we should be as eager to detain them as if
they were robbers carrying off our savings.

No art is learned without a master. Even dumb
animals and herds of wild beasts follow leaders of
their own. Bees have rulers, and cranes fly behind
one of their number in the shape of the letter Y.
There is one emperor, and one judge for each province.
When Rome was founded it could not have two
brothers reigning together, and so it was inaugurated
by an act of fratricide. Esau and Jacob warred
against one another in Rebecca's womb. [4] Each
church has but one bishop, one arch-presbyter, one
archdeacon; every ecclesiastical order is subjected
to its own rulers. There is one pilot in a ship, one
master in a house; and however large an army may
be, the soldiers await one man's signal. I will not
weary my reader with further repetition, for the
purpose of all these examples is simply this. I want
to show you that you had better not be left to your
own discretion, but should rather live in a monastery
under the control of one father and with many companions. From one of them you may learn humility,
from another patience; this one will teach you
silence, that one meekness. You will not do what
you yourself wish; you will eat what you are ordered;

quod iuberis, habeas, quantum acceperis, vestiaris, quod acceperis, operis tui pensa persolvas, subiciaris, cui non vis, lassus ad stratum venias ambulansque dormites, necdum expleto somno surgere conpellaris, dicas psalmum in ordine tuo—in quo non dulcedo vocis sed mentis affectus quaeritur scribente apostolo: ' Psallam spiritu, psallam et mente,' et: ' Cantantes in cordibus vestris ': legerat enim esse praeceptum: ' psallite sapienter '—servias fratribus, hospitum laves pedes, passus iniuriam taceas, praepositum monasterii timeas ut dominum, diligas ut parentem, credas tibi salutare, quidquid ille praeceperit, nec de maioris sententia iudices, cuius officii est oboedire et inplere, quae iussa sunt, dicente Moyse: ' Audi, Israhel, et tace.' Tantis negotiis occupatus nullis vacabis cogitationibus et, dum ab alio transis ad aliud opusque succedit operi, illud solum mente retinebis, quod agere conpelleris.

16. Vidi ego quosdam, qui, postquam renuntiavere saeculo—vestimentis dumtaxat et vocis professione, non rebus—nihil de pristina conversatione mutarunt. Res familiaris magis aucta quam inminuta est; eadem ministeria servulorum, idem apparatus convivii; in vitro et patella fictili aurum come-

---

[1] 1 Corinthians, xiv. 15. [2] Ephesians, v. 19.
[3] Psalm xlvii. 7. [4] Deuteronomy. xxvii. 9.

you will take what you are given; you will wear the
dress allotted to you; you will perform a set amount
of work; you will be subordinate to some one you do
not like; you will come to bed worn out with weariness and fall asleep as you walk about. Before you
have had your fill of rest, you will be forced to get
out of bed and take your turn in psalm-singing, a
task where real emotion is a greater requisite than a
sweet voice. The apostle says: ' I will pray with
the spirit and I will pray with the understanding
also,' [1] and, again: ' Make melody in your hearts.' [2]
He had read the precept: ' Sing ye praises with
understanding.' [3] You will serve the brethren; you
will wash the feet of guests; if you suffer wrong you
will say nothing; the superior of the monastery
you will fear as a master and love as a father. Whatever precepts he gives you will believe to be whole-
some for you. You will not pass judgment upon your
elder's decisions, for it is your duty to be obedient
and carry out orders, according to the words of
Moses: ' Keep silence and hearken, O Israel.' [4]
You will be so busy with all these tasks that you will
have no time for vain imaginings, and while you
pass from one occupation to the next you will only
have in mind the work that you are being forced
to do.

I myself have seen some men who after they had
renounced the world—in garb, at least, and in verbal
professions, but not in reality—changed nothing of
their former mode of life. Their property has
increased rather than diminished; they have the
same number of servants to wait upon them and
keep the same elaborate table; though they drink
from glass and eat from plates of earthenware, it

ditur et inter turbas et examina ministrorum nomen
sibi vindicant solitarii. Qui vero pauperes sunt et
tenui substantiola videnturque sibi scioli, pomparum
ferculis similes procedunt ad publicum, ut caninam
exerceant facundiam. Alii sublatis in altum humeris
et intra se nescio quid cornicantes stupentibus in
terram oculis tumentia verba trutinantur, ut, si
praeconem addideris, putes incedere praefecturam.
Sunt qui, humore cellularum inmoderatisque ieiuniis,
taedio solitudinis ac nimia lectione, dum diebus ac
noctibus auribus suis personant, vertuntur in
μελαγχολίαν et Hippocratis magis fomentis quam
nostris monitis indigent. Plerique artibus et nego-
tiationibus pristinis carere non possunt mutatisque
nominibus institorum eadem exercent conmercia,
non victum et vestitum, quod apostolus praecipit, sed maiora quam saeculi homines emolu-
menta sectantes. Et prius quidem ab aedilibus,
quos ἀγορανόμους Graeci appellant, vendentium
cohercebatur rabies nec erat inpune peccatum, nunc
autem sub religionis titulo exercentur iniusta conpendia et honor nominis Christiani fraudem magis
facit quam patitur. Quodque pudet dicere, sed
necesse est, ut saltim sic ad nostrum erubescamus
dedecus, publice extendentes manus pannis aurum
tegimus et contra omnium opinionem plenis sacculis
morimur divites, qui quasi pauperes viximus. Tibi,
cum in monasterio fueris, haec facere non licebit et

---

[1] Images of the gods were carried on these litters in solemn
state.

[2] The *institores* were travelling merchants who dealt
largely in female finery. Cf. Horace, *Odes*, III. vi. 302; *Ep.*
XVII. 20.

[3] 1 Timothy, vi. 8.

is gold they swallow, and amidst crowds of servants
swarming round them they claim the name of hermit.
Others, who are poor and of slender means and think
themselves full of wisdom, pass through the streets
like the pageants in a procession,[1] to practise a
cynical eloquence. Others shrug their shoulders
and croak indistinctly to themselves, and with glassy
eyes fixed upon the earth they balance swelling
words upon their tongues, so that if you add a
crier, you might think it was his excellency the
governor who was coming along. Some, too, by
reason of damp cells and immoderate fasts, added
to the weariness of solitude and excessive study,
have a singing in their ears day and night, and
turning melancholy mad need Hippocrates' fomen-
tations more than any advice of mine. Very many
cannot forgo their previous trades and occupations,
and though they change its name carry on the same
pedlar's[2] traffic as before, seeking for themselves not
food and raiment, as the apostle directs,[3] but greater
profits than men of the world expect. In the past
the mad greed of sellers was checked by the aediles,
or as the Greeks call them, market-inspectors, and
men could not cheat with impunity : to-day under
the cloak of religion such men hoard up unjust gains,
and the good name of Christianity does more wrong
than it suffers. I am ashamed to say it, but I must
—at least we ought to blush at our disgrace—we
hold out our hands in public for alms while we have
gold hidden under our rags, and to every one's surprise
after living as poor men we die rich with purses well
filled. In your case, since you will be in a monastery,
such conduct will not be allowed; habits will
gradually grow on you, and finally you will do of

inolescente paulatim consuetudine, quod primum
cogebaris, velle incipies et delectabit te labor tuus
oblitusque praeteritorum semper priora sectaberis
nequaquam considerans, quid alii mali faciant, sed
quid boni tu facere debeas.

17. Neque vero peccantium ducaris multitudine et
te pereuntium turba sollicitet, ut tacitus cogites:
' Quid? ergo omnes peribunt, qui in urbibus habitant?
Ecce illi fruuntur suis rebus, ministrant ecclesiis,
adeunt balneas, unguenta non spernunt et tamen in
omnium flore versantur.' Ad quod et ante respondi
et nunc breviter respondebo: me in praesenti opusculo non de clericis disputare, sed monachum insti-
tuere. Sancti sunt clerici et omnium vita laudabilis.
Ita ergo age et vive in monasterio, ut clericus esse
merearis, ut adulescentiam tuam nulla sorde con-
macules, ut ad altare Christi quasi de thalamo virgo
procedas et habeas de foris bonum testimonium
feminaeque nomen tuum noverint, vultum nesciant.
Cum ad perfectam aetatem veneris, si tamen vita
comes fuerit, et te vel populus vel pontifex civitatis
in clerum adlegerit, agito, quae clerici sunt, et inter
ipsos sectare meliores, quia in omni condicione et
gradu optimis mixta sunt pessima.

18. Ne ad scribendum cito prosilias et levi ducaris
insania. Multo tempore disce, quod doceas. Ne

---

[1] Cf. p. 412, n. 1.

your own accord what was at first a matter of compulsion; you will take pleasure in your labours, and
forgetting what is behind you will reach out to that
which is before; you will not think at all of the
evil that others do, but only of the good which it is
your duty to perform.

Do not be influenced by the number of those that
sin, or disturbed by the host of the perishing, so as
to have the unspoken thought: ' What? Shall all
then perish who live in cities? Behold, they enjoy
their property, they serve in the churches, they
frequent the baths, they do not disdain unguents,
and yet they flourish and are universally respected.'
To such reasonings I have replied before, and will
now do so briefly again, merely remarking that in
this present short treatise I am not discussing the
behaviour of the clergy, but laying down rules for a
monk.[1] The clergy are holy men, and in every case
their life is worthy of praise. Go then and so live
in your monastery that you may deserve to be a
clergyman, that you may keep your youth free from
all stain of defilement, and that you may come forth
to Christ's altar as a virgin steps from her bower;
that you may be well spoken of abroad, and that
women may know your reputation but not your
looks. When you come to ripe years, that is, if life
be granted you, and have been appointed as a clergyman either by the people or by the bishop of the city,
then act as becomes a cleric, and among your col-
leagues choose the better men as your models. In
every rank and condition of life the very bad is
mingled with the very good.

Do not rashly leap into authorship, and be led
by light-headed madness. Spend years in learning

credas laudatoribus tuis, immo inrisoribus aurem ne
libenter adcommodes, qui cum te adulationibus
foverint et quodam modo inpotem mentis effecerint,
si subito respexeris, aut ciconiarum deprehendas post
te colla curvari aut manu auriculas agitari asini aut
aestuantem canis protendi linguam. Nulli detrahas
nec in eo te sanctum putes, si ceteros laceres. Accu-
samus saepe, quod facimus, et contra nosmet ipsos
diserti in nostra vitia invehimur muti de eloquentibus
iudicantes. Testudineo Grunnius incedebat ad loquendum gradu et per intervalla quaedam vix pauca
verba capiebat, ut eum putares singultire, non
proloqui. Et tamen, cum mensa posita librorum
exposuisset struem, adducto supercilio contractisque
naribus ac fronte rugata duobus digitulis concre-
pabat hoc signo ad audiendum discipulos provocans.
Tunc nugas meras fundere et adversum singulos
declamare; criticum diceres esse Longinum censo-
remque Romanae facundiae notare, quem vellet, et
de senatu doctorum excludere. Hic bene nummatus
plus placebat in prandiis. Nec mirum, qui multos
inescare solitus erat factoque cuneo circumstre-
pentium garrulorum procedebat in publicum intus
Nero, foris Cato, totus ambiguus, ut ex contrariis
diversisque naturis unum monstrum novamque
bestiam diceres esse conpactum iuxta illud poeticum:

---

[1] Closely copied from Persius I. 58–60.

[2] A character in the mime *Porci Testamentum* : here the
reference is to Rufinus, once Jerome's friend but afterwards
for theological reasons his bitter enemy. Cf. App. II, p. 498 ff.

what you are to teach. Do not believe your flatterers, or rather do not lend an ear too readily to
mockers; such men will warm your heart with ful-
some praise and make you in a fashion lose control
of your mind, but if you turn round quickly you will
see them making stork-necks behind your back, or
flapping their hands like a donkey's ears, or putting
out the tongue like a mad dog.[1] Never speak evil
of any man or think that holiness consists in attacking
others. Often we accuse our neighbour of what we
do ourselves, and eloquently inveigh against vices
of which we too are guilty, dumb men trying to criticize orators. When the Grunter[2] came forward to
address an audience he used to advance first at a
snail's pace and utter a few words at such long inter-
vals that you might have thought that he was
gasping for breath rather than making a speech.
He would put his table in position and arrange on
it a pile of books, and then frowning and drawing in
his nose and wrinkling his forehead he would call his
pupils to attention with a snap of his fingers. After
this prelude he would pour out a flood of nonsense,
declaiming against individuals so fiercely that you
might imagine him to be a critic like Longinus or the
most eloquent of Roman censors, and putting a black
mark against any one he pleased to exclude him from
the senate of the learned. He had plenty of money,
and was more attractive at his dinner-parties. And
no wonder; he hooked many with this bait, and
gathering a wedge of noisy chatterers about him
he would make public progress, Nero at home,
Cato abroad, a complete puzzle, so that you might
call him one monster made up of different and
opposing natures, a strange beast like that of which

' Prima leo, postrema draco, media ipsa chimaera.'

19. Numquam ergo tales videas nec huiusce modi hominibus adpliceris, ne declines cor tuum in verba malitiae et audias : ' Sedens adversus fratrem tuum detrahebas et adversus filium matris tuae ponebas scandalum,' et iterum : ' Filii hominum dentes eorum arma et sagittae,' et alibi : ' Molliti sunt sermones eius super oleum et ipsi sunt iacula,' et apertius in Ecclesiaste : ' Si mordeat serpens in silentio, sic, qui fratri suo occulte detrahit.' Sed dicis : ' Ipse non detraho, aliis loquentibus facere quid possum ? ' ' Ad excusandas excusationes in peccatis ' ista praetendimus. Christus arte non luditur. Nequaquam mea, sed apostoli sententia est : ' Nolite errare ; Deus non inridetur.' Ille in corde, nos videmus in facie. Salomon loquitur in Proverbiis : ' Ventus aquilo dissipat nubes et vultus tristis linguas detrahentium.' Sicut enim sagitta, si mittatur contra duram materiam, nonnumquam in mittentem revertitur et vulnerat vulnerantem illudque conpletur : ' Facti sunt mihi in arcum pravum,' et alibi : ' Qui mittit in altum lapidem, recidet in caput eius,' ita detractor. cum tristem faciem viderit audientis, immo ne audientis quidem, sed obturantis aures suas, ne audiat iudicium sanguinis, ilico conticescit, pallet vultus, haerent labia, saliva siccatur. Unde idem vir

---

[1] Lucretius, V. 905, describing the Chimaera.
[2] Psalm l. 20.   [3] Psalm lvii. 4.
[4] Psalm lv. 21.   [5] Ecclesiastes, x. 11.   R.V. margin.
[6] Psalm cxli. 4.   [7] Galatians, vi. 7.
[8] Proverbs, xxv. 23.   [9] Psalm lxxviii. 57.
[10] Ecclesiasticus, xxvii. 25.
[11] Cf. Isaiah, xxxiii. 15 (of the righteous man): *qui obterat aures ne audiat sanguinem.*

the poet tells us: ' In front a lion, behind a dragon, in the middle a very goat.' [1]

Therefore you must never look at men such as he was, or have any intercourse with fellows of this kind, lest you turn your heart aside unto words of evil and hear the words: ' Thou sittest and speakest against thy brother; thou slanderest thine own mother's son,' [2] and again: ' The sons of men whose teeth are spears and arrows,' [3] and in another place: ' His words were softer than oil, yet were they drawn swords,' [4] and more clearly in Ecclesiastes: ' Surely the serpent will bite where there is no enchantment, and the slanderer is no better.' [5] But you may say: ' I myself am not given to detraction, but if other people say things, what can I do?' Such a plea is only an excuse to ' practise wicked works with men that work iniquity.' [6] Christ is not deceived by such a trick. It is not I but the apostle who says: ' Be not deceived; God is not mocked.' [7] God looks upon the heart, we only see the face. In the Proverbs Solomon says: ' As the north wind driveth away rain, so doth an angry countenance a back-biting tongue.' [8] As an arrow, if it be aimed at a hard substance, sometimes rebounds upon the archer and wounds the wounder—and so the word is fulfilled: ' They were turned aside like a deceitful bow,' [9] and in another place: ' Whoso casteth a stone on high casteth it on his own head' [10]—so when a slanderer sees that his hearer is looking surly, and so far from listening is stopping up his ears so that he may not hearken to the blood judgment,[11] he for his part at once falls silent, his face turns pale, his lips stick fast, and the moisture dries up within his mouth. Wherefore the same wise man says: ' Meddle not

433

sapiens: ' Cum detractatoribus,' inquit, ' non conmis-
cearis, quoniam repente veniet perditio eorum; et
ruinam utriusque quis novit?' Tam scilicet eius,
qui loquitur, quam illius, qui audit loquentem.
Veritas angulos non amat nec quaerit susurrones.
Timotheo dicitur: ' Adversus presbyterum accusa-
tionem cito ne receperis. Peccantem autem coram
omnibus argue, ut et ceteri metum habeant.' Non
est facile de perfecta aetate credendum, quam et vita
praeterita defendit et honorat vocabulum dignitatis,
verum, qui homines sumus et interdum contra annorum maturitatem puerorum vitiis labimur, si me
vis corrigi deliquentem, aperte increpa, tantum ne
occulte mordeas: ' Corripiet me iustus in misericordia et increpabit me, oleum autem peccatoris non
inpinguet caput meum. Quem enim diligit dominus,
corripit, flagellat autem omnium filium, quem
recipit.' Et per Esaiam clamat Deus: ' Populus
meus, qui beatos vos dicunt, seducunt vos et semitas
pedum vestrorum supplantant.' Quid enim mihi
prodest, si aliis mala mea referas, si me nesciente
peccatis meis, immo detractationibus tuis alium vul-
neres et, cum certatim omnibus narres, sic singulis
loquaris, quasi nulli alteri dixeris? Hoc est non me
emendare, sed vitio tuo satisfacere. Praecipit dominus peccantes in nos argui debere secreto vel ad-
hibito teste et, si audire noluerint, referri ad ecclesiam habendosque in malo pertinaces quasi ethnicos
et publicanos.

---

[1] Proverbs, **xxiv.** 21 Vulgate.
[2] 1 Timothy, v. 19 (slightly altered).
[3] Psalm cxli. 5.   (Septuagint cxl. 5.)
[4] Hebrews, **xii.** 6.   [5] Isaiah, iii. 12 (Septuagint).

with them that are given to detraction: for their
calamity shall rise suddenly; and who knoweth the
ruin of them both?'[1]—that is, the ruin of him who
speaks and him who listens. Truth does not love
corners nor does she seek out whisperers. To Timothy
it is said: 'Against an elder receive not an accusa-
tion suddenly; but him that sinneth rebuke before
all, that others also may fear.'[2] When a man is of
ripe years you should not readily believe evil of
him; his past life is a defence and so is the honourable title of elder. Still, as we are but men and
sometimes in spite of our mature age fall into the
sins of youth, if I do wrong and you wish to correct
me, rebuke me openly and do not indulge in secret
backbiting. 'Let the righteous smite me, it shall
be a kindness, and let him reprove me; but let not
the oil of the sinner enrich my head.'[3] 'Whom
the Lord loveth, he chasteneth, and scourgeth every
son whom he receiveth.'[4] By the mouth of Isaiah
God makes proclamation: 'O my people, they who
call you happy cause you to err and destroy the
way of your paths.'[5] What benefit is it to me if
you tell other people of my misdeeds, if without my
knowledge you hurt another by the story of my sins
or rather by your slanders, if while really eager to
tell your tale to all you speak to each individual as
though he were your only confidant? Such conduct
seeks not my improvement but the satisfaction of
your own vice. The Lord gave commandment that
those who sin against us should be arraigned privately
or else in the presence of a witness, and that if they
refuse to listen they should be brought before the
Church, and those who persist in wickedness should
be regarded as heathens and publicans.

20. Haec expressius loquor, ut adulescentem meum et linguae et aurium prurigine liberem, ut renatum in Christo sine ruga et macula quasi pudicam virginem exhibeam sanctamque tam mente quam corpore, ne solo nomine glorietur et absque oleo bonorum operum extincta lampade excludatur ab sponso. Habes ibi sanctum doctissimumque pontificem Proculum, qui viva et praesenti voce nostras scidulas superet cotidianisque tractatibus iter tuum dirigat nec patiatur te in partem alteram declinando viam relinquere regiam, per quam Israhel ad terram repromissionis properans se transiturum esse promittit. Atque utinam exaudiatur vox ecclesiae conplorantis: ' Domine, pacem da nobis; omnia enim reddidisti nobis.' Utinam, quod renuntiamus saeculo, voluntas sit, non necessitas, et paupertas habeat expetita gloriam, non inlata cruciatum. Ceterum iuxta miserias huius temporis et ubique gladios saevientes satis dives est, qui pane non indiget, nimium potens, qui servire non cogitur. Sanctus Exsuperius, Tolosae episcopus, viduae Saraptensis imitator, esuriens pascit alios et ore pallente ieiuniis fame torquetur aliena omnemque substantiam Christi visceribus erogavit. Nihil illo ditius, qui corpus domini canistro vimineo, sanguinem portat vitro, qui avaritiam proiecit e templo, qui absque funiculo et

---

[1] Bishop of Marseilles.

[2] Isaiah, xxvi. 12 (Septuagint).

[3] Bishop of Toulouse in the beginning of the fifth century, and a friend of Jerome. He lived at Rome before his episcopate (Letter LIV, 11).

[4] 1 Kings, xvii. 12.

I have spoken thus definitely because I wish to free a young friend of mine from an itching tongue and itching ears, so that I may present him born again in Christ without spot or roughness as a chaste virgin, holy both in body and in mind. I would not have him boast in name alone, or be shut out by the Bridegroom because his lamp has gone out for want of the oil of good works. You have in your town a saintly and most learned prelate, Proculus,[1] and he by the living sound of his voice can do more for you than any pages I can write. By daily homilies he will keep you in the straight path and not suffer you to turn right or left and leave the king's highway, whereby Israel undertakes to pass on its hasty journey to the promised land. May the voice of the Church's supplication be heard: 'Lord, ordain peace for us, for thou also hast wrought all our works for us.'[2] May our renunciation of the world be a matter of free will and not of necessity! May we seek poverty as a glorious thing, not have it forced upon us as a punishment! However, in our present miseries, with swords raging fiercely all around us, he is rich enough who is not in actual want of bread, he is more powerful than he needs be who is not reduced to slavery. Exuperius,[3] the saintly bishop of Toulouse, like the widow of Zarephath feeds others and goes hungry himself.[4] His face is pale with fasting, but it is the craving of others that torments him, and he has spent all his substance on those that are Christ's flesh. Yet none is richer than he; for in his wicker basket he carries the body of the Lord and in his glass cup His blood. He has driven greed from the temple; without scourge of ropes or chiding words he has overthrown the tables

437

increpatione vendentium columbas, id est dona
Spiritus Sancti, mensas subvertit mammonae et
nummulariorum aera dispersit, ut domus Dei domus
vocaretur orationis et non latronum spelunca. Huius
e vicino sectare vestigia et ceterorum, qui virtutum
illius similes sunt, quos sacerdotium et humiliores
facit et pauperiores, aut, si perfecta desideras, exi
cum Abraham de patria et de cognatione tua et
perge, quo nescis. Si habes substantiam, vende et
da pauperibus, si non habes, grandi onere liberatus
es; nudum Christum nudus sequere. Durum,
grande, difficile, sed magna sunt praemia.

CXXVII

AD PRINCIPIAM VIRGINEM DE VITA SANCTAE MARCELLAE

1. SAEPE et multum flagitas, virgo Christi Principia, ut memoriam sanctae feminae Marcellae
litteris recolam et bonum, quo diu fruiti sumus, etiam
ceteris noscendum imitandumque describam. Satis-
que doleo, quod hortaris sponte currentem et me
arbitraris indigere precibus, qui ne tibi quidem in

---

[1] This letter is really a memoir of Marcella, the noble lady
in whose house on the Aventine Jerome used to meet his
female disciples while he was living in Rome. The chief
facts of her life are given here by Jerome, who concludes
with an account of the sack of Rome in A.D. 410. In 408 the
Goths, who had been settled in Dalmatia, by Theodosius
(379-395), taking advantage of Stilicho's death, marched into
Italy under Alaric, and forced Rome to pay ransom. The
process was repeated in the next year and in 410 the city
was stormed and sacked, although the Goths, who were

of mammon of those that sell doves, that is, the gifts of the Holy Spirit; he has scattered the money of the money-changers, so that the house of God might be called a house of prayer and not a den of robbers. Follow closely in his steps and in those of others like him in virtue, men whom their holy office only makes more humble and more poor. Or else, if you desire perfection, go out like Abraham from your native city and your kin, and travel whither you know not. If you have substance, sell it and give it to the poor. If you have none, you are free from a great burden. Naked yourself follow a naked Christ. The task is hard and great and difficult; but great also are the rewards.

LETTER CXXVII

To Principia

Marcella [1] *and the sack of Rome*

Written A.D. 412

You have often and earnestly begged me, Principia, virgin of Christ, to honour in writing the memory of that saintly woman Marcella, and to set forth the goodness we so long enjoyed for others to know and imitate. It is, however, something of a grief to me that you should spur a willing horse,[2] or that you should think I need

Christians, spared the churches. Soon afterwards Alaric died in South Italy, his sudden end being used as a warning to Attila in 452 by Leo the Great. For Marcella and her circle, cf. Appendix I.

[2] A proverb: Cic. *Att.*, xiii. 45. 1: *quod me hortaris . . . , currentem tu quidem.*

eius dilectione concedam multoque plus accipiam
quam tribuam beneficii tantarum recordatione
virtutum. Nam ut hucusque reticerem et biennium praeterirem silentio, non fuit dissimulationis,
ut male aestimas, sed tristitiae incredibilis, quae ita
meum obpressit animum, ut melius iudicarem tacere
inpraesentiarum, quam nihil dignum illius laudibus
dicere. Neque vero Marcellam tuam, immo meam
et, ut verius loquar, nostram, omniumque sanctorum
et proprie Romanae urbis inclitum decus, institutis
rhetorum praedicabo, ut exponam illustrem familiam,
alti sanguinis decus et stemmata per consules et
praefectos praetorio decurrentia. Nihil in illa laudabo, nisi quod proprium est et in eo nobilius, quod
opibus et nobilitate contempta facta est paupertate
et humilitate nobilior.

2. Orbata patris morte viro quoque post nuptias
septimo mense privata est. Cumque eam Cerealis,
cuius clarum inter consules nomen est, propter
aetatem et antiquitatem familiae et insignem—quod
maxime viris placere consuevit—decorem corporis ac
insignem temperantiam ambitiosius peteret suasque
longaevus polliceretur divitias et non quasi in uxorem
sed quasi in filiam vellet donationem transfundere
Albinaque mater tam clarum praesidium viduitati
domus ultro appeteret, illa respondit: 'Si vellem

your entreaties, seeing that I do not yield even
to you in love for her. In recording her signal
virtues I shall indeed receive more benefit myself
than I confer upon others. That I have kept silence
up till now, and have allowed two years to pass
without speaking, has not been due to any wish to
repress my feelings, as you wrongly think, but
rather to my incredible grief; which has so overwhelmed my mind that I judged it better to remain
silent for the moment than to produce something
unworthy of her fame. And even now I shall
not follow the rules of rhetoric in praising your,
mine, or to speak more truly, our Marcella,
the glory of all the saints and peculiarly of the
city of Rome. I shall not describe her illustrious
household, the splendour of her ancient lineage,
and the long series of consuls and praetorian pre-
fects who have been her ancestors. I shall praise
nothing in her save that which is her own, the
more noble in that, despising wealth and rank,
by poverty and lowliness she has won higher
nobility.

On her father's death she was left an orphan, and
she also lost her husband seven months after marriage.
Thereupon Cerealis, a man of high consular rank,
paid her assiduous court, attracted by her youth,
her ancient family, her modest character, and those
personal charms which always find such favour with
men. Being an old man he promised her all his
money, and offered to make over his fortune as
though she were his daughter, not his wife. Her
mother Albina was excessively anxious to secure so
illustrious a protector for the widowed household,
but Marcella's answer was this: ' If I wished to

nubere et non aeternae me cuperem pudicitiae dedi-
care, utique maritum quaererem, non hereditatem.'
Illoque mandante posse et senes diu vivere et iuvenes
cito mori eleganter lusit: ' Iuvenis quidem potest
cito mori, sed senex diu vivere non potest.' Qua
sententia repudiatus exemplo ceteris fuit, ut eius
nuptias desperarent. Legimus in evangelio secundum Lucam: ' Et erat Anna prophetissa, filia
Phanuhelis, de tribu Aser et haec provectae aetatis
in diebus plurimis. Vixeratque cum viro annis
septem a virginitate sua et erat vidua annis octoginta quattuor nec recedebat de templo ieiuniis et
obsecrationibus serviens nocte ac die.' Nec mirum,
si videre meruit salvatorem, quem tanto labore
quaerebat. Conferamus septem annos septem mensibus, sperare Christum et tenere, natum confiteri et
in crucifixum credere, parvulum non negare et virum
gaudere regnantem: non facio ullam inter sanctas
feminas differentiam, quod nonnulli inter sanctos
viros et ecclesiarum principes stulte facere consuerunt,
sed illo tendit adsertio, ut, quarum unus labor, unum
et praemium sit.

3. Difficile est in maledica civitate et in urbe, in
qua orbis quondam populus fuit palmaque vitiorum,
si honestis detraherent et pura ac munda macularent,
non aliquam sinistri rumoris fabulam trahere. Unde

---

[1] St. Luke, ii. 36.

marry and did not rather desire to dedicate myself to perpetual chastity, I should in any case look for a husband, not an inheritance.' Cerealis urged that old men might possibly live long and young men die early, but to that she wittily retorted: ' A young man may possibly die early, but an old man cannot possibly live long.' This definite rejection warned other men that they had no hope of winning her as wife. In the Gospel according to Luke we read: ' There was one Anna, a prophetess, the daughter of Phanuel, of the tribe of Aser: she was of great age, and had seen many days; and she had lived with an husband seven years from her virginity; and she was a widow of about fourscore and four years, which departed not from the temple but served God with fastings and prayers night and day.'[1] It is not strange that she earned the vision of the Saviour whom she sought so earnestly. Let us now compare the two cases. Anna was married for seven years, Marcella for seven months. Anna hoped for Christ, Marcella held Him fast. Anna confessed Him at his birth, Marcella believed in Him crucified. Anna did not deny the child, Marcella rejoiced in the man as king. I am not drawing distinctions of merit between two saintly women, as some people foolishly do between saintly men and heads of churches. The point of my claim is this; as these two shared one labour so they will gain one reward.

In a slander-loving place, and in a city where the people once was the world, and it was the triumph of vice to disparage virtue and to defile all that is pure and clean, it is difficult not to drag along some fables of calumnious gossips. Therefore

quasi rem difficillimam ac paene inpossibilem optat
propheta potius quam praesumit dicens: ' Beati
inmaculati in via, qui ambulant in lege domini,'
inmaculatos in via huius appellans saeculi, quos
nulla obscena rumoris aura macularit, qui obpro-
brium non acceperint adversus proximos suos. De
quibus et salvator in evangelio: ' Esto,' inquit,
' benivolus '—sive ' bene sentiens '—' de adversario
tuo, dum es cum illo in via.' Quis umquam de hac
muliere, quod displiceret, audivit, ut crederet?
Quis credidit, ut non magis se ipsum malignitatis et
infamiae condemnaret? Ab hac primum confusa
gentilitas est, dum omnibus patuit, quae esset vi-
duitas Christiana, quam et conscientia et habitu
promittebat.

Illae enim solent purpurisso et cerussa ora depin-
gere, sericis nitere vestibus, splendere gemmis,
aurum portare cervicibus et auribus perforatis Rubri
Maris pretiosissima grana suspendere, flagrare mure,
et tandem dominatu virorum se caruisse laetentur
quaerantque alios, non quibus iuxta Dei sententiam
serviant, sed quibus imperent. Unde et pauperes
eligunt, ut nomen tantum virorum habere videantur,
qui patienter rivales sustineant, si mussitaverint, ilico
proiciendi. Nostra vidua talibus usa est vestibus,
quibus obstaret frigus, non membra nudaret, aurum
usque ad anuli signaculum repudians et magis in
ventribus egenorum quam in marsuppiis recondens.
Nusquam sine matre, nullum clericorum et mon-

---

[1] Psalm cxix. 1.   [2] St. Matthew, v. 25.

it is for a thing difficult and almost impossible that the prophet hopes rather than thinks to win when he says: 'Blessed are the undefiled in the way who walk in the law of the Lord.'[1] He means by the undefiled in this world's way those whom no breath of scandal has sullied and who have incurred no reproach from their neighbours. So too the Saviour in the Gospel says: 'Agree with [or be kindly to] thine adversary whilst thou art in the way with him.'[2] Whoever heard anything displeasing about Marcella that deserved belief? Who that believed such a tale did not rather convict himself of malice and backbiting? She put the Gentiles to confusion by showing to all what sort of thing that Christian widowhood is which she revealed in every thought and look.

Gentile widows are wont to paint their faces with rouge and white lead, to flaunt in silk dresses, to deck themselves in gleaming jewels, to wear gold necklaces, to hang from their pierced ears the costliest Red Sea pearls, and to reek of musk. Rejoicing that they have at length escaped from a husband's dominion, they look about for a new mate, intending not to yield him obedience, as God ordained, but to be his lord and master. With this object they choose poor men, husbands only in name, who must patiently put up with rivals, and if they murmur can be kicked out on the spot. Our widow, on the other hand, wore clothes that were meant to keep out the cold, not to reveal her bare limbs. Even a gold signet ring she rejected, preferring to store her money in the stomachs of the needy rather than hide it in a purse. Nowhere would she go without her mother, never would she interview without

achorum—quod amplae domus interdum exigebat
necessitas—vidit absque arbitris. Semper in comitatu
suo virgines ac viduas et ipsas graves feminas habuit
sciens ex lascivia puellarum saepe de dominarum
moribus iudicari et, qualis quaeque sit, talium
consortio delectari.

4. Divinarum scripturarum ardor incredibilis, semperque cantabat: ' In corde meo abscondi eloquia tua,
ut non peccem tibi,' et illud de perfecto viro: ' Et in
lege domini voluntas eius et in lege eius meditabitur
die ac nocte,' meditationem legis non replicando,
quae scripta sunt, ut Iudaeorum aestimant Pharisaei,
sed in opere intellegens iuxta illud apostolicum:
' Sive comeditis sive bibitis sive quid agitis, omnia
in gloriam domini facientes' et prophetae verba
dicentis: ' A mandatis tuis intellexi,' ut, postquam
mandata conplesset, tunc se sciret mereri intelle-
gentiam scripturarum. Quod et alibi legimus:
' Quia coepit Iesus facere et docere.' Erubescit enim
quamvis praeclara doctrina, quam propria repre-
hendit conscientia, frustraque lingua praedicat paupertatem et docet elemosynas, qui Croesi divitiis
tumet vilique opertus palliolo pugnat contra tineas
vestium sericarum. Moderata ieiunia, carnium abstinentia, vini odor magis quam gustus propter sto-

---

[1] Psalm cxix. 11. [2] Psalm i. 2.
[3] 1 Corinthians, x. 31. [4] Psalm cxix. 104.
[5] Acts, i. 1.

witnesses one of the monks, or clergy, which was often necessary for the needs of her large household. Always her retinue consisted of virgins and widows, and they were all staid women; for she knew that a saucy maid is a reflection on her mistress' character, and that women usually prefer the company of people like themselves. Her ardent love for God's Scriptures surpasses all belief. She was for ever singing: ' Thy words have I hid in my heart that I might not sin against thee ';[1] and also the passage about the perfect man: ' His delight is in the law of the Lord; and in his law he doth meditate day and night.'[2] Meditation in the law meant for her not a mere reperusal of the Scriptures, as the Jewish Pharisees think, but a carrying it out in action. She obeyed the apostle's command: ' Whether therefore ye eat or drink or whatsoever ye do, do all to the glory of God ';[3] and also the words of the prophet: ' Through thy precepts I have got understanding.'[4] She knew that only when she had fulfilled those precepts would she deserve to understand the Scriptures. So we read in another place ' that Jesus began both to do and teach.'[5] However fine a man's teaching may be, it is put to the blush when his own conscience reproves him; and it is in vain that his tongue preaches poverty and teaches almsgiving, if he himself is swollen with the wealth of a Croesus, and though he wears a coarse cloak fights to keep the moths from the silken robes in his cupboard.

Marcella practised fasting, but in moderation; and she abstained from eating meat. The scent of wine was more familiar to her than the taste, for she drank it only for her stomach's sake and her

machum et frequentes infirmitates. Raro procedebat ad publicum et maxime nobilium matronarum vitabat domus, ne cogeretur videre, quod contempserat, apostolorum et martyrum basilicas secretis celebrans orationibus et quae populorum frequentiam declinarent. Matri in tantum oboediens, ut interdum faceret, quod nolebat. Nam cum illa suum diligeret sanguinem et absque filiis ac nepotibus vellet in fratris liberos universa conferri, ista pauperes eligebat et tamen matri contraire non poterat monilia et, quicquid supellectilis fuit, divitibus peritura concedens magisque volens pecuniam perdere quam parentis animum contristare.

5. Nulla eo tempore nobilium feminarum noverat Romae propositum monachorum nec audebat propter rei novitatem ignominiosum, ut tunc putabatur, et vile in populis nomen adsumere. Haec ab Alexandrinis sacerdotibus papaque Athanasio et postea Petro, qui persecutionem Arrianae hereseos declinantes quasi ad tutissimum communionis suae portum Roman confugerant, vitam beati Antonii adhuc tunc viventis monasteriaque in Thebaide Pachumii et virginum ac viduarum didicit disciplinam nec erubuit profiteri, quod Christo placere cognoverat. Hanc multos post annos imitata est Sophronia et aliae, quibus rectissime illud Ennianum aptari potest:

---

[1] 1 Timothy, v. 23.

[2] For Athanasius see F. A. Wright, *Later Greek Literature*, pp. 331-333. Peter succeeded him at Alexandria. For "Pope" cf. p. 308, n. 2.

frequent infirmities.[1] She seldom appeared in public
and carefully avoided the houses of ladies of rank,
that she might not be forced to see there what she
herself had rejected; but she frequently visited the
churches of the apostles and martyrs for quiet
prayer, avoiding the people's throng. To her
mother she was so obedient that occasionally she
did for her sake things that went against her own
inclination. For example, Albina was devoted to
her own kinsfolk, and wished to leave all her property
to her brother's children, being without sons and
grandsons: Marcella would have preferred to give
it to the poor, but still she could not go against
her mother, and handed over her necklaces and
other effects to people already rich for them to
squander. She chose rather to see money lost than
to vex her mother's feelings.

At that time no great lady in Rome knew anything of the monastic life, nor ventured to call herself a nun. The thing itself was strange and the
name was commonly accounted ignominious and
degrading. It was from some priests of Alexandria
and from Pope Athanasius[2] and from Peter afterwards, who to escape the persecution of the Arian
heretics had all fled to Rome as being the safest
refuge for their communion, that Marcella was told
of the life of the blessed Antony, then still in this
world, and of the monasteries founded by Pachumius
in the Thebaid, and of the discipline laid down there
for virgins and widows. She was not ashamed to
profess a life which she knew was pleasing to Christ;
and many years later her example was followed by
Sophronia and by some other ladies, to whom the
lines of Ennius may most fitly be applied:

449

Utinam ne in nemore Pelio.' Huius amicitiis fruita est Paula venerabilis, in huius nutrita cubiculo Eustochium, virginitatis decus, ut facilis aestimatio sit, qualis magistra, ubi tales discipulae.

Rideat forsitan infidelis lector me in muliercularum laudibus inmorari : qui si recordetur sanctas feminas, comites domini salvatoris, quae ministrabant ei de sua substantia, et tres Marias stantes ante crucem Mariamque proprie Magdalenen, quae ob sedulitatem et ardorem fidei ' turritae ' nomen accepit et prima ante apostolos Christum videre meruit resurgentem, se potius superbiae quam nos condemnabit ineptiarum, qui virtutes non sexu sed animo iudicamus. Unde et Iesus Iohannem evangelistam amabat plurimum, qui propter generis nobilitatem erat notus pontifici et Iudaeorum insidias non timebat, in tantum, ut Petrum introduceret in atrium et staret solus apostolorum ante crucem matremque salvatoris in sua reciperet, ut hereditatem virginis domini virginem matrem filius virgo susciperet.

6. Annis igitur plurimis sic suam transegit aetatem, ut ante se vetulam cerneret, quam adulescentulam fuisse meminisset, laudans illud Platonicum, qui philosophiam meditationem mortis esse dixisset. Unde et noster apostolus : ' Cotidie morior per vestram salutem,' et dominus iuxta antiqua exemplaria : ' Nisi quis tulerit crucem suam cotidie et secutus

---

[1] The phrase, used here as an expression of regret for the loss of two noble women, comes from the opening lines of Ennius' translation of the *Medea* (Ennius, *Medea*, fr. 1 : *utinam ne in nemore Pelio securibus | Caesa accidisset abiegna ad terram trabes*).

[2] Magdala means ' tower.'   [3] St. John, xviii. 15–16.

[4] Plato, *Phaedo*, 67. E. τῷ ὄντι ἄρα . . . οἱ ὀρθῶς φιλοσοφοῦντες ἀποθνήσκειν μελετῶσιν.

[5] 1 Corinthians, xv. 31.

' Would that ne'er in Pelion's woods ! ' [1]

Her friendship was also enjoyed by the revered Paula, and in her cell that paragon of virgins Eustochium was trained. Such pupils as these make it easy for us to judge the character of their teacher.

Those unbelievers who read me may perhaps smile to find me lingering over the praises of weak women. But if they will recall how holy women attended Our Lord and Saviour and ministered to Him of their substance, and how the three Marys stood before the cross, and particularly how Mary of Magdala,[2] called ' of the tower ' because of her earnestness and ardent faith, was privileged to see the rising Christ first even before the apostles, they will convict themselves of pride rather than me of folly, who judge of virtue not by the sex but by the mind. Therefore it was that Jesus loved the evangelist John most of all; for he was of noble birth and known to the high priest, but he feared the Jews' plottings so little that he brought Peter into the priest's palace,[3] and was the only apostle who stood before the cross and took the Saviour's mother to his own home, a virgin son receiving the Virgin Mother as a legacy from Our Virgin Lord.

So Marcella lived her life for many years, and found herself old before she ever remembered that once she had been young, approving Plato's saying, who declared that philosophy is a preparation for death.[4] Wherefore our own apostle also says : ' For your salvation I die daily.' [5] So Our Lord too, according to the ancient copies, said : ' Whosoever doth not bear his cross daily and come after me

fuerit me, non potest meus esse discipulus,' multoque
ante per prophetam Spiritus Sanctus : ' Propter te
mortificamur tota die, aestimati sumus ut oves
occisionis ' et post multas aetates illa sententia :
' Memento semper diem mortis et numquam pecca-
bis,' disertissimique praeceptum satirici :

> ' Vive memor leti, fugit hora, hoc, quod loquor,
> inde est.'

Sic ergo—ut dicere coeperamus—aetatem duxit et
vixit, ut semper se crederet esse morituram. Sic
induta est vestibus, ut meminisset sepulchri, offerens
hostiam rationabilem, vivam, placentem Deo.

7. Denique, cum et me Romam cum sanctis ponti-
ficibus Paulino et Epiphanio ecclesiastica traxisset
necessitas—quorum alter Antiochenam Syriae, alter
Salaminiam Cypri rexit ecclesiam—et verecunde
nobiliarum feminarum oculos declinarem, ita egit
secundum apostolum ' inportune, oportune,' ut
pudorem meum sua superaret industria. Et quia
alicuius tunc nominis aestimabar super studio scripturarum, numquam convenit, quin de scripturis
aliquid interrogaret nec statim adquiesceret, sed
moveret e contrario quaestiones, non ut contenderet,
sed ut quaerendo disceret earum solutiones, quas
opponi posse intellegebat. Quid in illa virtutum,
quid ingenii, quid sanctitatis, quid puritatis inve-
nerim, vereor dicere, ne fidem credulitatis excedam

---

[1] St. Luke, xiv. 27.   [2] Psalm xliv. 22.
[3] Ecclesiasticus, vii. 36.   [4] Persius, V. 153.
[5] In A.D. 382.   [6] 2 Timothy, iv. 2.

cannot be my disciple.'[1] Indeed ages ago the
Holy Spirit by the mouth of the prophet declared:
'For thy sake are we killed all the day long; we
are counted as sheep for the slaughter.'[2] And
again after many generations we have the proverb:
'Remember ever the day of death and you will
never go wrong.'[3] Lastly there is the satirist's
shrewd precept:

'Live thou remembering death, for time flies fast.
This moment's speech I snatch before 'tis past.'[4]

Well then, as I began to say, Marcella in all the
days of her life remembered that she must die.
Her very dress reminded her of the tomb, and she
offered herself as a living sacrifice, reasonable and
acceptable unto God.

Lastly, when the needs of the Church brought me also
to Rome[5] in company with the holy pontiffs Paulinus
and Epiphanius, directors respectively of the churches
of Syrian Antioch and of Salamis in Cyprus, I in my
modesty was inclined to avoid the gaze of ladies of
rank. But Marcella was so urgent 'both in season
and out of season,'[6] as the apostle says, that her
persistence overcame my timidity. At that time I
had some repute as a student of the Scriptures, and
so she never met me without asking me some question about them, nor would she rest content at once,
but would bring forward points on the other side;
this, however, was not for the sake of argument,
but that by questioning she might learn an answer
to such objections as she saw might be raised. What
virtue and intellect, what holiness and purity I found
in her I am afraid to say, both lest I should exceed
the limits of men's belief, and also that I may not

et tibi maiorem dolorem incutiam recordanti, quanto bono carueris. Hoc solum dicam, quod, quicquid in nobis longo fuit studio congregatum et meditatione diuturna quasi in naturam versum, hoc illa libavit, hoc didicit atque possedit, ita ut post perfectionem nostram, si aliquo testimonio scripturarum esset oborta contentio, ad illam iudicem pergeretur. Et quia valde prudens erat et noverat illud, quod appellant philosophi τὸ πρέπον, id est decere, quod facias, sic interrogata respondebat, ut etiam sua non sua diceret, sed vel mea vel cuiuslibet alterius, ut et in ipso, quod docebat, se discipulam fateretur—sciebat enim dictum ab apostolo: ' Docere autem mulieri non permitto '—ne virili sexui et interdum sacerdotibus de obscuris et ambiguis sciscitantibus facere videretur iniuriam.

8. In nostrum locum statim audivimus te illius adhaesisse consortio et numquam ab illa ne transversum quidem unguis, ut dicitur, recessisse eadem domo, eodem cubiculo, una usam cubili et omnibus in urbe clarissima notum fieret et te matrem et illam filiam repperisse. Suburbanus ager vobis pro monasterio fuit et rus electum propter solitudinem. Multoque ita vixisti tempore, ut imitatione vestri et conversatione multarum gauderemus Romam factam Hierosolymam. Crebra virginum monasteria, monachorum innumerabilis multitudo, ut pro frequentia

---

[1] 1 Timothy, ii. 12.

increase the pain of your grief by reminding you of the blessings you have lost. This only will I say; all that I had gathered together by long study, and by constant meditation made part of my nature, she first sipped, then learned, and finally took for her own. Consequently, after my departure from Rome, if any argument arose concerning the testimony of the Scriptures, it was to her verdict that appeal was made. She was extremely prudent and always followed the rules of what philosophers call τὸ πρέπον, that is, propriety of conduct. Therefore, even when her answers to questions were her own, she said they came not from her but from me or some one else, admitting herself to be a pupil even when she was teaching—for she knew that the apostle said: ' I do not allow a woman to teach '—[1] so that she might not seem to do a wrong to the male sex, and sometimes even to priests, when they asked questions on obscure and doubtful points.

I have heard that you at once took my place as her close companion, and that you never left her side even for a finger's breadth, as the saying goes. You lived in the same house, and had the same cell and bed, so that every one in the great city knew that you had found a mother and she a daughter. A farm near Rome was your monastery, the country being chosen because of its loneliness. You lived thus together for a long time, and as many other ladies followed your example and joined your company, I had the joy of seeing Rome become another Jerusalem. Monastic establishments for virgins were founded in many places, and the number of monks in the city surpassed all counting. Indeed, so great was the crowd of God's servants that the

455

servientium Deo, quod prius ignominiae fuerat,
esset postea gloriae. Interim absentiam nostri
mutuis solabamur adloquiis et, quod carne non
poteramus, spiritu reddebamus. Semper se obviare
epistulae, superare officiis, salutationibus praevenire.
Non multum perdebat, quae iugibus sibi litteris
iungebatur.

9. In hac tranquillitate et domini servitute heretica
in his provinciis exorta tempestas cuncta turbavit et
in tantam rabiem concitata est, ut nec sibi nec ulli
bonorum parceret. Et quasi parum esset hic universa movisse, navem plenam blasphemiarum Romano
intulit portui invenitque protinus patella operculum
et Romanae fidei purissimum fontem lutosa caeno
permiscuere vestigia. Nec mirum, si in plateis et
in foro rerum venalium pictus ariolus stultorum
verberet nates et obtorto fuste dentes mordentium
quatiat, cum venenata spurcaque doctrina Romae
invenerit, quos induceret. Tunc librorum περὶ ἀρχῶν
infamis interpretatio, tunc discipulus ὄλβιος vere
nominis sui, si in talem magistrum non inpegisset,
tunc nostrorum διάπυρος contradictio et Phari-
saeorum turbata schola. Tunc sancta Marcella, quae
diu coniverat, ne per aemulationem quippiam facere
crederetur, postquam sensit fidem apostolico ore
laudatam in plerisque violari, ita ut sacerdotes

---

[1] The movement, led by Rufinus and Macarius, to bring
Origen's teaching before the Roman public. Cf. App. II, p. 498ff.

[2] ' Like to like,' a favourite proverb with Jerome.

[3] For Origen (A.D. 185–254) and his writings see F. A. Wright,
Later Greek Literature, pp. 317–320. The *De Principiis* is the
first systematic account of Christian theology and the most
profound work of serious philosophy which the third century
produced.

[4] Macarius (μακάριος—ὄλβιος). Jerome here, as often, plays
upon words.

name, which previously had been a term of reproach, was now one of honour. Meanwhile we consoled ourselves for our separation by an interchange of conversation, discharging in the spirit the debt that we could not pay in the flesh. Our letters always crossed, outvied in courtesies, anticipated in greetings. Separation brought no great loss, since it was bridged by a continual correspondence.

In the midst of this tranquillity and service rendered to God, there arose in these provinces a tempest[1] which threw everything into confusion, and finally swelled to such heights of madness that it spared neither itself nor anything that was good. As though it were not enough to have disturbed all our community here, it despatched a ship laden with blasphemies to the port of Rome. There the dish soon found a cover to match it,[2] and muddy feet fouled the clear fountain of the Roman faith. It is not surprising that in the streets and market-places of the city a painted quack can strike fools on the buttocks and knock out the teeth of objectors with a blow from his stick, seeing that this poisonous and filthy teaching found dupes at Rome to lead astray. Then came the disgraceful version of Origen's book *On First Principles*,[3] and that disciple[4] who might truly have been called ' Felix ' if he had never fallen in with such a teacher. Next followed my supporters' fiery confutation which threw the whole school of the Pharisees into confusion. Finally our saintly Marcella, who for a long time had closed her eyes to all this lest she should be thought to put herself in rivalry, finding that the faith which the apostle once praised was now in many people being endangered, came forward

457

quoque nonnullos monachorum maximeque saeculi
homines in adsensum sui traheret hereticus ac sim-
plicitati inluderet episcopi, qui de suo ingenio ceteros
aestimabat, publice restitit malens Deo placere quam
hominibus.

10. Laudat salvator in evangelio vilicum iniquitatis,
quod contra dominum quidem, attamen pro se pru-
denter fecerit. Cernentes heretici de parva scintilla
maxima incendia concitari et suppositam dudum
flammam iam ad culmina pervenisse nec posse latere,
quod multos deceperat, petunt et inpetrant eccle-
siasticas epistulas, ut communicantes ecclesiae
discedere viderentur. Non multum tempus in
medio, succedit in pontificatum vir insignis Anastasius, quem diu Roma habere non meruit, ne orbis
caput sub tali episcopo truncaretur; immo idcirco
raptus atque translatus est, ne semel latam sententiam precibus suis flectere conaretur dicente
domino ad Hieremiam: ' Ne oraveris pro populo
isto neque depreceris in bonum, quia, si ieiunaverint,
non exaudiam preces eorum et, si obtulerint holo-
causta et victimas, non suscipiam eas ; in gladio enim,
fame et pestilentia ego consumam eos.' Dicas:
' Quo hoc ? ' ad laudem Marcellae. Damnationis
hereticorum haec fuit principium, dum adducit
testes, qui prius ab eis eruditi et postea ab heretico
fuerant errore correcti, dum ostendit multitudinem

---

[1] Pope Siricius.   [2] St. Luke, xvi. 8.   [3] A.D. 398.
    [4] ' The head of the world ' is Rome, sacked in 410.
                [5] Jeremiah, xiv. 11.

openly on my side. As the heretic was drawing to his cause not only priests, monks and above all laity, but was even imposing on the simplicity of the bishop,[1] who judged other men by himself, she publicly withstood him, choosing to please God rather than men.

In the Gospel the Saviour praises the unjust steward, because, though he cheated his master, he acted wisely for himself.[2] The heretics in the same way, seeing that a small spark had kindled a great fire, and that the flames which for a long time had been hidden were now at the housetops, so that the deception practised on many could no longer be hid, asked for and obtained letters from the church of Rome, that it might seem that they were in full communion until the day of their departure. Soon after this the great Anastasius[3] succeeded to the pontificate; but Rome was not privileged to have him long, lest the head of the world should be struck off[4] while so noble a man was bishop. He was indeed swiftly removed from this earth that he might not seek by his prayers to avert the sentence which God once for all had passed. For the Lord said to Jeremiah: 'Pray not for this people for their good. When they fast I will not hear their cry; and when they offer burnt-offering and oblation, I will not accept them; but I will consume them by the sword and by the famine and by the pestilence.'[5] You may say: 'What has this to do with the praise of Marcella?' The answer is that she took the first steps in getting the heretics condemned. It was she who brought forward as witnesses those who first had been instructed by them and afterwards had seen the error of their heresy. It was she who revealed the numbers they had deceived, and

deceptorum, dum inpia περὶ ἀρχῶν ingerit volumina,
quae emendata manu scorpii monstrantur, dum
acciti frequentibus litteris heretici, ut se defenderent,
venire non ausi sunt tantaque vis conscientiae fuit,
ut magis absentes damnari quam praesentes co-
argui maluerint. Huius tam gloriosae victoriae
origo Marcella est tuque caput horum et causa
bonorum, quae scis me vera narrare quae nosti
vix de multis pauca dicere, ne legenti fastidium
faciat odiosa replicatio et videar apud malivolos sub
occasione laudis alterius stomachum meum digerere.
Pergam ad reliqua.

11. De occidentis partibus ad orientem turbo trans-
gressus minitabatur plurimis magna naufragia.
Tunc inpletum est: ' Putas, veniens filius hominis
inveniet fidem super terram?' Refrigerata caritate
multorum pauci, qui amabant fidei veritatem, nostro
lateri iungebantur, quorum publice petebatur caput,
contra quos omnes opes parabantur, ita ut ' Barnabas
quoque adduceretur in illam simulationem,' immo
apertum parricidium, quod non viribus sed voluntate
commisit. Sed ecce universa tempestas domino
flante deleta est et expletum vaticinium prophetale:
' Auferes spiritum eorum et deficient et in pulverem
suum revertentur. In illa die peribunt omnes
cogitationes eorum,' et illud evangelicum: ' Stulte,
hac nocte aufertur anima tua abs te; quae autem
praeparasti, cuius erunt?'

---

[1] Rufinus.　　　　　　　　[2] St. Luke, xviii. 8.
[3] Galatians, ii. 13.
[4] The allusion is perhaps to John of Jerusalem, with whom
Jerome was frequently at variance: but this is only a
conjecture, though a probable one.
[5] Psalm civ. 29.　　　　[6] Psalm cxlvi. 4 (slightly altered).
[7] St. Luke, xii. 20.

brandished in their faces the impious books *On First Principles*, which as emended by that scorpion's [1] hand were then openly on view. It was she finally who in a succession of letters challenged the heretics to defend themselves; a challenge which they did not dare to accept, for so strong was their consciousness of sin that they preferred to be condemned in their absence rather than appear and be proved guilty. For this glorious victory Marcella was responsible; she with you was the source and cause of this great blessing. You, who know that my story is true, understand that I am only mentioning a few incidents out of many, lest a tedious repetition should weary the reader. Moreover, I do not wish malignant people to think that under pretence of praising another I am giving vent to my own rancour. I will now proceed to the rest of my tale.

The hurricane passed from the Western world into the East and threatened very many with dire shipwreck. Then were fulfilled the words: 'Thinkest thou that when the son of man cometh he shall find faith on earth?' [2] The love of many grew cold, but a few who loved the truth of faith rallied to my side. Their lives were openly sought and every means was used to attack them, so that indeed 'Barnabas also was carried away with their dissimulation,' [3] and committed plain murder,[4] in wish at least if not in deed. But lo! the Lord blew and all the tempest passed away, and the prediction of the prophet was fulfilled: 'Thou takest away their breath, they die, and return to their dust.' [5] 'In that very day their thoughts perish.' [6] With it also the Gospel words were accomplished: 'Thou fool, this night thy soul shall be required of thee: then whose shall those things be, which thou hast provided?' [7]

12. Dum haec aguntur in Iebus, terribilis de occi-
dente rumor adfertur obsideri Romam et auro
salutem civium redimi spoliatosque rursum circumdari, ut post substantiam vitam quoque amitterent.
Haeret vox et singultus intercipiunt verba dictantis.
Capitur urbs, quae totum cepit orbem, immo fame
perit ante quam gladio et vix pauci, qui caperentur,
inventi sunt. Ad nefandos cibos erupit esurientium
rabies et sua invicem membra laniarunt, dum mater
non parcit lactanti infantiae et recipit utero, quem
paulo ante effuderat. ' Nocte Moab capta est, nocte
cecidit murus eius. Deus, venerunt gentes in hereditatem tuam, polluerunt templum sanctum tuum,
posuerunt Hierusalem in pomorum custodiam,
posuerunt cadavera servorum tuorum escas volati-
libus caeli, carnes sanctorum tuorum bestiis terrae.
Effuderunt sanguinem ipsorum sicut aquam in circuitu Hierusalem et non erat, qui sepeliret.'

' Quis cladem illius noctis, quis funera fando
Explicet aut possit lacrimis aequare dolorem ?
Urbs antiqua ruit multos dominata per annos
Plurima perque vias sparguntur inertia passim
Corpora perque domos, et plurima mortis imago.

13. Cum interim, ut tanta confusione rerum,
Marcellae quoque domum cruentus victor ingre-

---

[1] The Canaanite name for Jerusalem.
[2] Isaiah, xv. 1.　　　　　[3] Psalm lxxix. 1-3.
[4] Virgil, *Aeneid*, II. 361-5 and 369.

LETTER CXXVII

While these things were taking place in Jebus,[1] a dreadful rumour reached us from the West. We heard that Rome was besieged, that the citizens were buying their safety with gold, and that when they had been thus despoiled they were again beleaguered, so as to lose not only their substance but their lives. The speaker's voice failed and sobs interrupted his utterance. The city which had taken the whole world was itself taken; nay, it fell by famine before it fell by the sword, and there were but a few found to be made prisoners. The rage of hunger had recourse to impious food; men tore one another's limbs, and the mother did not spare the baby at her breast, taking again within her body that which her body had just brought forth. ' In the night was Moab taken, in the night did her wall fall down.'[2] ' O God, the heathen have come into thine inheritance; thy holy temple have they defiled; they have made Jerusalem an orchard. The dead bodies of thy servants have they given to be meat unto the fowls of the heaven, the flesh of thy saints unto the beasts of the earth. Their blood have they shed like water round about Jerusalem; and there was none to bury them.'[3]

' Who can tell that night of havoc, who can shed
        enough of tears
    For those deaths? The ancient city that for many
        a hundred years
    Ruled the world comes down in ruin: corpses lie in
        every street
    And men's eyes in every household death in countless phases meet.'[4]

Meanwhile, as you might expect in such a turmoil, the blood-stained conquerors burst their way into Marcella's house.

ditur—' Sit mihi fas audita loqui,' immo a sanctis
viris visa narrare, qui interfuere praesentes, qui te
dicunt in periculo quoque ei fuisse sociatam—intre-
pido vultu excepisse dicitur introgressos; cumque
posceretur aurum et defossas opes vili excusaret
tunica, non tamen fecit fidem voluntariae paupertatis.
Caesam fustibus flagellisque aiunt non sensisse tormenta, sed hoc lacrimis, hoc pedibus eorum egisse
prostratam, ne te a suo consortio separarent, ne sustineret adulescentia, quod senilis aetas timere non
poterat. Christus dura corda mollivit et inter
cruentos gladios invenit locum pietas. Cumque et
illam et te ad beati Pauli basilicam barbari deduxis-
sent, ut vel salutem vobis ostenderet vel sepulchrum,
in tantam laetitiam dicitur erupisse, ut gratias ageret
Deo, quod te sibi integram reservasset, quod pauperem illam non fecisset captivitas, sed invenisset,
quod egeret cotidiano cibo, quod saturata Christo
non sentiret esuriem, quod et voce et opere loqueretur: ' Nuda exivi de ventre matris meae, nuda et
redeam. Sicut domino visum est, ita et factum est.
Sit nomen domini benedictum.'

14. Post aliquot menses sana, integra vegetoque
corpusculo dormivit in domino et te paupertatulae
suae, immo per te pauperes reliquit heredes claudens
oculos in manibus tuis, reddens spiritum in tuis
osculis, dum inter lacrimas tuas illa rideret consci-

---

[1] Virgil, *Aeneid*, VI. 266.   [2] Job, i. 21.

[3] This passage may have inspired the lines by Sir William
Jones (1746–1794) 'to a friend on his birthday':

' On parents' knee a naked newborn child
Weeping thou sat'st, while all around thee smiled;
So live that sinking to thy life's last sleep,
Calm thou mayst smile, while all around thee weep.'

Cf. Letter LX. 13.

' Be it mine to say what I have heard,' [1]

nay, rather to relate what was seen by those holy
men who were present at that hour, and found you,
Principia, at her side in the time of danger. They
tell me that she confronted the intruders with fear-
less face, and when they asked her for gold and
hidden treasures pointed to her coarse gown. However, they would not give credence to her self-
chosen poverty, but beat her with sticks and whipped
her. She felt no pain, but throwing herself in tears
at their feet begged them not to take you from her
or force your youth to endure the fate which her old
age had no occasion to fear. Christ softened their
hard hearts, and even among blood-stained swords
a sense of duty found place. The barbarians escorted
both her and you to the church of the apostle Paul,
for you to find there either safety or a tomb. There
she burst into cries of joy, thanking God for having
kept you unharmed for her. ' By heaven's grace,'
she said, ' captivity has found me a poor woman,
not made me one. Now I shall go in want of daily
bread, but I shall not feel hunger since I am full of
Christ and can say in word and deed : " Naked came
I out of my mother's womb, and naked shall I return
thither : the Lord gave and the Lord hath taken
away ; blessed be the name of the Lord." ' [2]

Some months after this she fell asleep in the
Lord, sound in mind and not suffering from any
malady, with her poor body still active. She made
you the heir of her poverty, or rather she made
the poor her heirs through you. In your arms
she closed her eyes, your lips received her last
breath ; you were weeping, but she smiled,[3] conscious of having lived a good life and hoping for a

465

entia vitae bonae et praemiis futurorum. Haec tibi,
Marcella venerabilis, et haec tibi, Principia filia, una
et brevi lucubratione dictavi non eloquii venustate sed
voluntate gratissimi in vos animi et Deo et legentibus
placere desiderans.

CXXVIII

AD PACATULAM

1. CAUSA difficilis parvulae scribere, quae non
intellegat, quid loquaris, cuius animam nescias, de
cuius periculose voluntate promittas, ut secundum
praeclari oratoris exordium spes magis in ea laudanda quam res sit. Quid enim horteris ad continentiam, quae placentas desiderat, quae in sinu
matris garrula voce balbuttit, cui dulciora sunt mella
quam verba? Audiat profunda apostoli, quae anilibus magis fabulis delectatur? Prophetarum αἰνίγματα
sentiat, quam tristior gerulae vultus exagitat?
Evangelii intellegat maiestatem, ad cuius fulgura
omnis mortalium hebebatur sensus? Ut parenti
subiciatur, horter, quae manu tenera ridentem
verberat matrem? Itaque Pacatula nostra hoc
epistulium post lectura suscipiat; interim modo
litterularum elementa cognoscat, iungat syllabas,

---

[1] Cicero, *De Republica*, fr. 5.

reward hereafter. This letter to you, revered Marcella, and to you, my daughter Principia, I have dictated in the wakeful hours of one short night. I have used no charms of eloquence; my one wish has been to show my gratitude to you both, my one desire to please both God and my readers.

LETTER CXXVIII

To Pacatula

Feminine training

Written A.D. 413

It is a difficult matter to write to a little girl who will not understand what you say, of whose mind you know nothing, and whose inclinations it would be dangerous to warrant. To use the words of a famous orator's preface—' in her case praise is based on expectation rather than accomplishment.' [1] How can you urge self-control on a child who still craves after cakes, who babbles softly in her mother's arms, and finds honey sweeter than words? Can she pay attention to the deep sayings of the apostle, when she takes more pleasure in old wives' tales than in them? Can she heed the dark riddles of the prophets when her nurse's frown is sufficient to frighten her? Can she appreciate the majesty of the Gospel when its lightnings dazzle all men's senses? How can I bid her to be obedient to her parents, when she beats her laughing mother with baby hand? So my little Pacatula must read this letter herself in days to come; and in the meantime learn her alphabet, spelling, grammar, and syntax. To get her to

discat nomina, verba consociet, atque, ut voce tinnula ista meditetur, proponatur ei crustula mulsi praemia et, quicquid gustu suave est, quod vernat in floribus, quod rutilat in gemmis, quod blanditur in pupis, acceptura festinet; interim et tenero temptet pollice fila deducere, rumpat saepe stamina, ut aliquando non rumpat, post laborem lusibus gestiat, de matris pendeat collo, rapiat oscula propinquorum, psalmos mercede decantet, amet, quod cogitur dicere, ut non opus sit, sed delectatio, non necessitas, sed voluntas.

2. Solent quaedam, cum futuram virginem sponderint, pulla tunica eam induere et furvo operire palliolo, auferre linteamina, nihil in collo, nihil in capite auri sinere re vera bono consilio, ne habere discat in tenero, quod postea deponere conpellatur. Aliis contra videtur. ' Quid enim,' aiunt, ' si ipsa non habuerit, habentes alias non videbit ? Φιλόκοσμον genus femineum est multasque etiam insignis pudicitiae, quamvis nulli virorum, tamen sibi scimus libenter ornari. Quin potius habendo satietur et cernat laudari alias, quae ista non habeant. Meliusque est, ut satiata contemnat, quam non habendo habere desideret.' Tale quid

repeat her lessons in her little shrill voice she must have a prize of a honey cake offered to her. She will do her work quickly if she is going to receive as reward some sweetmeat, or bright flower, or glittering bauble, or pretty doll. Meanwhile, too, she must learn to spin, drawing down the threads with tender fingers; and though at first she may often break the yarn, she will one day cease to do so. Then, when work is over, she may indulge in play, hanging on her mother's neck and snatching kisses from her relations. Let her be rewarded for singing the psalms aloud, so that she may love what she is forced to do, and it be not work but pleasure, not a matter of necessity but one of free-will.

Some mothers, when they have vowed a daughter to virginity, are wont to dress her in dark clothes, to wrap her up in a little black cloak, to take away her linen garments, and to let her wear no gold ornaments on her head and neck. In reality this method is a wise one, for the child does not then become accustomed to things which afterwards she must lay aside. Other mothers think differently. ' What is the use,' they say, ' of her not having pretty things? Will she not see other girls having them? The toilette appeals to all women, and we know that many whose chastity is beyond reproach take pleasure in dressing not for men but for themselves. Nay rather, let her grow sated with having, and let her see that others are praised, who have not. And it is better that she should despise through being sated, than that by not having she should want to have.' ' This,' they argue, ' is the plan that the Lord used with the people of Israel. They craved after the flesh-

et Israhelitico fecisse dominum populo, ut cupienti-
bus Aegyptias carnes usque ad nausiam et vomitum
praeberet examina corturnicum, multosque saeculi
prius homines facilius carere experta corporis
voluptate quam eos, qui a pueritia libidinem nesciant; ab aliis enim nota calcari, ab aliis ignota appeti,
illos vitare paenitendo suavitatis insidias, quas
fugerunt, hos carnis inlecebris et dulci titillatione
corporis blandientis, dum mella putant venena noxia
reperire; mel enim distillare labiis meretricis
mulieris, quod ad tempus inpinguet vescentium
fauces et postea amarius felle inveniatur. Unde et
in domini mel sacrificiis non offerri ceraque contempta, quae mellis hospitium est, oleum accendi in
templo Dei, quod de amaritudine exprimitur olivarum, pascha quoque cum amaritudinibus comedi
in ' azymis sinceritatis et veritatis,' quos qui habuerit,
in saeculo persecutionem sustinebit. Unde et propheta mystice cantat: ' Solus sedebam, quia amaritudine repletus sum.'

3. Quid igitur? Luxuriandum est in adulescentia,
ut postea luxuria fortius contemnatur? Absit,
inquiunt; ' Unusquisque,' enim, ' in qua vocatione
vocatus est, in ea permaneat.' ' Circumcisus quis,'
id est virgo, ' vocatus est: non adducat praeputium,'
hoc est non quaerat pellicias tunicas nuptiarum,
quibus Adam eiectus de paradiso virginitatis indutus

---

[1] Proverbs, v. 3.   [2] 1 Corinthians, v. 7, 8.
[3] Jeremiah, xv. 17 (Septuagint).
[4] 1 Corinthians, vii. 24, 18.   [5] Genesis, iii. 21.

pots of Egypt, and so He sent them swarms of
quails until they gorged themselves and were
sick. Many worldlings who have tried all the
pleasures of the senses find it easier to give them
up than do those who from youth have known
nothing of desire. The one tread underfoot what
they know, the others are attracted by what is
unknown. The one penitently avoid the snares of
pleasure from which they have escaped, the others
are allured by the delights of the body and the
titillation of the flesh until they find that what they
thought was honey is really deadly poison. For we
know that " the lips of a strange woman drop as an
honeycomb, which for the moment is as oil in the
eater's mouth, but is afterwards found more bitter
than gall." [1] Therefore it is that honey is never
offered in the sacrifices of the Lord, that the wax
in which honey is stored is held in contempt, and
that oil expressed from the bitter olive is burned in
God's temple. Moreover, the passover is eaten
with bitter herbs and with ' the unleavened bread of
sincerity and truth.' [2] Those who take thereof shall
suffer persecution in this world. Wherefore the
prophet sings symbolically: " I sat alone, because
I was filled with bitterness." ' [3]

Well, is wantonness to be encouraged in youth,
so that in later life it may be the more firmly
rejected? ' Heaven forbid! ' they say, for ' let
every man, wherein he is called, therein abide.'
' Is any called being circumcised—that is, a virgin—
let him not become uncircumcised ' [4]—that is, let
him not seek in marriage the ' coats of skins,' wherewith Adam clothed himself when he was expelled
from the paradise of virginity.[5] ' Is any called in

471

est. ' In praeputio quis vocatus est,' hoc est habens uxorem et matrimonio pelle circumdatus: non quaerat virginitatis et aeternae pudicitiae nuditatem, quam semel habere desivit, sed utatur vase suo in sanctificatione et pudicitia bibatque de fontibus suis et non quaerat cisternas lupanarium dissipatas, quae purissimas aquas pudicitiae continere non possunt. Unde et idem Paulus in eodem capitulo de virginitate et nuptiis disputans servos carnis vocat in matrimonio constitutos, liberos eos, qui absque ullo nuptiarum iugo tota domino serviunt libertate.

Quod loquimur, non in universum loquimur, sed in parte tractamus, nec de omnibus, sed de quibusdam dicimus. Ad utrumque sexum, non solum ad vas infirmius, noster sermo dirigitur. Virgo es: quid te mulieris delectat societas? Quid fragilem et sutilem ratem magnis committis fluctibus et grande periculum navigationis incertae securus ascendis? Nescis, quid desideres, et tamen sic ei iungeris, quasi aut ante desideraveris aut—ut levissime dicam —postea desideraturus sis. ' Sed ad ministerium iste sexus est aptior.' Elige ergo anum, elige deformem, elige probatae in domino continentiae. Quid te adulescentia, quid pulchra, quid luxuriosa delectat? Uteris balneis, cute nitida, rubicundus incedis, carnibus vesceris, affluis divitiis, pretiosa veste circumdaris et iuxta serpentem mortiferum

---

[1] 1 Thessalonians, iv. 4.   [2] Cf. 1 Corinthians, vii. 22.

uncircumcision '—that is, having a wife and covered
with the skin of matrimony: let him not seek the
nakedness of virginity and of that eternal chastity
which he has forfeited once for all. Let him rather
possess his vessel in sanctification and honour;[1] let
him drink from his own fountain and not seek in
brothels those broken cisterns which can never contain the pure water of chastity. Therefore Paul
again in the same chapter, when he is discussing the
question of virginity and marriage, calls those who
are married slaves of the flesh, but those who are
not under the yoke of wedlock freemen serving the
Lord in all liberty.[2]

What I am saying now I am not saying as a
universal truth; I am treating of but a part of this
subject, and am speaking of some men only, not of
all. Moreover, my words are addressed to both
sexes; not merely to the weaker vessel. You, my
brother, are a virgin: why then do you find pleasure
in a woman's society? Why do you risk your
frail, patched barque in heavy seas, and lightly face
the danger of a hazardous voyage? You know not
what you desire, and yet your union is as close as
though you either desired her before or, to put it
as lightly as possible, were going to desire her in
the future. ' Her sex,' you will say, ' is particularly
suitable for household service.' Choose an old
woman, then, chose one who is misshapen, choose
one of proved continence in the Lord. Why should
you take pleasure in a young girl, pretty and volup-
tuous? You frequent the baths, you walk abroad
with rosy cheeks and sleek skin, you eat meat and
you abound in riches, you dress in costly clothes;
and do you fancy that you can sleep safe beside a

securum dormire te credis? An non habitas in
eodem hospitio, in nocte dumtaxat? Ceterum totos
dies in huiusce modi confabulatione consumens
quare solus cum sola et non cum arbitris sedes?
Cum etiam ipse non pecces, aliis peccare videaris,
ut exemplo sis miseris, qui nominis tui auctoritate
delinquant. Tu quoque, virgo vel vidua, cur tam
longo viri sermone retineris? Cur cum solo relicta
non metuis? Saltim alvi te et vesicae cogat necessitas, ut exeas foras, ut deseras in hac re, cum quo
licentius quam cum germano, multo verecundius
egisti cum marito. Sed de scripturis sanctis aliquid
interrogas: interroga publice; audiant pedisequae,
audiant comites tuae. ' Omne, quod manifestatur,
lux est.' Bonus sermo secreta non quaerit, quin
potius delectatur laudibus suis et testimonio pluri-
morum. Magister egregius contemnit viros, fratres
despicit et in unius mulierculae secreta eruditione
desudat.

4. Declinavi parumper de via occasione aliorum
et, dum infantem Pacatulam instituo, immo enutrio,
multarum subito male mihi pacatarum bella suscepi.
Revertar ad propositum. Sexus femineus suo iunga-
tur sexui; nesciat, immo timeat cum pueris ludere.
Nullum inpudicum verbum noverit et, si forte in
tumultu familiae discurrentis aliquid turpe audierit,

---

[1] Ephesians, v. 13.
[2] *Pacatula, male pacatae :* a play on words.

deadly serpent? Do you say that you do not live
in the same house with her, at least at night? Well,
you spend whole days with her in this sort of conversation. Why do you sit alone with her and
without any witnesses? Why, even if you do not
sin yourself, do you seem to others to be sinning,
leading poor wretches into error by the authority of
your name? You also, my sister, whether you are
a virgin or a widow, why do you spend so many
hours in talking with a man? Why are you not
afraid to be left with him alone? The needs of
nature should at least compel you to go out sometimes and leave him. You were more modest with
your husband, and even with your brother you did
not behave with such freedom as this. You say
that you are asking him some question concerning
the Holy Scriptures. Ask it publicly; let your
maidservants and attendants hear it. 'Everything
that is made manifest is light.'[1] Honest words
seek no quiet retreat; nay rather, they take pleasure
in a crowd of witnesses, and in the praise which they
win. He must be a fine teacher who despises men,
scorns his brethren, and labours in secret to instruct
one weak woman!

Other people's conduct has made me wander
somewhat from my path, and in instructing, or rather
nursing, the baby Pacatula, I have in a moment
incurred the enmity of many ladies who will be hard
to pacify.[2] I will now return to my subject. Females
should only mix with their own sex; they should
not know how to play with boys, nay, they should
be afraid to do so. A girl should have no acquaint-
ance with lewd talk, and if amid the noisy bustle of
a household she hears an unclean word, she should

non intellegat. Matris nutum pro verbis ac moni-
tum pro imperio habeat. Amet ut parentem, subiciatur ut dominae, timeat ut magistram. Cum
autem virgunculam et rudem edentulam septimus
aetatis annus exceperit et coeperit erubescere, scire,
quid taceat, dubitare, quid dicat, discat memoriter
psalterium et usque ad annos pubertatis libros Salomonis, evangelia, apostolos ac prophetas sui cordis
thesaurum faciat. Nec liberius procedat ad publicum nec semper ecclesiarum quaerat celebritatem.
In cubiculo suo totas delicias habeat. Numquam
iuvenculos, numquam cincinnatos videat vocis dulce-
dine per aures animam vulnerantes. Puellarum
quoque lascivia repellatur, quae quanto licentius
adeunt, tanto difficilius evitantur et, quod didicerunt,
secreto docent inclusamque Danaen¹ vulgi sermonibus
violant. Sit ei magistra comes, paedagoga custos
non multo vino dedita, non iuxta apostolum otiosa
ac verbosa, sed sobria, gravis, lanifica et ea tantum
loquens, quae animum puellarem ad virtutem insti-
tuant. Ut autem aqua in areola digitum sequitur
praecedentem, ita aetas mollis et tenera in utramque
partem flexibilis est et, quocumque duxeris, trahitur.
Solent lascivi et comptuli iuvenes blandimentis,
affabilitate, munusculis aditum sibi per nutrices ad
alumnas quaerere et, cum clementer intraverint, de
scintillis incendia concitare paulatimque proficere ad

---

¹ Danaë was imprisoned by her father to keep her unmarried.
² 1 Timothy, v. 13.

not understand it. Her mother's nod should be as
good as speech, her mother's advice equivalent to
a command. She should love her as her parent,
obey her as her mistress, fear her as her teacher.
At first she will be but a shy little maid without all
her teeth, but as soon as she has reached her seventh
year and has learned to blush, knowing what she
should not say, and doubting what she should say,
she should commit the psalter to memory, and until
she is grown up she should make the books of
Solomon, the Gospels, the apostles, and the prophets
the treasure of her heart. She should not appear in
public too freely nor always seek a crowded church.
Let her find all her pleasure in her own room. She
must never look at foppish youths or curled cox-
combs, who wound the soul through the ears with
their honeyed talk. She must be protected also
from the wantonness of other girls. The more freedom of access such persons have, the more difficult
they are to shake off; the knowledge they have
acquired they impart in secret and corrupt a secluded
Danaë with vulgar gossip.[1] Let her teacher be her
companion, her attendant her guardian, and let her
be a woman not given to much wine, one who, as
the apostle says, is not idle nor a tattler,[2] but sober,
grave, skilled in spinning, saying only such words
as will train a girl's mind in virtue. For as water
follows behind a finger in the garden, so soft and
tender youth is pliable for good or evil, and can be
drawn wherever you guide it. Spruce gallants often
try the effect of soft words, affable manners, and
trifling gifts upon a nurse in order to win access to
her charge. After succeeding in a gentle approach,
they blow the spark into a flame and become

inpudentiam et nequaquam posse prohiberi illo in se versiculo conprobato: 'Aegre reprehendas, quod sinas consuescere.' Pudet dicere et tamen dicendum est: nobiles feminae nobiliores habiturae procos vilissimae condicionis hominibus et servulis copulantur ac sub nomine religionis et umbra continentiae interdum deserunt viros, Helenae sequuntur Alexandros nec Menelaos pertimescunt. Videntur haec, planguntur et non vindicantur, quia multitudo peccantium peccandi licentiam subministrat.

5. Pro nefas, orbis terrarum ruit et in nobis peccata non corruunt. Urbs inclita et Romani imperii caput uno hausta est incendio. Nulla regio, quae non exules eius habeat. In cineres ac favillas sacrae quondam ecclesiae conciderunt et tamen studemus avaritiae. Vivimus quasi altera die morituri et aedificamus quasi semper in hoc victuri saeculo. Auro parietes, auro laquearia, auro fulgent capita columnarum et nudus atque esuriens ante fores nostras in paupere Christus moritur. Legimus Aaron pontificem isse obviam furentibus flammis et accenso turibulo Dei iram cohibuisse; stetit inter mortem et vitam sacerdos maximus nec ultra vestigia eius ignis procedere ausus est. Moysi loquitur Deus: 'Dimitte me et delebo populum istum.' Quando dicit 'dimitte me,' ostendit se teneri, ne

---

[1] Publilius Syrus, *Sent.*, 180, already quoted, cf. p. 356.
[2] 2 Numbers, xvi. 46–48.   [3] Exodus, xxxii. 10.

gradually more and more shameless. It is then impossible to stop them, and they prove the truth of the line:

' You can hardly blame a habit which yourself you
    have allowed.'[1]

I am ashamed to say it, and yet I must; women of rank who could have suitors of even higher station cohabit with men of the lowest class and even with slaves. Sometimes in the name of religion and under a cloak of continence they desert their husbands, and like another Helen follow their Paris without any fear of Menelaus. Such things are seen and lamented, but they are not punished, for the multitude of sinners gives licence to sin.

Shame on us, the world is falling in ruins, but our sins still flourish. The glorious city that was the head of the Roman Empire has been engulfed in one terrific blaze. There is no part of the earth where exiles from Rome are not to be found. Churches once held sacred have fallen into dust and ashes, and still we set our hearts greedily on money. We live as though we were doomed to death on the morrow, but we build houses as though we were going to live for ever in this world. Our walls glitter with gold, gold gleams upon our ceilings and upon the capitals of our pillars: yet Christ is dying at our doors in the persons of His poor, naked and hungry. We read that Aaron the high priest faced the furious flames and with his burning censer stayed God's wrath. In the might of his priesthood he stood between life and death, and the fire did not dare to pass his feet.[2] God said to Moses: ' Let me alone and I will consume this people,'[3] showing by the words ' let me alone ' that he can be stayed

faciat, quod minatus est; Dei enim potentiam servi preces inpediebant. Quis, putas, ille sub caelo est, qui nunc irae Dei possit occurrere, qui obviare flammis et iuxta apostolum dicere : ' Optabam ego anathema esse pro fratribus meis '? Pereunt cum pastoribus greges, quia, sicut populus, sic sacerdos. Moyses conpassionis loquebatur affectu : ' Si dimittis populo huic, dimitte; sin autem, dele me de libro tuo.' Vult perire cum pereuntibus nec propria salute contentus est. ' Gloria ' quippe ' regis multitudo populi.'

His Pacatula est nata temporibus, inter haec crepunlia primam carpit aetatem ante lacrimas scitura quaun risum, prius fletum sensura quam gaudium. Necdum introitus, iam exitus; talem semper fuisse putat mundum. Nescit praeterita, fugit praesentia, futura desiderat. Quae ut tumultuario sermone dictarem et post neces amicorum luctumque perpetuum infanti senex longo postliminio scriberem, tua me, Gaudenti fratri, inpulit caritas; maluique pirum quam nihil omnino poscenti dare, quia in altero voluntas oppressa luctu, in altero amicitiae dissimulatio est.

---

[1] Romans, ix. 3. [2] Exodus, xxxii. 32.
[3] Proverbs, xiv. 28. [4] Pacatula's father.

from carrying out his threat; for the prayers of His
servant hindered God's power. Who, think you, is
there now under heaven able to face God's wrath,
to meet the flames, and to say with the apostle:
' I could wish that I myself were accursed for my
brethren ' ? [1] Flocks and shepherds perish together,
because the priest is now even as the people. Moses
in his compassionate love said: ' Yet now if thou
wilt, forgive their sin; and if not, blot me, I pray
thee, out of thy book.' [2] He wished to perish with
the perishing, and was not content to win salvation
for himself; for indeed ' in the multitude of people
is the king's honour.' [3]

Such are the times into which our Pacatula has
been born, these are the rattles of her infancy. She
will know of tears before laughter, she will feel
sorrow sooner than joy. Scarcely has she trod the
stage before the curtain falls. She thinks that the
world was ever thus, she knows not of the past, she
shrinks from the present, she fixes her desires on what
is to come. After mourning incessantly for my dead
friends I have at length recovered composure, and my
affection for you, brother Gaudentius, [4] has induced
me to dictate this rough discourse and in my old
age write a letter to an infant. I preferred to
answer your request inadequately rather than not
to answer it at all. As it is, my own inclinations
have been paralysed by my grief; in the other case
you might have doubted the sincerity of my friendship.

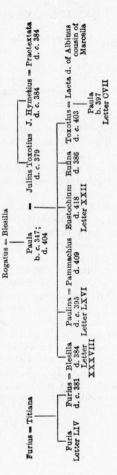

TABLE SHOWING THE RELATIONSHIP OF SOME OF JEROME'S CORRESPONDENTS AT ROME AND OF PERSONS REFERRED TO IN THE LETTERS IN THIS VOLUME

Furius = Titiana

Furia
Letter LIV

Furius = Blesilla
d. c. 381
Letter
XXXVIII

Rogatus = Blesilla

Paulina = Pammachius
d. c. 395   d. 409
Letter LXVI

Paula = Blesilla
b. c. 347;
d. 404

Julius Toxotius   J. Hymetius = Praetextata
d. c. 379   d. c. 384

Blesilla   Eustochium   Rufina   Toxotius = Laeta d. of Albinus
d. 394   d. 418   d. 386   d. c. 403   cousin of
Letter   Letter XXII   Marcella
XXXVIII

Paula
b. 397
Letter CVII

APPENDIX I

ON JEROME'S CORRESPONDENCE
WITH ROMAN WOMEN

JEROME had many friends at Rome whose names
occur frequently in his correspondence,[1] but some
of his most interesting letters are addressed to his
women friends in that city. Of these, those to
Marcella are the most numerous,[2] and she and her
circle had a great influence on the life and work
of Jerome from 382 onwards.

[1] Among such names are Pope Damasus (Introd., p. viii);
the senator Pammachius, a member of the Furian family
and a cousin of Marcella, whose friendship with Jerome dated
from their student days, when they had together attended
the lectures of Victorinus (cf. Letter LXVIII. 1, and preface
to Hosea); Pammachius was an ardent churchman and as
much interested in theological controversy as Jerome himself;
Oceanus, another layman, was connected with the great
Fabian family and was probably also a senator (cf. esp.
Letter LXVII.); his friendship with Jerome, like that of two
other Roman correspondents, Desiderius and Domnio (Letters
XLVII. and L.), seems to have begun after Jerome's second
visit in 382.

[2] About one-fifth of Jerome's letters are addressed to women,
most of them to Marcella. Besides the extant letters to her,
there was a collection which has been lost. Jerome says in
the catalogue of his works (*De viris ill.* 135) that he cannot
count his letters to Paula and Eustochium, as he wrote every
day. Most of these letters were impersonal and entirely
devoted to the interpretation of passages of scripture or
points of doctrine.

483

At the time of his second visit to Rome, in that
year, there was already established on the Aventine
Mount a community of women, presided over by
Albina and her daughter Marcella, leading a form
of conventual life, the first impulse to which at Rome
had been given many years before by Athanasius,[1]
the famous opponent of Arianism, who had been
driven from his see at Alexandria about 341 and spent
some years in exile at Rome. He and two Egyptian
monks who accompanied him, Isidore[2] and Ammon,
had been welcomed and entertained by Albina, a
noble and rich widow, at her palace on the Aventine,
and her daughter Marcella, though only a child,
was deeply impressed by the personalities of the
Eastern bishop and his companions and by their
tales of the wonderful lives led by the hermits and
cenobites, men and women, who already peopled
the deserts of Syria and Egypt. When Athanasius
departed he left with the child as a parting gift
his life of St. Antony, the study of which inspired
her with a deep admiration and desire for the monastic
life. Marcella grew up and married, but when her
husband died, after only seven months of married
life, leaving her a childless widow, she refused all
further offers of marriage, and, while continuing
to transact the necessary business connected with
her household and property, she henceforth tried
to lead, though staying at home with her mother,

---

[1] Letter CXXVII. 5.

[2] Probably the monk of Nitria referred to in Letter XXII.
33. When Paula visited Alexandria in 385 he was governor
of the pilgrims' hospice there; later he was involved in the
quarrel between Jerome and John, Bishop of Jerusalem, and
died, a very old man, in 403.

the kind of life for which she had always longed. She wore the plainest of clothes, fasted often and devoted most of her time to prayer and study of the scriptures. Gradually she collected around her a number of like-minded women, virgins and widows, who all lived together and looked up to Albina as a common mother. Among these was Marcellina, the sister of Ambrose, Bishop of Milan, who wrote for her his famous treatises on virginity. She had received the veil from Pope Liberius in 352, but lived for many years after with her own mother, and only after her death joined Marcella's community. Other members of the household, Sophronia, Felicita and another Marcella, are known to us by name only, but of Asella more is told. She was perhaps a sister [1] of Marcella, perhaps only a kinswoman, but when a mere child of ten she vowed herself to a life of virginity, and when her mother refused to buy her the plain brown dress worn by those dedicated to the religious life, Jerome tells us how the child sold her gold chain and bought the clothing for herself. Thenceforward she lived a life of fasting and of prayer, hardly seeing her own sister, only going out to visit the martyrs' shrines, and making for herself a hermitage in the midst of the busy life of Rome.[2] Such solitude and austerity were exceptional, and Marcella herself kept in touch with the world and welcomed as visitors at her home women whose tastes and interests were the same as her own. One of these friends was Lea,[3] a widow, who was at the head of another community

Letter XLV. 7.   [2] Letter XXIV.
[3] Cf. Letter XXIII.

485

of women; others, such as Titiana and her daughter Furia, were still living their normal life in the Roman society of the day.[1] Another member of the circle was Fabiola, who had married young and unhappily, and after divorcing her first husband had married again. Strictly speaking the Church did not recognize such a union, but legally it was valid, and no slur seems to have rested upon her. After her second husband's death, however, Fabiola's conscience troubled her for having contracted the marriage, and she astounded the world of Rome by publicly appearing as a penitent to expiate the sin of her second marriage. After receiving absolution she devoted her life and fortune to the care of the sick and poor, not only at Rome, but throughout Italy.[2]

But of all Marcella's circle, the most famous was her kinswoman the rich patrician Paula.[3] Her parents, Rogatus and Blesilla, were probably both

[1] Letter LIV.

[2] Cf. Letter LXXVII. The date of this public penance is uncertain. Jerome's account seems to make it clear that it took place before her visit to Palestine in 394, and it is tempting to place it during, or soon after, Jerome's stay in Rome (382–5) and to ascribe it to his influence. The description of the ceremony suggests the public act of penance which Bishop Ambrose exacted from the Emperor Theodosius in 392 and it may have been inspired by that. M. Thierry (*Life of S. Jerome*, II. p. 20 ff.) thinks it took place after Fabiola's visit to Palestine and connects it with a letter (LV.) written by Jerome to the priest Amandus in 394 in answer to a query about the validity of such a marriage as Fabiola's.

[3] For Paula and her family cf. Gibbon, Chs. XXXI. and XXXVII.: also Letter CVIII. 1. Gracchorum stirps, suboles scipionum, Pauli heres, cuius vocabulum trahit, maeciae Papiriae, matris Africani, vera et germana progenies.

APPENDIX I

Christians, but her husband Toxotius had been a pagan.[1] The marriage was apparently a very happy one in spite of the difference of religion, and during his lifetime she had led the usual life of a Roman matron of high rank, but after his death in 379 she tried to find consolation in a life of the strictest asceticism, and she spent so much money on charity that she was reproached for squandering her children's inheritance.[2] Jerome draws a vivid picture of the austerities which she practised and contrasts them with her previous life of luxury,[3] but she still maintained her household on a scale that enabled her to offer hospitality to Bishop Epiphanius during his stay in Rome in 382.[4]

The family life of Paula illustrates the struggle between Christianity and paganism in the Roman society of the day.[5] Her four daughters were all Christians. Blesilla, the eldest of them, had married Furius, a son of the devout Titiana, and had been left a widow before she was twenty, but as yet she was indifferent to her religion and enjoyed to the full the life of gay luxury which her wealth and position offered to her. Julia or Eustochium, the third daughter, had wished from a child to take the veil and much of her time had been spent with

[1] Cf. Letter CVIII. 3 ff.
[2] Letter CVIII. 5.
[3] Letter CVIII. 4. Cf. Letter CVIII. 15.
[4] Cf. Letter CVIII. 6.
[5] In Marcella's own family there was a similar division; Albina had been a Christian for many years, but her kinsman Albinus was not only a pagan, but a pontiff of Jupiter, though his wife and daughter were both Christians, and it was only years later that his Christian grandchild finally converted the old man (Letter CVII. 1–4).

487

Marcella, whose instruction and example had confirmed her natural bent. Paula sympathised with
this desire, but it was strongly opposed by the
child's uncle Hymetius, her father's brother. He
had been a favourite of the Emperor Julian and he
and his wife Praetextata held fast to the old religion,
and their influence and authority kept Paula's
only son, the young Toxotius, at this time a child
of nine or ten, from becoming a Christian. They
invited Eustochium to visit them, and by dressing
her in fine clothes and giving her a glimpse of the
social life in which she would naturally take part,
they tried to detach her from opinions which to them
seemed fanatical and unnatural. To modern minds
the scheme seems but a natural attempt to let the
child—she was only fourteen or fifteen—see something of the world which she was so determined to
abjure, but Jerome, writing of the incident twenty
years later, exults in its failure and denounced the
wickedness of the worldly uncle and aunt, whose
death, which occurred soon after, he ascribes to the
direct judgment of Heaven for this attempt to turn
the young virgin from her chosen path.[1]

Marcella and her circle were not only all wealthy
and well born, but they were also women of cultivated
intellect, and the visit of the Eastern bishops [2] with
whom Jerome came to Rome in 382 was an event
of great interest to them. Jerome at first, as he
tells us himself, avoided the society of women, but
Marcella and her friends longed to meet and to be

[1] Letter CVII. 5.
[2] Paulinus of Antioch (cf. Introd., p. viii) and Epiphanius
of Salamis in Cyprus. Cf. Letter CVIII. 6.

taught by one whose reputation for sanctity and learning stood so high. The letters written from his hermitage had been circulated in the West as well as in the East, and like the treatises of Ambrose of Milan and of Pope Damasus [1] had formed part of the reading of Marcella's circle. Many years later Jerome tells us [2] how Fabiola knew by heart and recited to him the letter in praise of the ascetic life which he had written to his friend Heliodorus in 374. He could not refuse to teach such eager disciples, and in response to Marcella's earnest request he gave a series of lectures and readings to her and her friends and finally became their director and spiritual guide.[3] He found his pupils intelligent and sympathetic and intensely interested in all questions of scriptural interpretation and theological controversy. Probably they all knew Greek and Paula and her daughters studied Hebrew as well,[4] so as to be able to help him in his great work of translating the Bible into the vulgar tongue. Long letters to Marcella, Paula and others [5] explain passages of scripture or points of doctrine and some essays on Jewish observances originated in the eager questions of Fabiola.[6] Not only many of Jerome's letters but some of his most important treatises were inspired by Marcella and her friends. During his stay in Rome a certain Helvidius, a lay-

---

[1] Cf. p. 102 and note 3.

[2] Letter LXXVII. 9, written 399.

[3] Cf. esp. Letter XXX. 14 (to Paula), saluta reliquum castitatis chorum et domesticam tuam ecclesiam.

Letters XXXIX. and CVIII.

[5] E.g. Letters XXXIII. and XXXIV., also LXIV.

[6] Letters LXIV. and LXXVIII., and p. 329, note.

man, wrote an attack on the celibate life, extolled
by Jerome as the highest, placing the estate of
marriage above it.[1] Such an attack struck at the
root of the life of celibacy which Marcella and her
friends were leading and trying to induce others
to lead, and it was probably in response to their
entreaties that he wrote in 383 his treatise against
Helvidius. It was certainly at Marcella's request
that ten years later Jerome, from his monastery
at Bethlehem, denounced the similar teaching of
the renegade monk Jovinian, who again made an
attempt to discredit the celibate life which Jerome
had done so much to encourage, and with such
success that by that time, as he exultantly writes,
Italy was full of nunneries and the number of monks
in Rome was past counting.[2]

But interesting as these general treatises and
letters are, it is in the more personal letters on life
and conduct that the influence of Jerome's ardent
and magnetic personality on his disciples is best
seen. That influence was especially strong on
Paula and her family. He confirmed the young
Eustochium, Paula's third daughter, in her desire
to take the veil,[3] and his famous letter to her in
praise of virginity, much of which reads strangely
when we remember that it was addressed to a child
of fourteen or fifteen, was really intended for a larger
public and was a defence of the celibate life and
an attack on its opponents. The marriage of Paulina,
Paula's second daughter, to his friend the senator

---

[1] Cf. esp. Letter XXIV. 1.
[2] Letter CXXVII. 8. Cf. also Palladius de Opiano.
[3] Letter XXII., written in 384.

Pammachius, a man of more than twice her age, was approved by him, but it was on the life of Paula herself and her eldest daughter Blesilla that his influence was strongest.

Ever since the visit of Epiphanius to her house in 382,[1] Paula had longed to abandon her life in Rome and to visit the Holy Land and the famous solitaries of Egypt and the East, and there to adopt a conventual life. Such a desire, involving, as it did, the abandonment of her children, two of whom were still quite young, and the loss to them of much of their inheritance, naturally aroused strong opposition among Paula's family and friends, part of which was directed against Jerome, to whose influence it was ascribed; and just at this time Pope Damasus, his friend and patron, died. Siricius, his successor, was jealous of his predecessor's friend, and perhaps frightened by the unpopularity which his uncompromising principles had aroused—his advocacy of asceticism, his exaltation of monastic as opposed to family life, and the violence of his attacks on those who disagreed with him. This unpopularity was brought to a head by the death of Blesilla towards the end of the year 384, shortly after that of the Pope. For nearly two years Paula and Jerome, her spiritual director, had striven to turn the gay young widow to a more serious way of life, but it was only after a dangerous illness in the summer of 384 that Blesilla was converted and threw herself into a life of self-denial and study with the same ardour with which she had previously pursued a life of pleasure. Her health was delicate and a few

[1] Letter CVIII. 6.

months later she died. The populace ascribed her illness to the fasting and asceticism advocated by Jerome, and clamoured for the expulsion of the monk [1] whose austere teaching was held responsible for her death.[2] Darker accusations still were brought against him, and it was openly declared that the friendship between him and the dead girl's mother was only the cloak for a more guilty relation.[3] Jerome exposed the lie and the slanderer confessed his falsehood, but no doubt an atmosphere of suspicion remained, and as he now no longer had the Pope's friendship and protection, Jerome decided to leave Rome. He embarked at Ostia with his brother Paulinus and his friend the priest Vincentius in August 385, and wrote thence a letter of farewell to his women friends and disciples, which he addressed, not to Paula or Marcella, but to the virgin Asella,[4] perhaps because she, absorbed in a life of prayer and contemplation, was unaffected by the atmosphere of slander and suspicion which was surrounding him.

A few months after Jerome's departure, Paula finally made up her mind to start on her long-wished-for journey to the East. The storm of anger and disapproval which the death of Blesilla and her friendship with Jerome had brought upon her, added to her natural grief at the loss of her child, had

[1] Cf. Letter XXXIX. 6.

[2] Letters XXXVIII. and XXXIX.

[3] Cf. Letter XLV. 2 where Jerome alludes somewhat obscurely to this incident. Who the accuser was is unknown. Apparently legal proceedings were taken against him for the slander, and the mention of torture suggests that he was a slave.

[4] Letter XLV.

reduced her to a condition of deep depression and despair from which Jerome had tried in vain to rouse her,[1] and he himself seems to have been sincerely fond of his young disciple, whose memory, he promised, should be kept alive wherever his works were read.[2] Paula and Eustochium and the band of widows and virgins who went with them were escorted to the port of embarkation by a crowd of friends and relations, hoping, we may think, even to the last to dissuade them from the journey.[3] Jerome movingly describes how the young Toxotius stood on the shore stretching out his arms to his mother as he implored her to return, and how her youngest daughter vainly begged her to stop till she should be settled in marriage. But no family ties could now keep her back from her pilgrimage.

Such journeys were not without precedent; about thirteen years before, Melania, a wealthy widow of Spanish origin, had left Rome, abandoning her home there and her only child, to travel in the East and establish a convent on the Mount of Olives; associated with her on her travels and in her life at Jerusalem was Rufinus, the friend of Jerome's youth, and later his bitter enemy. Jerome was perhaps at Rome when Melania thus exiled herself, though there is no certain evidence [4] that he knew her or had influenced her conduct, but he no doubt

[1] Letter XXXIX., written to Paula on the death of Blesilla.

[2] *Op. cit.* section 7.

[3] Letter CVIII.

[4] The fact that Melania's freedman Hylas was one of the band of ascetics with Jerome at Aquileia, and accompanied him to Syria, suggests that he knew Melania when in Rome as a student.

had used this precedent to confirm Paula in her
purpose, for in his eyes, as his letters prove,[1] no
home ties or duties should prevail once the vocation
for the religious life had been felt. There still
exists a guide written for the assistance of such
pilgrims as Paula and Melania which gave a list of
inns and hospices and the best route to follow,[2]
and perhaps aided by some such itinerary, Paula
and her companions made their way through the
Aegaean islands to Salamis in Cyprus, where they
stayed with the venerable Bishop Epiphanius, and
thence to Antioch, where they met Jerome and his
monks, who accompanied them to Egypt, where
the monk Isidore entertained them, and afterwards
to Jerusalem. Here they probably stayed at the
monasteries on the Mount of Olives with Jerome's
old friend Rufinus and Melania, whose experiences
had been so like Paula's own life.[3] But this is not
expressly told us; when Jerome wrote the history
of these travels,[4] the bitterness of theological con-

[1] Cf. esp. Letter XIV.

[2] *Itinerarium a Bordigala Hierusalem usque*, written 333 A.D.
(ed. Tobler and Molinier, Geneva, 1879 and by P. Geyer in
Itinera Hierosolymitana, Vienna, 1898).

[3] It was the death of her husband and two of her children
which had led Melania to leave her home in Rome and her
only remaining child and to go on a pilgrimage to the East,
where she lived for nearly a quarter of a century. Jerome
couples the names of the two women together in a letter
written in 385 (Letter XLV. 4 and 5), but the most striking
parallels in their lives were then still in the future—Paula's
journey to the East, her convent at Bethlehem beside Jerome's
monastery, like Melania's at Jerusalem beside the monastery
of Rufinus. Melania, however, revisited Rome in 397 and
lived there with her son Publicola and his family for eleven
years, ultimately persuading her grand-daughter the younger
Melania and her husband Pinianus to return with her to the East.

[4] Letter CVIII., *circ.* 404.

troversy had estranged him for ever from the friend
of his youth. Finally, the pilgrims came to Bethlehem, where they settled, and in the monasteries
built there Jerome carried on his literary work,
Paula and Eustochium acting as his secretaries, and
kept up a constant correspondence, not only with his
disciples in Rome, but with friends all over the world.
To Marcella, especially, he wrote constantly, and
when her mother died, Paula and Eustochium
urged her to join them in Palestine.[1] She, however,
had no wish to leave Rome and continued to live her
life there, somewhat more austere and more definitely
conventual after the loss of her mother, till she
died after the sack of Rome by Alaric in 410, which
Jerome graphically describes in a letter in praise of
her life, written to the virgin Principia who had
taken Eustochium's place as Marcella's constant
companion.[2] Fabiola, however, came to visit her
friends at Bethlehem, and under the escort of her
kinsman Oceanus, Jerome's friend and correspondent,
made a pilgrimage through the Holy Land and even
thought of settling down there for the rest of her
life, but the threatened invasion of the Huns in
394, the danger of which was so imminent that the
monks and nuns of Bethlehem left their monasteries
and took refuge on the sea-coast, caused her to
abandon this idea and she returned to Rome.[3]

Jerome's letters show how close a connection
the solitaries of Bethlehem kept up with their
Roman friends, and he still acted as a spiritual
director to his disciples, exhorting one against a

[1] Letter XLVI., 386 A.D.
[2] Letter CXXVII. Cf. Letter LXV.
[3] Letter LXXVII. 7 and 8.

second marriage,[1] instructing others on the education
and upbringing of their children,[2] condoling with
others on the loss of friends or relations.[3]

Paula too kept in close touch with her children
and felt deeply the successive loss of those whom
she had left in Rome. Her youngest daughter
Rufina had died a year or two after her mother's
departure;[4] and in 394 her second daughter Paulina
died. Pammachius, heartbroken at the death of
his young wife, gave away all her fortune to the
poor and himself assumed the habit of a monk;
though he continued to take his seat in the senate
and fulfil his public duties, he devoted his life to
the care of the poor and joined with Fabiola, till
her death in 399, in maintaining a hostel for pilgrims
at Ostia.[5] The marriage of Toxotius brought
Paula some comfort. Soon after her departure he
became a Christian, and afterwards married Laeta,
a devout Christian, though her father Albinus,
Marcella's cousin, was a pagan. There was one
child of this marriage, a second Paula who was
dedicated to the cloister from her birth. Her
mother asked Jerome for advice on her education;[6]
and it was by his counsel that she was sent to
Bethlehem to be brought up in the convent there.
But before this her father and grandmother were
both dead. The peace of Paula's last years had
been disturbed, not only by the death of her children,
one after the other, and by her own ill-health caused

[1] Letter LIV.
[2] Letters CVII. and CXXVIII.
[3] Letters LXVI. and LXXVII.
[4] Letter CVIII.
[5] Cf. Letters LXVI. and LXXVII. 10.   [6] Letter CVII.

by the austerities which she practised, but also by the theological disputes which had alienated Jerome from his early friend Rufinus and which caused dissension throughout the Christian world.

After Paula's death in 404 Eustochium took over the government of the nunnery, and continued to work as Jerome's secretary; his correspondence was as active as ever—with Rome, Gaul, Spain and Africa. In 418 Eustochium too died and was succeeded by her niece the younger Paula, and it was she who nursed the aged Jerome in his last illness in the following year.

Note.—In addition to the works referred to, pp. xv–xvi, an interesting account of Jerome's circle in Rome is given in Mrs. Oliphant's "Makers of Modern Rome," Chs. I.-VI., and in Lady Herbert's "Wives and Mothers in the Olden Time" (Bentley, 1885); and especially in Copland Perry's "Sancta Paula" (London, 1902).

APPENDIX II

JEROME AND ORIGENISM

" THE tempest " [1] which disturbed the earlier years of Jerome's monastic life in Bethlehem arose from the revival of Origenism [2] in the East [3] and the attempt to introduce its doctrines in the West; the theological controversy led to personal quarrels with his old friend and fellow-student Rufinus [4] and with John, Bishop of Jerusalem,[5] the bitterness of which was reflected in many references to them in his later letters.[6]

Jerome in his earlier years had been an enthusiastic admirer of Origen; he had translated some of

[1] Letter CXXVII. 9; cf. LXXVII. 8.

[2] The following were the chief points of Origen's teaching which were deemed heretical : the pre-existence of soul; the denial of the resurrection of the body; the limitation of eternal punishment; and the possibility of salvation even for the devil. Cf. Letter LI. Epiphanius to John of Jerusalem, translated by Jerome.

[3] Origen's works had always been much admired in his native country, Egypt, and many of the monks there were Origenists.

[4] Rufinus (of Aquileia) (c. 344–410) was a member of Jerome's first band of ascetics at Aquileia; when this broke up he accompanied Melania to Palestine and founded, with her, monastic establishments on the Mount of Olives, where he carried on literary and educational work. He was still on friendly terms with Jerome in 392.

[5] Since 385.

[6] In this volume cf. pp. 431, 461, note 4.

APPENDIX II

Origen's works and brought them to the knowledge of Pope Damasus, writing of them with unqualified approval.[1] It was perhaps the consciousness of this which induced Jerome to defend his own orthodoxy fiercely against a certain Aterbius, who visited Palestine in 395 and charged him, together with Rufinus and Bishop John, of being adherents of Origenism. The vehemence of his defence alienated him from his friend and from his bishop, who declined to answer the charge which, in their opinion, Aterbius had no authority to bring against them. When, therefore, in the following year, the aged bishop of Salamis, Epiphanius, who was the leader of the movement against Origenism, visited Jerusalem and denounced the errors of the heresy in Bishop John's own church, Rufinus sided with John in the ensuing controversy between the bishops, while Jerome and his monks took the side of Epiphanius.[2]

John appealed to Theophilus, the Patriarch of Alexandria, who at first sided with the Origenists; the monasteries at Bethlehem were practically placed under an interdict, and the bishop even tried to induce Rufinus,[3] the powerful minister of Theodosius, to banish Jerome from Palestine. This danger, however, passed away with the assassination of Rufinus at the end of 395, and soon after Theophilus changed his views and made peace with Jerome, whom he reconciled also with John. They worked together

[1] Cf. the preface to his translation of Origen's two homilies on the Song of Songs (383); also Letter XXXIII. written to Paula in 384. As late as 392 he wrote of Origen in terms of the highest admiration (Preface to Micah).

[2] The particulars of this controversy are given in Jerome's treatise " against John of Jerusalem " and in Letter LI.

[3] To be distinguished from Jerome's friend, p. 1, note 4.

against the teachings of Origenism[1] and finally
secured its condemnation in the East.[2]

While Jerome's dispute with Bishop John was still
at its height, Rufinus (of Aquileia) decided to leave
Palestine and return with Melania to Italy; before
his departure he was solemnly reconciled to Jerome
at Easter 397, perhaps through the intervention of
Melania.[3]

The reconciliation between Jerome and Rufinus
was probably sincere, but it did not stand the test of
a further controversy on Origenism which arose in
Italy. On his arrival there Rufinus was strongly
urged to translate the speculative works of Origen
into Latin by a certain Macarius of Pinetum, a
Roman of good position, perhaps a senator.[4] The
recrudescence of Origenism in the East had aroused
interest in his works all over the Christian world, and
in spite of Jerome's translations, the Western Church
seems to have known little about him.[5] Rufinus,
who always remained his fervent admirer, was glad
of the opportunity to make his works known, and
translated two books of the *De Principiis*, Origen's
most controversial work, softening down or altering
many passages which had been condemned as heretical, on the ground that these were not in the original

[1] Jerome translated the encyclicals of Theophilus into
Latin (Letters LXXXV., LXXXVI. and LXXXIX.). Letter
CXXVII. alludes to this.

[2] In A.D. 400 Letters XC., XCI. and XCII.

[3] Jerome, *Apol.* 111. 33. For Melania's part in it cf.
Palladius, *Hist. Laus.*, ch. 1.

[4] Cf. p. 457 and Letter LXXX. (from Rufinus to Macarius).

[5] Pope Anastasius, when he condemned Origen's works as
heretical, stated that he had never read them (Letter to John
of Jerusalem).

work.[1] He published this work in the spring of 398,
and added a preface in which he clearly referred to
Jerome, though not by name, speaking of him in
terms of the highest praise as a translator and
admirer of Origen.[2] Such a description, though true
of Jerome's opinions a few years before, was mani-
festly misleading in view of his attitude during the
recent controversy in Palestine, and was strongly
resented by Jerome's friends in Rome, especially
Pammachius, Oceanus and Marcella, who sent a copy
of Rufinus' work to Bethlehem.[3] Jerome replied by
making a literal translation of the first two books of
the *De Principiis* and sending it to Pammachius at
Rome with a letter defending his own orthodoxy,[4]
with which he enclosed a personal and not unfriendly
letter to Rufinus.[5] This letter, however, which
might have averted an open breach, never reached
Rufinus. When it got to Rome, circumstances there
had changed; the pope Siricius, never favourably
disposed to Jerome and his circle, was dead,[6] and his
successor. Anastasius, was under the influence of
Jerome's friends; after considerable controversy,
which seems to show that the teachings of Origen
had made some headway in the West, Origenism
was formally condemned as heretical in 400.[7] Rufinus
had left Rome on the death of Siricius and settled
first at Milan and then at Aquileia, where he lived on

[1] Such licence in translators was not uncommon and is
defended by Jerome (by whose example Rufinus justifies his
own methods) in Letters LVII., LXI. and LXVI.

[2] Letter LXXX.   [3] Letter LXXXIII.

[4] Letter LXXXIV.   [5] Letter LXXXI.

[6] A.D. 398.

[7] Letter XCV. In Letter CXXVII. 9 and 10, Jerome
ascribes this chiefly to Marcella.

friendly terms with Jerome's friend, Bishop Chromatius, for about ten years. It was there that he read the attack which Jerome had made on him in the letter sent to Pammachius, who seems to have suppressed the personal letter addressed to Rufinus himself.[1] A bitter controversy ensued in consequence between Jerome and Rufinus.[2] Their friends tried in vain to reconcile them [3]; and Jerome's anger against his former friend did not end even with the latter's death.[4]

[1] In *Apol*. 111. 28, Jerome defends this action of Pammachius.

[2] Jerome, *Apology*, and Rufinus, *Apology*.

[3] Chromatius of Aquileia; Augustine also deplored the quarrel (CX. 6). Melania was included in Jerome's wrath (Letter CXXXIII. 3).

[4] A.D. 410. Cf. the preface to the commentary on Ezekiel (written 410-14) and to Jeremiah (written 417-19); also Letter CXXV. (p. 431).

INDEX OF PROPER NAMES

A

AARON, 209, 319, 479
Abel, 151
Abigail, 191
Abisama, 401
Abishag, 191, 195, 199
Abraham, 55, 93, 97, 151, 159, 191, 269, 271, 279, 333, 439
Abundantius, 301
Adam, 269, 347, 471
Aegaean sea, 494
Aelius Donatus. Cf. Donatus.
Aemilian family, viii
Aeneas, 338
Africa, 496
Africanus, 486
Ahab, 319
Ahasuerus, 421
Alans, 301
Alaric, 438, 439
Albina (mother of Marcella), 187, 441, 449, 484, 485, 487
Albinus, Pontiff of Jupiter, 338, 339, 487, 496
Alexander, 147
Alexander the Great, 349; gates of (i.e. Caspian Gates), 329
Alexandria, 308, 343, 448, 484, 499
Alps, 5, 301
Altinum, xiv, 188, 282, 283, 295
Amalek, 305
Amandus, 486
Ambrose (bishop of Milan 374–397), 17, 102, 103, 170, 485, 486, 489
Ambrose (a friend of Origen), 171
Ammon (son of Noah), 73, 79
Ammon (an Egyptian monk), 484
Amos, 47, 167
Ananias, 219, 279
Anastasius (Pope 398–402), 459, 500, 501

Anaxagoras, 273
Anna, 27, 157, 259, 263, 443
Antimus, 119
Antioch, vii, viii, xii, 2, 16, 303, 308, 331, 453, 488, 494
Antony, St. (born in Egypt c. 250, after living as a hermit for many years he left his solitude to become the founder of monasticism in N. Egypt), 143, 449, 484
Aquileia, vii, 2, 23, 27, 308, 493, 498–502
Arabia, 303, 400
Arcadians, 303
Arcadius (emperor of the East 395–408), 300
Argus, 245
Arian (heresy), 17, 27, 299, 449, 484
Aristotle, 53, 349
Armenians, 343
Arnobius, 287
Asella, 178, 179, 187, 485, 492
Aser (tribe of), 259, 443
Asia, 405
Assa, 301
Assyria, Assyrians, 105, 167, 305
Assyrian king, 61
Atellan (farces), 190, 191
Aterbius, 499
Athanasius (Patriarch of Alexandria and the principal opponent of Arianism, d. 373), 365, 448, 449, 484
Athens, Athenians, Attic, 173, 303, 307, 405
Atlantic Ocean, 271
Attalus (king of Pergamum), 21
Attila, 439
Aufidii, 275
Augiensis (Turicensis), xv
Augustine (the Great; Bishop of Hippo, d. 432), xii, xiv, 502

503

INDEX OF PROPER NAMES

Auxentius (Bishop of Milan), 17
Aventine, viii, 439, 484
Azov, sea of, 329

B

Babylon, 23, 63, 67, 186, 187, 247, 341, 353, 371
Babylonian, 365
Bacchus, 247
Balaam, 327
Barak, 261
Barnabas, 461
Basil, St., 412
Basle, xv
Bathsheba, 77, 191
Beelzebub, 167
Belial, 125
Belshazzar, 105
Benedictine (edition), xv
Benjamin, 158, 159, 279
Berolinensis, xv
Bessians (tribe of), 273
Bethlehem, ix–xii, 178, 227, 255, 264, 313, 330, 338, 490, 494, 495, 496, 499, 501
Bezaleel, 291
Black Sea, 337
Blesilla (d. of Paula), viii, ix, 83, 158, 159, 161, 167, 231, 311, 487, 490, 491, 492
Blesilla (mother of Paula), 486
Bonosus, vii, 21, 23
Brahmans, 257
Britain, 271, 335
Bruti, 275
Burdigala (Bordeaux), 493

C

Caesar, 317. Cf. Nero.
Camillus (Furius), 229, 233, 337
Canaan, 135
Cannae, 19
Canticles, xi
Capitol, 341
Cappadocian, 210
Caracalla (emperor), 314
Carmelite, 415
Carneades, 273
Carthage, 102
Caspian, 328
Cato, Catos, 195, 431
Caucasus, 303, 329

Cenobites, 137
Cerealis, 441, 443
Ceres, 247, 363
Chalcis (desert of), vii, 18
Chaldaean, xi, 55, 65, 167, 411
Charybdis, 39, 401
Chimaera, 433
Chremes, 230, 231
Chromatius (Bishop of Aquileia), 19, 27, 309, 502
Chronicle (of Eusebius), xii
Chronicles (the), 305, 319
Cicero, Ciceronian, xii, xiii, 125, 127, 213, 233, 273, 275, 419
Cleanthes, 195
Clitomachus, 273
Coloniensis, xv
Constantinople, 8, 298, 301, 308
Constantius (Emperor), 398, 399
Corinthians, 153, 215, 303, 339
Cornelia, 233
Cornelius (Centurion), 47, 281, 401
Crantor, 273
Crassi, Crassus, 25, 275
Croesus, 287, 415, 447
Cybele, 175, 361
Cydnus, 303
Cyprian (Bishop of Carthage, fl. 258), 102, 103, 287, 365
Cyprus, 453, 488, 494

D

Dacia, 301
Dalilah, 77
Dalmatia, vii, 19, 301, 438
Dalmatian Islands, 283
Damasus (Pope 366–384), viii, 102, 103, 183, 483, 489, 491, 499
Danae, 476, 477
Daniel, xi, 13, 47, 75, 113, 247
Dardania, 301
Darius, 287, 329
David, 47, 51, 77, 191, 203, 217, 233, 275, 319
Deborah, 261
Deiphobus, 168
Democritus, 195, 273
Demosthenes, 213
Desiderius, 483
Didymus, xii, 170
Dinah, 109, 353
Diogenes, 273
Diomede, 120, 121

504

INDEX OF PROPER NAMES

Dives, 97
Domitius, 209
Domnio, 483
Donatus, Aelius, vii

E

Ecclesiastes, xi
Egypt, Egyptians, 21, 53, 77, 107, 135,
    169, 187, 273, 283, 303, 322, 327,
    329, 335, 343, 359, 419, 471, 484,
    491, 494, 498
Eli, 353
Elijah, 59, 73, 91, 99, 133, 259, 319
Elis, 290
Elisha, 59, 73, 99
Ennius, 297, 449, 450
Epaphras, 277
Ephesians, xi
Epicurus, 213
Epiphanius (Bishop of Salamis in
    Cyprus), 453, 487, 488, 491, 494, 498,
    499
Epirus, 301
Erasmus, xv
Esau, 279, 423
Essenes, 141
Esther (roll of), 365
Ethiopia, 57, 343
Ethiopians, 67, 329
Etna, 243
Etruscan Sea, 325
Eugenius, 298, 301
Euphrates, 23, 167, 303
Euripides, 213
Europe, ix
Eusebius (Bishop of Caesarea), xii
Eusebius (brother of Chromatius), 19,
    27, 308
Eusebius (father of Jerome), vii
Eusebius Hieronymus. Cf. Jerome.
Eustochium (Eustochia), viii–x, 53,
    57, 111, 178, 187, 227, 231, 232, 338,
    351, 367, 450, 451, 483, 487, 488, 490,
    492, 494–496
Euxine (Black Sea), 3, 337
Evagrius, 16, 17, 19
Eve, 93, 99
Evilat, 403
Exuperius (Bishop of Toulouse), 228,
    249, 437
Ezekiel, x, xi, 77, 167, 239, 502
Ezra, 187, 365

F

Fabiola, 308–337, 486, 489, 495
Fabius (Q. Fabius Maximus), 313
Fabius (Q. Fabius Pictor), 291
Felicitas, 187, 485
Felix.   Cf. Macarius.
Felix (Minucius), 287
Freemantle (Canon), xi, xv
Fronto, 419
Furia (d. of Titiana), 228, 229, 232,
    486
Furius.   Cf. Camillus.
Furius (son of Titiana), 487

G

Gabriel, 147, 355
Gainas, 300
Galatians, xi
Galen, 245
Galli (the), 275
Gallius, Quintus, 213
Ganges, 403
Gaudentius, 481
Gaul, xi, 299, 371–372, 405, 496
Gauls (the), 337
Gaza, 342, 343
Genesis, 197
Gennesaret (Lake), 411
Getae, 343
Gotha, xv
Gothic (War), 299
Goths, vii, 273, 301, 438
Gracchi, 232, 235, 349
Gracchorum stirps (of Paula), 486
Gracchus (Prefect of Rome), 341
Gratian, 298, 299
Greek, xi, 143, 165, 195, 273, 303, 349,
    405, 421, 489
Gregory Nazianzen, viii, 211
Gregory of Nyssa, viii
Gymnosophists, 357

H

Habakkuk, 61, 75
Halys (River), 303
Haman, 101
Hannah, 345, 369, 411
Hannibal, 19
Hebrew, Hebrews, 273, 419, 489

505

INDEX OF PROPER NAMES

Hecuba, 297
Helen, 479
Heliodorus (Bishop of Altinum), xiv, 29, 188, 189, 199, 265, 311, 331, 488
Helvidius, xii, 101, 489, 490
Heptateuch, 365
Herbert, Lady, 496
Hercules, 175
Herodotus, 329
Hesiod, 195, 297
Hezekiah, 105, 159, 305
Hieronymus, Eusebius. Cf. Jerome.
Hilarion (a hermit), xii, xiii
Hilary (Bishop of Poitiers, fl. 360), 287, 367
Hilberg, xiv, xv
Hippias (of Elis), 290
Hippocrates, 225, 427
Hiram, 291
Holofernes, 101, 261
Holy Land (the), 331, 495
Homer, 195
Horace, 125
Hortensius, 349
Hosea, 269, 483
Huns, 301, 304, 309, 329, 343, 495
Hylas, 487, 493
Hymetius, Julius Festus, 351, 487–488
Hyrcanian, 33

I

Iconium, 156
India, Indians, 271, 273, 343, 403
Innocentius, 2, 3
Isaac, 191, 269, 279, 367
Isaiah, xi, 111, 145, 157, 167, 261, 435
Ishmael, 279
Isidore, 135, 484, 494
Isis, 361
Isocrates, 195
Israel, 63, 73, 109, 191, 263, 271, 305, 333, 469
Italy, 295, 329, 438, 439, 486, 490, 500

J

Jacob, 61, 77, 97, 135, 153, 239, 269, 275, 333, 423
James, St., 101
Jebus (cf. Jerusalem), 463
Jehoshaphat, 305
Jephthah, 279
Jeremiah, x, xii, 99, 143, 167, 249, 391, 459, 502

Jericho, 197
Jerome, vii ff., 2, 16, 18, 19, 24, 54, 74, 77, 88, 178, 188, 192, 196, 214, 228, 264, 308, 309, 338, 352, 396, 430, 436, 438, 456, 460, 483, 484, 486–496, 498–502
Jerusalem (Jebus), vii, 25, 55, 97, 113, 125, 157, 167, 181, 186, 187, 203, 308, 321, 327, 331, 419, 455, 463, 493, 494, 498–500
Jesse, 93
Jews, Jewish, 53, 55, 143, 153, 161, 185, 186, 187, 217, 275, 357, 399, 401, 411, 447, 451
Jezebel, 73
Job, xi, 61, 77, 365
John of Jerusalem, xii, 460, 484, 498–500
John (the Baptist), 77, 143, 161, 271, 345, 409
John (the Evangelist), 23, 101, 451
Jonadab, 410, 411
Jonah, 267, 321
Jones, Sir William, 464
Jordan, 279, 327, 409
Josedech, 187
Joseph, 159
Josephus, 143
Joshua, 95, 187, 275
Jove, 341
Jovian, 299
Jovinian, xii, xiii, 265, 490
Jovinus, 19
Judaea, vii, 105, 215, 261, 411
Judah, 131, 271
Judas, 47, 145, 239, 399
Judith, xi, 101, 261
Julia. Cf. Eustochium.
Julian, 23, 25
Julian Alps, 301
Julian (Emperor), 298, 299, 488
Jupiter, 53

K

Kenites, 197
Keturah, 97

L

Labriolle, P. de, xvi
Lacedæmonians, 303
Lactantius, 287
Laeta (dau.-in-law of Paula), 338, 339, 496
Lake Gennesaret, 411

INDEX OF PROPER NAMES

Lateranus, 317
Latins, xiv, 273, 275
Lazarus, 97, 267, 269, 277, 325
Lea, 485
Leo the Great, 439
Leonides (tutor of Alexander), 349
Levite, 187, 201
Liberius (Pope 352-365), 485
Ligurian, 5
Livy, xii, 143
Longinus, 431
Lot, 57, 71
Lot's wife, 57
Lucifer, Luciferian, xii, 61
Lucilius, 25, 372, 373
Lucius Paulus, 275
Luke, St., xi, 211, 259, 347
Lupicinus, 24, 25
Lyons, Lugdunensis, xv, 298, 299

M

Macarius (a monk of Nitria, probably
    the same as one mentioned in a
    letter to Rufinus dated 374, ep. III),
    135
Macarius (a Roman Christian, disciple
    of Rufinus), 456, 457, 500
Maccabees, 27
Macedonia, 301, 371
Maecia. Cf. Papiria.
Magdala (Mary of), 451
Malchus (hermit), vii, xii, xiii
Malta, 335
Manasseh, 319
Manes, Manichaean, 81, 149
Marah, 73, 415
Marcella, viii, x, 117, 158, 159,
    166, 167, 171, 177, 187, 263, 343,
    438, 439, 441-467, 483-490, 492,
    494-496, 501
Marcella, perhaps sister of the above,
    187, 485
Marcelli (the), 275
Marcellina (sister of Ambrose), 102,
    103, 187, 485
Marcellus, 19
Marcomanni, 301, 303
Maria Maggiore (church of), x
Marianus Victorius, xv
Marii (the), 275
Marnas, 343
Marseilles, 436
Martha, 107
Martianay, xv

Mary (mother of Christ), 91, 99 101,
    147, 155, 199, 329, 345, 355, 357,
    367, 451
Mary of Magdala, 450, 451
Mary (sister of Martha), 167, 451
Massagetae (tribe of), 329
Matthew, St., xi, 347
Maximi (the), 275
Maximus (emperor), 298, 301
Maximus, Quintus Fabius. Cf.
    Quintus.
Medea, 450
Medes, Media, 299, 329
Melanium (or Melania), 183, 185, 493,
    494, 498-502
Melania (granddaughter of the above),
    494
Menander, 213
Menelaus, 479
Mesopotamia, 167, 283
Metelli (the), 275
Methuselah, 207, 295
Micah, 499
Migne, xv
Milan, 17, 170, 485, 489, 501
Minucius, Felix, 287
Miriam, 253, 321
Mithras, 341
Moab, Moabite, 73, 261, 463
Moeris, 191
Monacensis, xv
Montanus, 321
Mopsus (Mopsucrene, near Tarsus),
    299
Moses, 73, 95, 107, 191, 269, 275, 283,
    305, 321, 327, 411, 425, 479, 481

N

Nabal (the Carmelite), 415
Naboth, 319
Naevius, 297
Naomi, 261
Nazianzen. Cf. Gregory.
Neapolitanus, xv
Nebuchadnezzar, 23, 99, 187, 305, 341
Nepotian, xiv, 31, 188, 189, 227, 265,
    277, 279, 281-289, 291, 305, 309, 311,
    413
Nero, 253, 316, 317, 431
Nestor, 195
Nicolas, Nicolaitanes, 47
Nineveh, 269, 319
Niobe, 297
Nitria (Egypt), 135, 484

507

INDEX OF PROPER NAMES

Noah, 71, 95
Nola, 19
Novatius, 321
Numantia, 337
Nyssa. Cf. Gregory.

O

Oceanus (kinsman of Fabiola, correspondent of Jerome), 308, 309, 311, 483, 495, 501
Oedipus, 195
Olives, Mt. of, 493, 494, 498
Oliphant, Mrs., 497
Olympus, 243
Onasus (of Segesta), 166-169
Ophite (heresy), 47
Origen of Alexandria (185-253), xi, 170, 171, 173, 456, 457, 498-502
Orontes, 303
Orpheus, 387
Ostia, 178, 309, 492, 496

P

Pacatula, 467, 475, 480, 481
Pachumius, Pachomius (d. c. 349; the founder of Monasticism in Upper Egypt and one of the first to collect solitary ascetics under a rule; his sister founded a convent for women), xiv, 449
Palestine, ix, x, 303, 309, 372, 486, 495, 498-501
Pambos (d. 393; a monk of Nitria; he entertained Melania on her visit there and was a prominent supporter of the Nicene doctrine), 135
Pammachius (son-in-law of Paula and correspondent of Jerome), 264, 309, 311, 333, 483, 490, 496, 501, 502
Pannonia, 136, 301
Papinian, 315
Papiria, Maecia, 486
Papirius, 337
Paris, Parisinus, xv
Paris, 479
Parthians, 335
Paul, St., 33, 35, 49, 61, 71, 125, 147, 153, 156, 158, 159, 169, 211, 215, 217, 239, 247, 279, 315, 339, 465, 475
Paula, viii-x, 178, 181-187, 231, 232, 277, 309, 338, 367, 369, 371, 450, 451, 484, 486-496, 499

Paula (grand-daughter of the above), 338-371, 496
Paulina (d. of Paula I), 309, 311, 333, 490, 495
Paulinian, or Paulinus (brother of Jerome), 178, 492
Paulinus (bishop of Antioch), viii, 453, 488
Pauli heres (of Paula), 486
Paulus (Lucius), 275
Paulus (a hermit), xii, xiii, 142, 143
Pelion, 450-451
Pergamum, 21
Pericles, 273
Persia, Persian, 273, 298, 343, 421
Persius, 171
Peter, St., 35, 47, 133, 159, 209, 217, 317, 401, 451
Peter (Patriarch of Alexandria), 448, 449
Phanuel, 157, 259, 443
Pharaoh, 107, 155, 253, 401
Phares, 197
Pharisee, 321, 447, 451, 457
Philemon, xi
Philip (of Macedon), 349
Philo, 143
Phison, 403
Phoenicia, 303
Phygellus, 147
Pinetum, 500
Pinianus, 494
Pisos (the), 275
Pityus, 301
Plato, 53, 143, 195, 273, 295, 451
Plautus, 125
Pliny, xiii, 419
Pompey, 337
Posidonius, 273
Pouget, xv
Praetextata (wife of Hymetius), 351, 488
Principia (companion of Marcella), 439, 465, 467, 495
Procopius, 298, 301
Proculus (Bishop of Marseilles), 437
Ptolemy, 21
Publicola, son of Melania, 494
Publius, 335
Pulvillus, 275
Pythagoras, 195, 273, 354, 355

Q

Quadians, 301

INDEX OF PROPER NAMES

Quintilian, 419
Quintus Fabius, 291
Quintus Gallius. Cf. Gallius.
Quintus Maximus. Cf. Fabius.

R

Rachel, 99, 153
Rahab, 149, 197
Rebecca, 191, 423
Rechab, 197
Red Sea, 155, 401, 445
Remnouth, 137
Rogatus (father of Paula), 486
Rome, Romans, vii, xii, xv, 17, 19, 53, 67, 83, 119, 125, 133, 152, 169, 175, 183, 195, 232, 254, 255, 263, 275, 277, 299, 301–309, 316, 317, 325–337, 363, 364, 367, 405, 423, 436–441, 449, 453–465, 479, 483–496, 500, 501
Rufina (d. of Paula), 495
Rufinus (of Aquileia), xii, 430, 456, 493, 494, 496, 498–502
Rufinus, 301, 499
Rusticus (Bishop of Narbonne), 396, 397, 399

S

Salamis (in Cyprus), 453, 488, 494, 499
Sallust, 305, 337
Samaria, Samaritans, 53, 73, 167, 187, 231, 399
Samnites, 337
Samson, 77, 345
Samuel, 27, 345, 367, 411
Saracens, 19
Sarah, 157, 191
Sardanapallus, 253
Sarmatians, 301
Satan, 45, 75, 131, 165, 181, 183, 255, 317
Sauhes, 137
Scaevolas (the), 275
Scauri (the), 275
Scipio, 337; Scipionum suboles (of Paula), 486
Scylla, 39, 401
Scythia, 301, 325, 343
Segesta, 169
Seneca, xiii
Sephora, 191
Serapis (Temple of), 342, 343
Sharon, 93

Sharpe (Rev. Father), xvi
Shumanite, 191, 192, 193, 197
Simonides, 195
Sion, 23, 65, 97, 187
Siricius (Pope 384–398), viii, 491, 501
Socrates, 213, 273
Sodom, 57
Solomon, 57, 79, 83, 151, 193, 203, 225, 365, 399, 419, 433, 477
Sophocles, 195
Sophronia, 449, 485
Sophronius, 119
Spain, 496
Spinaliensis, xv
Stephen, St., 47
Stesichorus, 195
Stilicho, 438
Stridon (Dalmatia), vii, 24
Susannah, 13, 246
Syria, Syrians, 19, 131, 342, 453, 484, 493

T

Tanais, 329
Telamon, 273
Terence, 230
Tertullian, 103, 287
Thamar, 79
Thebaid (Egypt), 449
Thecla, 157
Theodosius (a hermit), vii
Theodosius I (emperor 379–395), 298, 300, 438, 486
Theophilus (Patriarch of Alexandria), 499, 500
Theophrastus, 194
Thessaly, 301
Thierry, xv, 486
Thrace, Thracians, 272, 299, 301
Thucydides, 305
Tiber, ix
Timasius, 301
Timothy, 71, 219, 247, 283, 435
Tishbite, 319
Titiana, 229, 487
Titus, xi, 339, 369
Tobit, xi
Torcello, 282
Toulouse, 228, 436, 437
Toxotius, Julius (husband of Paula), 338, 486
Toxotius (son of the above), 338, 339, 369, 488, 493, 496
Tyre, Tyrian, 291, 331

INDEX OF PROPER NAMES

U

Uzziah, 105

V

Valens, 298, 299
Valentinian, 204, 298, 299
Valerian (Bishop of Aquileia in 370), 25
Vallarsi, Dominic, xv
Vandals, 301
Vashti, 421
Vaticanus, xv
Venetia, 282
Venus, 175, 247
Vercellae, 5
Verona, xv
Vesuvius, 243
Victorinus, 287, 483
Victorius. Cf. Marianus.
Vigilantius, xii

Vincentius (a priest, friend of Jerome), 178, 492
Virgil, 33, 125
Volscian (Province), 325
Vulcan, 169, 243

W

Wright, F. A., xvi, 448, 456

X

Xenocrates, 195
Xenophon, 273
Xerxes, 307

Z

Zarephath, 133, 259, 437
Zechariah, 199
Zeno, 195
Zöckler, O., xv